The Mullendore Murder Case

The Mullendore
Murder Case

BY JONATHAN KWITNY

Farrar, Straus and Giroux · New York

Second printing, 1975

Printed in the United States of America
Published simultaneously in Canada by Doubleday
Canada Ltd., Toronto
DESIGNED BY HERB JOHNSON

Library of Congress Cataloging in Publication Data

Kwitny, Jonathan.
The Mullendore murder case.
1. Mullendore, E. C., 1937–1970.   2. Murder—
Oklahoma—Case studies.   I. Title.
HV6533.06K84   1974   364.1′523′0924 [B]   74–14652

We would like to express our appreciation to The Tulsa Tribune,
especially to Windsor Ridenour, Royce Craig, Dick Grant, Jean Hope,
and Kathy Callahan, for many of the photographs used in this book.

For Carolyn and Susanna

and in memory of Joshua

The Characters

Family

E.C.—*the scion and murder victim*
"We aren't scared of all these threats, are we?"
LINDA—*his wife, the Jackie Kennedy of Osage County*
"I always signed everything that E.C. put in front of me."
GENE—*his father, the patriarch of the ranch*
"You're goddamn right I'll run the son of a bitch. Who do you think built the son of a bitch up?"
KATHLEEN—*his mother, an Indian chief's granddaughter*
"Whatever you want to do, E., is sure fine with all of us."

AND

ERD—*the grandfather and empire builder*
JENNIE—*Erd's wife, the lieutenant-governor's sister*
KATSY MECOM—*E.C.'s sister, a beauty contestant who proudly wore the Mullendore brand*
JOHN MECOM, JR.—*E.C.'s brother-in-law, the Texas oil heir and pro-football impresario*
EDNA VANCE—*the disapproving mother-in-law*

Ranch employees and associates

CHUB ANDERSON—*the handsome, powerful manservant and bodyguard . . . and a convicted cattle rustler*
"He told me that we would be meeting some pretty tough people. . . . He said they were connected with the Mafia."
DALE KUHRT—*the ranch manager*
"I was just looking at blood and wondering who was gonna get shot next."
PAUL KELLY—*the farm manager*
"E.C. told me he was fooling around with a bunch of gangsters. I said, 'I am going home.'"

PAUL BURCHETT—*the bookkeeper*
"*At no time did I ever ask E.C. a point-blank question.*"

AND

MIKE BURKHART—*the assistant foreman*
GEORGE RAY—*the cattle salesman*
JOHN ARRINGTON, JR.—*the Okie lawyer with a
    $19 million insurance case*
JULIA GILKEY—*the maid at the mansion*
LULA HARRISON—*the best cook in the U.S.A.*
KAY SUTTON—*Mrs. Harrison's granddaughter*
PAUL JONES—*the hay-baling contractor and rancher*
WADE NAVARRE—*the horse trainer*
DON McMOY ⎫ *the pilots-for-hire*
BIG ED ⎭

Moneyfinders and their friends

LEROY KERWIN—*the Atlanta insurance agent who had the Mafia
    after him*
"*Tell that son of a bitch E.C. he better not die.*"
LEON COHEN—*Kerwin's partner, a convicted rapist and swindler*
"*One man in Ohio has sold more insurance, but that man is
    seventy years old.*"
TALMADGE KOLB—*the high-salaried financial adviser*
"*I wasn't interested in the shoot-out at the O.K. Corral.*"
MORRIS JAFFE—*the Texas financier*
"*I would be willing to stick my neck out to guarantee Mr.
    Kerwin.*"

AND

CARLOS MARCELLO ⎫ *the Mafia bosses*
MILWAUKEE PHIL ALDERISIO ⎭
LEO "THE MOUSE" RUGENDORF ⎫ *Alderisio's henchmen*
LARRY ROSENBERG ⎭
MICKEY MANTLE—*the baseball star striking out as
    a businessman*
FLOYD SMITH ⎫ *Dallas agents promoting*
JAMES DUNNE II ⎭ *Mantle's mistake*
JIM JACKSON ⎫ *gun-toting ex-cons on the*
KENT GREEN ⎭ *lookout for loans*
GINNY MUELLER—*Green's girl friend who had a loaded purse*
DAVID TAYLOR—*lawyer, preacher, or con man,
    depending on the need*

GEORGE AYCOCK—*the loan finder who wanted a mere 10 percent of the $15 million*

HAROLD AUDSLEY
BYRON PRUGH } *the master swindlers, based in Fort Lauderdale*
PHILIP WILSON

JAMES FOREMAN—*president of United Family Life Insurance Company*

ED MILLER—*the credit investigator who was only $35 million or so off base*

MICHAEL SCHLOSSBERG } *the insurance doctors for people without time to be examined*
ARNOLD B. RUBENSTEIN

Creditors, townspeople, and cops

HAROLD COPPER—*president of the Production Credit Association*
"To the best of my knowledge I told him that my action would probably be in a foreclosure way."

LARRY SILVER } *the ambulance drivers*
GENE KLUTTS
"Well, let's not rush into anything here, right real quick."

BILL DUNLAP—*the state trooper*
"Chub kept referring to, that it was the Mafia, and he asked me if I will pull the shade."

T. F. DUKES—*the prosecutor*
"Too many motives and clues."

AND

GEORGE WAYMAN—*the sheriff*
RICHARD KANE—*the lawyer-rancher*
FRANK RALEY—*the rancher-druggist*
DE LOS PETTIT—*the game ranger*
JAMES STURDIVANT—*the insurance lawyer*
ARNOLD MOORE—*the mortician*
VIP CROWE—*the old-time trial lawyer*
RUDY BRIGGS, GEORGE HUGHES, AND BILL MITCHELL—*the deputies*
And the bankers who found out their loans weren't so secure after all:
  WILLIAM B. HILL, *Arkansas City, Kansas*
  FRANK C. "COKE" HARLOW, *Coffeyville, Kansas*
  KENNETH ALEXANDER, *Lawton, Oklahoma*
  JESSE T. COLLINS, *Atlanta, Georgia*
  GEORGE SCHUMACHER, *Dewey, Oklahoma*

The Mullendore Murder Case

The Osage dwarfed its settlers as if they lived in the palm of a great hand. And as Sheriff George Wayman stood near the entrance of the Cross Bell Ranch that September day in 1970, he could almost feel the fingers of the hand closing in. This was the day E. C. Mullendore would be buried.

The land had taken shape more than 35,000 years before. Southwest of the Ozark Mountains, between the Arkansas and Caney rivers, the ice age had squashed the green hillocks of the Osage curiously flat, so that a man could see great distances over their tops.

And everything Sheriff Wayman could see, in any direction, belonged to the Mullendores. It was September 29, and the blue-stem grass already was flecked with autumnal yellow. When the sun broke between the clouds, the wind-rippled green pastures sparkled as if they had been showered with ambers. Few trees, sparse herds of cattle, and only a distant feed shed or cowboy's house blocked the clean line of the horizon. The sky seemed bigger in the Osage than elsewhere.

Sheriff Wayman tugged his white, broad-brimmed hat lower, covering more of the graying hair around his ears. He straightened the crease of his suit pants over the tops of his cowboy boots and let a long brown swill of tobacco juice slip slowly from his lips and trail into the reddish dust of the Mullendores' four-mile driveway. The first cars already were rumbling up the drive, more outsiders than normally passed this way in a month. And it would be Sheriff Wayman's job this Tuesday afternoon to

3

see that the cars got safely in and out without clogging route 10, the narrow strip of state-owned blacktop that looped north from Bartlesville to Pawhuska, through Mullendore country. When the afternoon was done, the sheriff would return to his office to begin solving the biggest murder case in the history of northeastern Oklahoma. But for now, he considered it perfectly natural to lay aside that job and supervise traffic for the murdered man's funeral.

At the opposite end from route 10, the driveway made a wide oval turn past the main compound of houses at the ranch and enclosed an evenly manicured lawn. On the flagpole at the center of the lawn a white banner occasionally unfurled with the breeze, displaying the Cross Bell brand, sewn in crimson. The Mullendore family flag had been raised only to half-mast.

The visitors parked their cars along the drive and began to congregate on the grassy mall, near the imposing shadow of the elder Mullendores' huge stone mansion. Inside the mansion, under a blanket of yellow roses that cost $638.60, was a coffin containing the body of E. C. Mullendore III, thirty-two-year-old scion of the most famous family in the Osage. He was dressed in Levi pants and a tailor-made, monogrammed shirt. The gashes in his scalp had been stitched closed, and he would have been happy to learn that the mortician had rather deftly concealed the bald spots. There was no room in the coffin for the big white hat that normally covered them. He was, as always, wearing cowboy boots crafted for his feet by Lou Casey, the bootmaker he flew to San Antonio to patronize. And in E.C.'s forehead, just above his nose, and slightly off center to his right, was the hole, made by a .38-caliber bullet.

Some of the people gathered outside knew E.C. as a tireless worker, devoted to his ranch, protective of his wife and four children, generous to a fault with his employees and respectful of his aging parents. They resented the way the newspapers were depicting him as a playboy. But others knew E.C. as a two-fisted, whiskey-soaked, insult-hurling, barroom-brawling, reckless-driving rogue who had sought out the Mafia in his relentless and often successful pursuit of trouble.

George Ray, a livestock salesman, who had visited the ranch much more often than Sheriff Wayman had, knew E.C. was both breeds, plow horse and bronco. In fact, of the people he saw gathered at the mall for the funeral, Ray figured he knew E.C. as well as anyone. The slender, graying salesman had worked cattle with E.C. when the Mullendore boy was still in school. From early in his career, Ray had invested time counseling children's 4-H groups, and when the youngsters grew into ranch owners, they often commissioned him to sell their cattle. Ray had sold for E.C. in the good years. He also had sold for E.C. in the last year, at significant risk to himself, when E.C. rapidly was losing access to other old friends. Now there was talk that those cattle sales had been illegal, and that the federal prosecutor was investigating. Ray was, frankly, a little nervous. But if anybody came around asking him questions, he would just tell them the truth: He had done what his friend asked him to; if the cattle sales were crooked, well, that was a matter E.C. had resolved for himself. Ray certainly hadn't coaxed anybody into selling anything. Despite what he knew about the cattle sales, and despite all the rough characters he had seen around E.C. that summer, George Ray certainly hadn't figured to become a pallbearer for the young man so soon.

Ray spotted a recently familiar face in front of E.C.'s house, across the mall from the mansion of the elder Mullendores. With a tug at his tooled brown-leather belt, Ray ambled over to try to find out why Kent Green was still on the ranch. Kent Green: a burly, bull-necked, cigar-chomping graduate of four penitentiaries, whose jacket was cut just short enough to show the curved wooden handle of the pistol that protruded from his hip pocket. E.C. had brought Green to the ranch to attract some Cosa Nostra money. But E.C. was gone now and Ray figured Green ought to be gone, too.

Ray didn't know it, but Green had a few problems on his own mind. For one thing, if the local police investigating the murder ever bothered to look up Green's record and found out that he was a felon, there would be some explaining to do about that .38 in his pocket. For another, Green had been having a little trouble balancing his checking account. A couple of weeks ago, his bank in Kansas City had notified him that he was overdrawn by about $3.7 million. But hours after the murder the elder Mullendores had assigned Green to guard their son's house, and there he stood.

Ray and Green exchanged nods.

"What'd it look like to you?" Green asked.

"It doesn't look like a professional job," Ray observed.

"It doesn't look that way to me either," Green said.

Green ought to know.

George Ray, the loyal veteran cattle salesman, made a strange conversational match for Kent Green, the hoodlum. But William B. Hill made an even stranger one. Hill was the executive vice-president of the Union State Bank at Arkansas City, Kansas. He actually was in charge of the bank because its president, Robert Docking, was away on another job. The other job was being governor of Kansas. Kansas recently had issued a warrant for Kent Green's arrest on three counts of first-degree kidnapping and illegal possession of firearms. But Hill, who was running the governor's bank, evidently wasn't aware of that as he and Green amiably passed the time at E. C. Mullendore's funeral.

Naturally enough, they discussed E.C.'s money problems. The young rancher's debts of more than $10 million included hundreds of thousands to the Arkansas City bank. Some was for loans that Hill had approved; the rest represented checks that E.C. had bounced there. Hill recalled that, throughout the summer of 1970, he "talked to Mr. Mullendore once or twice a week on the phone" about repayment. E.C. would "say that he thought they would have something the next day or the next week or something like that." Then, five days before his death, E.C. had visited Hill at the bank. "He said he would have his money within a week. He told me he wouldn't tell me where the money was coming from. I assumed he wouldn't tell me because he thought it was coming from some place that wasn't through the regular channels."

So Green informed Hill exactly where E.C. was getting the loan to refinance the Cross Bell Ranch. "I had the money for E.C.," Green said. "Eight million. I was going to deliver it Sunday morning if he hadn't been killed."

Many ranch employees had gathered on the mall for the funeral, including Damon "Chub" Anderson, the handsome, paroled cattle rustler E.C. had hired, first as a welder, later as his personal companion, bodyguard, and manservant. Chub's shoulder was freshly bandaged to protect the bullet wound he had received in the shoot-out Saturday night when E.C. was killed.

The cowboys were there, waiting to ride in the funeral procession. Jerry Don Harper was not there, although he had intended to be. Harper, twenty-three years old, had quit his eight-dollar-a-day job at the ranch in April for better pay digging ditches with a road crew. He typified the drifters who had worked at the Cross Bell over the decades. Harper had been brought up at a state orphanage in Pryor, Oklahoma. On August 28, 1968, he married the former Kathy May Walden, who lived just outside of Pryor. Kathy May had turned twelve years old just three months before the wedding. When he got his job as a feed hauler with the Mullendores, Harper moved into a house on the ranch with his wife, their son and a friend—an AWOL soldier on probation for receiving stolen property.

The day before E.C.'s funeral, the Tulsa papers and television newscasts bubbled with speculation about the murder, and Jerry Don Harper returned to the ranch to hear what the hands were saying. He stopped at several houses for the lowdown, but got the fullest explanation from Paul Kelly, who had been hired to supervise the farming E.C. had begun on the ranch. As they watched the Monday Night Football game on television, Kelly recounted for Harper that E.C. and his mother had gone to Caney, Kansas, to watch the stock-car races the previous Saturday night. E.C. had promised to drive one of the cars in a race, but was too drunk. When they came home, they found Chub Anderson, E.C.'s manservant, waiting at the mansion with the elder Mr. Mullendore.

Kelly had heard the rest of the story from Chub. He repeated it for young Harper, unmindful that Chub himself was about to become a prime suspect in the investigation. As Harper remembers the manservant's story, E.C. and Chub "were going to eat supper or something over at E.C.'s house. E.C. went downstairs and Chub was going to fix some bath water, and Chub heard some shots from downstairs and went to see what had happened. He seen E.C. on a couch, or chair, or something." Then, the account continued, Chub caught a glimpse of two mysterious intruders. "They shot Chub in the back and, when Chub came to, they were going upstairs. Chub followed them and they were going out a glass door and Chub fired five shots at them as they were going out. Chub followed them on outside and shot at them again."

That, at least, was Chub's story. It had yet to be scrutinized by the law, the press, or the dozens of lawyers who were about to descend on the Osage to struggle over E.C.'s insurance.

Says Jerry Don Harper: "Kelly told me that all phones had been cut off up there 'cause they had not paid their bill, and E.C. had been drinking quite a bit, and he said that he thought from the beating they gave E.C., even if they hadn't shot him, the beating would have killed him anyway. He said that he thought it was somebody wanted money and they probably figured he had a big life insurance policy and it would be taken care of. They figured it was the only way they could get the money. We talked about E.C.'s wife. I asked him if he thought she might have had something to do with it, [considering] the trouble they were having . . . He said that he didn't think that Linda had anything to do with it.

"I asked them about the funeral," Harper recalls. "I wanted to come up. And Paul said it would be the next day and that I was welcome if I wanted to come." But Harper and his wife had been working on a six-pack of Coors; and on the drive back to Tulsa that night, the transmission began to go out on their Ford. Harper was going through a second six-pack, this time without any help, and Kathy May finally had to drive, even though she wasn't old enough to have a license. Somehow, they never made it back to the ranch for the funeral the next day.

Inside the mansion, the patriarch, Gene Mullendore, fat and fiery, half-blinded by cataracts and half by rage, held court before the funeral of his only son. He sat in his chair by the great stone fireplace in the sixty-foot living room, several handguns visibly within his reach as usual, his Cross Bell belt buckle gleaming in the center of his domelike belly. Gene had two jobs to tackle, in between receiving the condolences of Osage County citizens, which really meant very little to him. First he had to quell rumors among the cowboys and hired hands that the ranch was bankrupt and on the verge of folding. Ever since the payroll checks had bounced—and the maid had found the .38 hidden under E.C.'s sofa cushion—the help had been deserting the ranch. So Gene bellowed at the old-time employees that the loan to save the Cross Bell was ready to sign; it was just delayed by the shooting.

Paul Kelly, the farm manager, remembers being told, "They had this loan all through and everything. All they had to do was sign it Monday morning and the money would be there, and everything was going ahead as usual, no changes. He told me this the day of the funeral, and I thought it was a bunch of baloney, because there isn't anyone up there capable of loaning the money."

The patriarch's second task was to separate his daughter-in-law from the $16 million worth of life insurance and get her off the Cross Bell Ranch—forever. (Gene, in his vanity, might have found considerable solace that day had he known that the insurance industry would record the case of E. C. Mullendore III as the largest single life insurance claim in the history of American underwriting. But he wouldn't find that out until later.) The important thing now, he thought, was to divert the money to the ranch and away from the no-good bitch who had run out on his son a week ago.

But stopping Linda Mullendore would not prove easy. A goggle-eyed credit investigator had appraised dark, leggy Linda in September 1969 and noted on his report that she had "an hourglass figure." In the ensuing $8 million negligence suit that the insurance companies filed against the credit company, this notation about Linda's shape was one of the few items on the investigator's report that no one challenged. The credit investigator, however, like a lot of other people, had failed to observe the more pertinent truth about Linda: she was perhaps the only person in the Osage with a will and an ambition comparable to Gene Mullendore's.

She took everything Gene had to throw at her that day, in the mansion living room, among the flowers, her husband not yet in the ground; and if she flinched, nobody saw it. He called her a bitch and worse, and blamed her for E.C.'s death. He demanded that she sign a contract immediately, settling the disposition of the ranch and the insurance money. She listened with the long-necked, high-chinned, pursed-lipped dignity of the princess she considered herself to be. If her role was to play the Jacqueline Kennedy of Osage County, she would play it to the hilt.

Most difficult of all was when her oldest son, chubby, nine-year-old E. C. Mullendore IV, was brought in to pay his respects to his grandfather. Linda, at the urging of her mother, with whom she was staying, had forbidden the lad to watch television or read a newspaper over the past three days and he had learned only that morning the reason why. Now he walked to where his grandfather sat, and the brief scene that followed etched itself indelibly in the memories of Linda and of George Ray, who also heard.

"I'm sorry, Grandpa," the little boy said.

Gene cast him a bitter glance and answered, "If you'd have been here with your father instead of running off to Tulsa, it wouldn't have happened."

Linda Mullendore left the house without signing anything.

Lula Harrison had been watching gospel singers on television at about 9 a.m. that Sunday, September 27, when the phone rang. Her son Ben answered. "And I seen an expression on his face," she recalls. "He knew it would hurt me, and he looked at me before he told me. He said, 'This woman told me to tell you that E.C. was killed last night.'"

Mrs. Harrison had known E.C. and Linda since they were children, and despite the inability of her large, sixty-year-old frame to move around much or climb stairs quickly, they had hired her as cook in 1961. E.C. frequently declared she was "the best cook in the U.S.A.," and called her "U.S.A." as a nickname. She had stayed on until the week of the murder, when she decided there was "too much tension." After Linda moved to Tulsa with her mother, she summoned Mrs. Harrison to care for the children.

Linda's mother, Edna Vance, though sixty-two years old, had preserved her trim figure and young woman's features. She blackened her hair with dye and maintained a severe demeanor —George Ray called it "stately"—and successfully encouraged both these habits in her daughter. About the only thing Edna Vance shared in common with the elder Mullendores the day of the funeral was the feeling that her offspring had selected an unworthy marriage partner.

"The thing that bothers me," Lula Harrison says now, "is Mrs. Vance never did seem to be upset. The death didn't bother her." Mrs. Harrison vividly recalls Mrs. Vance in front of the mansion shortly before the funeral service, remarking to a friend, "Now Linda will have all the money she needs. I want her to kick them out of here. That's her house and she has a right to get them out of that house." (Linda says she never heard her mother make any such remark.)

E.C.'s coffin was solid bronze, though its silver color led guests to believe it was solid silver. George Ray was momentarily stunned when he and the other pallbearers tried to pick it up. "It was the heaviest casket I ever lifted. We couldn't hardly carry the casket out of the house to the funeral car," he says.

The service took place on the mall in front of the house. There was a large spray of red and white carnations arranged on an easel to duplicate the family flag, with the ranch brand in the center. The Reverend Byron Wolff, pastor of the First Methodist Church of Enid, Oklahoma, performed the ceremony with some Indian verse, as requested by Gene Mullendore. Remarks Mrs. Ray about the ceremony's non-religious slant: "I don't think Gene believes in a higher deity than himself."

The Mullendores and their in-law were seated uneasily together under a tent. Icy-faced Edna Vance sat beside seventeen-month-old Linda Mullendore, Jr., the youngest of Linda's four children. During the ceremony, the little girl began to cry. "Shut that damn kid up," Gene barked. Without looking back, Mrs. Vance picked up the child, carried her out of the tent, and took a seat among the several hundred guests. "Mrs. Vance didn't talk to Gene that day," George Ray recalls. "It was the end of her being in the family."

E.C.'s body was driven to a high spot about one and a half miles southeast of the compound of houses. The cortege included forty mounted cowboys and E.C.'s own horse, saddled but riderless. After the burial, Gene stood on a rock and shook hands with each of the cowboys as they passed in procession. Then the crowd returned to the mall for drinks, a spread of hors d'oeuvres, and a catered dinner. (Linda did not attend.) The affair cost more than $10,000.

Meanwhile, out in the parking lot, Sheriff Wayman prepared to find out whether justice could still be done in the Osage, nearly eighty years after Erd Mullendore, Gene's father and E.C.'s grandfather, had established a family empire there.

Two   ERD C. MULLENDORE STRUGGLED WITH A BLANKET to shoo the dust from his horse's face. Great choking clouds of dust rolled in from the parade of buckboard hacks arriving from Arkansas City, unloading thousands of spectators who had come to watch the second great Oklahoma Land Rush. It was 10:30 a.m., September 16, 1893, and Erd had trained his horse for too many weeks to appreciate this useless interference.

Historians would write that it was 106 degrees in the shade, which was nonsense; there wasn't any shade. Every half hour or so through the morning of waiting, Erd would slice one of the watermelons that young boys had distributed and suck some moistness into his throat. But he worried mostly about the horse. Erd had dieted off twenty pounds and honed his animal to an edge of strength for these few hours, which would determine the course of many men's lifetimes. In his own case, though he didn't know it, the dash south would determine the course of a dynasty.

Thousands of other contestants felt the same irritation. The shouts and insults they hurled at the hacks full of spectators, soon escalated into a barrage of watermelon rinds as hundreds of young men, their fortunes at stake, pelted the throngs of citizenry with the only weapon handy. The watermelon throwing subsided at eleven, when the soldiers announced that contestants could approach the starting line.

They wedged themselves into rank, shoulder to shoulder. Ahead of them lay six million acres, two hundred miles wide by fifty-seven miles deep: the Cherokee Strip. Erd never thought of himself as part of a last generation of frontier Americans. He was just an Indiana farm boy, the oldest surviving son of John Mullendore. John and his wife had brought forth about fifteen children. An accurate count didn't exist. Four or five died of diphtheria in a single winter in Franklin, Indiana, about thirty miles south of Indianapolis. The bodies of two of them lay a week in their ice-locked cabin before they could be removed for burial. What remained of the family finally packed up for Kansas. They settled on a farm near Howard, not far from the Oklahoma line where Erd now stood.

The federal government had surveyed the Cherokee Strip and platted it into farms of 160 acres. At the center of each farm stood a white wooden stake. The first man who wrote his name on that stake would own the farm, if he stayed to work it. Erd nervously eyed the cavalry soldier assigned to his section of the line. At noon, the soldier was to fire his pistol in the air to signal the start of the rush. But the wait proved too intense, and if the soldier fired his pistol at noon, Erd never heard it. At about two minutes to twelve, the line eastward began to break. The men glanced quickly at each other and the dash was on.

The contestants had not been allowed into the Strip before the rush, but maps were available. One night in the farmhouse at Howard, Erd had stabbed his finger at a bend in the Chikaskia River where the soil ought to be rich, and now he rode for that spot. The impatient raced ahead, often casting scornful glances. He let them pass. Over the next two hours he would come upon many of these men, their dehydrated horses near death.

Pacing his steed almost perfectly, Erd broke over a crest just before 2 p.m. and saw beyond him the Chikaskia, where it turned. He picked his point and aimed for it. He could see only a few other riders in front of him now. One of them almost disappeared over the side of his mount, and Erd saw the ends of a broken saddle cinch flapping under the horse's belly. The rider still clung to his panicking horse, beating it furiously, as Erd galloped past.

Many men wrote of their adventures that day and in the days to come. Though Erd Mullendore wasn't one of them, their experiences probably are an accurate gauge of his own. He almost certainly came to know W. E. Knapp, who selected a farm near the same river bend.

By 3 p.m., Knapp wrote, "the whole river bottom was a mass of humanity." Soon after Knapp and his boss, with whom he rode, had staked their claim, another man arrived and said, "Partners, I think you are on my claim."

"Didn't you see that flag when you rode in?" Knapp says he asked.

"No," the stranger replied.

"Well, you see it now," Knapp said, his hand near his gun. "That's my flag. Now, do you have any particular objections to our staying here?"

They stared at each other for a while until finally the other man rode off. He turned out to be the first of many to gallop up and announce, "Say, mister, you are on my claim."

Wrote another participant: "On the morning of the run, the country was a wilderness; in the evening, [it was] a land of many people with here and there a tented townsite and thousands of campfires. The next day the plows began to turn the virgin soil, while the merchant, banker and professional men opened shop beneath the roofs of canvas or in rough board shanties."

In the days after the rush, men returned to Kansas for supplies and to register their claims at the government land office. W. E. Knapp was surprised to find that another man, a foreigner, had registered the claim where Knapp and his boss had settled. One day the boss's son discovered the foreigner unpacking his belongings on a section of the claim. The boss approached with a gun in each hip pocket, and Knapp recalled the conversation, mocking the foreigner's accent.

"This is my claim. I have the batent in my bocket," the newcomer reportedly said.

"You get off here," the boss replied. The man left, but returned later, and eventually the boss had to pay him fifty dollars to vacate.

Erd often told his daughter, Mrs. Mildred Mullendore Adams, how cold it was that first winter on the Cherokee Strip. W. E.

Knapp writes that his boss had gone to Ponca City, Oklahoma, to buy lumber when a blizzard struck. The boss returned nearly frozen to death. As Knapp built a fire to revive him, the boss explained that the pack horse had been left seven miles behind. "We had to go back with the lantern to find the horse or it would have frozen overnight," Knapp wrote.

One man reportedly lived the winter in a hole on a creek bank. Some comforts were available, if expensive. "You could get a shave for a nickel, if you had the nickel," Knapp wrote. "Money was scarce."

The town that rose near where W. E. Knapp and Erd Mullendore staked their claims was called Blackwell, after its founder, A. J. Blackwell, an exceptional entrepreneur. While other men trained horses for the land rush, Blackwell quietly bought up prairie hay, until he had cornered 300,000 tons of it. That fall, a series of mysterious fires burned off the hayfields along the Chikaskia River, stranding settlers without feed for their livestock—except, of course, what A. J. Blackwell would sell them. Blackwell raised his price to previously unexplored altitudes, first one dollar, then $1.25 a bale.

Blackwell also owned the church where interdenominational services were held. There soon followed the Blackwell Hotel, which dominated the entertainment market. For enlightenment, people read the *Blackwell Lion*. But Blackwell was not the settler who would make the biggest fortune or the biggest mark on history. Mullendore was.

Erd built a lean-to, then a sod house. He cooked for himself for several years, but was little inclined toward domestic pursuits. One day a visitor from near Stillwater mentioned that George Berry, a farmer in the area, had brought a sister onto his claim to handle kitchen chores. The idea appealed to Erd, but instead of sending for one of his own sisters, he decided to go after George Berry's, who, it was reported, was well qualified to perform other duties as well.

"Someone told Daddy that Jennie Berry was a most attractive person," recalls Mrs. Adams, Gene Mullendore's sister. "So Daddy made plans he'd like to meet her. And he made a trip down there." Erd and Jennie married in 1897. Some years later, George Berry was elected lieutenant governor of Oklahoma, a post he retained for eighteen years, longer than anyone else ever has.

Falling in love with a girl whose brother soon would wield powerful political influence was merely the first of many fortuitous events in Erd's life. The next occurred in 1901, when he and Jennie decided to sell their two small claims—his near Blackwell and her share of the Stillwater property—and buy a larger farm near Cleveland, Oklahoma, across the Arkansas River from the Osage. Two years later it was discovered that Cleveland's foundation was a lot less solid than anyone had imagined. In fact, much of the town was sitting on pools of a thick black liquid for which Easterners would pay millions of dollars. Erd decided to invest some of his farm income in oil leases and soon displayed an uncanny sense of where those underground pools were located.

J. Paul Getty, who made hundreds of millions of dollars from the Oklahoma and Texas oil discoveries of that period, has written that he and his father discovered a secret method for determining where to lease property. They watched trains run along a seemingly flat stretch of land; if at one point the trains suddenly seemed to increase speed, just slightly, it indicated an otherwise imperceptible crest on the property. Under such a crest, Getty wrote, was likely to be oil.

Unlike Getty, Erd Mullendore espoused no particular theories or secret strategies to account for his success. To some people, the oil seemed to follow Erd around, always reposing under a tract he filed a lease on. With the oil money, he bought more land, and some Hereford cattle to graze on it, and he bought stock in banks at Cleveland, Pawnee, Cushing, and Hominy. His brother became president of the Hominy bank.

"People that are thrifty, they save money," says Mrs. Bessie M. Johnson, Erd's eldest daughter. "It was a gradual thing. He didn't get it all overnight."

But he got it. Thirty million dollars' worth.

He built a large brick house on a sixteen-acre tract overlooking the Arkansas River. (The house still stands, although a flood-control project has spoiled the view of the once swift-flowing waterway.) Erd filled the house with marble fireplaces, heavy, carved furniture, stained-glass windows, and one of the first central vacuum-cleaning systems, with an outlet in every room and a suction device in the basement. Jennie gave birth to Bessie (Mrs. Johnson), then Billy, who died at age two from contaminated drinking water, then Gene, then Mildred (Mrs. Adams), then Dale, then Patience.

Mrs. Adams remembers the day her father took her to the fields to watch explosives being lowered into the ground. There was no "boom," just a faint rumble, she says, "but oil would come shooting over the top of the derrick, and he would get covered with it—his hat, his shirt—then they'd cap the well and rig up a pump." When Erd and Mildred got home, Jennie would fuss over the ruined shirt and the little girl's oil-splattered dress, "and he would laugh at that." As long as the oil came in, they could afford plenty of shirts and dresses to waste in celebration.

But most of the money Erd made from oil and banking did not go to buy shirts or dresses; it went to buy land—land for cattle, land for crops, land just to ride over. Often he would roam it on horseback, or sometimes in his early-model Ford, the rocks in the pastures clanging against the oil pan (which occasionally ruptured). "When people connected him to the oil business, he always told them he was just a dirt farmer," Mrs. Adams recalls. "He didn't like people who put on airs or weren't down to earth." He rose early for walks in the orchard by his house, and would pick the peaches when they ripened. He wore bib overalls. Trips to town were saved for later in the day.

"He looked just like a farmer," says L. C. Mueller, who went to work for Erd's Cleveland National Bank as a teenager. "He'd come in here with his boots on from out working cattle, and you'd never guess he was a millionaire."

Mueller, who at sixty-six remains at the bank as vice-president, a green eyeshade on his forehead, remembers Erd as five feet, ten inches, muscular and trim, "a snappy talker and walker. There wasn't anything poky about him. He was very businesslike, didn't do much socializing. Once he had a dry hole at Crescent [Oklahoma] and he stopped for a beer on the way back. It surprised the heck out of me. It was the only time I ever saw him drink.

"E.C. [only Jennie called him by his first name, Erd] was everywhere. He was on the ranch, in the oil fields, and in here and out there—at one time he was president of three different banks, and an oil and gas company. A real wheeler and dealer. You couldn't keep up with him."

But Mueller also remembers Erd's concern for individual employees, and his generosity. "When I came here, I didn't have a dime. I wasn't even twenty-one yet. He said, 'How would you like to buy some stocks?' I said, 'I don't have any money.' He said, 'You can sign a note, can't you? I'll loan you the money.' Well, I signed a note, the stocks went up, and I made a heap of money. The other employees did the same thing." Of course, Mueller and his colleagues might have sung a different tune if the stocks had gone *down*. But Erd Mullendore's stocks never went down.

Bank ownership provided Erd with advance notice of where land would become available and how much it would cost. He used the knowledge often. He bought mostly on the south bank of the Arkansas River. North of the river lay the Osage—an Indian reservation until 1907, after which the law still kept substantial land in possession of the Indians.

Indians often visited south of the river. Along with old wooden buildings and mud streets in Cleveland, they contributed to the frontier atmosphere in which the Mullendore children grew up. One of the hobgoblins of their youth was an Indian called John Stink, who came from Pawhuska, capital of the Osage. Legend said that John Stink's family had decided he was near death during an epidemic and had taken him to the hills for an Indian burial, with rocks piled on either side of his body. But some time later John Stink woke up well and walked back to Pawhuska. "Everybody thought he was a ghost," according to Mrs. Adams. "They told him to stay away. So he lived in the hills as an outcast and kept a pack of wild dogs for company." Because the other Indians would have nothing to do with him, John Stink came to Cleveland from time to time to buy goods from the white man. Then he disappeared back into the Osage.

That wild country north of the river beckoned to Gene Mullendore. Gene learned one lesson well from his father. Mrs. Adams recalls that Erd repeated it often: "If you just hold on to land—pay your taxes—you won't need to worry. They're not making any more land."

Three LINDA MULLENDORE SAYS SHE CAN'T REMEMBER when her father-in-law wasn't overweight and ornery. But Gene's sisters say that back in high school he was a handsome rake.

He had been spoiled almost from the day he was born in 1903. "Daddy was overly generous with all of us, to a fault," Mrs. Adams says. "If we'd ask him for a quarter, he'd give us fifty cents. I'd meet him at the bank after school—Gene did too—to get money for pop or candy."

Classrooms held little attraction for Gene, a partygoer and girl charmer. In an effort to mature him, Erd packed him away to Kemper Military Academy and later to Wentworth Military School, both in Missouri. At Kemper, for the first time, Gene was confronted by people who wanted to know his middle name. Erd had gone through life with only the initial "C." and gave no more to his son. But Gene spotted a picture of the steamship *Clermont* and appropriated it for his own. To this day, neighbors in the Osage think his middle name is Clermont. He also began to add "Jr." to his name, even though *that* wasn't literally true, either.

But while military school changed Gene's name, it failed to change his attitude. He made the football team, not the honor roll. Mrs. Adams was attending a girls' boarding school in Nashville which Gene liked to visit. "The girls all swooned at him," she recalls. He also liked to visit home, where he and his brother Dale drove their own Cadillacs.

"I was never allowed to go to the public dances," Mrs. Adams says. "It was an oil community. A lot of the young fellows were drinking. Gene liked that kind of thing."

Dale, younger, quieter, always looked to his more popular brother for guidance. Then, at age nineteen, Dale died of a ruptured appendix. His bedroom was sealed off, the furniture still in it, and not reopened until the house was sold, a half century later.

Gene attended the University of Oklahoma, joined Beta Theta Pi fraternity, and left after a few years without graduating. His father tried to make a banker of him. For more than two years, Gene toiled as a clerk behind the counter at Cleveland National. "He was like a bull in a china shop," Mrs. Adams recalls.

"Gene was bookkeeping in the bank, but he didn't like it," says L. C. Mueller, who worked shoulder to shoulder with Gene. "Gene liked to be outside. He worked cattle. He worked on horseback."

True enough, Gene hankered to ranch on his own. But his dissatisfaction fed on something more solid than an inclination toward the outdoors—which, after all, he shared with his father. Gene's ever-deepening rivalry with A. C. Adams, a rivalry that ultimately would drive a wedge through the Mullendore family, contributed in large part to his restlessness.

A.C.—or "Ad," as he was known—was a contemporary of Gene's in Cleveland, but grew up in decidedly different circumstances. While Gene spent his teen years touring the party circuit in his Cadillac, Ad shined shoes in local barbershops. Among the shoes he shined were those of Erd Mullendore, who determined that the special ministrations of young Adams brought an exceptionally high gloss to the leather. This extra elbow grease, if that's what it was, paid off handsomely for the youngster.

While still a senior in high school, A. C. Adams graduated from shining shoes to clerking in the Cleveland National Bank, upon invitation of the bank's president. By the time Gene Mullendore arrived from his three years at the university, A.C. had risen to a capacity in which he supervised both Gene and another contemporary, L. C. Mueller. Not only that, but A.C. Adams was about to become the boss's son-in-law.

"A. C. Adams never went to college," Mildred Mullendore Adams says of her husband. "Daddy always told him, 'Personally, I'd rather have a son of mine work in the bank and get business training.' Daddy wanted him to know business, and he always said that you could learn business better in a small bank than in any business school."

"Mr. Adams was the person who, above all in the world, Erd Mullendore had confidence in," says Linda Mullendore, recounting the family history. "Erd handpicked him to run the bank." One can imagine Gene Mullendore's reaction to his swift replacement as number-one son. He longed for a life of his own.

At a dance in Bartlesville, Gene met a trim brunette named Kathleen Boren, whom Mueller describes as "one of the prettiest gals you ever saw in your life." Not only that, she had land in her family. Her father, Melvin Boren, generally known as "Buck," had driven cattle north from his ranch in Texas to fatten on the bluestem grass of the Osage until one trip when he met Blanche Brown and decided that, between the girl and the grass, he really had no reason to go back to Texas. Blanche's father—Kathleen's grandfather—was Charlie Brown, one eighth Osage Indian, the only half-breed ever elected primary chief of the tribe, an office he held from 1918 to 1920.

When writers concern themselves with the mistreatment of Indian tribes in the United States, they don't talk about the Osages, who got their luck from the same place Erd Mullendore got his. In the mid-nineteenth century, the tribe migrated south from Missouri and Kansas in a series of land-swapping treaties with the government. Unlike some other tribes, the Osages never became sentimental over a particular piece of real estate and had moved around a lot even before the white men came. But shortly after the Civil War, when they received their third or fourth eviction notice from Washington—because Union soldiers wanted to farm the tribal property in Kansas—the Osages decided to find a real home once and for all.

Two chiefs expressed opinions on where they ought to go. Wah-Ti-Ankah suggested west. But Paw-Hiuskah observed that as long as they kept moving west onto good farmland, the white men were going to keep following them and chasing them off. He suggested they move south into northeastern Oklahoma, generally regarded as poor for crop growing. A very thin layer of soil covered a thick bed of limestone. Only an optimist would plant wheat, and corn was out of the question. The Cherokees had been living there—the land lay at the end of the famed Trail of Tears—but were unhappy and preparing to move to where the farming would be better.

To the profound relief of their descendants, the Osages chose to follow Paw-Hiuskah, and eventually named their capital for him. The Cherokees, history's losers, turned over the reservation, which henceforth would be called the Osage.

It was 1872, and there were two important facts nobody knew regarding this land. First, new breeds, with more tender meat, would come to dominate the cattle industry, and these breeds would graze better on Osage bluestem than on any other natural ground cover—or so a lot of people would contend. Second, pocketed in that thick bed of limestone was something a lot more valuable than wheat or corn—3,447,000,000 barrels of oil.

In 1906, with statehood just a year away, Congress decided the white and Indian territories would have to be merged. The original idea was simply to divide the Osage land among individual tribesmen, many of whom would then choose to sell out to white settlers. But the Osages argued their long-held belief that property should be owned communally, not individually. After long negotiations, the tribe and the government reached a compromise. The land would be owned individually, and the minerals—all that oil—collectively. All Osages on the official rolls as of June 30, 1907, would receive one headright, or share, in the communal income. When the day came, there were 2,229 headrights to be awarded. Each Osage received 657 acres, $3,819.76 as his share of the tribal trust fund, and $\frac{1}{2,229}$ of future revenue from any oil wells drilled on the land that had been the reservation and that now would be known as Osage

County. Income from each headright totaled about $15,000 a year through the oil boom, a princely sum in the 1920's. The quarterly income checks dropped to ninety dollars in 1936, but by 1956 had risen to $2,700. In 1972, the owner of each Osage headright still received quarterly checks of $685. Although Indians were forbidden by law to sell their headrights, they could will them. If a white man inherited a headright, he could sell it, so a market developed and the price for a headright reached more than $100,000 in the 1920's.

Kathleen Boren was born in 1905, just in time to qualify for a headright. When Gene Mullendore met her, Kathleen's 657-acre allotment and that of her mother were being ranched by her father, Buck Boren, who had acquired thousands of acres contiguous to those allotments. The Indians generally were uninterested in ranching. To protect against exploitation, the law measured carefully the amount of land Indians could sell, and required many Osages to retain at least part of their allotments for decades. But when Buck Boren couldn't buy land, he leased it, and his was one of the larger ranches in the Osage when his daughter married Gene Mullendore December 21, 1926. Kathleen moved to Cleveland, where her husband continued to sulk away at his bank clerk's job.

Like many a New York snowstorm, the panic that reached Wall Street in 1929 had been born much earlier on the Great Plains. As chronicled in song by Oklahoma's "dust-bowl balladeer," Woody Guthrie, the agricultural panic began "back in nineteen twenty-seven" when the "rain quit and the wind got high, and a black old dust storm filled the sky." The farmer in Guthrie's song "swapped my farm for a Ford machine" and drove off to California.

Buck Boren couldn't even get a Ford machine for his ranch in 1927. It was mortgaged, and when Boren couldn't meet the payments, the bank put it on the auction block. Boren had been ranching in the area since Indian Territory days, and began building his Osage spread at statehood. Whoever bought it out from under him in foreclosure would earn his undying enmity.

Gene Mullendore, his son-in-law, bought it.

Boren "moved to San Antonio to start a new ranch and never set foot on the Mullendore property again," says Linda. Only after his death, decades later, did his widow return to the ranch and resume ties with Kathleen and the grandchildren.

That was the beginning of the Cross Bell Ranch. Not only did

Gene buy it for a song, but he borrowed the tune—a $2 million advance from his father on his inheritance. Gene carried over the Cross Bell brand from his mother's family. It had been an old Mexican mission brand, and according to tradition, the first Berry cattle were driven up from Mexico with the Cross Bell already burned into their hides.

Lawyer John Arrington, Jr., who, like his eighty-year-old lawyer-father, has represented the Mullendore interests on many occasions, says that Gene bought substantially all of the main ranch in that initial transaction and did very little to improve it. "When you go in with no debt, essentially, as he originally did, with money which today would be worth probably $8 million in buying power, it was not difficult to continue to operate," Arrington says.

Gene swears he "built the son of a bitch up myself." On the open market, he bought the Pawhuska Ranch, about nine thousand acres plus about four thousand leased acres, and the Fairfax Ranch, about seven thousand acres. He also added numerous small tracts to the main ranch.

The Cross Bell Ranch lies just north of the tiny hamlet of Hulah, Oklahoma. It also lies just east of Hulah, just south of Hulah, and just west of Hulah. It spreads beyond the Osage into Washington County, Oklahoma, and up into Kansas. Gene once told a newspaper reporter that the ranch contained about 100,000 acres—or "it might be just 50,000. I've never found a cowboy with wind enough to step it off." The reporter, writing in 1950, observed how difficult the ranch was to locate from the highway. "It's best to find it with an airplane," he noted.

Gene had long since built a runway and bought an airplane. The state law requiring a crisscrossing grid of public roads, east-west and north-south, one mile apart, never applied to the Osage. So the Mullendore land rolls on, its beauty uninterrupted, its boundaries unapparent. The view from overhead is said to be breathtaking.

Gene hired his old co-worker L. C. Mueller several hours a week to keep books for the ranch. "He just didn't have his nose to the grindstone till he got his ranch," Mueller remembers. "He was real busy after that, though."

Mrs. Adams recalls that when her brother moved to the ranch, he eschewed the bib overall costume that Erd wore and adopted Western-style dress, with fancy shirts and tooled-leather belts. Gene "always did like nice clothes," Mrs. Adams says.

Gene and Kathleen moved first into a small bunkhouse, but soon work began on the feudal mansion that still stands at the heart of the Cross Bell. A newspaper reporter who visited it in 1939 wrote, "Step up the stone walk, across the long front porch, and you find yourself in a huge front room, a treasure spot of Western luxury. The high walls are paneled in knotty pine to the heavy-beamed ceiling, and the shiny hardwood floor has black walnut pegs instead of nails. Crackling flames in the large rock fireplace cast a soft glow across the mounted cow-hides and Indian woven rugs. The red-flowered divan, opposite the fireplace, matches the heavy drapes. Nearby is a pine coffee table with a thin copper sheet top. Another divan and chair set is upholstered [with] beautiful white Navajo rugs, enlivened by turquoise blue designs. Even the electric lights in old-fashioned coal oil lamp brackets rise from a replica of a big wagon wheel.

"Mullendore's own bedroom has furniture with his original design. The pine beds have the 'M' and Cross Bell brand worked into huge [patterns] which form the head and base. Mrs. Mullendore's bedroom is definitely feminine and very modern. The color scheme of chartreuse and rose is carried out in the thick carpet and the drapes. Just a step away is the sleeping porch with nine beds. Each has a matching spread with one letter to spell out 'Cross Bell.' "

His boots planted firmly in the Osage soil, Gene transformed his flighty rakishness into dedication. His new character displayed itself in everything about him: his clothes, his house and his discovery of the true god—land.

"Land was Gene's main interest," says Mrs. Adams. "There never was a piece of land he didn't want to own."

"It's like Lincoln said," declares Frank Raley, searching to dignify the philosophy of Osage ranchers like himself. "I don't want all the land. I just want the land adjoining mine. Of course, then I want the land adjoining *that*, too. I think we're all grasping and reaching at heart. I own race horses, and I like to win every race I start. I never heard of Gene Mullendore stealing anything, but he played as hard as he could."

Gene kept close watch on foreclosures and tax liens, and acquired a lot of land through forced sales. Court records show that former owners, including some of Indian descent, occasionally tried to reassert claims to this land but seldom if ever were successful.

Gene used his skill at maneuvering and his superior financial

23

resources to "freeze people out"—a practice that many less successful ranchers regard as disreputable. "If you surround a guy," says Frank Raley, "buy all the land around him, the law says you have to give him the right-of-way. But sooner or later they're going to sell. There's such a thing as psychological claustrophobia. You know that no matter what you do, you ain't going nowhere. Everybody that's in this business is in it because he thinks he's going to grow. You crowd a man into a corner and he'll pay to get out. Gene made some enemies like that."

Richard Kane, an Oklahoma lawyer-rancher as was his father, says, "Gene acquired a lot of land on a zero basis. He didn't pay anything for it. It's called adverse possession. You just occupy five or ten acres and physically prevent the owner from getting in." Kane says his father, John H. Kane, once "stood up to" such a ploy and refused to surrender a patch of land Gene had surrounded. Ultimately, Gene swapped him an equivalent tract bordering the Kanes' ranch. "Gene respected my father more after it was over, somebody who could not be cowed. The other people weren't strong enough to fight."

Mrs. Eugenia Tucker has owned land bordering the Mullendore ranch for thirty-three years, and according to George Ray, who was married to Mrs. Tucker in 1970 and divorced from her later, there were constant disputes. "It was over everything you can think of," he says. "Fencing. Prairie fires." Mrs. Tucker won't comment about the Mullendores now.

Osage ranchers frequently accuse each other of starting prairie fires on each other's property. Gene Mullendore was accused in court of using prairie fires to drive a man off some land Gene wanted, but the case never was proven. Pawhuska people say Gene once settled a land dispute by riding to a neighbor's house with twelve armed cowboys on horseback behind him. The difference of opinion reportedly was resolved on the spot.

"I've never heard of one rancher shooting another one over land or anything else," says John Arrington, Jr. "There's a lot of litigation. Pawhuska, a town of five thousand people, once had like fifteen or twenty lawyers who made a living."

In a 1958 court suit, Leonard Shook said he bought some land bordering the Mullendore ranch. Gene had been using a strip of the land as a driveway and parking area for a cowboy's house. Shook says he warned Gene not to use the strip any more, then cleared his property and piled the collected refuse on the strip in question. The next week he returned and found the refuse scattered as before over the rest of his property. So again he piled the refuse on the strip Gene had been using, and once more it was scattered over the rest of the property. The next time Shook went back, he was greeted by the cowboy's wife, who held a .22 rifle on him while the cowboy "verbally abused" him, the suit charged. After that, cowboys' vehicles blocked all access to Shook's entire property. After a court hearing, Judge Jesse J. Worten issued an order restraining Gene personally from interfering with Shook's access to the property.

Over the years Gene successfully found paths through the forest of rules the government had created to protect Indian lands. According to these rules, a white man can buy from an Indian only with permission from the Bureau of Indian Affairs office in Pawhuska. The bureau requires open bidding to guarantee the seller the best price available. If you want to buy land, Frank Raley explains, "the real-estate man at the Indian agency puts your name on a list. The Indian has to petition for a permit to sell land. The bureau makes an appraisal and must determine if there is a need to sell the land. If they approve, they'll send out a bulletin [to the people on the list] with the data on it. You send your bid with a certified check for 10 percent of what you're willing to pay. But if you're real smart, or you know someone in the real-estate department, you can determine pretty close to what the appraised value is. I'm talking about getting it from the person who made the appraisal. You can get a pretty good idea."

In addition, says Raley, "The bank official who sold the certified checks knows what the other people are bidding. When you see a check's been made out to the Bureau of Indian Affairs, you know that's 10 percent of what the man who bought the check is going to bid. I'm telling you, there are ways."

One way or another, Gene put together what the Tulsa newspapers called "Oklahoma's greatest ranching empire." There may have been larger ranches, but not run as a family enterprise by one man. Despite his poor eyesight, Gene hired no managers or full-time bookkeepers. "He knew his people, he knew how many trucks he had and generally what shape they were in," Raley says. "He knew it in his head. If he'd have written a note to himself, he couldn't have read the note."

Like every rancher, Gene needed cowboys to mend the fences, to bring hay, salt, and minerals to the cattle in winter, to doctor the calves, to separate the cows, yearlings, and bulls into appropriate pastures and to round them up before shipping. But

Gene paid his hired cowboys substantially less than other ranchers did. According to Linda, even in the later years of his reign, Gene paid only $70 a month plus room and board "for a single boy, another $23 for a married man. Depending on how many children he had. If he had eight or ten, he might make $150. They all [the children] worked on the ranch."

And unlike other ranchers, Gene regularly was able to truck in convicts from McAlester and other Oklahoma prisons to handle whatever chores presented themselves. Reportedly, he paid nothing for this labor—unless you consider his annual contributions to the Democratic Party.

Gene's lawyer, State Senator Gene Stipe, a personal friend of U.S. Speaker of the House Carl Albert, has been one of Oklahoma's most powerful political figures for several decades. Gene's family also was a legal client of the Edmondson family, which has produced an Oklahoma governor and a congressman in recent times.

Not all of Gene's relations with government bore the fruit he desired, however. Twice over the years, government lawsuits forced Gene to violate the guiding principle of his life: Never sell land. Even under court order, Gene refused to sign the deeds of sale; judges had to perform this act for him. In 1949, the Army Engineers decided they needed 2,045 acres from the Cross Bell Ranch for the federal government's Hulah Dam and Reservoir project. The government offered Gene $37.50 an acre and told him if he wanted more he could go to court and ask a jury for it. Gene took the opportunity to go to court, but didn't ask for more money. He simply offered to pay the government $50 an acre for the entire 21,000 acres set aside for the project. After listening to his performance, the jury voted him $58.75 an acre for his ranch property. Gene almost spurned the check, even after the judge signed away his land. "He didn't want to get paid," says Frank Raley. "He wanted that land."

Worse yet was in 1956, when the city of Pawhuska condemned a corner of Gene's Pawhuska Ranch for what is now Blue Stem Lake, which furnishes the city's water. He couldn't understand why his neighbors weren't cowed after all these years. "Gene feels like he gets a bad deal, he don't know anything to do but fight," Raley recalls. "He like to run all over town after Claude Carter, the city manager, but he never did catch him. Carter . . . was ducking in and out of his office whenever somebody saw Gene's Cadillac in town. When they built that lake, Gene got so mad he wouldn't come back to town for a while. He stopped buying his Cadillacs here. Sid Shook sold him Cadillacs, and Gene thought Shook should have helped him out with the lake. He bought his Cadillacs in Bartlesville until E.C. took over.

"Don Stewart, the president of the First National Bank, said he'd appraise the land for $175 an acre," Raley adds. "Gene said, 'But you got $2,000 an acre for some land here recently.' Don said, 'I know, but the people who bought it had to have it. The city can condemn yours.'"

Gene tried to prevent the engineer from coming on the property to begin the necessary surveying. Judge Jesse J. Worten had to sign another injunction to make Gene stand aside. The case went to trial in May 1957, and the jury voted to raise Gene's compensation from $24,682—the price determined by Stewart and two other appraisers—to $35,000. Gene demanded a new trial but never got it.

Ironically, Sid Shook's son Doc, who now owns the Ford agency in Pawhuska, became a boyhood friend of Gene's son E.C. Doc is one of the few people around who will defend some of Gene's idiosyncrasies—such as patrolling his vast acres of well-stocked forest with armed cowboys to administer their own violent justice on any trespassing hunters. "He just wouldn't allow fishing or hunting on his place and that's why a lot of people don't like him," Doc Shook says. "But long before this ecology thing got started, he brought the deer and pheasant and quail into this country. He wanted to take care of those animals. That's why he had the buffalo. He wanted to see those things come back."

Linda Mullendore thinks there is another explanation for why Gene brought herds of deer, buffalo, and longhorn cattle onto the ranch, and kept them at great expense. "He wanted them because no one else had them," she says.

A hundred years ago, in the days described by pulp Westerns, longhorns dominated the American cattle industry. "The longhorns could live on nothing," says John Arrington. "And you could drive them to market, and it didn't hurt them because they weren't any good to begin with. You could drive them all the way from Texas to Abilene." But in the twentieth century, new kinds of cattle—Hereford, Angus, and Charolais—moved their more romantic predecessors aside. "The longhorns didn't put on weight," Arrington explains of the breed's decline. "A tremendous percentage of their size was in unusable things. There was a tremendous weight loss in the head. They're mean. They're

27

vicious. They kill people. They kill horses. They hook each other with their horns and kill each other. They tear fences down."

While the deer on the Cross Bell Ranch merely tormented hunters, the buffalo and longhorns destroyed property wantonly. But whatever their cost, the exotic relics of America's past helped nourish the legend Gene Mullendore built around himself. As late as 1950, a bug-eyed Tulsa newspaper reporter would visit the Cross Bell and tell his readers: "Mullendore's ranch is so big it will cost him $30,000 this spring just to phosphate the place. He owns his own grain elevators; grinds all his feed; has eight or ten trucks, fifteen hundred head of horses, a private airplane, and a ranch house as big as a medieval mansion. The [pinewood] dining room table is as long as some towns' air strips. When a cowboy wants another slice of bread, there's no passing—he just sends a jeep down for it. The Cross Bell's dozens of cowboys are served steaks for every meal. And I said STEAK:—something about the size of a saddle blanket, garnished with eggs. Mullendore, in addition to thousands of cattle, owns a herd of buffalo, plenty of deer, two hundred head of goats, and a couple of children. Entertaining at the Mullendore ranch is on such a scale that the main guest room contains nine beds. . . . 'We like to think of our guest's comfort,' says Mullendore. 'If he falls out of one bed, he has eight others to get back into.' "

Gene wanted a place for the ranch and for himself in history. The Cross Bell's slowness to replace horses with pickups owed as much to Gene's vanity as to his frugality. Once he invited a troupe from Hollywood to film a grade-B shoot-'em up on the ranch and set townfolk talking about the lavish parties he threw for the cast. Not all the talk about the Cross Bell was respectful, of course.

Sheriff Wayman: "There's no way that you could put a ranch of that size together without trompin' on some people's toes. You buy the land of a small rancher or a small farmer, you drive him out, and that's what happens. You run a lot of hunters and fishers off your land, and they're not gonna like it."

Some of the people Gene alienated most were named Mullendore. After Erd's death in 1938, the bitterness intensified between Gene on the one hand, and his sisters and their husbands on the other. Erd's will left his son-in-law A. C. Adams in charge of the trust fund for the Mullendore children. But most irritating of all to Gene, Erd and Jennie placed their ranches under the supervision of Adams and their other son-in-law, Ralph Johnson, even while Jennie continued to live.

"Gene was taking on as the ranching expert," Mrs. Adams says. "He used to call down and tell Mother when to sell the cattle, how many pounds of feed per head of cattle to use— My husband had run his own ranch and he didn't want to run it the way Gene ran his."

The argument over how and when to ship cattle to market typified the essential difference in outlook between Gene and the rest of the family. "Instead of shipping one load of thirty or forty cattle," Mrs. Adams says, "he would wait to get nine or ten carloads, then go into Kansas City, and it would make headlines. The biggest cattle shipment [that] ever came to town. The big rancher from Oklahoma. He liked to make a splash, he liked the publicity. Of course, it would break the market. Everybody would read about it and the price would drop. But he didn't care." A. C. Adams cared. He was selling cattle for profit, not pride.

According to Mrs. Adams, Gene's ornery attitude split him from his mother and sisters, and visiting between them stopped. "We just kind of hoped he'd stay over there and not bother our business, and we wouldn't bother his," she says.

When A. C. Adams wound up administering Erd Mullendore's estate, Gene could hardly stand the blow. He must have felt that the father he had struggled to impress, whose name he adopted for his own, had neither loved nor respected him. Outsiders seldom understood the depth of resentment within the family. When Gene took over the Little Chief Ranch in Fairfax, Oklahoma, which had been in Jennie Berry Mullendore's family for decades, local residents assumed the ranch was part of Gene's inheritance. The truth is, he bought it on the open market by submitting the highest bid when A. C. Adams decided to sell.

Ironically, neither Mrs. Adams nor L. C. Mueller interpret Gene's exclusion from his parents' estate with the same harsh connotations that Gene himself drew. They say the $2 million that Erd gave Gene to start his ranching career represented the bulk of what Gene had coming to him. As far as they are concerned, Gene was denied administrative power over the Mullendore trust simply because most of what remained in the estate belonged to his three sisters. "Gene wanted to have his cake and eat it too," Mrs. Adams says. "He wanted his ranch, and he also wanted a share of the Mullendore trust."

After Jennie Mullendore died in 1952, Adams and Bessie Mullendore Johnson decided to sell some of the family holdings (including the Little Chief Ranch) and divide the profits among the trust beneficiaries. Gene raged against selling family property and pleaded with his youngest sister, Patience Mullendore McNulty, to intervene. Mrs. McNulty had moved to New York, where her husband practiced law. She cast her vote in a letter that A. C. Adams later submitted to a court to justify his decision. "Of course, I know certain members of the family are against selling," Mrs. McNulty wrote, "but I believe you agreed with me once that it is the logical and practical thing to do. We are not concerned any more with who is going to be the biggest cattleman in the state, or any other vain ideas."

Later, however, Mrs. McNulty became dissatisfied with the way the trust's money was distributed, and she joined Gene in a lawsuit against Adams and Mrs. Johnson. Gene insisted that his dynasty-building program was the true way to pursue Erd Mullendore's goals. The lawsuit charged Adams with mismanaging the trust. After weeks of hearings, Mrs. Adams recalls proudly, Judge Royce Savage announced his decision with these words: "I hope at the time of my death I will have someone to look after my estate as well as A. C. Adams looked after the Mullendore Trust."

Despite this bitter defeat, Gene continued to protest whenever he got the chance. In 1955, Mrs. Johnson had to return to court to obtain permission to divide some property that Erd had left to the four children in common. Gene again refused to approve any sale of land. The judge appointed appraisers, auctioned the property, and divided the proceeds.

Whatever animosity Gene failed to spend on his shotgun-toting neighbors and land-selling relatives, he reserved for the oilmen. Every rancher in the Osage is bound by the Indian tribe's oil-rights agreement. Federal law requires landowners to allow drilling, as determined by the tribe. The Indians get the money, which has sparked deep resentment among the cattlemen.

Richard Kane, Osage rancher and lawyer: "Texas ranchers were always bailed out by the oil income. Osage ranchers had to live from cattle, which is a cyclical business. Beef prices rise and fall. I don't suppose there's been a rancher without alternate sources of income who didn't fall into lean times on two or three occasions because of the cyclical nature of cattle prices."

During those lean times, the spectacle of hard-pumping oil machinery across the landscape tends to bubble the blood of cowmen. The rules allow them only one outlet for their anger—litigation. The Indians and oil companies must guard against damage to the ranches they drill on. If fences break, or if the cattle drink oil and die, the landowners can sue for damages. These constant lawsuits fortify the Osage legal industry against any lean times of its own.

Nobody ever had to coax Gene Mullendore into court, and plenty of lawyers have found work arguing over who was responsible for damage to or from oil equipment on the Cross Bell Ranch. Once Gene paid an out-of-court settlement to the Tidal Oil Company because of a lawsuit charging him with running a bulldozer over Tidal's pipes and other equipment in an effort to render an oil operation unworkable. Later he was charged with physically preventing another oil company's men from laying pipes on his land. He, like other ranchers, would accuse the companies of starting fires or causing other destruction in the course of their work.

Over the years, Osage ranching has changed in ways that tended to cramp Gene's flamboyant style of operation. By the 1950's, the beef industry had discovered it could obtain more meat for its money by fattening cattle on corn and other grains for six months or so after a year of grazing. Instead of selling direct to the packinghouses in Kansas City, Osage ranchers started selling to feed-lot operators who would come to Oklahoma from their headquarters in Kansas, Iowa, or Indiana. The U.S. Department of Agriculture restricted its "prime" and "choice" grades mostly to cattle that had fattened on high-protein grains. Cattle that went to slaughter direct from grazing on even the best bluestem grass could earn no higher designation than "good." In the old days, cattle could graze for four or five years to attain their weight at slaughter. Now, with housewives demanding smaller cuts of meat, packers wanted smaller animals with a higher percentage of beef. This meant quick fattening for a rendezvous with the butcher after a mere eighteen months. So ranching became less personalized—there was no such thing as a direct-to-table Mullendore steak (although Linda Mullendore recalls a day in the mid-1960's when a motorist collided with a stray calf, providing the family with an unexpected barbecue; she contends the meat was "terrific").

Along with the revolution in beef marketing, science was

discovering foreign grass strains, such as Bermuda, brome, and fescue, that could graze many more cattle per acre than the native bluestem. None of these developments was going to destroy Osage ranching. But they were going to change it.

Into this changing world came E. C. Mullendore III.

Four

E. C. MULLENDORE III WAS BORN OCTOBER 26, 1937. Initials were all the name E.C. ever got, because Gene had nothing more than initials from his father's name to pass on. Erd was in the Mayo Clinic the fall that E.C. was born, but managed to come to Oklahoma and meet his grandson once. Erd died in January 1938.

"The Mullendores want to bring up their son in the right atmosphere," a newspaper reporter wrote after a trip to the ranch in February 1939. "Here is a bright-eyed little youngster who will take care of the family name and traditions in the next generation. The baby was scarcely out of his crib before he had, made to order, a cowboy outfit with tiny boots and chaps. A glimpse at the youngster's favorite toys (saddles and guns and Western stuff) is convincing that the son will follow in his father's footsteps. Before the boy could talk, he was shaking a pair of miniature boxing gloves on his tiny fists. 'Yes,' his father chuckled, 'the boy will have to learn how to meet the hard knocks which come in every business.' "

E.C. was 1/64 Osage Indian, and Gene wanted him to have a headright. Since Kathleen's would go to the boy only upon her death, Gene bought E.C. 7/12 of a headright on the open market. As late as 1970, it was valued at $9,000.

E.C. "went to the little country school at Hulah," instead of being driven to Pawhuska or Bartlesville as other ranchers' children were, Linda Mullendore says. "Mr. Mullendore used to hire people with large families to work on the ranch. The children of these people that worked there, those were E.C.'s friends."

"Nobody from Pawhuska or Bartlesville went up there and visited as children," John Arrington, Jr., recalls. "Not until E.C. was a teenager, and even then . . . he never really had a good time. He had to work like a dog his whole life. While others would be whooping it up in the usual teenage fashion, he'd be driving back and forth to the ranch and working till dark. Everybody always talked about how hard E.C. worked, and how hard Gene worked him from the time he was a stripling."

Of course, E.C. seldom required coaxing. Gene assigned him considerable responsibility, not just menial chores. The boy's aunt, Mildred Adams, recalls that "Gene often sent E.C. with the cowboys to Kansas City to sell the cattle. He sent E.C. out to buy land when he was still a youngster. Most any place I'd see him, he'd be in his cowboy clothes. Woolf Brothers [a high-priced Kansas City department store] once advertised in the Kansas City papers that E.C. had brought the cattle up there from the Cross Bell Ranch and they were outfitting him in the best Western attire. He was only ten or twelve years old then."

George Ray, the livestock salesman, remembers that "as an infant he rode with his dad to oversee operations in a pickup truck. In 1952, E.C. went to my auction and bought ninety-some bulls at a sale. Gene was with him, but E.C. did the bidding. I can remember him ordering cars, railroad cattle cars, when he was fifteen years old. You'd see him in town with his Levi's and boots on, and he had been out working with the rest of the guys."

Ranchers segregate their bulls, mother cows, and salable yearlings in separate pastures, and try to arrange calf crops in February–March, and again in September–October. Love sometimes proves stronger than fences, and the science isn't exact. But about six weeks after the calf crop is due, the cowboys round up the herd, count them, and "shape," or segregate, them.

Often E.C. himself would perch atop one of the wooden sides of the shaping chute as the cattle were run past, single file. As each animal passed, he would determine its sex, and whether it ought to be kept for breeding or sold as a yearling. If a female calf, or heifer, were kept, she would be expected to calve annually for ten or twelve years before infertility condemned her to processing as a very thoroughly ground luncheon meat. How large a cow herd a rancher built depended on how much grazing land he owned and how much he needed the cash he could get by selling his heifers as yearlings. At the end of the shaping chute, a cowboy manipulated a gate that could lead each animal to one of several pens. As E.C. or the foreman signaled, the gateman would close off the chute accordingly, and the animal would join his selected mates. The biggest job came when the male calves were penned off. These were the cattle that had to be worked into steers after all the yearlings were sorted.

As each steer-to-be ran down a second chute, it reached a point where the sides closed upon it mechanically and squeezed so tight the animal could move neither forward nor backward. The machine would turn each male calf on its side, whereupon four cowboys would descend the walls of the chute. One would sizzle the Cross Bell brand deep into the animal's hide. A second would castrate him, and a third would clip off his horns at their roots with a specially designed tool, while a fourth doused the horn area with blood-stopping powder and vaccinated the animal. Then the mechanical pincers would flip the steer back on his feet, as the cowboys leaped clear. After this, of course, the steer seldom had to be asked twice to leave.

A crew of cowboys could shape about 2,100 head of cattle, or work about four hundred steers in a day. E.C. taught himself to handle each job, even the messy castrating and dehorning.

Frank Raley, the Osage rancher who owns a drugstore in Pawhuska: "Four of us went out on the lake one weekend for a drunken poker party. E.C. said, 'I borrow a million dollars every year from the Federal Reserve Bank in Kansas City for 7 percent.' I said, 'Why would you pay that much interest?' He said, 'Hell, I can make more money every year than that.' E.C. was only about fifteen or sixteen years old then.

"Gene told about this oil lease some Indians were trying to sell. The owner of the lease would get ⅞ of the royalties, and the Indians would get a ⅛ override. They sold the lease to two Jewish guys from Bartlesville, but every hole came up dry. Gene figured out they just hadn't gone down far enough. Well, these two Jewish guys were complaining and Gene asked how much they'd take for the lease. They said $10,000. Gene said, 'E.C., how fast can you write a check?' Then Gene drilled down two hundred more feet and made a fortune."

Linda Vance's father Leo worked for Murray Tool & Supply Company in Cleveland, Oklahoma, back when the sound of Erd Mullendore's Ford rumbling down the main street still brought the town to attention. After Murray Tool folded, Vance moved to Pawhuska and became an independent oil-drilling contractor. When somebody bought an oil lease, Vance was the man they called to drill the hole. He got paid whether it was dry or wet.

He did rather well at it, but died of illness when Linda was thirteen.

Vance's wife, Edna, contributed some Cherokee Indian blood to their only child. The blood gave Linda no claim to Cherokee oil, the Cherokees long ago having turned over their valuable oil rights to the Osages. Mildred Mullendore Adams, who knew the Vances well when they lived in Cleveland and kept track of them later, remembers that Edna always was very conscious of appearances, and that from earliest childhood Linda's clothes not only were expensive but were selected and arranged with great attention.

Linda: "My mother and father knew Gene before he married Kathleen. His mother, Jennie, was very fond of my mother, and his father was fond of my father, before either one of us [herself and E.C.] was born. So I'd always known them. Mrs. Mullendore [Jennie] came up to be with my mother when my father died. I'll never forget it—she couldn't get out of the car, she was so crippled. She died that same year.

"E.C. came to Pawhuska to high school as a freshman. We started dating when I was fifteen and he was fourteen. I had a driver's license and he didn't. They used to joke and say that was the only reason [that he went out with me]. So we dated all through high school."

Classmates recall neither one of them as even an averagely bright student, although pressures may have been greater on them than most. E.C. was the son of the biggest rancher in the Osage, and Linda was his girl friend.

Linda saw the Cross Bell Ranch when she was fourteen. "I'd never been up there. He took me up one morning after he had just put on the wheat in a field there in the bottom. You know, so green. And we went to see the cattle. He was so proud of it.

"He worked after high school. He hayed until dark, and then came into town so exhausted that he would lie down on the floor to watch television and go to sleep, and get up and go home at eleven o'clock."

Edna Vance's daughter required a degree of finishing that Pawhuska High School was unprepared to render, so Linda was packed off to Hockaday, an exclusive Dallas boarding school, for her junior and senior years.

Meanwhile, E.C. was becoming a bit of a cutup back home. He made friends with Doc Shook, son of the Cadillac dealer who enraged Gene during condemnation of Gene's ranchland for the

Pawhuska city reservoir. "E.C. was one of the smartest people I ever knew, but school didn't concern him a whole lot," young Shook says. "He used to be chunky and hard to handle. Several times I thought he was about to get us both killed starting fights."

Linda says E.C. "never wanted to go" to the University of Oklahoma, and would have chosen to learn scientific ranching at Oklahoma State instead. But Gene insisted otherwise, and E.C. followed his father's footsteps, not only to the O.U. campus at Norman but to Beta Theta Pi fraternity. Linda went, too, and joined Pi Beta Phi.

"He wore cowboy boots and tailored Levi's, while the rest of us wore Ivy League clothes," recalls Jim Sturdivant, a classmate who one day would represent a consortium of insurance companies against the $19 million claim of Linda Vance Mullendore. "He had a reputation for taking a lot of people out to dinner and picking up the tab. He drove a Cadillac or Lincoln Continental as a freshman, and wore diamond stickpins. I didn't even have a bicycle."

Unlike his father and grandfather, who forged detailed impressions of themselves in the minds of everyone they met, E.C. often seemed faceless and ordinary. People who saw him frequently still have trouble recalling a single distinguishing aspect of his appearance. Even his cowboy clothing, which looked flamboyant away from home, was not extraordinary for the Osage.

A medical report puts his height at five feet, nine inches. Gene says he was five feet, eleven inches, and "very athletic." Linda says he "was very handsome," with "medium brown hair, hazel eyes, olive skin, lots of personality." Paul Jones a neighboring rancher who hauled hay under contract for E.C. for the better part of a decade, says E.C. was only five feet, eight inches tall, and "homely," with "dark hair, balding in back and front, pale complexion, sickly, milky-looking. He had a high, whiny voice, and sweared all the time. Always saying [in imitation whine], 'Goddamned sons of bitches . . .'" And so it goes. After dozens of interviews, no consensus emerges.

What people remember is his behavior. A frequent scrapper, he had a gold-capped front tooth as a souvenir from an old fight. Julia Gilkey, the maid in Gene and Kathleen's house, recalls that E.C. drank to excess as a youth, but cut way down "after he had that terrible wreck a long time ago. I have never known him to have a drinking problem since then."

He was in a coma for several days after the accident. His mother told neighbors that death was expected. Somehow he survived. Linda seldom left his bedside at the hospital. There are varying accounts of what caused the accident.

Linda: "It was August 26, 1958. We had a date [in Pawhuska, 32 miles from the ranch], and he left, and he always called me when he got home. Before, on one occasion, he had . . . got to feeling sort of tired, and . . . pulled off the road . . . and had gone to sleep. And so I called Kathleen and I said, 'Is E.C. there?' 'No, he isn't.' And I said, 'Well, I'll start from this end, you start from that end.' And he was just fine, you know. He was asleep that time. But this time I called and asked if he had gotten there yet, and she said no, that he had probably just pulled off like he had before, 'so don't come all the way up here. We'll go on down and look for him.' And he just went to sleep driving the car, missed a curve, and hit a big high-line pole."

"He was traveling a little fast for that country road," adds one neighbor.

But around Pawhuska there's a story that E.C. was at the local golf and country club that night and, as one resident put it, "got into a drunken brawl with a much older guy. Nobody got hurt in the fight, but that's the condition E.C. was in when he had the accident."

Then there was the night E.C. came home and saw a man with a rifle in the high grass near the driveway. A deer poacher, he thought, and decided to teach the man a lesson. But as he approached to chase the man off, two others emerged from the shadows and jumped him. They pummeled E.C. bloody with their rifle butts and left him for dead. But the doctors at the hospital put him together again.

"Most of the time, if he asked poachers to leave, why they would," says Linda. "On that particular night, all he did was get out of the car and say the same thing, and they were waiting for him. They tried to kill him. They tried to run over him with their car after they beat him." Linda says the men—who never were arrested—were enemies of the family. The story you hear in the Manhattan Café in Pawhuska, from people who don't want to be quoted, is that the men were relatives of a Bartlesville girl whom E.C. had made pregnant.

Occasionally E.C.'s reckless risk-taking had a happy ending.

Once when somebody stole a valuable stud horse from the ranch, E.C. trailed the thief for three days into Kansas. Finally he took the family airplane up and spotted his man, still in the saddle. Returning to the ground, E.C. cut the man off by automobile and retrieved his horse. The newspaper account didn't say what happened to the thief.

E.C. was in his fourth year at the university when cataracts shut off Gene Mullendore's vision. At least, that's the official explanation of why E.C., who always was more interested in cowhides than sheepskins anyway, quit school and came home to take over. Linda came with him, and they were married December 3, 1959. According to Frank Raley, who operated the Western Union franchise in Pawhuska at the time, the Mullendores were good enough friends of then Senate Majority Leader Lyndon Johnson to wire him instructions—apparently in jest—to reserve a bridal suite in Washington for the honeymoon.

At first the couple lived in a small apartment on the second floor of a brick garage behind the mansion. But Gene had been building a modernistic, flat-roofed, glass-fronted cabana and party house by the swimming pool across the mall from the mansion's front. So they changed the architect's drawings somewhat and converted the half-finished cabana into a home. E.C. and Linda moved into the bizarre-looking structure in the summer of 1960. It became known as the "little house," emphasis on "little," in contrast to the mansion, which was known as the "big house." According to Gene, the little house cost only $150,000.

Into it Linda would bring four children: E.C. IV, Clint, Eric, and Linda, Jr. They were not financially deprived. When Linda, Jr., was only six months old, Gene gave her a child's bracelet—with ten real diamonds in it.

"I gave E.C. all my bank stock," Gene says. "I gave him a headright and put it in his own name so he could have money to spend. He had to have money to operate on. Mrs. Mullendore gave him all of her money. It was all turned over to E.C."

At about this time, E.C.'s sister Katsy, who had become a sorority sister of Linda's at the university, began bringing her boy friend home for visits. Katsy was three years younger than E.C. George Ray remembers her as a strong performer in 4-H, winner of first place in the steer-calf division at the Osage County Fair when she was twelve years old. A newspaper reporter saw her seven years later in 1959 as "a sun-tanned, brown-haired, blue-eyed [actually brown-eyed] beauty" who had just been runner-up in the contest for Queen of the American Royal Horse and Livestock Show in Kansas City.

According to a petition she filed in Osage County Court in 1961, her name, a derivation of her mother's, "was originally placed on the birth certificate as Kaye Mullendore by a stubborn nurse who refused to recognize the fact that a person could be named Katsy. The petitioner has always used the name Katsy Kaye Mullendore."

The judge agreed to give Katsy the name she had always used, only to have her change it again a year later by marrying her boy friend and becoming Mrs. John Whitfield Mecom, Jr. Mecom had been a classmate of Katsy's at the universities of Texas and Oklahoma, but was little more of a student than the Mullendores were and apparently failed to graduate from any of the three universities he attended. He preferred to whack polo balls from ponyback, sponsor race cars at Indianapolis, and buy the New Orleans Saints football team. He could afford these hobbies because his father had amassed a quarter-billion-dollar fortune and had made Mecom, Jr., a full partner.

John Mecom, Sr., had obtained money essentially the same way Erd Mullendore had, by leasing land that always seemed to have oil under it. But Mecom carried none of Erd's inhibiting love for any particular piece of real estate, and felt no touch of Erd's moral longing to be known as an ordinary dirt farmer. As far as Mecom was concerned, the only thing better than being the third richest independent oil operator in the United States, which he was, would have been being the first or second (H. L. Hunt and Sid Richardson deprived him of that).

Mecom, Jr., happened to be dashingly handsome on top of his athletic proclivities and quarter-billion-dollar fortune. The entrance of this Prince Charming into the family obviously delighted Gene Mullendore. But for E.C., who had been outfitted with an oversized pair of boots to fill anyway, Katsy's wedding marked the beginning of a decade of ever more futile efforts to keep up with the Mecoms. The wedding took place on the mall between Gene's big house and E.C.'s little one, and each day afterward the distance across that mall seemed to grow just a bit greater.

Gene, for example, couldn't have been happier with young Mecom's talent for getting newspapers to plaster his picture on their pages alongside puffy descriptions of his latest activities. To Linda, he was a publicity hound, who presented more of himself to the public than a person in true society ought. The stories in the press disjointed her sense of propriety, which had genuine origins but was encouraged all the more by its handiness as a defense mechanism. "E.C.," she insists, "never called the papers. He wasn't a publicity seeker. He hated it."

There was, for example, the matter of the *uthu-pshe*, or cradleboard, ceremony. In Osage tradition, Gene held celebrations at the ranch for the firstborn of both his children, with forty or fifty invitees, all Indians. The child is wrapped in boiled cloth and given a crib and an Indian name. E. C. Mullendore IV, for example, was named *Hulah Kiheka*, or Eagle Chief. Osage gifting tradition is the opposite of the white man's; the celebrant of a great occasion distributes blankets, food, or other presents to his guests rather than receiving things from them. The Indians figure that if a man has good luck, he ought to share it, rather than expect his friends to compound it at their own expense.

The Tulsa newspapers never learned of the ceremony for E. C. Mullendore IV in 1962, but when John Mecom III came along a year later, his parents' preparations for the ceremony included ample notice to the press. Linda still recalls the resultant publicity, pointedly observing that the Mecom party was "probably not as elaborate" or as well attended as the one Gene threw for her own son. The shadow of the playboy brother-in-law in Houston hovered over E.C.'s house right up to the night of his murder.

According to Linda, a lot of things about E.C. never made the papers. Such as his philanthropy. She notes that he paid for the senior class at nearby Copan High School to travel to Kansas City for the American Royal Horse and Livestock Show and stay in a hotel. And he once went to Chicago to convince the Santa Fe Railroad to erect a warning light at an Osage County crossing where four people had just been killed. "If there was ever a cowboy who came to him crippled or with one eye or down on his luck, E.C. always hired him, gave him something to do, even if it was just a fire watch," Linda says.

Ranch management settled E.C. down the way it had his father. He dieted from 210 pounds on his wedding day to a trim 160, a weight he maintained the rest of his life. For at least five years he laid off the bottle and kept mostly out of trouble. His reading matter consisted of *The Farmer-Stockman, The Hereford Journal,* a hog magazine, a crop magazine, *The Kansas City*

Star, and *The Wall Street Journal.* He shunned hobbies and vacations.

"People used to ask him to take up golf because he worked too hard," Linda says. "He just thought that was ridiculous. He laughed at them. He was much happier talking to older men, businessmen, than he was talking to people our age, because he was bored with them."

"If you don't talk about golf, or hunting, or fishing, up in our country, you don't have much to talk about," notes John Arrington, Jr.

Despite his disinclination for hunting, guns seemed to fascinate E.C. Guns always had lain around the house when he was growing up—his father collected them. Jelly Bryce, the FBI agent-in-charge for Oklahoma, who specialized in quick-draw exhibitions, knew the Mullendores and presented the teenaged E.C. with a pistol. Another friend, Walter Spencer, gave E.C. two derringers and a .38. On their honeymoon, E.C. bought Linda an exceptionally big pistol, a .44 Magnum, and said, "This will protect us."

At one point E.C. decided to clear the guns out of the house for fear the children might find them. His collection—the relics—went back to the big house, where Linda says Gene liked to toy with them. E.C. stored the newer guns in another house he owned in Bartlesville, but they were stolen. Then Linda bought a pistol in a Bartlesville store for her own protection and they stashed it in the children's closet. "He and I were the only ones that knew where it was," she says. "It was plastic-handled, and E.C. laughed at the time I bought it and said, 'Why did you ever buy one like that? It will probably explode in your hand.'"

Packing a pistol in the glove compartment of one's car has become common practice in the Osage, where people believe that coyotes and other potential sources of irritation should be shot on sight. George Ray says E.C. carried a fancily engraved automatic in his glove compartment. "I don't know what caliber it was. I have seen him with that little over-and-under I gave him. I have given him several guns myself. God, he had a lot of them. I gave him a .22 derringer, one of those Magnums. I also gave him a 6 mm. Remington deer rifle. And I gave him a German Mauser I would sure like to have back."

Linda says E.C. wanted his three sons "to learn how to hunt and fish, 'cause he remembered that he didn't know how to do any of these things. Because no one had ever shown him. And he wanted them to be well rounded, to be able to do everything."

So E.C. bought his oldest son a .410-gauge shotgun on the lad's sixth birthday. The boy hunted squirrels and frogs. "Kathleen loved to eat squirrel," Linda recalls, "and so she'd say, 'Well, I'd like to have a squirrel,' and off they'd go. Of course, the others [the two younger boys] were too little, but they went, too."

In at least one respect, Linda adapted to Mullendore life as if she had been born with the family's blood: she knew how to spend money. From the time Gene had bought the Cross Bell, extravagance had been the family trademark. While Gene ran the ranch, the family flew its plane to Kansas City to shop for groceries. The Mullendores wanted practically everything they touched to be custom-made and monogrammed with the family brand, a passion they often carried to ridiculous extremes. The swimming pool was in the shape of the Cross Bell brand. Richard Kane, a lawyer-rancher, insists he learned from a source in a local lingerie shop that before Katsy Mullendore departed for her freshman year at the University of Oklahoma, she ordered two dozen pairs of panties and slips emblazoned with Cross Bells.

Almost anywhere in Osage County one can hear gossip that Linda Mullendore flew to Dallas regularly to have her hair done. Actually, she says, this happened only twice. Mrs. Harrison, the cook, vouches that Linda often did her own hair at home, because Mrs. Harrison recalls carrying out the dye-blackened bath towels afterward. But there is no doubt Linda spent money in the best Mullendore tradition. "I don't think a store's got as many clothes as Linda," Mrs. Harrison says. "I never seen so many clothes. Some of them, the tags wasn't even took off of them. I've seen her have a party and the flowers made it look like a funeral parlor. E.C. once said to me, 'She wants to spend more money than I can make.'" Despite E.C.'s disinclination for golf, the Mullendores were members of a lavish country club in Bartlesville, replete with an indoor garden and river that follows the main staircase down in a cascade of waterfalls. There they could socialize with Phillips Petroleum Company executives.

Linda stored her clothes in several different buildings, both on the ranch and in Bartlesville. George Ray says he visited the ranch one day when men were shifting some of the clothes from one building to another. "They had a Hertz truck with a twenty-foot bed with nothing but her clothes on racks," he says. Intrigued, Ray inspected and says he found $300 to $800 price tags still dangling from about half of them. He says E.C. once estimated that day-to-day living expenses for the two houses came to $120,000 a year. The figure seems conservative.

Linda regularly ordered dresses, shoes, and handbags costing hundreds of dollars and apparently thought nothing of spending $5,000 or more on an item of jewelry. She shopped antique stores, and remembered college friends with $32.50 floral bouquets. The Neiman-Marcus store in Dallas seemed to affect her dramatically. Every time the changing winds from the south carried the store's scent toward the ranch, it cost E.C. several thousand dollars. The pad of bills that Neiman-Marcus filed in connection with E.C.'s estate constitutes a remarkable document. Purchase of a $1,000 evening dress merely necessitated the purchase of a $200 handbag and a $125 pair of shoes to match. Linda ordered dozens of shirts for E.C., mostly monogrammed, at an average price of about $20 each. The unending pressure the younger Mullendores felt to keep pace with flashy, free-gifting Mecoms kept Neiman-Marcus clerks hopping. For Katsy's birthday in 1968, for example, Linda had Neiman-Marcus send a floral arrangement for $127.50, a white straw hat for $102, and a Dior wool costume for $576.30—and that was a pale token of what happened at Christmas, when the whole family had to be taken care of in similar style. Kathleen was no stranger to Neiman-Marcus either. On June 17, 1968, for example, she spent $506.15 on five nightgowns and a bathrobe. Two weeks earlier, the routine purchase of five bras, one pair of panties, and three girdles had come to $208.

"People just expected the Mullendores to live like that," comments one Oklahoman who knew them. "It's almost like they felt they had to do it."

Besides E.C., Linda, and their growing family, two other persons became virtual members of the Mullendore household during the decade that preceded the young rancher's final turbulent year: Edna Vance (Linda's mother) and Chub Anderson.

Mrs. Vance did not exactly blend in unnoticed.

Says Kathleen: "She was always nice, very nice, but she was a bitch when [E.C.] couldn't put out all the money she could spend."

Mrs. Harrison, the cook: "Linda was all right as long as her mother was away from there. Linda was nice to be around until her mother came. Mrs. Vance was something else. She followed [E.C.] around the house, telling him what to do like she was his wife. Sometimes E.C. would run her off. Sometimes she would pack a bag and come up there and stay. Make all the help unhappy. I told her I wouldn't work for her if I didn't have anything but bread and water. I couldn't stand her. And Linda would say to me when it would get rough, 'Well, me and my mother didn't get along all the time when I was a little girl.' " One time, Mrs. Harrison says, Mrs. Vance came to visit while E.C. was in Los Angeles on business. "E.C. called from L.A. and told [Linda] to have her mother gone from his house by the time he got back."

But Linda recalls that "E.C. loved my mother. He never drove through the Fairfax or Pawhuska ranch without stopping to see her."

George Ray: "Edna visited often and tried to school the children to her way of thinking. The older Mullendores disapproved of her and she disapproved of them. They never had gotten along. She considered herself better than people doing work for the Mullendores. She considered herself better than me. She considered those children like you would the crown prince."

To Mrs. Vance, the Mullendore flamboyance was no substitute for true class, and she recoiled from the coarseness she often observed on the ranch. "The kids swore a blue streak, and E.C. encouraged it," Ray says. Ray recalls hearing the young rancher try to teach E.C. IV "to say 'goddamn,' and 'son of a bitch,' when he could scarcely say 'Mama' and 'Papa.' "

One visitor remembers seeing E.C.'s two eldest sons trying to saddle a stubborn horse. As four-letter words filled the air, E.C. laughed and said, "My father taught me like that, and if they didn't talk like that, he'd throw 'em off the ranch." Mrs. Vance reportedly was apoplectic over the incident.

While Mrs. Vance played the traditional disapproving mother-in-law, Chub Anderson's role in the family was strange indeed. Chub had a history of trouble when he came to the ranch in 1966, just before his twenty-fifth birthday. He had beaten up some other boys in high school. He had married young, and his wife bore children in 1962 and 1964; but in 1965 he entered the state penitentiary at Granite, Oklahoma, where he served eleven months of a seven-year sentence for livestock theft. "I don't recall the [victim's] name," he says. "There were three different things involved in it. We went down and got a load of wild hogs; they were ear-notched [indicating they belonged to somebody], and got a bull up by I don't recall exactly where, but it was up in Kansas. The fellow with me and I had got a horse from Washington County [Oklahoma]. I was tried in Washington County —didn't have a jury trial. These other places agreed to drop their charges if I would agree to a seven-year sentence on this horse."

After his parole, Chub took a job as a welder in Dewey, where he had been born and raised. Dewey is in Washington County, adjoining the Osage on the east; part of the Cross Bell Ranch lops over into Washington County. A contractor with an assignment to build a hay barn on the ranch hired Chub to help him, and when the barn was finished, E.C. invited Chub to stay on.

Square-jawed, curly-haired, endowed with movie-star good looks and built (as one neighbor put it) "like Mr. America," Chub hardly deserved his unflattering nickname, which had been thrust upon him before he was a year old. Authorities investigating the Mullendore murder would try unsuccessfully to link Chub to E.C. prior to 1965. At one point, Chub said that before going to work for E.C., "I knew who he was, but I didn't know him." Another time, he said, "I have known him since my high school days, not personally too well, but I have seen him to know who he was."

Initially, Chub's job was "just welding, and then they would tear up machinery. I would weld on them, on their trucks; and we were overhauling a horse barn for him, building it all out of steel inside, and I was working on it. When they would tear something up, I would weld on their trucks. I think about '67 or '68, somewhere in there, I started taking his boy to school. He had started preschool, just went half a day. Bartlesville. His oldest son. Just on Tuesday and Thursday at first."

Linda Mullendore: "It was when E.C. [IV] was in the first grade and I had been driving him to school in Bartlesville and I was expecting Eric [their third child], and it got to where I couldn't drive. [Chub] had been working out there on the ranch, and E.C. liked him and he said, 'I know who you can get to drive the children that would be good and take care of them,' and that was when he got the job. As near as I can remember."

Soon Chub was driving two children to school, and when he passed through Dewey and Bartlesville, he picked up the groceries for both families at the ranch. "The maids would call the orders in and they would always have them waiting on me. All I done was pick them up." Chub's marriage was dissolving—the divorce became official in 1968—and he moved into the spacious "bunkhouse" apartment over the ranch machine shop. His salary was raised from $3 to $3.50 an hour, in addition to which E.C.

45

gave him money for clothes and bought him a Chevrolet for his personal use. Chub often ate meals with the family.

George Ray: "[E.C.] trusted Chub 100 percent, I think. As much as he trusted anyone in the world, he trusted Chub Anderson. The fact that he entrusted his children to him, and that he entrusted his money with him. Chub made large deposits for him, large deposits that were endorsed checks."

Despite his parole, Chub carried a .38 pistol. "Sometimes when he would sit in the house," says Lula Harrison, "I would find long bullets, but I didn't pay any attention to what caliber they was. They was under the pillows of the couch."

Linda: "E.C. always said that Chub didn't have to be on parole. That he would get him pardoned. Probably he just never did get around to it." Chub still reported to an officer in Bartlesville.

Chub: "We would build corrals and things during the summer. During the winter, I would work most of the time going after his boys at school. I would usually have to babysit with them of an evening after they got out of school." If E.C. and Linda went out, even to the big house for dinner, Chub might sleep the night in a spare bed in one of the boys' rooms or on the couch.

Mrs. Harrison says Chub was at the house "whenever he didn't have to drive E.C. or take the boys to school, and when they would go to parties and things, he would have to stay and put the boys to bed. The oldest boy was hard to handle." Mrs. Harrison says Linda would give orders to Chub "just like she would us, to stay and bathe the boys and put them to bed, and when E.C. was away, if she would go to the big house, he would have to stay with them and make them go to sleep." In the afternoons, Chub would teach the boys to ride or take them frog hunting, and on occasion Linda would go with them. Chub had a regular spot at the family dining table. Sometimes he ate there with the family while E.C. ate in an easy chair from a TV tray. "I would serve them all their breakfast in the kitchen," Mrs. Harrison says. "E.C. wouldn't eat usually. If he would, it would be in the middle of the day. He would come in and I would fix him a little something to eat."

Ranch hands began to joke about the amount of time the handsome, broad-shouldered, wasp-waisted employee was spending around the boss's wife. "You know, people think something is wrong when there isn't nothing wrong," Mrs. Harrison says. "When they was together, the boys was all with them." But

Mrs. Harrison disapproved of the way Linda appeared before Chub in nightclothes when E.C. was out on the ranch. "She would say he was one of the family, so she just treated him like one in the family. I know, if it had been me, I would have been fully dressed or something."

Kay Sutton, Mrs. Harrison's seventeen-year-old granddaughter, who also helped with the household chores: "Chub used to sit down and talk to my sister and myself, and we would get to giggling. I figured he was an okay guy. Sometimes you would think Linda would be jealous, and by the tone of her voice she didn't like it or something. She didn't want me around him."

Mrs. Harrison: "She wanted them to call him Mr. Anderson. I would say, 'You'd better not call him Mr. Anderson. He is a little convict on parole.' I would say, 'He's not even a citizen.' I spoke it out loud so she would hear me."

Kay Sutton: "Sometimes me and Chub would be up there by ourselves and Mrs. Vance [Linda's mother] always had something to say about it. She was trying to make something out of it that it wasn't. She didn't think Chub should talk to us."

Mrs. Harrison: "E.C. worked constantly on the ranch. He would come back to the house, and there would be Linda and Chub swimming. He'd just stand and look. When Chub went hunting, taking the boys, she'd go with him. Mr. Mullendore [Gene], he didn't like it worth a dime. When she'd go swimming and sunbathing with Chub, he'd get mad."

Linda says she went swimming with Chub only once.

Five

"SHEEEEEEE—IT!" E. C. MULLENDORE SAID, AND pounced on the brake, jerking the yellow Continental to a halt. The ranch terrain was rough on the car, but there would be a new Continental or Cadillac next year. E.C. reached into the glove compartment for a pinch of Copenhagen tobacco and stuffed it behind his lower lip. He replaced the can, then flung open the door, setting off the whining alarm system that came with this year's model to remind him that the ignition key was still in place. "Damn!" he said, yanking the key loose and wondering if he could get somebody to disconnect the alarm system. He got out into the pasture, pulling his white hat across the seat behind him and settling it on his head by habit. Although a stranger can't detect the difference, Osage County residents insist that every man has a distinguishing style of wearing his hat and that E.C. wore his a touch low, front and rear.

The sun was fully over the hills now and the last beads of dew rubbed themselves on E.C.'s brown boot tops as he approached the horse barn. He took hold of the barn door, whose top hinge was busted off the frame, and he yanked upward to see if the door would lift off the ground and swivel on the bottom hinge. It wouldn't. A man galloped up on horseback, one of the oldest and best cowboys the Cross Bell had. He was up early because he knew E.C. was always on the ranch by sunrise and that the young boss wasn't going to be pleased today. E.C. whacked his hand against the broken door and looked up at the cowboy.

"This new boy, Mickey," the man said.

"Hell, he tore the same door off last week, didn't he?"

"Same door," the man said.

"Well, somebody else gonna have to drive that hay truck for a while. What the hell's the matter with the guy? He drunk?"

"Nope. Just new," the cowboy said. "No damage. 'Cept we'll have to fix it."

" 'Cept you'll have to fix it," E.C. repeated. "What else you gonna do today?"

"Well, there's some broken fence not far from the main gate down by route 10."

"Damn, I *know* there's some broken fence down by route 10. I *seen* it."

"Well, we'll fix her. Couple of the boys said they was a few strays yesterday afternoon. They got 'em back. I don't think there's much."

"You know what they're doing now? They're goin' out with helicopters. Damn helicopters! It was in the paper a couple days ago. These guys had a truck, see. And this helicopter would tell the guys down below in this truck where the strays were. By two-way radio. They'd be packed up and gone before anybody knew they was there."

The cowboy gave a tiny smile. "We'll get her fixed today," he said.

"Well, you take care now." E.C. strode back to the Continental and drove off.

One time, George Ray recalls, a Cross Bell cowboy was caught stealing cattle off the ranch. "The guy asked [E.C.] to please go easy," Ray says. "E.C. cursed him out. He says, 'You son of a bitch, you stole my cattle and you're going to jail.' The cowboy was 220 pounds and all muscle. I was afraid we were going to have to smoke that guy off of E.C. But E.C. wasn't afraid of the devil himself. He had guts."

The yellow Continental pulled alongside the big house. E.C. spat tobacco juice into a tin can he kept on the floor of the car and walked to the heavy main door. He didn't knock. His father was dressed and waiting for their morning talk. Many days, when Gene didn't feel well, he stayed upstairs longer and the conversations took place in his bedroom. But the conversations always took place. Julia Gilkey, the maid, says the two men sometimes conferred from early morning until noon. She says at times she caught the tone of the discussion, though seldom the subject matter. Gene, she notes, "has his bad days. He calms down pretty quick if you let him have his way, just agree with him whether he is right or wrong and he will calm down. I have never heard E.C. raising hell [at these meetings]. He wasn't like his daddy. His daddy will just speak out and maybe curse, but E.C., never." At least, not to his father.

George Ray says he attended many of the sessions over the years, although he says "there would be a point when they would ask me to leave the room." Ray describes the portion of the meetings that he saw: "Gene would say, 'Now, E.C., how are those cattle over in the north pasture doing?' And he would say, 'Well, Dad, the water's all right. They're doing all right.' "

According to Ray, E.C. would report, "We're gonna work the cattle out of [a certain] pasture today," and they would discuss what work or which pasture ought to take precedence. E.C. would ask, "What do we do with the old cows?" and they would discuss whether to pasture them separately or sell them, and where and how they might bring the best price. "If there was ever a disagreement," Ray says, "his father's word was the law."

One disagreement was over the buffalo. "The buffalo were tearing down fences. E.C. would tell his father, 'The buffalo got out again today, tore down so many fences, grazing off the wheat that wasn't ready.' They were tearing down people's gardens and clotheslines. Gene would say, "Well, goddamnit, fix the fences.' His words were always, 'Goddamnit, get that goddamned thing done.' He said they were keeping the buffalo and the longhorns [despite E.C.'s complaints], and he absolutely held E.C. responsible if anything went awry. The buffalo and the longhorns and the quail were his thing. And the acquisition of more land."

Linda Mullendore didn't attend those morning sessions, but she could hardly escape the disagreement over the buffalo. "He built all these fences and the buffalo would tear them down. It was discouraging," she recalls. "He left the gate open so they could go in the gate. They'd never go in the gate. The buffalo would take the top two wires off the fence. They were just always out. Once they got away across the Kansas border, and there's an old cemetery up there. They got in and pushed the tombstones out. And we had to go get them and bring them back, and E.C. and the cowboys had to go up there and put up the tombstones again. They went up in a pickup with horses in that, and [herded] them back. They scared a few motorists."

"And the so-called cattalo," John Arrington, Jr., says. "I think one newspaper said they were the product of careful breeding. Well, they weren't at all. A buffalo just got away and bred a cow and it was a big mess, because it killed the cow usually when she had one, because the thing's got that hump on him. The cattalo is just like a mule. It's a hybrid that can't breed, and it's a monstrosity. Whenever you have buffalo running around, it's going to happen." Cattaloes, he adds, are inedible.

"I'm sure he [Gene] didn't think the buffalo could make money," Linda says. "Nobody could think that. They're a hobby. E.C. hated them. They eat as much as a Hereford cow, or more. And feed is expensive. And finally, to keep them from tearing the fences down and have the cowboys waste their time chasing them, he built the buffalo fence—$26,000 worth of fence. And then, of course, they couldn't get to the grass and had to be fed [with store-bought feed]."

She says E.C. often suggested getting rid of the buffalo, "but not to his father. He would say to me, 'I wish we could get rid of them, and one of these days we will.' But he felt that if his dad, you know, wanted the buffalo and the longhorn, well, 'That's something Dad wants, you know, I'll just have to put up with it.' "

After the buffalo and longhorns came the quarter horses. In the fall of 1968, Linda says, Gene got it into his mind "to build the best quarter-horse racing stable in the United States. When he got a bee in his bonnet, you know, one day he'd get [what he wanted]."

The quarter horse is the basic Western working horse, but

50

some have been specially bred with thoroughbreds for racing. "E.C. did object the first time," Linda says. "His father said, 'No, I want to go ahead and have some race horses.' E.C. always did everything his father asked him to. The worst [example] would be the race horses." So they bought six or seven horses for about $60,000, the beginning of a nearly half-million-dollar investment.

"E.C. didn't like race horses," Linda says. "He didn't believe in it. The first horses they bought were at a sale in Florida, and he came back and said, 'Well, we bought the horses. That's one investment that will lose money.'"

Although Gene retained title to most of the land, he gave E.C. power of attorney over the ranch. Linda says she saw the document shortly after they were married but doesn't remember when it was dated. Kathleen at times says that E.C. "never did do anything without first consulting his dad." But at other times she says her son "was pretty close-mouthed" and "never wanted to worry his dad or me."

Linda argues that her father-in-law was really running the ranch. "E.C. had to make all the decisions on borrowing the money. But if there were six cowboys out working the pasture and Mr. Mullendore—this really happened—wanted a door hung on this old outhouse over here, they'd stop and go hang the door."

Says John Arrington, Jr., "No one would think of not obeying his order. He was still the big boss. If he told a cowboy to do something, or he ordered something, it would never enter anybody's head to say, 'I'd have to check it with E.C.'"

For a while the ranch continued as it had for decades. "Nobody up there had a real business education," says James Sturdivant, the insurance lawyer who went to college with E.C. "There was just always enough income to keep going. There was always enough up there, it didn't matter. Nobody was concerned about business economics. They knew well how to breed cattle, fertilize pastures, and so forth."

"You'd have to have seven auditors to figure out his operation," Frank Raley says of E.C. "He's got horse paddocks here, cows over there, he's buying land here, leasing it there." E.C. didn't hire a full-time bookkeeper until 1970. Linda: "I kept all the books for the payroll, and an accountant in Pawhuska [an insurance agent working in his spare time] kept the other accounts. I wrote their name down and how much they made.

Paid them twice a month. Took out their social-security tax and this sort of thing. It was very simple. Uncomplicated. Kathleen kept them until E.C. and I were married."

Gene was still his old, ornery self. After E.C. and Linda married and plans for the bathhouse-cabana were revised to make a home for the young couple, Gene tried to dodge payment of the original architect. In 1963, Robert Caldwell, the architect, sued for $5,769.91, including $87.77 for the kitchen sink, which he had furnished. The Mullendores denied that they had ever hired Caldwell. They refused to show up for depositions in Caldwell's court case, arguing that Gene (in the words of his doctor) "has an affliction with respect to his eyesight which makes it very difficult to find his way even about familiar premises and it would be very dangerous for him to be un-attended away from his place of abode." Kathleen also could not appear, because she "has been in constant attendance on her husband at their residence and has herself become almost completely exhausted because of the sickness, and she is not well herself and would not be able to attend court or any other place outside of their home for the purpose of giving a depo-sition."

Judge J. C. Cornett twice threatened the Mullendores with contempt of court if they didn't show up at a designated time to testify, but deputies couldn't locate the Mullendores to serve the summonses. The case finally came to trial in December 1964, and at its end, Judge Cornett told Gene, "There are times when it is necessary that a public official's duty must transcend friendship. Last Friday, unfortunately, while the court was still in session, you engaged in words and actions which rendered your conduct in contempt of this court. Your offensive language was directed at a . . . member of the bar [Caldwell's lawyer]. This . . . is not a place where you may take the law into your own hands. As long as I preside over this court . . . I shall permit no one in court to resort to or threaten violence except under penalty of law." The judge fined Gene $50 and sentenced him to ten days in jail, but suspended the jail term on condition of an apology and good behavior. Worse, the jury awarded Caldwell $2,887.77.

In general, E.C. treated employees much better than Gene had. There was no more convict labor. By 1970, salaries had increased to $250 a month, plus an individual house—most of the cowboys' houses were substantially improved under E.C.'s administration—plus meat, plus $15 a month for every child that worked. Says George Ray: "He would help employees when their wives were about to give birth. If a man was in jail, he was there to bail them out and he defended them. Gene would never do that."

The employees seemed to agree. James Gose, a cowboy: "He was sure a good guy to work for. He was always wanting to know if you needed anything. He would get you just about anything. Since I have come there, he never did get on a horse and work cattle, but he would drive by."

Chub Anderson: "Everybody that ever worked for him got along with him real well. If they ever got in any financial bind, he would loan them the money and they would pay it back out of their checks. Some of them would holler they wanted a bathroom in their house. He would try to work that out."

Dale Kuhrt (pronounced "court"), the professional ranch manager E.C. hired in October 1969: "Most of the hands, the only one they would get mad at was me. E.C. was always advancing them money, and the first day I went to work I told them there wouldn't be any more advances. Before I went out there, you could go to the Pig Stand or anywhere and charge a beer or anything you wanted, and E.C. would pay for it. He was too bighearted with the help."

Linda tells of one time the new ranch manager threatened to have one of the hands arrested for driving a pickup truck recklessly. E.C. was away at the time, so Linda says she intervened against calling the police "because E.C. always tried to protect all the boys and Lonnie [the culprit] was just a welder and a hay hand."

A sporting-goods store clerk in Pawhuska says Linda and E.C. came in one year and bought $6,000 worth of shotguns, saddles, and other equipment for the cowboys for Christmas. (Linda says he's probably exaggerating.)

Relations with outsiders, however, generally failed to improve. Even in 1970, *The Tulsa Tribune* would report about the Cross Bell, "Ranch hands still ride with a rifle in the saddle, and trespassers often hear the whine of a warning shot." In 1969, the Mullendores still were haggling in court with Sohio Petroleum Corporation over whether the company's carelessness with its power lines caused a bad grass fire that allegedly killed cattle and crops and destroyed fences. In 1967, the family still was in court with Gene's sisters and A. C. Adams over Erd's estate. And about the same time, Richard Kane says, E.C. tried to acquire some Indian land adjoining the Kanes' pastures for "less than reasonable prices." Kane says he and his father "backed him down," and the Indian bureau disapproved the sale to E.C.

"It was the same inconsistent, Dr. Jekyll–Mr. Hyde situation," Kane says. "When they wanted to be hospitable, the Mullendores were the most hospitable you could be. But when they wanted to be mean, they could be meaner than anybody. They'd beat up oil-company employees walking their pipelines. Gene and E.C. would travel around with the cowboys. The cowboys would hold the guy and E.C. would beat him. Poachers, too. But this exposed them. This is why E.C. got beaten up, why they were burned out a few times. All somebody has to do is throw a burning piece of paper in your pasture in the fall and he can wipe you out. E.C. was the same kind of mixture [as Gene]. You'd meet him socially and he was as nice and gentlemanly as he could be. But in business, the stories are that he was otherwise." The difference between E.C. and his father, Kane says, was that "E.C. could never quite carry it off."

Six   No one could have told E.C. exactly how much money he was worth, because land has so little liquidity. For almost half a century, the price of land in Osage County had been determined largely by what the Mullendores were willing to pay for it. Estimates varied wildly as to the Cross Bell's value—and even as to how many acres it contained. According to papers the family filed in U.S. District Court, Tulsa, in April 1971, the main ranch consisted of about 42,300 owned acres; the Little Chief Ranch at Fairfax, 6,772 acres; the Pawhuska Ranch, 9,626 acres; and a ranch that E.C. bought for $330,000 in 1963, in Sedan, Kansas, near the Cross Bell, 7,439 acres (including some leased acres). The total exceeds 66,000 acres. This figure would seem to be the most accurate available, because the 1971 filing, unlike others, contained a pasture-by-pasture assessment of the various ranches. (The pastures that were totaled up had names like North Nigger, South Nigger, West Whistler, Timmors Trap, Coon Creek, Wildlifeland, East Fronkier, West Fron-

Gene Mullendore

Linda Mullendore

E. C. Mullendore

Kathleen Mullendore

Katsy Mullendore Mecom (E.C.'s sister), with one of her children

Linda and E.C. with their children from left to right: Linda Jr. (infant), Clint, E.C. IV, and Eric

Chub Anderson

House and grounds of the Cross Bell, set up for a party, as would be seen from E.C.'s house

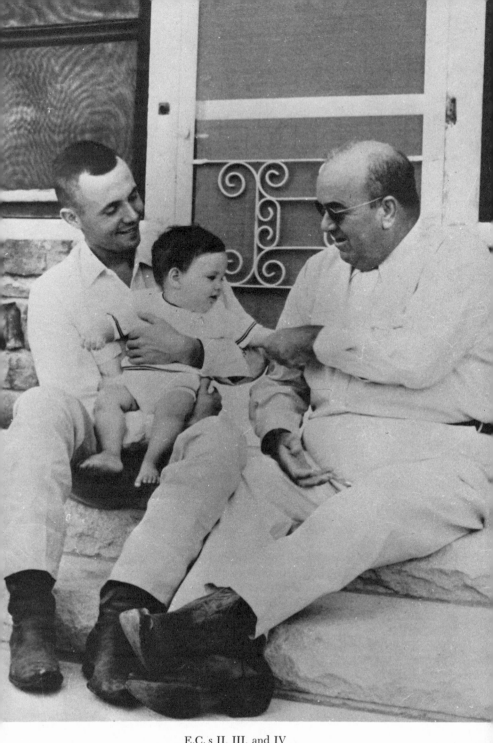

E.C. s II, III, and IV

E.C. with Clint and E.C. IV

kier, Skull Creek, Hickory Creek, Railroad Brown, North Slaughter, East Slaughter, and South Slaughter.)

Besides the acres owned outright, the Mullendores leased thousands of acres. The terms of the leases differed and the total is hard to tabulate. John Arrington says, "E.C. probably doubled the leased land under Mullendore control during his administration, because there were people around who liked E.C. well enough to lease to him where [the land] had not been available to lease before." Also, the Mullendores owned 1,280 acres in Pecos County, Texas, and had grazing leases on 15,000 acres there—apparently part of Kathleen's inheritance from her parents, the Borens. At E.C.'s death, *The Tulsa Tribune* soberly estimated that the young rancher managed 130,000 acres.

Now as to value: as recently as 1967, courthouse records indicate, E.C. was buying ranchland for about $200 an acre. Farmland in Osage County is generally valued at about $500 an acre, because it takes a heavy investment in bulldozers and labor to convert ranchland into farmland—and most ranchland lacks the potential for such improvement. For four or five years before his death, E.C. had invested heavily to clear the thickets off the Cross Bell's best bottom land and make it tillable. The Mullendores' farmland expanded from almost nothing to about 6,750 acres, including at least 2,325 acres of wheat, 700 of barley, and 470 of alfalfa.

Thus, if you took the best estimates of land owned outright in 1968–70 and multiplied by then current prices, you would have about 60,000 ranch acres at $200 each, or $12 million, plus about 7,000 farm acres at $500 each, or $3.5 million, a total of $15.5 million. Of course, if the Cross Bell had suddenly gone on the market at any particular moment, competition among bidders might have raised the price much higher than $15.5 million; or a lack of interest might have forced the sale at a price much lower. Lease value is even harder to estimate objectively.

E.C.'s livestock was worth several million dollars or more. A count by a federal agency in December 1968 showed 15,419 head of cattle, 1,138 hogs, and 335 horses (most of them work horses, not race horses). A similar count one year later showed 16,670 head of cattle, 1,215 hogs, and 379 horses.

The young Mullendore also tried to diversify his holdings beyond land and livestock. The results make a pretty good argument for sticking to what you know. When John Mecom, Sr., bought control of the National Bank of Commerce in Tulsa, E.C. bought some stock and became a director. Later, Mecom sold to Jimmie J. Ryan, who also controlled Community National Life Insurance Company, with headquarters in Tulsa. At Ryan's suggestion, E.C. bought stock in Community National Life and became a director. But Jimmie J. Ryan turned out to be a con man. In 1969, the insurance company went into receivership. Most of its purported $26 million in assets was found to consist of worthless securities churned off the printing presses of a gang of professional swindlers. Among these worthless securities, for example, was a purported deed to vast timber acres in North Carolina, valued on the balance sheet at $5.2 million. Regulatory authorities later discovered that the vast timber acres actually consisted of the Great Smoky Mountains National Park and a nearby Cherokee Indian reservation, and were subject to a firm competing claim by the United States government. An insurance agency controlled by Ryan's family had taken hundreds of thousands of dollars in real cash out of Community National, purportedly as commissions for the sale of insurance policies paid for with these phony "assets." The worthless insurance policies, in turn, were used to collateralize large loans, and some major banks lost millions of dollars when the loans weren't repaid. Ryan and several others pleaded guilty to fraud. Naturally, E.C. wasn't involved in the scandal—Ryan apparently had used him to provide a few thousand dollars in capital and some prestige from the Mullendore name—but E.C.'s investment with Ryan wasn't what you'd call a winner.

Neither was his investment with Wally Noel, a short, blond, Germanic-looking Kansan whom E.C. met in 1967. Noel claimed to be active in revenue-bond financing, and proposed a joint venture with E.C. to market revenue bonds for various communities and the state government. Somewhere along the line, however, Noel switched interests from revenue bonds to Italian gastronomy, and E.C. ended up backing a chain of Pizza Hut franchises with $100,000 to $150,000. But the big highway restaurant franchise boom, which started with McDonald's hamburgers and Kentucky Fried Chicken, quickly fizzled out when dozens of imitators selling everything from pizzas to tacos to fish and chips discovered there was a limit to how much motorists could eat.

E.C.'s investments on and off the ranch caused a great outflow of cash, and to provide it, E.C. rapidly escalated the

Cross Bell's debt. In 1954, Gene had signed an $890,000 mortgage on the ranch, and on October 11, 1963, the family replaced it with a $1.2 million mortgage to the Metropolitan Life Insurance Company—still a relatively small mortgage for the value of the property. In August 1966, Met Life increased the mortgage to $2.1 million.

In the fall of 1967, E.C. needed more money, and apparently Metropolitan Life thought the loan E.C. had in mind was too close to the ranch's potential for repayment. E.C. mentioned to his in-laws that he needed a new lending source. So at the wedding of John Mecom, Jr.'s sister Lannie in Houston, Mecom, Sr., introduced E.C. to E. M. Radcliffe, a West Memphis, Arkansas, loan broker. Radcliffe had helped the Mecom family find loans to finance some of its projects.

Loan brokers like Radcliffe are supposed to know which insurance companies, pension funds, or other sources of revenue are cash-heavy and looking for places to invest. For a fee, the brokers negotiate loans for whoever hires them—either the businessmen needing loans or the lending institutions. E.C. and Radcliffe arranged a meeting later at John and Katsy's house.

"We discussed a lot of figures," Radcliffe recalls. "E.C. was in the process of bringing his ranch up to the highest potential of getting the most out of it. He was clearing land, putting it into grain crops, and he was very ambitious and wanted to get the ranch rolling in the highest state of cultivation for both pastures and fields. He wanted me to be a consultant to work with him in bringing the ranch up to the place where he wanted it to be."

So Radcliffe and some men from Northwestern Mutual Life Insurance Company, with which Radcliffe had a working arrangement, went to the ranch to take a look. While they negotiated a long-term mortgage, Radcliffe helped E.C. obtain interim loans of $100,000 from McEloy Bank in Fayetteville, Arkansas, and $275,000 from a bank in Lubbock, Texas.

In November 1967, Northwestern Mutual lent the Cross Bell operation $4 million, to be repaid over twenty-five years. Part of this money retired the two interim bank loans, and part of it paid off the mortgage of Metropolitan Life, which charged a prepayment fee of 2 percent, or $33,600. Part of the new money repaid some smaller mortgages E.C. owed on individual parcels of land he had been buying over the years. In addition, Radcliffe charged E.C. an $80,000 commission for negotiating the Northwestern Mutual loan. After deducting this commission, and the amount needed to pay off E.C.'s existing debts, Radcliffe said

E.C. was left with $759,000 "for operating capital to improve the ranch." Radcliffe's $80,000 commission, coupled with the $33,600 penalty fee to Metropolitan Life, plus normal higher interest costs, meant E.C. was paying quite a premium to get $759,000 in "new" money—an indication that E.C.'s grand plans already were pressing him toward improvidence.

And even then, the Northwestern Mutual loan was not enough. After committing all this money to long-term improvements—new land, transformation of pastures or wooded acres into farmland, construction of new storage buildings and cowboys' houses, etc.—E.C. still needed cash on which to operate—to buy feed, to pay wages, to meet the payments on the long-term loans, and, of course, to buy groceries, new cars every year, diamond jewelry, and thousand-dollar evening dresses.

One might expect the twice-yearly sale of cattle to keep a rancher in the black, but E.C. had to meet the cost of stocking his new pasture before he could receive income from it. And he was expanding capacity not only by purchasing more land but also by planting new strains of grasses that would graze many more cattle per acre than the native bluestem. In the middle 1960's, E.C. began withholding all his yearling heifers from market, planning to use them for brood cows to enlarge his herd.

Moreover, E.C.'s personal living expenses were beginning to rival those of a colonial-era maharajah. But Linda Mullendore would rather concentrate on the ranch expansion to explain why E.C.—having just received a long-term capital loan from Northwestern Mutual—also needed a second loan to cover short-term operating expenses.

At the suggestion of George Ray, E.C. went to the Production Credit Association in nearby Ponca City, Oklahoma, to see about an operating loan. Production Credit is a cooperative formed under the Farm Credit Act of 1933 to lend short-term money to farmers and ranchers. Production Credit Associations (PCA's) were formed in agricultural areas all across the country. The one in Ponca City gets its money from the Federal Intermediate Credit Bank in Wichita, which, in turn, raises cash by selling interest-bearing debentures on the public market. The members of PCA are its borrowers, each of whom must invest 9 percent of his loan to buy stock in the PCA. Each borrower receives one vote for the board of directors of the local PCA, and the board hires a professional president to handle the actual loan applications, disbursements, and repayments.

In December 1967, a month after obtaining his long-term loan from Northwestern Mutual Life, E.C. applied for and won a $1.4 million line of credit from the Ponca City PCA. And on January 12, 1968, he withdrew his first cash: $707,600 "to refinance bank indebtedness, general operating expense, beef stock, and a loan service fee," according to Harold Copper, the PCA president. Actually, it appears that E.C. used most of the money to pay off a $525,000 loan from Commerce Trust Bank in Kansas City. Gene had kept a revolving loan account at Commerce Trust for many years, usually for much smaller amounts. After E.C. paid off the loan in January 1968, the Mullendores never borrowed from Commerce Trust again. Whether the bank pressured its big ranching customer to close accounts because of financial distrust has never been disclosed.

Through the spring of 1968, the Mullendores continued to withdraw money at Ponca City to buy livestock, pay taxes, pay lease fees, buy feed, pay contracted labor, and so on. In exchange, PCA held a mortgage on the Mullendores' cattle. Thus, whenever E.C. sold any cattle, the money was supposed to go back to the PCA to reduce the loan there. The PCA also held a secondary mortgage on the Mullendores' land, so that if the ranch was ever foreclosed on, PCA would be entitled to the real-estate assets remaining after Northwestern Mutual had been paid off.

John Arrington, Jr.: "When E.C. took this thing over, [he] set out to do what he felt his father wanted, and what he himself took over as the ideal from his father, of having the best ranch—certainly in this whole area of the state, if not in the entire United States. And the only way to do that was to spend substantial sums of money, both for land acquisitions to increase the size of your base that you had to put the cattle on, [and] to clear bottom land—farmland—in order to raise your [own] feed so you wouldn't have to be at the mercy of what you had to pay for feed in the winter. The more feed that you could raise and work through your elevator there, the less you had to buy."

Linda: "And he had to buy thirty new bulls every year [to maintain the quality of the herd]. The veterinary bill was $50,000 a year."

John Arrington says he was told that the calf crop under Gene's administration had never exceeded 70 to 80 percent, but E.C. was able to raise it to 90 percent. "If you keep your good heifers and ship away your culls," Arrington explains, "it takes a number of years, but ultimately you get to the point where 90 percent of your cows are having calves. Well, that means if you have ten thousand cows, then you have nine thousand calves, and they're selling them in the market today [1972] for between $400 and $500 a calf. You see what kind of income [you'd get]—and E.C. set out to do this. He paid higher prices for land, but when it was land next to his place, that he needed to add to his ranch, he felt that the value of the land would continue to increase as inflation occurred. What seemed to be too high a price in a particular time would later prove to be a very reasonable price. When you bought land at $35 an acre, $125 an acre sounded high. But now the same land that he would buy for $125 an acre is appraised at $150 or $175 an acre.

"You can't work your breeding, you can't keep your yearlings separate, you can't manage them with a minimum number of cowboys, unless your pastures are a reasonable size. You've got to build new fences. You've got to replace fences that haven't been replaced since the twenties. There are fences up there that are fifty years old, that were put up by Mr. Boren, that have never been replaced. E.C. replaced those. You have to build houses and silos and things where you can store the feed that you're growing. E.C. did that. It's terribly expensive. All this was during that period in the sixties when interest rates started going up and up and up. Every single thing he did was directed toward making this not just a showplace but something that would produce and would be there for his sons. Fifty years from now. When he built a gate, he built it with steel posts and had it welded. He didn't just build a wooden gate with two-by-fours and two-by-sixes."

E.C.'s capital expenditures during 1967 far outraced the net proceeds of the loan from Northwestern Mutual. So he continued borrowing from banks. The theory, says John Arrington, was that as soon as the capital investments started producing more income, E.C. would get another big twenty-five-year insurance company loan to pay off the short-term bank loans.

But the theory wasn't working out, and ultimately E.C. was trying to borrow money from almost any bank he could find that would lend to him. He had met William B. Hill, executive vice-president of the Union State Bank at Arkansas City, Kansas, socially in February 1967. Over the next few years, Hill says, E.C. obtained "ten different loans, and that doesn't include renewals" from the bank. The first was a $30,000 loan April 7, 1967, renewed in October.

Gene had banked at the First National Bank of Dewey, Oklahoma, for twenty-five years without borrowing money, but E.C. took out a loan of $35,578 on July 21, 1967, to buy real estate—the "old Floyd Carpenter place." Over the next few years, E.C. made payments on his loans, but he borrowed more than he paid, and the debt gradually climbed toward the bank's $90,000 lending limit.

Frank C. "Coke" Harlow had been president of the Coffeyville (Kansas) State Bank since its inception in October 1967. When the bank's first anniversary rolled around, Harlow decided he could get a lot of publicity by celebrating with a buffalo barbecue. There was only one likely place to get a buffalo. E.C., of course, was more than happy to give one free to the bank, and the beast was slaughtered and served up to guests at a party. During their conversations, E.C. took the opportunity to ask Harlow about a loan. He borrowed $70,000, and agreed to invest $10,000 to buy stock in Harlow's bank. He paid interest on the loan for a while, but after May 1969, it fell into arrears.

In December 1968, E.C. borrowed $60,000 from the First National Bank of Tulsa. By the next September, he had returned to borrow $100,000 more to buy cattle, possibly breeding bulls.

The failure of the Cross Bell Ranch to operate in the black under E.C.'s administration was becoming apparent. A lot of people, blessed with hindsight, have tried to figure out why he lost money.

Paul Jones, who contracted to supply hay and services for E.C.: "Gene chiseled and cut corners and burned people out and got them mad. E.C. just paid high prices. You can sit here and figure out how much you're paying for an acre, and you put a $400 cow on it, and there's no way you can make any money."

Frank Raley, the rancher-druggist: "He'd go to a man's house and say, 'Well, we know it's worth $125 an acre. I'll tell you what I'll do. I'll give you $175 tonight. You pack up by the end of the month. I just want to get it closed.' That's the rancher's mentality. He just wants that land."

Richard Kane, the lawyer-rancher: "E.C. would lease a ranch at $7 an acre when [from] anybody else [the owner] would have felt happy getting $5. He bought land at $500 an acre when the going price was $300. He would rent land, and his operations wouldn't even cover the amount of the rent, let alone the cost of the labor. He had life plans [for] all of this. [But] times change. The days of the robber baron were over. His father, for all of his faults, never paid more for land than it was worth. He often paid nothing for it. The tactics [E.C.'s] father and grandfather used just weren't possible in the sixties. Ethics are much more closely watched now."

If E.C.'s land purchases were of doubtful astuteness, so were his decisions about grazing grass. Osage bluestem grows straight up in thin stalks lined with sprouts of tiny leaves. It will reach as high as six feet if left ungrazed. Bermuda, a slightly more brilliant green, crawls in runners along the ground and makes a thick, matted carpet that squashes and springs up as you walk on it.

Kane: "Bluestem grass needs no fertilizer. It just grows naturally, the native ground cover. Bluestem can feed one cow per six to ten acres. Other grasses, fescue or brome or Bermuda, will feed one cow on one acre. But you need cultivation and labor. So the rancher goes with his native pasture. But one of E.C.'s problems, he cleared the wooded areas to introduce Bermuda grass [and] some fescue. It would make the land much more productive, but it turns into more farming than ranching. You need all sorts of equipment, fertilizing costs every year. Then the alfalfa has to be baled and fed [to the cattle] over the winter. So he was doing things a lot different than his father ever did."

E.C. had six or seven rented bulldozers at a time clearing land for conversion to Bermuda grass or alfalfa. Other Osage ranchers now sharply divide over the wisdom of converting from bluestem to Bermuda, and chances are it will take more experiments to prove whether or not conversion is viable. Beef prices bounce along in a jagged graph, making planning difficult. A rancher can't know what this year's calf crop will bring in next year's market.

Still, ranch trustee Joe Jarboe says the grass conversion was "not one of E.C.'s mistakes. In many cases it will pay off. On a particularly large ranch like that, you need these small traps or pastures, for weaning calves. You may put a thousand head on 150 acres for a month or six weeks. It keeps them away from their mothers. [Otherwise] they'll crawl through the fences to get back and suck. You have to take them away from the mother every year so she can have another one."

Paul Jones: "It wasn't on his grass plantin' that he went wrong—unless someone rickadooed him puttin' it in. Even at

$100 an acre [and Jones thinks it should cost considerably less than that], it's still cheap. He just did it way too quick. He should have made a ten- or twenty-year deal out of it instead of in a couple or three years."

Jones also thinks E.C. got "rickadooed" on many of his purchases for the ranch. "Where it would have cost me $400 a mile to build fence, he paid somebody $700. The cowboys stole feed off of them, sold it to someone they knew could use it. Maybe steal a ton at a time, would cost $65 to $70, the cowboys would sell it for maybe $35. People didn't like [the Mullendores], they had a lot of enemies, so they would have sugar in their tractor fuel tanks sometimes. The cattle was stolen, too." Jones says the Mullendores could have stopped the thievery by keeping better records, as other ranchers did.

Jones: "Cowboys would take E.C.'s trailers, use E.C.'s gas, to participate in rodeos. Four pickups might be gone in one week. To Kansas, Tulsa. During working hours, they'd just take off and go to rodeos. They hired a fencing contractor to do the fencing when the cowboys should have been doing it. The farming end of it was the same way. They should have had cowboys doing some farm work. Instead, the Muller Construction Company [an independent contractor] did the farm work—plowing and ground preparation—when the Mullendore tractors would be setting. He couldn't get the hired hands to do it. He'd tell them to take care of his cattle, and they'd take care of one pasture and go and do what they pleased. It was a loose operation.

"For instance, he called me one time to bring some hay, he was out of feed. I unloaded 450 bales, there was four hundred head of cattle. About sixty came over. There was no cowboys there to call the cattle in. He was there and he saw what was happening. I talked to the cowboys later, and they lost five hundred cattle that winter [1967–8]. The food was there. It just wasn't distributed right. The cowboys—half of them would be in town, drunk. E.C. didn't care, really. The Mullendores have always lost cattle. Gene was mean to his labor and got a lot out of them. E.C. was nice to them, improved the quarters, and they took advantage of him. If Gene had known what was going on, he'd have put a stop to that. I've heard cowboys remark about not letting the Old Man catch them at something.

"E.C. would just call me and say, 'Bring over some hay.' It didn't matter about the price. He could have gotten a much better deal if he'd have done some horse trading. He had plenty

63

of pickups [to get the hay himself]. But it was just too much trouble. I was happy to go along. There was a lot of profit in it."

Says Sheriff Wayman: "He spent money on stuff that didn't produce. A $125,000 grain elevator, for instance." Says Osage ranch trustee and Buick dealer Eddie King: "They did a lot of good. The gates, the fences—it's all very nice if you could afford it. But when I get in a pinch, I don't spend so much of my money on extracurricular activities."

Some associates think E.C.'s psychological problems were getting the better of him and contributing to the Cross Bell's deficits. Paul Jones says E.C. "was a spoiled kid. Nobody liked him. He was trying to buy his friends by being so nice to his hired hands, and all they were doing was robbing him. People he liked and wanted to get something out of, he was nice to them. But if he didn't think he could get something out of them, he treated them like dirt."

Jones also detected a strong jealousy of Chub Anderson in E.C. "He would have liked to have been like Chub. That's why he took on with him. E.C. would discipline Number Four [as they called his son, E.C. IV] by saying, 'Goddamn, if you don't straighten up, I'm going to get Chub after you.' "

E.C. also tended to be more open and demonstrative than his tight-lipped, charm-schooled wife, and this may have bothered him. Says Dale Kuhrt, the ranch manager: "Whenever I was with E.C., he would call her up every two or three hours. He's got more affection than I probably have. Every time he would call her, he would say, 'I love you.' " Mrs. Harrison, the cook, recalls, "E.C. was always trying to kiss her, putting his arms around her when they would come to the kitchen. She would stand there and let him hug and kiss her." Asked if Linda ever responded to E.C.'s affection, Mrs. Harrison replies, "No."

George Ray argues that E.C. had "a Napoleonic complex. As far as this county's concerned, and the livestock business, he intended to control it." Ray notes that E.C. had a three-foot marble bust of Napoleon at the entrance to the little house, and several more small busts of Napoleon inside. (Linda says the busts blended with the house's French décor and that she doubts E.C. even knew very much about Napoleon.)

But by all odds, E.C.'s main psychological challenge was trying to please his father—the same challenge that had plagued Gene Mullendore himself a generation before. E.C. must have looked up to Gene with awed frustration, just as

Gene had regarded Erd. E.C., like Gene before him, pursued the image he thought fate had prescribed, but E.C. had neither the grandfather's genius nor the father's meanness. As E.C.'s friend Doc Shook puts it in the local idiom, "E.C. and his father were just different turned" (though Shook adds, "E.C. got a lot more like his father as he got older").

Says James Sturdivant, the lawyer: "His father cast such an image of greatness that E.C. was dogged by it." And George Ray's wife says, as her husband nods assent, "Gene wanted to perpetuate everything through E.C. He wanted him to walk on water. If he fumbled, he was a so-and-so. And if he made it, it was an excuse for Gene to say, 'Look how great *I* am.'"

Linda's loose ways with a dollar helped strain E.C.'s relations with his parents all the more. Mrs. Gilkey, the only maid at the big house, recalls that during the morning conferences with E.C., "Gene hollered continuously that she was spending too much and wasting."

Moreover, just as Gene had felt a rivalry with his brother-in-law A. C. Adams over Erd's affections, E.C. at times felt the same rivalry with his own brother-in-law, the flashy Texas oilman. Says Linda: "He was sick and tired of hearing from Gene about Mecom, Mecom, Mecom. This was held up as the high point of achievement. Race cars and safaris—this was all E.C. heard about—and he got up at five every morning and worked till seven. I think E.C. wanted to be worth as much money as John Mecom. When Katsy married John, he heard John praised all the time. He didn't like hearing about someone else with his race cars and importing animals from Africa and Indianapolis and football. [E.C.] worked hard and he resented it. He felt John hadn't had the same chance to make his own way. He never even considered John Mecom, Jr., his equivalent in business judgment or hard work. He liked John all right. He had immense respect for John Mecom, Sr."

Ironically, when E.C. became eager for more loans in the summer of 1969, the Mecom family, to whom he might have turned for help, faced trouble of its own. The Six-Day War had wiped out the Mecoms' substantial oil investments in Jordan, and with interest rates spiraling and money growing scarce in the United States, some of the Mecoms' bank creditors threatened to call their loans. In a little more than a year, the Mecoms would have to enter bankruptcy proceedings to stall off the creditors. Eventually they managed to reorganize their assets, make payments, and leave bankruptcy with their empire mostly intact. But even though the Mecoms lacked the liquidity to lend any money in the summer of 1969, they could provide advice. Over the July 4 weekend, when the Mecoms traditionally got together with the Mullendores, talk turned to getting a big new umbrella loan for the ranch. And John Mecom, Jr., suggested that E.C. call a couple of "super insurance men" the Mecoms knew in Atlanta.

Seven

EIGHT YEARS BEFORE JOHN MECOM RECOMmended him to E.C. as a "super insurance man," Leroy Sterling sat in the office of his Ford agency in Chicago. It was March 5, 1961, and Sterling was signing bills of sale and filling out forms to go to the company headquarters in Dearborn. He had signed so many bills of sale and filled out so many forms in twenty-four hours that his right hand hurt and his fingers could hardly hold the pen straight. In the corner a couple of 250-pound goons munched sandwiches and leafed slowly through old copies of *Time*. Sterling glanced out the window. It looked like a Chinese fire drill out there, he thought. Men were scurrying everywhere. So many cars were rolling off the lot that Milwaukee Phil had even sent over Leo "the Mouse" Rugendorf to direct the traffic. Rugendorf was Milwaukee Phil's loan-sharking partner. With all the hubbub, Sterling worried momentarily that the cops might show up. But Milwaukee Phil had probably gotten to somebody.

Guys would pull onto the lot in taxis, some well-dressed, some hoods with less class than Sterling himself. They would drop a small pile of hundred-dollar bills on the desk and look on suspiciously while Sterling scribbled through a few more forms. Then a desk drawer would open and swallow the money, and the customer would take one of the forms out to the lot and find his new car. The factory guarantees were still in the glove compartments. But the guarantees would never be used. Because the names on the forms Sterling filled out weren't genuine.

Even Sterling's own name was a temporary alias. The short, dumpy, balding man who sat behind the desk at the Ford agency that day had been born Leroy Albert Silverstein, May 27,

1930, in Chicago. By the time E. C. Mullendore III came to know him in 1969, he had changed his name again, this time legally, to Leroy Albert Kerwin.

Apparently he attended, but did not complete, junior college, where he played some football. The police found no reason to start a file on young Silverstein. But after he adopted the name Sterling, he became the focus of one of the most publicized Mafia escapades in Chicago since the 1930's. The financial crisis Kerwin suffered because of the Chicago car caper stayed with him, even years later, when his seemingly prosperous insurance racket snared E.C. and Linda Mullendore.

Back in 1960, Kerwin (then Sterling) and George Harris, another Chicagoan, founded an automobile dealership called Sterling-Harris Ford. How they met Mob boss Felix Alderisio—better known as Milwaukee Phil—never became clear in court. According to one police theory, they borrowed their original capital from Alderisio's syndicate and couldn't meet the juiced-up interest payments. Other police theorize that the car dealers were fronting for Milwaukee Phil from the beginning in a carefully planned bankruptcy swindle.

At any rate, on the weekend of March 4–5, 1961, Sterling-Harris Ford held one of the greatest automobile bargain sales in history. The dealership sold three hundred cars in two days, all for below cost. The buyers consisted almost entirely of Chicago Mafia members and their colleagues, relatives, and friends, who paid the agency a total of $225,000. The money disappeared, but police found records from the transactions in the basement of Apex Waste Company, which was owned by another Alderisio business partner, Lawrence Rosenberg—a lifelong friend of Leroy Silverstein/Sterling/Kerwin's.

Sterling-Harris closed its doors, bankrupt and unable to pay more than $700,000 that it owed to a finance company for the missing cars. Police retrieved some of the cars by staking out a wedding party for the daughter of Chicago Mob overlord Anthony "Joe Batters" Accardo. One after another of the Sterling-Harris cars pulled up and was impounded, to the chagrin of its well-pedigreed owner. In Sheboygan, Wisconsin, a Ford dealer spotted 150 of the new Fords in a lot and called his home office demanding to know why the company had allowed a new dealer into his territory. There was no new dealer—not authorized, anyway. The company called the police, who traced the cars to Sterling-Harris.

According to the Chicago Crime Commission, one of the

67

Sterling-Harris cars, a Thunderbird, showed up in Las Vegas in the possession of "a well-known singer and entertainer" and "was registered in the name of a record company owned by him." A source close to the crime commission reveals that the man in question was Frank Sinatra, but that his name was omitted from the commission's report because investigators couldn't prove that he knew the car had been obtained illegally.

Kerwin, Harris, Rugendorf, and Rosenberg all were convicted of bankruptcy fraud and given stiff sentences. The appeals courts reversed all the convictions on technicalities. The Justice Department retried and reconvicted the men, but some of these convictions were reversed. Kerwin wound up serving fifty-eight days in the U.S. penitentiary at Terre Haute, Indiana. Leo "the Mouse" Rugendorf pleaded guilty the third time around, in exchange for which the government agreed to reduce his sentence to six months; in 1971, he was convicted of extortion in another matter. The prosecutors declined to try Rosenberg a third time in the Sterling-Harris case, preferring to try him instead for the various loan rackets he had been running with Alderisio. In October 1971, a Chicago jury convicted him of fraud, but he continued to run a loan company while appealing his three-year sentence.

In the long run, the civil lawsuits that reverberated from the Sterling-Harris case may have affected the participants much more than the criminal prosecutions. Associates Discount Corporation, a reputable finance company, had lent Kerwin and Harris the money to pay Ford Motor Company for the agency's cars. Associates assigned Malcolm Gaynor, a lawyer, to convert the IOU's from Kerwin and Harris into cash. "I've been working on this for eleven years and it involves something in excess of two hundred lawsuits," Gaynor sighed to a reporter late in 1971.

Gaynor said that Associates received several hundred thousand dollars from the sale of the cars that authorities managed to recover, and filed suit for the rest of the money against Kerwin, Harris, Rosenberg, and Rugendorf. Kerwin and Harris then came to Gaynor and agreed to pay off the debt in installments if Associates would drop Rosenberg and Rugendorf from the lawsuit.

"They pleaded that Rosenberg and Rugendorf had been maligned unjustly. They said they wanted to pay the debt themselves. Whether that was the real reason or not, you can judge for yourself," Gaynor said. He said Associates accepted the deal because terrified witnesses were refusing to testify against

68

Rosenberg and Rugendorf. The deal with Associates left Kerwin responsible for paying nearly $250,000 to protect two of Milwaukee Phil Alderisio's prized henchmen.

Kerwin would have more than his conscience to worry about if he couldn't shield Rosenberg and Rugendorf from the debt collector. Several men are said to have double-crossed Alderisio over the years. Some of them were found murdered. Others never were found at all. Police consider him a prime suspect in at least fourteen killings. Hidden FBI microphones once caught Alderisio and several Mafia associates howling with laughter over how one victim had been suspended naked on a meat hook and tortured with electric prods and other instruments for several days until he finally died.

While appealing his criminal conviction in the Sterling-Harris case, Kerwin worked at a Gary, Indiana, correspondence school, Sanford Tech, marketing self-improvement courses for bored housewives and dissatisfied laborers. Then a friend who managed the correspondence school devised a scheme to sell insurance policies to the students. He and Kerwin looked around for an insurance man to help set it up. One day the friend brought Leon Cohen to Kerwin's office and Kerwin's life took a new direction.

Cohen, the son of a Detroit butcher, was a convicted rapist (the babysitter at a friend's house when he was twenty), and swindler (selling worthless stock in an Atlanta insurance firm in 1959, and promoting a $225,000 insurance racket in 1961). But Cohen varnished over his prison record with geniality. Despite his abbreviated five-foot, six-inch frame, he was a handsome, dark-haired charmer with a knack for developing intimate conversations with strangers. Ready to embark on a career as a respectable life-insurance salesman in Atlanta, he said he needed a partner and Kerwin was his man.

Kerwin, homely and carelessly dressed, looked at least ten years older than Cohen, although they both were nearing forty. But Kerwin, even with his propensity for profane speech and general rudeness to people, showed a keenness for what Cohen disdained: bookkeeping, money-management, and attentiveness to contractual details. So Kerwin moved to Atlanta. They called their agency Cohen, Kerwin, White & Associates. There were only two of them, but they believed in putting up a strong front.

It was the spring of 1969. The Internal Revenue Service was pursuing both men for hundreds of thousands of dollars in unpaid taxes, Cohen from his financial swindles and Kerwin from the Sterling-Harris Ford fiasco. Kerwin had just been sentenced to an eighteen-month term for income tax evasion, and was scrambling to keep out of jail, as he had been all decade. To catapult him out of trouble and into the big money, Kerwin relied on the formidable contacts that Leon Cohen had made in the insurance business.

Enter Morris Jaffe and Mickey Mantle.

Jaffe is one of those wheeling, dealing Texans who make proper New York bankers blush in defense of capitalism. In 1962, at age thirty-nine, after a fifteen-year career as a residential and commercial builder, Jaffe took over Billy Sol Estes's agricultural empire after Estes went to jail in the well-publicized $22 million government subsidy swindle. Morris Jaffe also spent eight years as president of Fed-Mart Corporation, a retail store–life insurance combine whose shares were traded on the American Stock Exchange. He stayed on as chairman of the life insurance company when it broke off from Fed-Mart, the department store company. At the same time, he assembled an extensive real estate and commercial building empire, which he runs from San Antonio. He caused a furor in Tulsa in 1966 when he attempted to erect a highly unpopular apartment project there; he ultimately developed houses in the area.

Among the other things Jaffe developed during the 1960's were more-than-nodding acquaintanceships with two men of influence: President Lyndon Johnson, to whose campaigns he contributed faithfully, and Carlos Marcello, the Mafia High Commission's man in Dixie, who operates from a base in New Orleans. Jaffe said in 1971 that he had known Marcello only "three or four years. The only dealing I have had with Mr. Marcello is in regards to purchasing real estate." The New Orleans Metropolitan Crime Commission reported that Marcello was making frequent trips to San Antonio. Jaffe says the Mafia don was a perfect gentleman during their tour of unexploited acreage near New Orleans, but that the real-estate deal fell through in 1971, when Marcello went to jail for slapping his FBI tail.

Although Jaffe personally had been more interested in stock averages than batting averages, professional baseball soon played a role in his search for ways to make money. Mickey Mantle, another good ol' Oklahoma country boy, was concluding a spectacular eighteen-year career with the New York Yankees. Mantle had been earning hundred-thousand-dollar-a-year sums,

70

and now that there was practically as much bandage as flesh on his once-speedy legs, he wanted to invest his savings and free time to provide an income secure from the curve balls that the future might throw him. What Mantle didn't know about business—which, as it turned out, was a lot—Morris Jaffe was ready to help with. Mantle had invested in Jaffe's life insurance concern and done promotional work for it as early as 1965.

Exactly who decided on fast-food franchising for Mantle's post-baseball career is something nobody is very eager to admit now. But Mickey Mantle's Country Cookin' Kitchens was formed, and Floyd Smith, a Dallas real-estate and insurance agent, was hired as president. Morris Jaffe agreed to become a director of the Mantle corporation and to start the first Country Cookin' Kitchen cookin' in a San Antonio shoppin' center that he owned.

Mantle and Smith each held 110,000 shares in the company, and Jaffe 100,000, for which they paid five cents a share. Then, as was the fashion in those bull-market days, they registered with the Securities and Exchange Commission to sell 200,000 shares to the public at $15 a share. The stock sold out on July 11, 1969, and Country Cookin' Kitchens netted $2,790,000 from some six hundred public investors who evidently figured that Mantle might become the Colonel Sanders of the 1970's. These investors no doubt were impressed and reassured about the project when they saw that Jaffe had persuaded an old friend and sometime business associate to join the board of directors and lend his prestige: John W. Mecom, Sr.

Mantle himself seemed genuinely enthused about the restaurants, and promised to appear personally wherever a new one opened up. "This will be my life when I quit playing ball. I really like it," he said at his final Yankee spring training. "For one dollar you get your choice of ham hocks and beans, chicken and dumplings, Irish stew, or pot luck."

James Dunne II, a Dallas insurance man Smith and Jaffe knew, went to work searching for investors who would open new restaurants in the chain. One of Dunne's insurance industry friends was Leon Cohen, who had rented an office with Leroy Kerwin in the prestigious MONY Building on Peachtree Street, Atlanta's main thoroughfare. Dunne dropped by the office one day to urge Cohen and Kerwin to buy a restaurant franchise.

"He was trying to sell it to us with directed stock," Cohen says. Apparently this means that after the Cohen-Kerwin agency invested enough cash to start a restaurant in Atlanta, the Mantle company would wind up owning the restaurant and the agency would wind up owning stock in Country Cookin' Kitchens. Cohen says Dunne "told us the stock would be worth more money than what it was on the market for. I told him, 'If I am going to buy any franchise, I think the Mantle corporation has to have insurance on Mickey Mantle.' "

So Cohen sold the firm a $1 million policy on Mantle's life with an annual premium of $19,200. After all, if the baseball star died, the company would have nothing left but a lot of dumplings and ham hocks. Because of this transaction, Leon Cohen and Leroy Kerwin were able to enter the life of E. C. Mullendore III.

Cohen had devised a clever get-rich-quick gimmick. Most old-line life insurance companies pay their agents a 55 percent commission on the first year's premiums for the life insurance policies they sell. In successive years, the agent receives a much smaller percentage of the renewal premiums. But some new companies, eager to establish themselves quickly, will offer special deals to high-producing agents.

One would-be growth company, Life Insurance Company of Kentucky, agreed to pay Cohen and Kerwin 90 percent of the first year's premiums as commissions on the policies they sold. Cohen, a convicted con man whose strong point is talking, convinced Life of Kentucky that he was a supersalesman who would bring in all sorts of heavy business. For one thing, Kerwin had a long-time friend in Chicago who was managing the business affairs of some professional athletes and enter-tainers, and the friend had agreed to channel life insurance deals on the celebrities to the agency in Atlanta. Among its clients, real or imagined, the agency listed boxer Muhammad Ali, football player O. J. Simpson, and singer Harry Belafonte.

Soon after receiving their 90 percent commission agreement, Cohen and Kerwin rewarded Life of Kentucky with the $1 million policy on Mickey Mantle. Just as fast, however, the agents abandoned Life of Kentucky for a more lucrative agree-ment with an Atlanta firm, United Family Life Insurance Com-pany. United Family pledged a 95 percent first-year commis-sion, with a 13.75 percent commission on renewals. In exchange, Cohen and Kerwin pledged to sign $25 million in business—a pledge they quickly kept. In six months with

United Family, Cohen and Kerwin wrote $39.5 million in insurance, with premiums amounting to $850,000, ranking them among the leading insurance agencies in the country, according to dollar volume. Then they moved on to an even better deal with another firm.

The life insurance companies, in their greed, failed to see Cohen's gimmick. If the commission on a policy was 95 percent, then the agents could allow customers to buy policies for as little as 5 percent of the premium, a relatively minor amount. The companies assumed that customers would want to keep renewing their insurance until it was paid up. This would provide a profit to the company in future years. But the renewals didn't materialize, because Cohen and Kerwin weren't really marketing insurance. They were helping people obtain loans.

If a businessman was having trouble borrowing money, a big insurance policy could help him in several ways. First, he could use the policy itself as collateral for a loan, since it would appear from face value to be worth considerably more than what the businessman paid for it (all that Cohen and Kerwin required in the way of cash payment was the 5 percent they had to remit to United Family, and perhaps a little extra for their own commission). Second, lenders might look more favorably on a borrower who could guarantee that insurance money would be available, at least upon his death, to repay the loan. Third, if a businessman were desperate enough to go to a Mafia loan shark, the sharks, especially around Chicago, often required the borrower to supply life insurance in the equivalent amount of the debt; the sharks then had the option of killing a recalcitrant borrower to collect. (Usually this was unnecessary, because the borrower was aware of the option and made sure he wasn't recalcitrant.)

By brokering loans for their clients, Cohen and Kerwin could compensate for the insurance commissions they had rebated. If Cohen and Kerwin didn't receive their 95 percent commission upon issuance of the policy, they could collect what was owing to them later by requiring the customer to share the proceeds of his loan. Insurance commissions, loan brokerage fees—it was all money. When the year ended, the policyholders would fail to renew and the insurance company would be upset. But there would be another insurance company to deal with. The plan was not exactly illegal. It just was not very nice.

"I am the front runner," Cohen declared. "I sell the policy.

Leroy carries it out." He explained that Kerwin played a large part in helping the customers get loans.

Although the life insurance companies failed to perceive Cohen's gimmick, it apparently did not have to be explained twice to Morris Jaffe. After Cohen and Kerwin sold a second $1 million policy on Mickey Mantle to the Country Cookin' Kitchens, this time placing it with United Family Life, Jaffe bought a $2.5 million policy on himself.

Jaffe also promised to introduce Cohen and Kerwin "to wealthy people who could afford large policies." Jaffe would receive 40 percent of the profits from the business he brought them, and would share the use of a DC-3 and a Lear Jet, plus pilots, with Cohen and Kerwin.

"I was told that Mr. Cohen was the largest producer of life insurance in the world," Jaffe says. "Mr. Cohen told me that he had been in trouble when he was twenty years old, but that he had pulled himself back up, had become a lawyer, a Phi Beta Kappa, received a full pardon, had letters of recommendation from top insurance companies, and had great compassion for a man like Kerwin and wanted to help him."

Floyd Smith, the president of Country Cookin', says he made a deal with Cohen and Kerwin for 30 percent of the profits on business he brought in. Smith says he bought a $1 million policy on himself and that Jaffe eventually bought $10 million, while "trying to arrange a loan of some sort with Mr. Cohen." Smith told Joseph E. Howell of *The Tulsa Tribune* that he forgot how much the premiums were and that he didn't pay beyond the first year, anyway. "My obligation," Smith told Howell, "was to pass on someone interested in insurance and then introduce them to Mr. Cohen. I presume . . . that he would forgo part of his first year's premium in order to write more insurance. He would be able to sell insurance in large blocks. The policy seemed like a bargain at the price that we paid. The cash value was extremely high."

When Kerwin went to Chicago to appeal his eighteen-month sentence for tax evasion, Jaffe went with him to plead on his behalf. "I would be willing to stick my neck out to guarantee Mr. Kerwin as I know him," the wealthy and influential Texan told the judge. "If there was some way I could personally take responsibility, I would do it."

The judge must have been impressed, because Kerwin, despite his prior record, had his prison term set aside. His only

74

punishment was to report to a halfway house in Atlanta every evening for ninety days, working at the insurance agency all the while. He and Cohen had plenty of work there to occupy their daytime hours.

Loan brokers all over the country heard about the Cohen-Kerwin agency and sent clients who had applied for business loans. Cohen believed that to hustle a first-class businessman, you had to treat him first class. So buying an insurance policy from the agency could be an exceedingly pleasant experience. One customer, George Peteler, operated a valet service that ferried passengers' baggage between the Miami airport and their hotels. He says he ran into a loan broker while lunching at his country club near Miami, and mentioned that he was looking for cash to expand the baggage service nationwide. Replied the broker: "That's a hell of an idea. I know just the people for you to go to. I know this insurance firm in Atlanta that loans money." (The loan broker involved later went to prison for a bank swindle.)

Peteler recalls that Cohen and Kerwin "picked us up at the airport in a chauffeur-driven Rolls-Royce. They probably blew $400 to $500 entertaining us. It's quite a show they put on there with the girls and the French restaurants and all. They have secretaries there like professional call girls. You walk in and you feel like you're being offered everything they own." Peteler says his lawyer backed him out of the deal when they learned that Cohen and Kerwin required purchase of a $1 million life insurance policy in order to obtain a $500,000 loan. The loan was supposed to come "through various people in Texas."

The most famous of the agency's miniskirted female employees was a receptionist who became known as "Linda Wonderful from Little Rock" because of her habit of answering the phone with the phrase "It's a *wonderful* day" in a voice that left most callers helpless against anything that Cohen might suggest.

In one case, Cohen and Kerwin helped bankrupt the First Citizens Bank of Covington, Georgia, by obtaining a $25,000 unsecured loan there for the owner of a provision store in Atlanta, and a matching $25,000 loan for themselves. They procured these loans, as they did other loans at various banks, by brokering a compensating deposit. This means they persuaded someone—usually an insurance company they were representing—to deposit cash in the bank to compensate for the money being loaned out. The brokered deposit made the loan possible—but it did not collateralize the loan. If the loan wasn't repaid, the deposit still could be withdrawn, leaving the bank short of cash. In the case of the Covington, Georgia, bank, Cohen and Kerwin brokered a $100,000 deposit from Mickey Mantle's Country Cookin' Kitchens—money raised by the Mantle corporation's public stock offering. Not a penny was repaid from the two loans induced by the Mantle deposit, and the bank collapsed under the weight of these and other losses. The superintendent of the Georgia Banking Department called such brokered loans "unethical" and said, "The scheme used here has resulted in the failure of at least eight banks in the past eighteen months."

Unaffected by bank closings, the Cohen-Kerwin agency prospered. Insurance companies competed with each other to get the fast-writing Atlanta boys under contract. Alexander Hamilton Life Insurance Company, near Detroit, gave them a whopping 117 percent commission agreement, which meant that every time Cohen and Kerwin wrote a policy, the insurance company would send *them* money. Notes from Kerwin's files indicate he was working on a deal with two fledgling companies to get 138 percent. Cohen and Kerwin also sought—and in some instances received—an insurance company's agreement to deposit some of its reserves in a particular bank specified by the agency. This would create a compensating balance to accommodate Cohen-Kerwin loan customers.

Kerwin found doctors who would vouch for the good health of the agency's customers without bothering to examine them. Rather than scrape up a few hundred dollars to pay the printing bills, Cohen and Kerwin simply issued their printer a $100,000 life insurance policy. The printer accepted with delight, because his doctor had discovered tumors on his bladder and other agencies had told him he was uninsurable. He says United Family Life refused to renew his policy when its two-year term expired. But, grateful as he was to Cohen and Kerwin, the printer—himself a twice-convicted fraud operator—refused to go along with the agents' next request. He says they brought him a $10,000 certificate of deposit on the Bank of Georgia and asked him to duplicate it in quantity. If Cohen and Kerwin were planning to peddle counterfeit banking certificates, they apparently couldn't get any other printers to go along either. The phony certificates never turned up.

The Cohen-Kerwin money-making apparatus included a

travel service, although not the customary variety. As an inducement to send their insurance business to Alexander Hamilton Life, that company's marketing subsidiary gave Cohen and Kerwin flight checks on the subsidiary's account with Eastern Air Lines. The bearer could fill in the amount of the check, sign it, and use it to pay any domestic airline fare. Cohen, Kerwin, White & Associates handed the checks out to a diverse list of friends and acquaintances, sometimes offering to sell the checks for a discount on the actual ticket price. Eastern eventually sued the agency for about $80,000 to cover the cost of unauthorized tickets that Alexander Hamilton refused to pay for. Alexander Hamilton sued for more than $400,000 it said it advanced to Cohen and Kerwin in commissions for insurance policies the company never issued because for one reason or another the deals fell through. (In 1972, though the cases weren't resolved, both Eastern and Hamilton appeared to be whistling in the dark.)

"The money we advanced to Leon Cohen was nothing more than we advanced to anybody else in the house," E. Keith Owens, Hamilton's chairman, says. "The only difference was that he had so much business. And he appeared to be bringing in *quality* business." Yet, because the customers were buying their policies to try to get loans, the premiums weren't renewed the second year on the overwhelming majority of Cohen's and Kerwin's business. Thus the insurance companies never started earning their profits.

The team of agents prospered, although Cohen always seemed to do better for himself individually than Kerwin did. Cohen (through his wife) owned 60 percent of the agency, while Kerwin owned only 40 percent. Cohen had married the attractive daughter of a prominent family in the Atlanta Jewish community and had settled in a plush house. Kerwin had married the short, plump (but Linda Mullendore says "vivacious") sister of a lawyer who had handled the affairs of Sterling-Harris Ford in Chicago. The Kerwins occupied a garden apartment with their two daughters, one of whom was retarded.

Kerwin also established a curious relationship with Nona, a twenty-four-year-old topless go-go dancer who had fled her bartender husband in Boone County, Indiana. She had gone to jail there as a traffic scofflaw and faked a suicide to win release. Kerwin kept Nona in a $300-a-month apartment in Atlanta, apparently never knowing that she was sharing it with another

77

man, who told police he used to hide in the closet when Kerwin visited and emerge later to help the go-go dancer eat the steaks Kerwin had brought.

The John Mecoms, Senior and Junior, were in Atlanta to meet Morris Jaffe one day in the winter of 1968–9. Mecom, Sr., was a director with Jaffe in Country Cookin' Kitchens, and Mecom, Jr., was a director of Jaffe's life insurance company in Texas. "I have known Mr. Jaffe, or my family has, for, oh, ten or twelve years, at least," Mecom, Jr., says. The trip to Atlanta concerned Satellite Three-in-One Corporation, "a fast-food franchise service . . . that Mr. Jaffe was trying to interest my father and I in." The Mecoms bought one thousand shares of Satellite Three-in-One stock, but the franchise deal never attained orbit. (Somehow Kerwin and Cohen later got their hands on the one thousand shares and used them to collateralize a bank loan.)

On the same trip to Atlanta, Jaffe introduced the Mecoms to Cohen. "He flew back to Houston with us that night," young Mecom says. "On the way, the first conversations I ever had with Mr. Cohen concerned helping work out some long-term financing for the football business. Cohen persuaded young Mecom that financing could be obtained for the Saints on the basis of life insurance policies the Mecoms could purchase. "I can't exactly say what Leon told me," young Mecom says, "but after the conversations we had, I felt confident that he could do it."

So Mecom bought more than $22 million in insurance from Cohen and Kerwin: $10 million on himself, $2 million on Katsy, $5 million on his father, $2 million on his mother, $1 million on Dr. Scott Glover (the family physician), $500,000 on Mrs. Glover, $500,000 on Vic Schwenk (the New Orleans Saints' general manager), an undisclosed amount on Mrs. Schwenk, and $500,000 each on two football players—Steve Stonebreaker and Doug Atkins. All the policies were written on United Family Life; none stayed in effect past the first year. Mecom says he had no further business dealings with Cohen, although he did invite Cohen to attend some Saints' football games. Mecom even supplied tickets to some of Cohen's friends. And he decided that E. C. Mullendore ought to talk to Cohen. He told E.C. about it when they got together over the July 4 holiday in 1969.

"I just felt that E.C. would benefit from this the same as we felt our family would," Mecom says. "I thought it was a good idea of security." Getting a loan? That "was brought up as one of the benefits of it. Frankly, on my acquaintance with Mr. Cohen, it was the first time that I ever halfway understood what life insurance was about and I felt that the explanations that he gave me and the reasons were very similar to what Mr. Mullendore should have, and I felt it was necessary that he should at least make the acquaintance. I checked Cohen's reputation and so forth with some friends in Atlanta and nothing seemed wrong. Mr. Jaffe, being a personal friend of the family's, represented that the man was a good insurance salesman and had something to offer, so we sat down and listened to it."

Two Postscripts

According to sources quoted by Joseph E. Howell in *The Tulsa Tribune*, Mickey Mantle had been unaware that two $1 million insurance policies would be issued in his name and was very unhappy when he learned about them. In 1969, Mickey Mantle's Country Cookin' Kitchens reported a net loss of $1,312,145. The firm opened six restaurants on its own, but sold only two franchises, and one of those apparently folded fast. Reported losses in 1970 totaled $696,654. The company then suspended restaurant operations and changed its name to Invesco International Corporation. It moved to Las Vegas and leased space for a gambling casino in a new hotel. Mantle resigned as chairman, but received a ten-year, $25,000-a-year contract for personal appearances. He put 90,000 shares of stock in trust for his children, and remarked to a sportswriter, "Mostly I've invested like I hit the last few years. I've made a lot of outs."

On June 1, 1972, the House Select Committee on Crime received a report about John Mecom, Jr.'s contacts with organized criminals. The report indicates that young Mecom was less naïve than his own account of his dealings in Atlanta might indicate. Aaron M. Kohn, director of the New Orleans Crime Commission, testified before the committee that Mecom, Jr., was a director and shareholder of two New Orleans corporations in association with Sam Lee Presley, Jr., who was convicted September 9, 1971, in Mississippi of federal gambling violations. Kohn said another associate in the New Orleans enterprises was Berald E. Sonner, who "has a considerable record of forming business partnerships with individuals who are also partners of Carlos Marcello or other major members of the Marcello structure." According to an Associated Press dispatch, Kohn testified that Mecom also was a close friend of James and Anthony Moran, owners of La Louisiane Restaurant in New Orleans' French Quarter, who had a "close and sometimes financial association" with the Marcello crime family.

Eight

AT SIX O'CLOCK ONE MORNING IN EARLY JULY 1969, the telephone rang in Leon Cohen's suburban Atlanta home. Cohen staggered out of bed to answer it.

"Hi!" said a voice on the other end of the line. "This is E.C."

Cohen blinked and rubbed his eyes. "E.C. who?" he said.

"Mullendore!" exclaimed the voice. "John's brother-in-law. Well, when are you coming to see me?"

Cohen remembered that over the July 4 weekend he had received a call from John Mecom, Jr. "He wants $10 million," Mecom had said. "He's Katsy's brother."

"It's not that easy," Cohen had replied, and figured he would talk to Katsy's brother later.

Now Cohen looked at his watch. Suddenly it occurred to him that if it was 6 a.m. in Atlanta, it was 5 a.m. in Hulah, Oklahoma.

"I'm an early riser," E.C. explained.

Cohen told E.C., "I'm busy, I'll get back with you," and returned to bed.

A few days later, Cohen says, Mullendore called again, also early in the morning (the calls persisted to where E.C. threatened to rearrange Cohen's whole metabolic cycle). The rancher said he and his son had climbed to the top of the new Jefferson Memorial Arch in St. Louis. "The thought of high places made him feel like he needed insurance," Cohen says.

So Cohen flew to San Antonio to meet Morris Jaffe, who had a 40 percent stake in any money Cohen could earn from E.C. Cohen and Jaffe then flew to Tulsa for lunch with the Mullendores at the fashionable Summit Club there.

E.C. applied to Cohen for a $10 million policy on himself, and a $5 million policy on Linda. "E.C. and I always laughed about the agent that sold it," Linda said later of Cohen. "He was the wheeler-dealer type and E.C. bought it so he could borrow money. They told him that if he bought this insurance that they would loan him this huge amount of money and he always said they were not any good."

E.C. said he wanted to check Cohen out, although according to Linda that investigation was eventually handled by John Mecom, Jr.'s personal lawyer.

Gene obviously knew about the deal. "The [loan] money had been promised," he said later. "They would get it in Atlanta, and that is why he took out the insurance policy."

Linda recalls the application session: "Leon Cohen gave both E.C. and me a stack of papers to sign in blank. He informed us that this was the way he and the insurance company always handled matters; that he would complete the papers since he had the necessary information. There were such a large number of blank forms, neither E.C. nor I paid any attention to what was contained on the forms. We simply assumed that it was a matter of formality which Leon and the insurance company had worked out to simplify their own office procedures. I don't know whether they were insurance forms or medical forms or what their purpose was. I always signed everything that E.C. put in front of me, and I hardly ever read it because I thought E.C. was doing the right thing."

Cohen himself had a surprise that day, he says. Here they were in a swanky private restaurant on the top floor of a large bank, when "I saw E.C. dip snuff [evidently the Copenhagen brand "smokeless tobacco" E.C. liked]. Here was a man who was impeccably dressed. I came unglued," Cohen says.

After the luncheon meeting, Jaffe flew the Mullendores to Dallas, apparently in his private plane, where they visited Gene, who was in Parkland Memorial Hospital. Gene loved to visit the mineral baths in Hot Springs, Arkansas, but that summer the steam rooms got a little too hot for him and he scalded his feet badly enough to require hospitalization.

On August 29, 1969, the Mullendores returned to Dallas, this time to the office of Dr. Ben R. Buford to be examined in connection with their insurance applications. Cohen waited outside during the thorough, one- or two-hour exams, Linda says. Cohen had ingratiated himself to the Mullendores to the point of accompanying them to visit Gene in the hospital. He later took them to Edwin Tarcus, his custom tailor, where on his recommendation E.C. ordered two suits and a sport coat. She says she and E.C. were unaware that the insurance company, United Family Life, required not one but two medical examinations for such large policies—or that Cohen and Kerwin had prison records.

The next formality was a visit to the ranch on September 4 by Ed Miller of the Retail Credit Company, which claims to be the largest consumer-credit rating service in the United States. Cohen had called the day before, Linda says, and told them "that a man was coming to investigate us as to this insurance policy." Miller arrived in time for lunch, after which "E.C. left and went upstairs or went to the office or some place, and Mr. Miller asked me about my health history and about—did I like to ride a horse and ski and, you know, about the children and their ages and everything, and I told him all of these things. The only thing I really recall is Mr. Miller going over, and framed on the wall above the television set, and I can remember vividly, he leaned over the television set, looked up, and read this article in the paper, the *Farm Journal,* with reference to [the Mullendores' owning] 130,000 acres. He didn't mention this to me, but I remember him reading it. A friend of ours had sent it to us, and E.C. thought it was a great joke, because it was erroneous, and it was a joke between us, and he framed it there and we laughed about it. And Mr. Miller read this article, and I think that is where he got his information that's in the erroneous Retail Credit report. E.C. would never tell anyone how much acreage he had, much less a total stranger like Ed Miller, even if it was for the purpose of obtaining insurance, and at that time he was having United Family checked out."

E.C. did spin Miller around the ranch in the family El Dorado, and the credit investigator recalls driving across one creek so deep that water came gushing into the sporty Cadillac. Miller noticed all the oil wells around, and asked how many there were on the property. E.C. told him: ninety, and Miller wrote it down. Miller didn't inquire about who received the royalties from the oil wells, so E.C. never had occasion to tell him it was the Osage Indian tribe, not the Mullendores.

Miller says he showed E.C. a recent financial statement indicating the Mullendores' net worth, assets minus debts, at $3,157,706. "I asked him if that was his total net worth. He said, 'Hell no, I'm worth ten times that amount.' I asked for a breakdown. He wasn't interested in going into details. He didn't see that it was any of the insurance company's business."

Retail Credit Company reported to United Family Life: "We

have estimated Mr. E. C. Mullendore III's net worth as $37,427,500. This is about as close as can be estimated with the knowledge at hand. This net worth is broken down as follows: land, $25 million; cattle and other livestock, $10 million; machines, vehicles, and equipment, $500,000; cash, operating capital, $500,000; oil and other investments, $1.4 million; cash in personal bank account, $10,000; 7/12 Osage Indian headright, $17,500."

The report continues: "For income tax purposes during 1968, Mr. E. C. Mullendore III had a net operating loss of $79,000. He had gross income, however, of $980,000, and it is estimated by very reliable financial sources that approximately $400,000 of the $980,000 was a net profit to Mr. Mullendore. However, the $400,000 was plowed back into his ranching operations in the form of purchasing additional land, more equipment, cattle, and building new fences. Much of this money was spent in the clearing operation of bottom land and rolling timberland to enable them to increase the farming capacity of this ranch." Retail Credit placed the combined worth of the two Mullendore men at between $55 and $60 million.

Actually, the Mullendores hadn't filed their 1968 tax return yet—and didn't until May 7, 1971, the same date they filed their 1969 return. Linda says the reports were late because, "as I recall, the bookkeeper did not have the books in order at that time." The 1968 return showed total income, apparently before expenses, of $222,473.

During 1969, the Mullendores had been meeting expenses by drawing on a new commitment from the Ponca City Production Credit Association for $3,820,000—which included principal and interest from the previous loan of $1.4 million. Withdrawals from the PCA money included—among other items— $73,500 for required purchase of PCA stock; $380,000 for payment on Northwest Mutual's mortgage (interest alone ran to $280,000 a year); $60,000 on contracts the Mullendores had signed to purchase new land; $320,000 to refinance open bank loans; $100,000 to pay bills; $40,000 to buy farm equipment; $30,000 for thirty breeding bulls; and $613,925 for "general expense."

In mid-1969, the family owed nearly $8 million to secured creditors and roughly half a million to unsecured creditors. Both figures were climbing because the Mullendores were operating heavily in the red. The value of the ranch, by any seemingly fair yardstick, remained double the amount of the debt; but this

83

doesn't mean the ranch could produce income enough to pay even the interest on the debt, and it doesn't mean the ranch could easily be liquidated to raise cash. Unless a buyer could be found who wanted to go into Osage cattle raising in a very big way, the ranch might have to be sacrificed at far below recent per-acre prices, which had been shored up by the Mullendores' eagerness to buy more land at almost any cost. But James Foreman, president of United Family Life, didn't know about that. Says Foreman, who personally reviewed the Mullendore applications and the Retail Credit Company report: "I wasn't worried about anybody with that much land. I can think back and see reasons for being alarmed, but I was not alarmed at that time. We knew nothing about Mullendore but what a phenomenal fellow he was—how wealthy. It was all over the office: He owned half of Oklahoma and had an option on the rest."

So United Family granted the $10 million policy to E.C.— actually it had to issue two $5 million policies because its computer was programmed to handle only seven figures. But the $5 million policy to Linda was delayed because her medical examination in Dallas had indicated a heart problem that might require a special rating.

Now it was time to shop for the big umbrella loan to refinance the ranch. Linda: "Mr. Kerwin came to the ranch and stayed for four or five days, and brought with him a typewriter and a calculator. He had told E.C. that he could assist in obtaining long-term financing. [He said] previous financial statements prepared by E.C. were understated with particular reference to the values placed on both real and personal property. For example, I can remember Kerwin asking E.C. what was the highest price paid in Osage County for farmland, and E.C. responded $750 an acre, so Mr. Kerwin prepared a financial statement which showed that all of E.C.'s farmland was valued at $750 an acre. The same was true of pastureland at $200, which Kerwin listed at $250."

Chub Anderson recalls flying to Atlanta with E.C. two or three weeks later: "I know he went to meet a Leon Cohen, but I don't know the business end of it. I went to the office and met Leon Cohen and two of his associates [including Kerwin]. We got there about dinnertime [lunchtime] and he sent his secretary with me to go eat, and they stayed at the office. [After lunch] we went back to Leroy's office. I sat in there and talked to this old girl for about two or three hours, I think. [Kerwin] would come out and get coffee. But E.C. and Cohen was in his office with the door shut. . . . I didn't hear any of their conversation. I just supposed it was probably something about insurance or a loan or something. I went out with [the secretary] that night, you know, looking Atlanta over. [We looked Atlanta over together] quite a bit.

"I remember that the new cars had just come out, because E.C. bought a new Mercury station wagon, off of Leon, I believe, some way, and I drove it back from Atlanta, Georgia, when I came back." E.C. had given him a credit card and some money.

First-year premiums on the initial $10 million in insurance that E.C. bought came to $167,000. On August 22, 1969, apparently the date of application, E.C. paid the Cohen-Kerwin agency $4,000. What, if any, arrangements they made for payment of the rest of the premium aren't clear. Ultimately, E.C. would owe the agency much more than $4,000, whether for insurance premiums or loan brokerage fees, but Cohen and Kerwin weren't worried about his credit. On September 1, John Mecom, Sr., the oil tycoon, presented the following to Cohen on personalized Mecom stationery:

> Dear Leon,
> This letter will serve as my personal guarantee that any and all monies up to a maximum of $350,000 will be paid by me in the event E. C. Mullendore III or Linda V. Mullendore fail to honor their obligation to you or your firm. At my option, if called upon, I can assign you 25-plus acres in Cobb County, Ga., at a value of $150,000.
> /s/ John W. Mecom

At the bottom of the letter, in different handwriting, was scrawled: "Additional guarantee: Morris Jaffe. Subject to limit of J. W. Mecom."

On September 30, Cohen and Kerwin persuaded the First National Bank of Atlanta to lend E.C. $175,000. From the proceeds, he immediately wrote the Cohen-Kerwin agency a check for $41,750, which Cohen later said was a brokerage fee. The rest of the money E.C. transferred to his accounts in Oklahoma. James Steele, vice-president of the bank, says Cohen and Kerwin prevailed upon Mickey Mantle's Country Cookin' Kitchens to deposit a $125,000 compensating balance at the bank to induce the loan to E.C. In addition, the bank received a lien on one of E.C.'s $5 million insurance policies as security. Byron L. Harris, another vice-president of the bank, says the two

85

agents told him the Mullendore loan "was the best loan we'd ever made."

The news of Linda's abnormal electrocardiograms sent her on a tour of doctors' offices. "We were concerned," she says, "because at that time Linda [Junior] was only six months old, and after you've had ten double masters and abnormal EKG's, you do tend to worry a little bit when you have four children."

Lula Harrison, the cook, says Linda had claimed for years that she had heart trouble. Mrs. Harrison noted that E.C. had been skeptical because "she got out of doing things he wanted her to do." A doctor in Tulsa referred Linda to the Cleveland Clinic, in Ohio, for extensive examination. On November 13, 1969, Linda flew to Cleveland with Mrs. Harrison's daughter; Leon Cohen met them, and E.C. and Katsy joined them the next day.

Linda: "They X-ray your heart and they inject a tube in the vein and run it up through the neck down into the heart and take pictures of the heart which go on a television screen, and examine the blood vessels and supply of blood to the heart to determine whether or not there really were abnormalities in the EKG, and whether or not this would show I had a bad heart condition."

John Mecom, Jr., said later that Katsy had paid $1,300 for Linda's expenses on the clinic trip, "but I think Mr. Mullendore reimbursed her for it. Mr. Mullendore offered to pay me and wrote a check to me that I tore up for this amount." But after E.C.'s murder, Katsy filed a claim against her brother's estate including $1,300 in expenses for the trip to Cleveland. Linda, executrix of the estate, denied the claim. And the Cleveland Clinic continued to bill the Mullendore family for $1,043.19, which it says nobody paid.

The test results showed that Linda's health was in no immediate danger, but the results still were abnormal enough to raise her insurance rating, which tacked an unacceptable surcharge onto her premium. So E.C., Cohen, and Kerwin came to another solution. E.C. would apply for a *third* $5 million policy on himself. It was issued in December. Both Kuhrt, the ranch manager, and George Ray say that E.C. thereafter boasted to practically everybody who might be interested that he now had nearly $16 million in insurance (including insurance he owned before buying the United Family policies). Apparently, however, E.C. never considered that his new application to United Family, on which the third $5 million policy was issued, might require two more medical examinations.

Nine

MICHAEL SCHLOSSBERG WENT TO HIGH SCHOOL in Brooklyn, received a B.A. from New York University and an M.D. from New York Medical College. He served his internship at Kings County Hospital and his residency at Brookdale Hospital, both in Brooklyn. Then the Army drafted Schlossberg and sent him to Fort McPherson in Atlanta in September 1967. He went in as a captain but became a major because "there was a law passed and everybody was raised one rank."

Leroy Kerwin was "a friend of a neighbor of mine." Schlossberg talked to Kerwin about insurance, and "I did eventually buy insurance from him. He asked me if I'd like to do insurance examinations and I said sure. I could have used the money. I [had done] them in New York, but very few. They were difficult to come by in New York."

So Schlossberg began doing these lucrative exams for Kerwin in 1968. Because he was moonlighting from the Army, he had to perform the exams at the Cohen, Kerwin, White & Associates office.

Then Kerwin mentioned the possibility of simply filling out medical examination forms without bothering to conduct the examinations. "It came about as a favor. In other words, he asked—he had mentioned this to me and said this is just a formality, and he—I had been doing examinations for him and I was very appreciative of the fact that he was giving me these examinations, and he said, 'This is just a formality and would you be good enough to do it for me?' He told me it was mainly for businessmen who were too busy to come down, millionaires, wealthy people. These were his words, and I said I would be willing to do it."

Schlossberg says he faked only about twenty examinations. He says he always thought the applicants had been examined by another doctor first. He would simply copy over and rephrase the first doctor's report. "I used to change it, very insignificant changes. For example, the weight [of Linda Mullendore], my weight was 140, Dr. Buford's weight [from the examination in

Dallas] was 143. The blood pressure was 120/86. My blood pressure was 130/85. Pulse rate was 72, mine. Dr. Buford's was 76. I wrote down, 'Physical exam for the past five years,' and he had, 'General exam each year for the past five years.' " In regard to E.C., Schlossberg wrote: "Weight, 155. That's my weight. Dr. Buford's weight was 153. My blood pressure was 120/80. Dr. Buford's was 112/82. My pulse was 72. Dr. Buford's was 80.

"Mr. Kerwin would say, well, this businessman is in town, and he's here at this time, but he's just too busy to be examined. It was explained to me by Mr. Kerwin that this was a formality and at that time I really didn't see that it was wrong, and number two, I needed the money.

"Mr. Kerwin used to have the urine specimens. He would tell me that this is the specimen of the patient. I believed him." Schlossberg says he never even shook hands with E.C. or Linda Mullendore. He says he had to stop doing insurance examinations on August 1, 1969, when he was discharged from the Army and went into private practice in Atlanta, because he specializes in obstetrics and gynecology. He says the OB-GYN Society considers it improper for its members to examine men.

Arnold B. Rubenstein went to high school in Chicago. He received his B.A. from the University of Michigan and his M.D. from Chicago Medical School. He served his internship at the Michael Reese Hospital in Chicago, then won a fellowship to the Mayo Clinic in urology. He completed his specialty training at three Northwestern University hospitals in Chicago and entered private practice July 1, 1969, in Atlanta.

"When I moved to Atlanta, I had a cousin by the name of Carol Korem Kerwin. When I first came down to a strange city, I developed a very close relationship with my cousins. [These cousins included not only the Kerwins but also Richard Korem, Carol Kerwin's brother and the lawyer for Sterling-Harris Ford, who also had moved to Atlanta.] Through my social relationship with Mr. Kerwin and his wife, . . . we sort of discussed business, me telling him about my medical practice and him telling me about his insurance business. [He asked me] would I mind doing some insurance examinations for him in that it was difficult to find . . . at various times during the day, weekends, night, physicians to examine some of his clients. It was—did not go along with my thinking. I was practicing urology and urology alone. But after a period of time and as our relationship grew, and with the environment that I was in—I was put in sort of a very glamorous type of environment and many favors were done for me, such as when Carol and Leroy and my wife and myself went out for dinner, I was supposedly the struggling young doctor and I could never pick up a check. Whenever he would buy a shirt for himself, or a raincoat and other minor things, he'd always just give— 'You take one too.' I was extremely impressed. Then, apparently, now, the conversation came up again about insurance examinations and I—he mentioned, 'Well, what's the difference? You could always use the $25 for each examination.' And I said, 'All right, if you have any trouble, let me—I'll be glad to help you out.'

"I performed some examinations at the office of Cohen, Kerwin, and White for the most part, but offhand I can remember some in hotel rooms. One examination sticks in my mind in the airport that was really not a—what I'd call a good physical examination. It was like a partial type of physical examination.

"I was introduced to Mr. Mullendore in the offices of Cohen, Kerwin, and White. I got the impression he was an important client of the firm, and I asked him just very— I guess you'd call them superficial social questions, such as how are things in Oklahoma."

Rubenstein performed no examination of any kind on E.C., but did fill out a medical form on the rancher based on information he found in the reports of Dr. Buford and Dr. Schlossberg. At one point in his report, where Schlossberg (who himself had been copying from Buford's report) had written an answer on the wrong line, Rubenstein carelessly repeated the mistake. He caught himself, crossed it out, and corrected it.

He says he thinks E.C.'s signature already "was on the form when I filled it out." Like Schlossberg, Rubenstein made sure the answers on his report were "different with no medically clinical significance—blood pressure, pulse. I changed the numbers which have no medical significance but would make the exam look better. For instance, five foot nine and a half on this examination signed by Dr. Schlossberg, and I have five foot nine. The blood pressure, his is 120 systolic, the [pulse] around 80, and the diastolic pressure being 75. Mine is 115, 80, 75." He also says the urine Kerwin gave him might have been anybody's.

Soon after Rubenstein arrived in Atlanta, Kerwin introduced him to Schlossberg. Says Rubenstein now: "Dr. Schlossberg and I refer patients to each other. Our wives are friends. We office in the same building, and Mike and I are friends. I had known that he had done work while he was in the Army at Fort McPherson for Mr. Kerwin and Mr. Cohen, but I had no idea that he had done the same thing that I had done.

"I took the money and I cashed the checks, but I sincerely believe that I did not do this for the money. I did this so as not to feel obligated in any way for the little things that were done for me, like if I needed an automobile, my car was in the shop and I—instead of renting a car I dropped by [Kerwin's] office and they'd give me a car. When it came time for the fight [Muhammad Ali's big comeback bout] in town, a lot of people don't spend fifty or a hundred dollars for a seat to see a boxing match, and, 'Here, Arnie, take two seats for you and Judy to the boxing match.' I mean, there's no way I could really repay anything like this. I didn't want them to think that I was, you know, like mooching off of them. I wanted to do them favors also."

So Dr. Rubenstein faked about ten examination reports to United Family and five to eight each to Alexander Hamilton and Life of Kentucky. He says he understood it was "common practice" to fake secondary reports on life insurance so long as there was a primary report.

Why did Dr. Rubenstein come to Atlanta? "That's a very interesting question. I had many opportunities in Chicago, sir. The primary reason I came to Atlanta—I don't even know if I should say this, but in my field of urology, fee splitting is rampant in Chicago. Look who's talking about morals. I didn't want to have any part of any fee splitting."

Ten   DUDLEY MCELVAIN OF BARTLESVILLE ARRIVED at the University of Oklahoma one year after E.C. did, and met the young rancher during fraternity rush. They formed a friendship that endured throughout the 1960's. McElvain and his wife would go out evenings with E.C. and Linda. McElvain had worked as trust officer of the First National Bank in Bartlesville, and in September 1968, he accepted a vice-presidency at the Home State Bank of Kansas City, Kansas.

In June 1969, E.C. called his friend and asked for a $50,000 loan to lease some ranchland. McElvain approved it without even an investigation. But because the money market was tight,

E.C. had to sign a $100,000 note to the bank, creating a $50,000 compensating balance account. He agreed to pay 7½ percent interest on the $100,000, but this amounted to 15 percent interest on the $50,000 that he actually received.

A month later E.C. asked for the other $50,000, "to pay insurance premiums for his father," McElvain says. On July 25, McElvain approved the advance, adding Gene's signature to the note.

Two weeks later, E.C. asked for $150,000 more, raising the loan to $250,000, the bank's legal lending limit. The bank rejected the request on the grounds the loan was too big for him to repay comfortably in two years. E.C. never explained why he wanted the money. The bank did agree to advance him $25,000 on August 6. On August 13, he asked for another $10,000. The bank's board of directors turned him down.

During the same period in 1969, E.C. continued to increase his loans at the First National Bank of Dewey and the Coffeyville (Kansas) State Bank, where E.C. promised that Leon Cohen would deliver a $100,000 compensating balance. Cohen didn't.

Despite the shortage of cash, the Mullendores' spending on personal items continued unabated—perhaps it even accelerated. Kathleen later contended that Linda concealed her heavy personal spending from E.C., but if she could do that, she must have been quite a camouflage expert. Here, for example, is a record of spending at one store, Le Marquis, Inc., beginning roughly when the Mullendores committed themselves to live on money that they borrowed from Ponca City Production Credit Association: November 30, 1967—one man's Bueche-Girod watch, $1,100; December 18, 1967—one enameled and diamond bracelet, $4,600; April 24, 1968—two Louis XV reproduction armchairs, $1,190; June 12, 1968—one Louis XV flat bureau, $2,850, and one silver biscuit box, $135; December 2, 1968—one Cybis ring-necked pheasant, $1,800, and one tea cart, $200. Total purchases—$11,875 in about one year.

They continued buying artifacts costing several hundred dollars each from Le Marquis. But that was nothing compared to what happened on a trip to New Orleans in June 1969, after E.C. had begun borrowing heavily from banks. Linda's purchases from the Manheim Galleries there on June 24 must have impressed even the Mecoms: one black lacquered sideboard, $12,000; two matched period récamier, $9,000; two Empire chairs with bronze mounts, $2,100; one Empire chair, $1,500; one pair of blackamoors, $4,250. The Mullendores paid $10,000 cash, and left the remaining $18,850 to be billed.

On July 25, 1969, the Mullendores went to Kansas City. While E.C. was collecting the last $50,000 that his friend Dudley McElvain could allow him, Linda visited Woolf Brothers and bought an $800 dress. On October 14, two weeks after E.C. had paid a nearly 25 percent commission to Cohen and Kerwin in order to obtain a loan from the First National Bank of Atlanta, Linda returned to Woolf Brothers and ran up a bill for $2,714.55, including a fur coat for $1,399. Two days later she stopped at Jaccard's, a jewelry store, and bought a cat's-eye ring for $3,275. (At Christmas she would return to the same store for a $2,000 coin bracelet watch. She says the ring and watch were gifts for E.C.)

But for sheer extravagance, the Neiman-Marcus purchases topped everything. Linda and E.C.'s account—which was separate from Gene and Kathleen's (although Linda says Kathleen often used it, too)—contains such items in 1968–69 as fourteen drinking glasses, at about $15 a glass, and five gold-plated electric percolators, dispatched as gifts at a cost of $100 each.

In August 1968, the account shows a $565.85 Dior suit; in September, five robes, a pair of shoes, and a purse, for a total of $642.75. But October was the month that E.C. never should have allowed Linda near Dallas. From her base at the Statler Hilton, she made repeated forays into the fitting rooms at Neiman-Marcus. On October 9, she bought two hostess robes for $400.85, a raincoat for $130, eleven scarves for a total of $185.12, and two nightshirts and two gowns for $167.70: a total of $883.67. The next day she tripled her effort, reaching $3,138.70 on miscellaneous items highlighted by a three-piece Galanos suit for $1,346.80, one Originala coat for $300, a clock as a gift to John Mecom, Sr., for $226.90, and thirteen pairs of shoes totaling $700. Gathering new energy on October 11, she rocketed to her third consecutive peak, racing through $4,420.29 of borrowed money to buy numerous trinkets, including a $1,051.40 topcoat and toys adding up to $391.91.

Linda returned to the intoxicating embrace of Neiman-Marcus on succeeding days, but never quite matched her earlier efforts. Her total spending there from October 9 through October 17—when she paused for a breather—adds up to $10,019.51.

Then, on October 20, the bills indicate, she returned with

Kathleen to start their Christmas shopping. That included everything from a merry-go-round (for the Mecom children) to two
armadillos (for Gene). Linda's own stocking was to contain a
$4,750 natural ranch mink coat. Breakfast at the Cross Bell
must have been a snazzy affair judging from the family's fas-
cination with bathrobes. Santa brought one $400 robe to Kath-
leen, three $300 robes to E.C., and three $200 robes to Linda.
Before Santa was done, the ranch accounts had been set back a
staggering $11,500, most of it charged to E.C. and Linda.

Linda says E.C. was not particularly concerned about letting
the Neiman-Marcus bill run up, because the store was charging
18 percent interest and therefore would not lose money. So the
Mullendores kept buying, even though their account was far in
arrears. April 9, 1969, four suits and three sport coats, $1,190.90.
May 12, four dresses, $925. May 15, one fan set, one blouse, one
jumper, $520. June 26, five pairs of shoes, $236.09. July 3, one
Nan Lee Longhorns and one easel sent to E.C. III, $480, and
one flowers-of-the-century to the Mecoms, $156. July 16, two
dresses, $575. July 18, one champagne bucket and stand to the
Mecoms, $312. July 19, one coat, three dresses, $861.60. August
16, one three-piece dress, $576.20. August 28 and 29, two bags,
$175.80. On October 13, a total of $2,450 was charged to one of
the Mullendore accounts for a watch and a bee pin to be sent to
Mr. and Mrs. Leon Cohen in Atlanta. Christmas 1969 included
an 18-karat yellow-gold wedding band with thirty diamonds,
twelve amethysts and twelve opals (the bill doesn't say who got
it) and a $1,200 portrait of one of the Mullendore men.

Julia Gilkey, the maid at the big house, insists that Linda was
responsible for the lion's share of the outflow. Kathleen, she
says, actually tried to curtail the spending when severe money
problems developed—evidently *after* Kathleen spent $900 on
lingerie in June alone. "Mrs. Mullendore [Kathleen] had cut
down considerably on things," Mrs. Gilkey says. "She would say,
'Julia, we can't afford this and we can't afford the other. I just
got to cut down.' She started telling me that way before Christmas [1969], that we are not going to do like we have been
doing, like we would fix those Christmas boxes for the cowboys
and all those different things. She would say, 'We just can't do it
this year. We aren't able.'"

Mrs. Gilkey says Linda "had Lula [the cook], she had Della
[the cleaning woman], she had that little granddaughter of
Lula's and sometimes that old big grandson of Lula's. Every day

she had three women over there besides Chub, where there was just me over at the big house, and I had a lady help me on Saturday, and that was all the help I had."

Whatever efforts Kathleen made toward economy, spending for Gene's quarter-horse racing project was unaffected. On October 17, 1969, E.C. bought seven or eight quarter horses at the famous Haymaker horse auction operated in Oklahoma City, by television star Dale Robertson and his brother Chet. Three times in that one afternoon E.C. set new records for bidding on quarter-horse mares. The old record price was $66,000, but E.C. bid $105,000 for Sea Nymph, then $110,-000 for Chickamona, and finally $125,000 for Paula Laico.

Dale Kuhrt, whom E.C. had just hired as ranch manager, has an interesting explanation of how E.C. mustered the courage to pay such high prices: the young cattle baron was plastered. Although E.C. had assumed a temperate posture in the early years of his marriage, he had begun drinking again as his financial problems worsened.

Of course, the high prices E.C. paid for horses that October 17 consisted mostly of credit. According to Kuhrt, Melvin Hatley of Purcell, Oklahoma, the seller, "came up the day after and I'm sure they worked it out. I think [E.C.] paid one third down." George Ray, however, recalls that a $130,000 check E.C. gave to Chet Robertson later bounced, and that Robertson "came up here and was kind of in a huff, and he and E.C. rode around on the ranch for a while and came back and everything was all right. I guess E.C. straightened it out with him—I don't know." Hatley took a mortgage on the horses to secure E.C.'s $250,000 IOU. E.C. made similar arrangements for his subsequent purchase of still more horses.

Buying horses initiated a series of expenses for shipping, stabling, and training them. For his trainer, E.C. hired Wade Navarre, a short, heavy Louisiana Cajun, whom Linda describes as "a former used-car salesman who was the uncle of somebody who knew somebody who knew either Gene or E.C." Navarre's stables were in Lafayette, Louisiana, and to haul the horses there, E.C. bought a tractor truck and semi-trailer horse van for $33,858.

Although Linda says E.C. entered quarter-horse racing reluctantly at Gene's insistence, E.C. and Linda instigated another big spending project all on their own. They decided to move off the ranch. They picked a house in Bartlesville, owned by Richard Kane, the lawyer-rancher, who had decided to move into an older, larger house. Linda says E.C. agreed to pay $200,000, of which $165,000 was financed by the First National Bank of Bartlesville. Kane, a director and stockholder of the bank, co-signed for the loan.

Trouble was, Linda says, much as E.C. liked the new house for its spacious, tree-shaded lot, the house had only two bedrooms and the Mullendores had four children. So in came $100,000 worth of architects, remodelers, landscapers, plumbers, and so on to put the place into the shape they desired.

Gene: "They never told *me* about building this goddamned house in Bartlesville. It wouldn't have struck me as the right thing to do under the circumstances."

Local gossipers said the Mullendores bought the house so they wouldn't have to commute to their posh country club in Bartlesville. Linda says they bought it "so the children could go to school in Bartlesville, so we wouldn't have to drive so far."

George Ray may have a deeper insight: "Gene and Kathleen took Linda and E.C. over completely. That's the real reason they wanted to move off the ranch and into Bartlesville. There was constant pressure from Gene over the ranch and their private lives. He was in touch with them constantly about E.C.'s drinking and Linda's spending. For a long time E.C. never took a strong drink at their house. E.C. sensed the dissension between Linda and his father. He wanted that house [in Bartlesville] very badly. He intended to run the ranch himself, but he intended to remove his family from the ranch so they would have a life of their own and not be under censure from day to day.

"E.C. was a fine young man. He just got caught in something that was over his head, that he just didn't understand. Finances. He didn't understand that you could overborrow. He didn't seem to realize that the cost of his borrowing, the interest, was over the profit you could hope to make from ranching."

In November, E.C. found and quickly exploited a new source of loans. Kenneth Alexander, an officer of the American National Bank in Lawton, Oklahoma, was a friend of Dale Kuhrt, E.C.'s new ranch manager. At E.C.'s request, Kuhrt called his banker friend and reported that E.C. owned thirteen thousand acres himself and leased another ninety thousand from Gene. Alexander noted it for the files. Among other errors, this estimate indicates that Gene owned roughly thirty-five thousand acres that E.C. actually leased from outsiders. But Alexander, impressed, agreed to meet E.C. at a livestock sale in Dewey.

Linda: "They came to the ranch and had dinner that night, and E.C. said, you know, that he would like to borrow some money, and Kenneth said, 'Fine, how much?' That's all I remember." The result was a loan of $100,000.

Then, according to Leon Cohen, E.C. dropped by the office in Atlanta and said, "Hey buddy, I need $40,000." So on November 16, 1969, E.C. received a check for $40,000, representing a loan from the Total Learning Institute, a purported correspondence school of which Cohen and Kerwin were officers. Did E.C. tell Cohen why he wanted the money? "Nope." Did Cohen take any security? "No. I have no idea how the funds were going to be used." Then, Cohen says, E.C. wanted to borrow an additional $50,000. "We didn't want to loan him any more." So Morris Jaffe, the Texas financier, borrowed the $50,000 from Cohen and Kerwin on his personal note. Then he endorsed the check over to E.C. so that the rancher's loan legally would be coming from Jaffe, instead of from Cohen and Kerwin. Cohen describes E.C. as "healthy, wealthy, and had the ability to pay," but says there is "a difference between having a man owe you $40,000 and having him owe you nearly $100,000. I wouldn't want my maid to owe me $50, but there are plenty of people I would just love to have owe me a million dollars." Apparently E.C. wasn't one of them.

The Mullendores continued to see Cohen and Kerwin, expecting an eventual big umbrella loan to pay off all the bank loans and refinance the ranch. The first Sunday in December, the New Orleans Saints were scheduled to play the Falcons at Atlanta, and the Mullendores and Mecoms decided to make a weekend of it. Saturday, December 6, E.C. went shopping with Cohen and Kerwin, and that night the young rancher and his wife attended a lavish bash in Cohen's house honoring the owner of the Falcons and the owner of the Saints (Mecom, Jr.) and many of their acquaintances. Linda says there were three or four hundred guests. Among them, according to law-enforcement sources, was a New Orleans football fan named Carlos Marcello. Cohen kept the reputed Mafia boss's telephone number in his pocket secretary.

Cohen and Kerwin continued to help E.C. in small ways, but never with the overall refinancing the young rancher sought. By winter, the agents had switched their representation from United Family Life to Alexander Hamilton Life, a Michigan-based firm. They sold E.C. a so-called "Jumping Juvenile" policy from Hamilton on each of the four Mullendore children. The policies covered the children's lives for $200,000 until they turned eighteen, after which the coverage jumped to $1 million. The four premiums totaled $33,820, but since Alexander Hamilton Life was paying Cohen and Kerwin a 117 percent commission, there was no need for E.C. to pay the premium, and apparently he didn't. Instead of a premium going in to Hamilton, the insurance company presumably sent Cohen and Kerwin the extra 17 percent of their commission, in this case $5,749.40. All four policies subsequently lapsed for non-payment of the second year's premium.

E.C.'s new insurance applications occasioned an update of the Retail Credit Company investigation. On October 24, Retail Credit announced that since the previous report on September 11, the ranch "appears to be about in the same shape." Noting that E.C. had just bought three quarter horses for a total of $341,000, the report concluded: "The subject appears to be financially stable." Another update on December 11 estimated the older and younger Mullendores' combined net worth at $37,427,500, and E.C.'s annual earned income at $980,000. (There is a discrepancy between this and the September report, but no one seems to have caught it. In September, Retail Credit said the $37,427,500 represented E.C.'s net worth alone, and that the combined net worth of the Mullendore men was $55 to $60 million.)

While Cohen and Kerwin fished for loans, E.C. became ever more desperate. He borrowed $78,028 from the First National Bank of Coffeyville, Kansas, in December 1969, $64,850 from the Coffeyville State Bank a few weeks later, and $30,000 from the First National Bank of Dewey, Oklahoma, on January 5.

He also appears to have begun resorting to what bankers call "check kiting," although as Coke Harlow, president of the Coffeyville State Bank, says, "that's a nasty word." In September 1969, a year or so after Harlow's guests had dined on Mullendore buffalo steak, E.C. opened a checking account at the Coffeyville bank as he had done at many other banks. Harlow admits that he and George Schumacher, an executive at the First National Bank of Dewey, were "suspicious of the kiting of checks, maybe. Sometimes you play on this float business, of giving a check today when you are not going to have [the money] deposited in the bank that you drew the check on, maybe until tomorrow or the next day, and knowing that the check might not be presented for payment for two or three days." Did E.C. kite checks? "Not knowingly; possibly did, but here again, that's a nasty word."

On September 30, 1969, E.C. made his first large deposit at the Coffeyville bank, $100,000 wired from the First National Bank of Atlanta (part of the proceeds of the loan Cohen and Kerwin had arranged for him). The $100,000 stayed in Coffeyville one day. When it arrived, checks for $60,000 and $35,000 already were waiting in Coffeyville to be covered. E.C. had written those checks on September 24 and September 28, prior to the deposit. Both checks were to his own account at the First National Bank of Dewey, where, presumably, still other checks were waiting to be covered.

On another occasion, E.C. wrote checks of $5,000, $2,500, and $4,000, all payable to his own account at Dewey. Then two or three days after writing the checks, he covered them with a $12,000 deposit—another check, drawn on his account at the Farmers & Merchants Bank of Dexter, Kansas. Sometimes E.C. would move checks for $20,000, or even $60,000, drawn on his bank accounts at Stillwater, Oklahoma, or on the Ponca City Production Credit Association account; the checks would stay in Coffeyville only one hour, then go out to Dewey. Apparently other checks already had been written for the money, and were waiting for collection. The more banks a check kiter uses, the longer he can postpone the date he will be called upon to make good.

According to William B. Hill, executive vice-president of the Union State Bank at Arkansas City—Governor Docking's bank— E.C. maintained a checking account with a normal balance of less than $100. Yet hundreds of thousands of dollars passed in and out of the account. As soon as deposit checks came in, withdrawal checks arrived to take the money out. Then the deposit checks, drawn on his accounts elsewhere, began to arrive late, and finally began to bounce. Early in 1970, Hill says, E.C. had a balance of about $350,000 in checks that wouldn't clear, and the Arkansas City bank "told him that they had been returned to us and that he would have to get something in here to take their place."

Then, on January 8, 1970, the appeals of Cohen and Kerwin persuaded Fulton National Bank in Atlanta to lend E.C. $250,000; as soon as the loan was funded, E.C. conveyed $83,125 from the proceeds to Cohen and Kerwin as a fee, and the rest to the bank in Arkansas City, apparently to relieve his bad check crisis. This still left about $200,000 in overdue checks.

Less than a week later, on January 13, the National American Bank in New Orleans lent the young rancher $200,000. National American, under control of the Roussell family, had become known as a swinging bank in the late 1960's, catering to an occasional wheeler-dealer. In E.C.'s case, the bank took such a plethora of collateral that it is hard to determine who or what actually pried loose the $200,000. An officer of National American said later that John Mecom, Jr.'s co-signature on the loan, making Mecom responsible if E.C. welched, convinced the bank to put up its money. Says Mecom: "He had a need and I felt I could help; that's all there was to it. [The money] was used for the operation of the ranch. I did not go into detail with E.C. on that."

Lula Harrison, however, remembers when Linda spread her jewelry over the dining-room table to tabulate for use as collateral in the loan. "We did not think it was unusual," Linda says. "My engagement ring was in New York [for repairs on the setting] or it would have gone, too. But I kept my wedding ring." Linda argues that the bank didn't even ask for the jewelry as security, but that E.C. decided to offer it anyway. "This is something we wanted to do and this is not unusual," she says. Most of the thirty or forty pieces of jewelry belonged to Linda, although a few pieces that Kathleen contributed made up about two thirds of the $250,000 appraised value. Says Linda: "E.C. and I went to the bank, met with Mr. Mishler, the president of the bank, and oh, John, Jr., his attorney Mr. Kelliger, and at that time we signed the note and left and made a list of the jewelry, and the whole thing took about fifteen minutes."

Notwithstanding the Mecom guarantee and the jewelry, Cohen, Kerwin, White & Associates also played a hand in the goings-on at National American. The agency brokered a $200,000 compensating deposit to encourage the bank's generosity; later the deposit was withdrawn. Kerwin displayed characteristic charm in negotiating the deal; writing to a bank officer—apparently Irish—Kerwin, formerly Silverstein, tacked on a P.S.: "In checking back on my family tree, I find that there was a Kerwin that came from Ireland." John Mecom, Jr., who also borrowed from National American, says he was aware Cohen and Kerwin had placed a $200,000 deposit in the bank, "but I cannot specifically say what for, whether it was for mine or for E.C.'s [loan]." The bank won't discuss the Cohen-Kerwin transaction or the loans.

On February 9, 1970, E.C. entered the hospital at Pawhuska, suffering, Linda says, from the flu.

Chub Anderson: "I don't know if it was the flu. I never did know, really. I thought it was kind of, you know, just run down, really." During the week before E.C. was discharged, Leroy Kerwin called the ranch and Chub answered the phone.

"Say, I hear E.C. is in the hospital," Kerwin said.

"That's right," Chub answered.

"Well," said Kerwin, "tell that son of a bitch he better not die."

Chub says he thinks Kerwin was joking, and that he declined to relay the message to E.C.

But soon afterward, Leon Cohen came winging in by private jet to pay his ailing client a bedside visit. Linda says Cohen "had a business appointment somewhere and he was . . . in a hurry, but he wanted to come and see E.C. and he flew into . . . the Pawhuska Airport and I met him." She says she thinks it was purely a social visit but that they may have talked business while she was out of the room.

Cohen and Kerwin seem to have been worried that their $15 million client might expire before his insurance policies did, thereby embarrassing their neat little operation. Or perhaps they were concerned about E.C.'s health because they hoped to soak him for more money, maybe even the unpaid $250,000 in insurance premiums. At any rate, Linda and E.C. were rapidly losing faith in both the agents and the policies. Says Linda: "We began to doubt, if [Cohen] couldn't provide the funds for the long-term financing that he had . . . promised, we began to doubt that the policies themselves . . . were any good . . . Mr. Cohen is very flamboyant, as you know. He was a wheeler-dealer type." Linda says she and E.C. laughed at the policies and considered them worthless.

They had reason to seek laughter where they could find it. The young rancher's back was nearing the wall. His $380,000 annual payment for principal and interest on the Northwestern Mutual Life mortgage, scheduled for November, had fallen into arrears. Northwestern naturally was getting edgy. Under normal circumstances, the Production Credit Association would have provided mortgage payments out of its loan budget. But E.C.

wasn't exactly keeping up his end of the budget. Instead of repaying the PCA, he kept increasing his loan by borrowing more money.

According to Harold Copper, president of the Ponca City PCA, any loan in excess of 15 percent of the capital structure of a local PCA requires approval from the nearest Federal Intermediate Credit Bank—in this case, the one in Wichita. Any loan in excess of 35 percent of the capital structure requires further approval from the Farm Credit Administration in Washington. Yet E.C. already had borrowed $3,820,000, including back interest, of the Ponca City PCA's total capital of $9.8 million. E.C. was budgeted to repay $1,419,900 by December 1969, and to continue paying at that rate until the debt was clean; but he hardly was in a position to do so.

During 1969, E.C. actually repaid (according to Copper) about $636,321, but all the while he had been drawing out more money.

Copper had been cooperative in the extreme. He had okayed the previous year's $380,000 payment to Northwestern Mutual. He hadn't winced when E.C. submitted a draft of $5,312.65 for a new Cadillac. He credited E.C. with $744,000 for increased value of livestock, which meant that the money needn't be repaid immediately in cash; actually the herd's value increased by only $426,000, according to Copper's account later. But this new advance of $380,000 for Northwestern Mutual was taking the loan a bit further into the void than Copper could go without an okay from Wichita and Washington.

After weeks of red tape, the PCA finally agreed to pay, and E.C. signed over the check at a ceremony February 17, 1970—three months late—at the Houston office of John Mecom, Sr. Present were E.C., Linda, Gene, Katsy, both Mecoms, and two representatives of Northwestern Mutual, Calvin Lemmon and William Manning.

Linda: "We were sitting around the table and I think Cal Lemmon said, you know, 'E.C., do you have the payment?' And he said, 'Yes, here it is.' And he handed him the check and they discussed, oh, grass conditions, the calf crop, how hard the winter had been, how the children were . . . I don't remember anything being said about the loan."

At the conclusion of the meeting, Linda—because E.C., she says, would have been too embarrassed—asked John Mecom, Sr., for a $20,000 loan to meet the payroll at the end of the month. He gave it to her.

On February 25, 1970, the Ponca City PCA underwent its periodic federal examination. The official report stated: "The Mullendore loan accounts for almost 40 percent of the total volume. Because of the impact, we encourage you to continue your best efforts in controlling the size of the loan and work toward a desired loan improvement."

Although it seems obvious that E.C.'s resources already were exhausted by the winter of 1969–70, his grand plans for the ranch never flagged. Linda says he envisioned a feed-lot operation for some of the bottom land the bulldozers were clearing; then the Cross Bell could bring cattle from other ranches for fattening before slaughter. Meanwhile, partly on the advice of John Mecom, Sr., he began hiring professional management. Dale Kuhrt, a dark-haired, thirty-eight-year-old six-footer, arrived in October 1969. Though without a college degree, Kuhrt had managed several ranches in the area successfully. "Well," he says, "when I went up there, I didn't know they were in a financial bind. He called me and asked me to come up and run the thing. The deal they offered me wasn't too much better than what I had with Coddings [his previous employer]." But Kuhrt says he wanted a change. E.C. gave him a five-year contract and an attractive yellow brick house just on the edge of the main compound. They established an office in a porchlike area adjoining the house, and equipped it with a telephone hook-up that allowed E.C. and Linda to divert from their own home the growing number of calls from discontented creditors.

Chub: "E.C. and [Kuhrt] seemed to get along real good to the best of my knowledge. Dale pretty well did what E.C. told him to do. I don't think Dale made any big decisions on his own. I think E.C. would lay out two or three days' plans and Dale would have them done."

Kuhrt: "Well, let me put it this way. They got the Montgomery lease right after I went there and we . . . would have been at full capacity. [But] they had a lot of junk. The first thing I did was wean calves and get all the trashy cows out of the bunch. The first of January I had as good a distribution of those cattle as they ever had. The right amount of cattle in each pasture. You would never have to move them. We had room for more cattle then. And there is a good inventory on January 1, 1970, and Production [the PCA] has a copy of it."

In consultation with Kuhrt, E.C. hired Paul Kelly as farm manager. Kelly, about five ten, blond, Scandinavian-looking, had a degree from Oklahoma State University and had been working as a county agent. "All I do is take care of the farming and make sure it gets done," he says.

Because he managed a crew of five men, Kelly was in a good position to observe the effect Dale Kuhrt had on the ranch. "My bunch [was] always griping they [didn't] get enough money," he recalls, "but . . . they [blamed] Dale, not E.C. Dale cut out their fringe benefits, their groceries and things they were accustomed to getting before Dale came along. Dale cut out their gravy train."

Early in February, after a haggle over salary, E.C. hired sixty-six-year-old Paul Burchett to be the ranch's first full-time book-keeper. Heavy-set, with a ruddy complexion and sandy-white hair, Burchett was completing long decades of bureaucratic ciphering for the county treasurer and later the county engineer. That scarcely prepared him for the mess he was called upon to clean up at the ranch. Until then Kathleen and Linda had written checks day to day, and the Cross Bell's records supposedly had been kept in formal order by a Pawhuska insurance agency. But the agency's work had been hopelessly inadequate. Income taxes hadn't been computed or filed since 1967. Bills lay unopened. Kuhrt observed that the Mullendores were writing ordinary counter checks to pay expenses, and often filed no record of them. He and Burchett quickly instituted a voucher system with carbon copies.

Burchett: "We more or less started new books, you know, set up an accounting system beginning in January 1970. [E.C.] was in the office every morning I went to work, quite an early riser. When he wasn't there I knew where he was, and very seldom a day went by without him calling the office, so I had what you would call close contact with the man."

Yet, as George Ray notes, "E.C. never told anyone about his business—never actually trusted anyone to tell them all his business." Neither Kuhrt nor Burchett believed in poking his nose where it wasn't wanted, which probably qualified them well for the jobs E.C. had in mind. Burchett picked up his hat and drove back to Pawhuska every day at 5 p.m. He kept only the cash accounts and did not concern himself with property, equipment, livestock, or most of the off-ranch investments, such as the Pizza Huts. Occasionally, E.C. would pass large checks directly to and from banks, so that Burchett could keep no record of them. Burchett says he wasn't even aware of E.C.'s drinking, which scarcely could have gone unnoticed by a close associate.

"E.C. and I got along real well," Burchett says. "But I let him tell me what he wanted to tell me. If he were gone for a week's time, when he came back we greeted each other just like you and I would, but at no time did I ever ask him a point-blank question: 'Did you borrow any money?' 'Did you buy any horses?' or 'Did you do any good?' When he came in, I waited for *him* to say. That was the reason I didn't know too much about his business back here."

Dale Kuhrt: "I guess it was the first of January before I realized how much of a bind he's in. After I got up there, I and Paul Burchett—I hired Paul Burchett to come up and help on the bookkeeping—we opened eight to ten boxes of letters that went back to May of 1969. Paul came up in February, when we really got to digging, and it was just a little different than what I was used to. Then when [E.C.] decided he was gonna have to make a good solid financial statement [to obtain a loan] it was up to Paul and I to get her done and that is when we really, that is when he had to divulge his finances to us and that is when we realized what the conditions were."

Eleven   E. C. MULLENDORE III WAS LOOKING FOR the same kind of debt-consolidation loan you can hear about on the radio every day: wrap all those pesky bills into one easy-to-meet payment, and even have some cash left over for those needed home improvements. But in E.C.'s case, by early 1970, those pesky bills came to $10 or $12 million.

He asked his friend George Ray for help in finding the loan, and Ray introduced him to Lloyd Tucker, a Tulsa insurance and real-estate agent who had done business with Ray. Tucker said he might be able to help E.C. locate a lender, in which case Ray and Tucker would split the finder's commission fifty-fifty.

Instead of finding a lender, Tucker just found another money finder: Talmadge Kolb. In his late fifties, about five feet eight or nine, Kolb had thinning gray hair and one eye that didn't track—some people speculated it was artificial. Linda remembers him as "dignified, quiet, well-spoken."

Kolb had been out of a steady job for about six months, since the bankruptcy of Community National Life Insurance Company in Tulsa. That was the scandal-ridden, Mafia-hooked company E.C. had been suckered into investing in, whose purported $26 million in assets were found to consist mostly of a deed to Great Smoky Mountain National Park and other worthless securities printed up by organized swindlers, causing millions of dollars in losses to banks and policyholders around the country. Kolb had been the chief financial adviser to Community National and to its president, Jimmie J. Ryan, who pleaded guilty to mail fraud.

Although they weren't intimate, Kolb and E.C. had met each other through Community National. In February 1970, while E.C. was still in the hospital, Kolb paid him a visit at Lloyd Tucker's request. They had a long bedside chat, with the result that Kolb succeeded Cohen and Kerwin as the young rancher's chief money finder of the moment. 1970 would see a series of such money finders, each of whom appeared temporarily to win E.C.'s complete confidence.

"Within two weeks after I went to work," recalls Paul Burchett, the bookkeeper, Kolb came into the office and "E.C. let me know [Kolb] was the man that was promoting a loan. He was there pretty often. He was drawing regular pay, $400 a week," which made him the highest-paid employee on the ranch. Burchett himself got only $850 a month. Asked what Kolb's job was, Burchett says, "Well, he didn't do very much."

Linda says she thinks Kolb worked out of his home instead of having an office, and remembers that he frequently turned up for dinner at the Mullendore table.

Dale Kuhrt: "I checked into his history right away for my own curiosity to see if he could do anything. What was the name of this insurance company busted in Tulsa? Well, he was connected with them and I never could find out, but I think if you check the records out, he turned state's evidence in that thing to save his neck. That was a pretty good mess, that thing was. Apparently the guy didn't have any money. Claimed he had a hard time paying his household things. When he first came up there, he was gonna get a lot of percentage [of the ultimate loan]. He was there about ten days and told [E.C.] how much he could work if E.C. would put him on a salary basis, and he could work faster and get it rolling. So E.C. do that, and [Kolb] didn't do any more than he did before. He always drove back and forth [to his house in Tulsa]. Every time he would get there, he would forget to get gas and would fill up at the ranch [where they had a private pump for ranch vehicles]. I let him do it about three times and then decided to let his memory get better."

"I am in the insurance business," says Talmadge Kolb, by way of introducing himself, "and have served as financial consultant to various businesses and people." Of his meeting in the hospital with E. C. Mullendore, he recalls, "We visited with the small talk and caught up on—reminded each other of meetings before, and he said that he was interested in obtaining a loan to consolidate his indebtedness and to take care of some short-term loans. The money market had gone [down since he got them], and he felt like that in consolidating he could get a little better interest picture . . ."

Kolb says he told E.C. to prepare a list of assets and liabilities (a financial statement) and a list of annual income and expenses (an operating statement) and to provide maps of the ranch, pictures of the livestock, and various other items. Kolb says E.C. promised to get what was asked for and to pay Kolb a fee of ½ percent of the total loan; Kolb would divide his fee with Lloyd Tucker, and Tucker would divide his partial share equally with George Ray.

"I had in mind going to the Union Bank in California," recalls Kolb solemnly. Adds the former adviser to a gangster-dominated insurance-fraud operation, "I know a couple of bank officers there who had been kind enough to listen to me from time to time."

Kolb says he went to the ranch a week later with Tucker. "These things I had asked for had not been gotten together, and I told [E.C.] that I did not have enough to start work on. He just didn't have all of his bills together, and frankly, I doubt if he knew the extent of his liabilities at that time. We toured the ranch to some extent and drove around. I saw cattle and horses and hogs and buffalo, longhorn steers.

"[The office was] what at one time had been the cook shack, a room behind the foreman's headquarters. They had ordered furniture and they [were using] card tables and had various boxes and baskets that had been or were being used as files until their furniture and equipment was delivered. They had papers segregated into boxes and no real filing system. Apparently E.C. knew what boxes were which, because when you asked for something, why he would reach in and get it."

Kolb says he returned to the ranch several times. "The materials had not been forthcoming that I needed, and I told him that he needed to get someone to do this work because I was wasting time coming to the ranch and not getting financial data. So he asked me, 'Well, can you do that?' And I said, 'Yes, but I will have to go on a fee basis, an income basis, until I get it done. If I'm going to travel back and forth to the ranch and put full time into it, then I'll have to have an income.' So he agreed to $400 a week." Kolb says he collected the salary until he resigned July 22. Burchett says Kolb had a five-year contract and stayed on the payroll until approximately August 15. In addition, Kolb says, E.C. "paid travel expenses on a couple of trips to California and trips to Atlanta, trips to St. Louis. There were times when he would say go to his gas pump and fill up with gasoline.

"He told me that when he made his arrangements with the Production Credit that they had told him that upon his going in over there that they would take care of all his short-term money and that subsequently it had become a little more difficult to deal with them and that they were not furnishing him this short-term money as he had understood it to begin with. He didn't tell me that he was in default [with the PCA]. He said that they were pressing him, that he was overextended as to their limits, and that they wanted . . . his loan reduced.

"He furnished some money for me to go up and make a debt reduction and work out a moratorium with Mr. Gray, the vice-president of the [First National] Bank at Coffeyville [which was pressing E.C. for payment of an overdue $70,000 loan]." Kolb says he made an appointment with Gray in mid-March but that E.C. and Linda failed to show up as the banker had insisted. Kolb says that when he questioned E.C. about the incident, E.C. had replied that "that's what he had me for, to handle those things." Kolb says he paid the $70,000 debt down to $50,000 and persuaded Gray to wait until a financial statement was complete.

"In the early stages of it, I spent my time sorting out the notes and delegating through E.C. to Paul Burchett to get to the leases and the deeds and the mortgages and all of the pertinent information that we needed for a financial statement . . . and Mr. Kuhrt to get us an inventory, and the farm manager to furnish us estimates on the hay and the crops and so forth. And we became busily engaged in trying to . . . come up with a true financial statement."

Kolb says he found piles of unopened envelopes, many of them containing duplicates of bills that had been arriving for months in other envelopes that hadn't been opened. "Mr.

Burchett opened two envelopes that had substantial checks in them"—including $6,000 in fees for items the Mullendores were storing for someone. Kolb says he found no record books or ledgers—nothing at all that showed assets and liabilities.

"The first week I had anything to do with E.C.," Kolb recalls, "he said, 'You ought to go get some of that Mafia money that you're supposed to know something about,' and I suppose he was referring to the statements that had been thrown around in the newspapers in connection with Community National Life. I told E.C. that I didn't know any Mafia people and that if I did I wouldn't become involved with them or get him involved with them; that neither he nor I were prepared to deal in that league.

"Once E.C. said, 'Why don't you just get on an airplane and go to Las Vegas and get me a loan?' And I said, 'Well, I don't know anybody in Las Vegas that will make a loan,' and he said, 'Well, I thought you knew some people out there,' and I said, 'You know as many people in Las Vegas as I do. If you want a loan out of Las Vegas you will have to go yourself.' "

Twelve   EDWARD KURTZ IS A SELF-EMPLOYED CERTI-fied public accountant in Tulsa. In February 1970, he was twenty-seven years old and working for his father's accounting firm, Sartain, Fischbein, Kurtz & Company. Talmadge Kolb, who had employed the firm on tax matters, came to see Kurtz about compiling a financial statement for E. C. Mullendore in connection with brokering a loan. According to Kurtz, Kolb said that E.C. was looking for $15 million, and that Kolb would receive a 1 percent fee (not the ½ percent that Kolb now remembers).

E.C. visited the accounting office with Kolb in February. Recalls Kurtz: "E.C. didn't necessarily have a concept of what a CPA was supposed to do. He had apparently been told that he needed one. [Kolb said] that he was sure that [E.C.] could get the money if he could get a statement that was prepared by a CPA. I somewhat cringed . . . I explained to him that certified statements are extremely expensive and that they take a great amount of time. Time was important to [E.C. and Kolb]. When they walked into my office, they would like to have had my statement a week ago.

"After looking things over up there and finding the condition that the records were in and the way things were being done, I told E.C. III and Talmadge Kolb that a certified statement could possibly take four months and cost $20,000 or in excess, and then it probably wouldn't accomplish what they wanted. A certified statement would have to be prepared on a cost basis of the assets involved . . . Judging by the nature of the thing, being a family-owned ranch and land being in the family for a substantial number of years . . . it appeared that many of the assets had been acquired years before at a very low cost. In a ranching-type situation, cattle are raised and, depending on the accounting type of system, may have a very, very nominal cost, to where a statement showing a net book value could actually be a deficit figure and not a fair representation of the worth of the organization.

"I felt like if they found somebody that would be interested in loaning them $10 to $15 million, and if those people were interested, then it would be worthwhile to expend the money to get a certified statement and follow it up with appraisals and so forth.

"I said the statement that we would prepare in this short time would not be certified. Mr. Kolb said, 'No I don't need a certified statement, all I need is one put in the proper form by a CPA.' Mr. Kolb said that an individual in California—he was very vague on who the particular individual was that he was contacting to try to place this loan—but that he had been told that this is what was needed. I urged Mr. Kolb to give me the name of the person so that I might call him and thus avoid poor communication and us prepare something that was completely irrelevant to this individual's need. Mr. Kolb told me later that he had contacted the man, and that the man said a statement of equity [a statement based on current appraised value rather than cost] would be fine. Accountants don't generally like to use a statement of equity," Kurtz says, "because it deviates from what most people consider generally accepted accounting principles."

Kurtz says he worked until March 27 to finish the statement. "A lot of times I would need to stay in [my] office just to somewhat regain my sanity, because things were a little hectic up there [at the ranch] at times. Working conditions in the [ranch] office were cramped. They had several people working in there.

"There had not been any books posted for a considerable length of time. . . . Mr. Kuhrt had definite ideas on what he wanted to do toward an accounting system. Mr. Mullendore didn't seem to be too concerned about it. It was very difficult to get [E.C.] to sit in one place for any length of time to give [me] the information . . . I had to get. [Kurtz finally decided that Dale Kuhrt was the most reliable source of information at the ranch.]

"E.C. felt like that there was substantial equity there for a $15 million loan; that the Northwestern Mutual loan would be paid off; that the Ponca City Production Credit loan would be paid off. It was the desire of Mr. Kuhrt that Ponca City especially be paid off to provide for a cash flow, in that [as long as the PCA was a creditor, the money from] all cattle sales and so forth went directly to Ponca City, and Mr. Kuhrt felt like that it tied up the ranch to too great an extent to be able to do the things that they wanted.

"I discouraged the figure of $15 million. Based on our projections that Mr. Kuhrt and E.C. and I sat down and worked out, the ranch would not repay a $15 million loan. [It was] $5 million too high."

Kurtz recalls that Talmadge Kolb "was very interested" in E.C.'s $15 million in insurance policies. Kolb, he says, wondered "how they came into existence, perhaps from a, well, as to what the initial cost was and so forth. E.C. had made representations as to how much it had cost him to acquire the policies, and Mr. Kolb [a former insurance agent] had made several insistences that he couldn't possibly have bought them [so cheaply].

Finally Kurtz decided to call Leroy Kerwin to check out the policies. E.C. placed the call and talked privately to Kerwin for about five minutes, then put Kurtz on the line. "I questioned [Kerwin] at some length about the existence of the policies and he was familiar with what E.C. was trying to do to raise money. He made some representations to me that I felt like weren't entirely truthful, and [I] questioned him at some length as to cash value.

"I was suspicious when he began telling me how they were set up to where E.C. could borrow on the policies and be able to deduct the interest on his tax return, and I questioned him with regard to the particular [tax] code sections, which provide that [such] interest is *not* deductible, and he said, 'Well, we have arranged it in such a way that they will never know.' And I said, 'Well, have you ever given thought to the fact that he doesn't really need tax deductions [because he was operating at a loss]?' Just trying to get a general idea as to whether I could believe this guy or not. He represented that there was some cash value [in the policies], but he followed it up by the comment,

'You aren't thinking of drawing those down, are you?' [Apparently, Kerwin was afraid that Kurtz might try to remit the policies for their purported dollar value, thereby alarming United Family Life about the Cohen-Kerwin operation.] He did state to me that the insurance company had a very in-depth report on Mr. Mullendore, that they had gone to great lengths to accumulate information on him, and that if Mr. Mullendore would request, he would forward a copy of this report to me to assist me in preparation of a loan package.

"I understood that the agents in Atlanta had waived their commission, which I understood was legal in Atlanta or in Georgia [it isn't most places], in order to get the residuals on the policies, and therefore the cost, the initial cost, was substantially less [than normal]." Kurtz says he learned all this from Talmadge Kolb.

Kerwin impressed Kurtz "that he was very good friends with E.C., that he thought very highly of him, and that he hoped they could work out their financial problems."

The statement Kurtz prepared showed assets of $16,386,948, and personal liabilities—those not secured by the ranch—of $1,763,666, leaving equity of $14,623,282. "About 95 percent of the cost figures were not available to me," Kurtz said. "They did not keep very good records. If the value of the assets [mainly land] was realized by sale, it would have probably been a substantial income tax liability [since most of the sale money would be taxable profit], and [inheritance taxes] would be a material factor in the estate should [Gene die]. So we at least mentioned that we had not made any provisions for [these potentially heavy taxes]. It somewhat puts the responsibility on the reader—at least he's aware that the contingent liability isn't in there."

After considerable agony, Kurtz put down $15,000 for E.C.'s cash position. "I ascertained that figure mainly as it was extremely difficult—I knew that there were certain checks that were in transit to the bank, certain overdrafts in the bank where the bank balance at that time was somewhat insignificant, but at that time E.C. was even carrying a check in his back pocket for $50,000 or $60,000. It was a personal check, in handwriting. He showed me the check with [his] thumb over the [signer's name]. 'What will I do with this?' E.C. asked. Kurtz says he thought the young rancher was trying to impress him. So the $15,000 was just "a roundabout figure that we had used. . . . There was substantial evidence of returned checks—substantial in number and to me in dollar amounts." Earlier, some banks had honored E.C.'s overdrafts—but no longer.

Kurtz's statement also listed assets of $575,000 in personal property; jewelry accounted for $200,000, and "the remainder was pretty much just set out by E.C. and didn't necessarily seem extravagant in comparison to what you saw around in his home. I didn't go into the big house. I tried to discourage socializing, which I felt would go on very easily, because everybody seemed pretty hospitable."

Kurtz's report created a possibly misleading impression by listing the ranch finances separately on a back page. Ranch assets were listed at $21.4 million and debts at $8.3 million. But only the resultant equity—$13.1 million—was carried to the main statement at the front of the report. The only liabilities listed in the main statement were $1.8 million in unsecured debts. Thus nothing but a thorough, cover-to-cover reading of the report would reveal the $7.5 million in secured debt to Northwestern Mutual and the PCA.

Kurtz says he separated the ranch equity from other assets because some of the others "might be considered unbelievable," for example, the race horses. "Certainly there was enough indication to require [prospective lenders] to at least independently check the values for themselves. The statement is the statement of the client's, and he felt like the quarter horses were important and that they made good reading, so they were included."

The Bartlesville house was listed at $300,000, the Texas land at $223,400 (on E.C.'s word), the Pizza Hut investment at $200,000, and the newest Cadillac at the sticker price of $8,500. Buildings and improvements counted for $1,308,450. Kurtz valued farmland at $750 an acre and ranchland at $200 an acre, based on what Kuhrt, Burchett, and E.C. said. Included in the liabilities were $132,885.68 in personal debts, to creditors such as ABC Baby Furniture, Beshara Floor Fashions, and, of course, Neiman-Marcus. Most of these debts were more than ninety days past due, Kurtz said.

When the statement was complete, John Arrington, Jr., the lawyer, stopped by the ranch to look at it and made no changes. Among the bills Kurtz found was one from Arrington's law firm for $7,000.

Kurtz says he supplied fifty copies of the statement and submitted a bill for $5,000, which was never paid; the bill Kurtz's firm filed later with the Mullendore estate was for

$6,550. Kurtz says the statement achieved wide circulation, because "when you talk about this amount of money, perhaps a finder's fee on it, it's pretty easy to find people that think they might know somebody." As Kurtz observes, however, such deals "don't necessarily pan out."

Finally, Kurtz decided to wash his hands of the whole mess. E.C. had asked him to go see an Oklahoma City lawyer who George Ray thought might help. The lawyer accused Kurtz's financial statement of being "worthless and ridiculous" because it wasn't certified. Kurtz says that at the time he made his exit, Talmadge Kolb was talking vaguely about getting a loan from somebody he knew at the Teamsters Union pension fund.

Thirteen   TALMADGE KOLB: "LIKE MANY PEOPLE, when I entered that situation, why of course the Mullendore situation was the Mullendore legend, and I didn't feel that he would have any difficulty, and I didn't have any idea that the indebtedness was [so] extensive, and I don't think that he did, really. Everybody that I had ever talked to just assumed that whatever necessary financial arrangements they needed to make, they could make it. I had heard the stories of E.C.'s first trip on selling cattle, sixteen years old, and of course had heard the stories of their extensive operations and their knowledge of the ranching business and so forth. I don't think E.C. knew—he started out talking to me about $9 million on a loan, and $9 million would not have taken care of the indebtedness—it later proved to come up at some $10.5 million.

"We talked at the office; we would get in the car and go out across the ranch or . . . we would be over in E.C.'s house, or we might run down to Dewey or over to Pawhuska, and these conversations took place catch as catch can. He was busy running a large operation, and I discussed these matters, maybe ten minutes, and maybe twenty minutes. [Occasionally George Ray or Edward Kurtz would be present.] His secured position was not terribly out of line, but his unsecured position made things difficult . . . I told him that the accounts payable and short-term bank loans were excessive for the income, in relation to the fact that he was under obligation to pay all income to the

PCA and I didn't see where his outside assets were going to be able to pay the short-term money to banks that he had borrowed. I questioned him as to what kind of income he felt the quarter-horse operation was going to bring, and he told me that he frankly didn't know. That he had some of the finest horses in the country, but he never did know which one was going to win a horse race, and so we determined that we couldn't depend on the income from the quarter horses unless he would agree to sell some of them. He didn't particularly want to sell any of them."

The Benson lumber company in Pawhuska filed a $60,000 lien against the Mullendores because of a past-due bill, but according to Kolb "Benson came out to the house, and they sat and talked and [Benson] agreed to just sit tight on this thing and not press the lien. I felt that all these [local creditors] were people that [E.C.] had traded with before, and I felt that they were going to sit tight on the situation. . . . But [I] felt that any lending agency was going to require that those [creditors] be paid when they funded the money, and that it was absolutely necessary to have the correct list. . . .

"[In addition to the $10.5 million in debts], I felt he was going to need in excess of a million in operating monies because once this new loan was made, he wasn't going to be able to go back. That's the way we arrived at the $12 million loan that we began to seek."

According to the 1969 profit-and-loss statement E.C.'s staff of advisers helped him concoct, the ranch required $1,115,000 a year to operate, and its income was falling roughly a quarter million dollars short. "I felt that there was some nonrecurring expenses in there that could be knocked out," Kolb says, but the debt service—the payments for interest and principal on this whopping new loan—would be tremendous.

"I told him I thought he was crowding, he was getting awful close to 66⅔ percent of his total assets, and that perhaps there would have to be some changes made in some of the things like longhorn steers and buffalo, and one thing and another, that were non-productive . . . He agreed that he was going to have to tighten the belt. He told me that he had been borrowing from one place and putting in another, but this was a normal situation for him. And he told me that the tight money, the rise in the prime rate and so forth, had upset his operations.

"He bought this house [in Bartlesville] and was remodeling it. He had run into this financial difficulty, and at the time it was shut down as far as reconstruction was concerned. But he said, 'Go get me a loan so I can get them back on the house and get it finished.' " So Kolb went "to the First National Bank in Bartlesville [to] see if I couldn't get an extension on a note that [E.C.] had there [for $165,000] and meet with Mr. Gorman, the contractor on the house, who had filed a lien [for $88,000]." But after Kolb talked to the president of the bank, he returned to E.C. with news "that they were threatening to sue, and that [the] suit in itself, because of its locality and the nature of it, was going to be harmful to his whole financial picture. E.C. just said, 'Well, I'll handle it.' How he meant to handle it, I don't know."

At E.C.'s behest, Kolb also journeyed to the Home State Bank in Kansas City and the Union State Bank in Arkansas City. "My role in visiting each and every one of these banks was to placate the banker and assure him that everything was going to be all right once we got this other loan. I got moratoriums in all respects except the Bartlesville bank."

When Kolb asked about the debts to the two Atlanta banks, he says E.C. "told me that he had 'a super insurance man' down there that had gotten him some loans in Atlanta. Every time I would ask him about Cohen and Kerwin, he would say, 'That's another matter,' and never give me any information about this transaction. The only thing that he ever told me was that they returned a portion of his premium to him on the original policies. I don't know [how much]. He said they had told him that they were interested only in the renewals on policies and, in order to make it more attractive for him, that they had returned a portion of the premium to him." E.C. also complained to Kolb about the failure of Cohen and Kerwin to produce the consolidation loan they had promised.

"I heard him over the telephone with Mr. Cohen or Kerwin, and the only thing I know is, he said, 'Well, I don't know whether you mailed it or not, but it never did get here and I don't have the money,' and at a later time he said, 'Well, apparently somebody's backed out because I haven't gotten the money.' Apparently he was at this point a little bit disenchanted with his arrangement over there and wasn't real anxious to fill me in on it."

E.C. also had Kolb talk to Harold Copper, president of the Ponca City Production Credit Association, "to get him to stand still" on the PCA's quest for a $2 million payment. "At that time," Kolb recalls, "why, Mr. Copper was going from first of the month to first of the month. He was going to demand payment the first of next month each month. But he never did make the demand.

"I told [E.C.] that unless I was successful in obtaining moratoriums from the short-term lenders, that we might have to seek protection of the reorganization act. Chapter 11 [of the federal bankruptcy law].

"He said, 'What is that?' And I told him, and that if we were going to pursue that, he should get an attorney. And he said, 'All right. Meet me tomorrow and I'll have a lawyer here.' "

The lawyer was John Arrington, Sr., nearly eighty years old. E.C. and Linda closeted themselves with Kolb and Arrington from 10 a.m. to 4 p.m. Says Kolb: "Mr. Arrington, Sr., concluded that there was a good possibility that I was right in my recommendation. He was surprised to the extent of the short-term indebtedness, and he suggested that Mr. Mullendore contact John, Jr.," who practiced law in Tulsa, where bankruptcy papers would have to be filed in federal court. There are reports that Arrington, Sr., became physically ill outside E.C.'s house that day, so great was the shock of his sudden exposure to the ranch's condition.

E.C. phoned Arrington, Jr., and asked him to come up the next day to discuss bankruptcy. "If we can avoid it," he told Kolb, "I don't want it. That's the last thing I want. But I'll have to talk to the attorneys about it." When Arrington, Jr., arrived, E.C. queried him about Chapter 11 and learned he would need a comprehensive inventory of liabilities. Chapter 11 allows a debtor to safeguard his assets from creditors until a federal judge either approves a new financial arrangement or orders a sale of the assets with each creditor receiving a fair share. If E.C. had entered bankruptcy, he would have gained time, but he would have surrendered control of the ranch to a court until the court was ready to give it back to him or sell it. "Well," E.C. told Arrington, Jr., "the thing to do is get it all together, what I need to do."

So Arrington compiled a list of creditors and drew up the voluminous formal papers that a bankruptcy entails. Then Arrington advised E.C. to sign.

At a deposition in 1971, Linda testified that the decision on bankruptcy belonged to E.C. "I was ready to do whatever he wanted. I would have approved of it had he approved of it." But E.C. refused to sign. "He was sure he could obtain adequate financing elsewhere, without going into Chapter 11." In an October 1972 interview, however, she said E.C. would have signed the papers "at that time, right then." But Gene and Kathleen "didn't want to do it. E.C. and I had long conversations about it, but he only talked to his parents about it one time. [They said], 'No, we won't consider it.' [Bankruptcy] was totally unacceptable as far as Gene was concerned. He wouldn't hear of it. Neither would Kathleen. She said, 'Oh, that's unbearable.' You know, such a disgrace. And that was all. [E.C.] told them . . . that this is the only way to save the ranch. But they didn't believe him."

Whoever objected, the papers weren't signed, and the Mullendores lost an important chance to save the ranch through a bankruptcy reorganization. From that point, the stock of the ranch became depleted, and E.C. was surrounded ever-increasingly by mobsters.

Fourteen   IN 1969, AT THE AGE OF FORTY-FOUR, Jesse T. Collins had risen to manager of the mortgage loan department at the Fulton National Bank in Atlanta and seemed to have a bright future before him. In the twenty years remaining until he would retire, he might even have had a shot at the presidency of this major Southern bank. That was before he met E. C. Mullendore.

In September 1969, Leon Cohen and Leroy Kerwin had asked the bank to finance E.C.'s life insurance premium. The bank refused on the grounds the money market was too tight for such a large unsecured loan. (First National Bank of Atlanta made the loan instead.) But Kerwin was invited to lunch in the executive dining room at Fulton National, where an officer of the bank explained the situation to him to preserve good relations with the prospering insurance agent. The lunch must have been amiable because two months later Kerwin returned.

Jesse Collins: "In November 1969, Mr. James Foreman [president of United Family] came into my office and brought with him Leroy Kerwin. United Family Life Insurance Company maintained excellent balances with us. They had in excess of $2 million on deposit with us and we were servicing for United Family at that time $32 million worth of permanent loans. It was the first time the president of a life insurance company had ever come to see me. Mr. Foreman told me that Mr. Kerwin had a proposition to make to the bank and for me to listen. With this sort of introduction, naturally I listened. . . ."

Kerwin said he had sold E. C. Mullendore some life insurance. "He was bragging about $15 million worth," Collins recalls. "Kerwin proceeded to submit that Mullendore wanted to borrow $250,000 for a home improvement loan. This was to renovate and modify and add to a house in Bartlesville, Oklahoma, and at that time, Kerwin told me that the house when completed would be worth $600,000. Along with asking for the loan, Kerwin assured me that the bank would be provided with $250,000 in cash in the form of a CD [certificate of deposit] in order to have the cash to make the loan. He also told me that we would be given an assignment of at least $300,000 worth of face-value life insurance. Mr. Foreman indicated to me that United Family Life would provide us with a take-out commitment [a promise that if the loan was not repaid by a certain time, United Family would pay off the bank and assume the debt itself] if we would preclose the loan in order to satisfy the request of his client."

Kerwin then showed Collins the Retail Credit Company report indicating that the Mullendores owned 130,000 acres and 25,000 head of cattle and were worth $37,427,500. "Mr. Foreman agreed that this is the [report] that they had used to base the issuance of the life policies on." Nobody mentioned E.C.'s other bank loans. Kerwin reported that the young rancher "owns half of Oklahoma."

Collins says Foreman sat next to Kerwin during their entire meeting and objected to nothing that Kerwin said. "If Mr. Foreman hadn't been present, we wouldn't have even considered the loan—a real-estate transaction out of our market area, something that we wouldn't ordinarily have handled. . . ."

Why did Foreman offer this decisive assistance? According to James Sturdivant, the Tulsa lawyer who later represented United Family Life, "He just got persuaded by Cohen. Jimmy Foreman is about fifty, as nice a guy as you could meet. There's an autographed picture of Billy Graham on his desk. He's a Christian, Southern fellow."

At any rate, Collins took the deal to his bank's loan committee. The $250,000 compensating balance arrived as promised, from Life Insurance Company of Kentucky, which still was soliciting Cohen-Kerwin business. Fulton National would pay 6¼ percent interest on the deposit and receive 9½ percent interest from E.C. on the loan—a neat, seemingly guaranteed profit.

United Family's letter of commitment to take over the loan also arrived, dated December 10, 1969. The bank essentially approved the loan December 15, and formally closed the deal January 8. Collins says that "Kerwin brought Mullendore by in January just to make sure I knew there was somebody alive named Mullendore. I didn't see Mr. Mullendore before we actually closed the loan."

Normally, banks disburse construction loans little by little, as work on the project progresses. In E.C.'s case, the entire $250,000 disappeared in four days. Asked how this happened, Collins replies, "Is it permissible for me to laugh? Leroy Kerwin called within a couple of days after we had closed the loan and told me that he had just come back from Bartlesville and talked to E.C. and that the house was about ready for them to move in and that everything was pretty well finished up and that we needed to go ahead and advance the money so E.C. could finish up paying the bills that he had to pay and go ahead and move on in the house. I called Mr. Mullendore and he gave me the same, virtually the same, story, that the house was ready and that I needed to go ahead and deposit the money and he would probably transfer some of it out into Oklahoma so it would be easier for him to pay up a few of the final bills. I took him at his word and disbursed the money to the checking account for him."

E.C. immediately drew the money out in three checks. One was to Cohen, Kerwin, White & Associates for $83,125, which caught Collins's eye. The loan manager called Kerwin, who explained that "they had loaned Mr. Mullendore some money." The other two checks were to E.C.'s account at the Union State Bank in Arkansas City, the first for $150,000, the next a day or so later for $16,875, which was everything left of the loan. In retrospect, E.C. clearly seems to have used the money *not* to pay off the debts on his new house—which were held by the First National Bank of Bartlesville—but to clear up some of his unpaid checks at Arkansas City. Just before the Atlanta loan was funded, the chief resident officer of the Arkansas City bank had told E.C. about his $350,000 in bounced checks and "that he would have to get something in here to take their place."

Richard Kane, the lawyer-rancher who was selling the house to E.C., co-signed for him on his note to the Bartlesville bank, because, in Linda's words, "Dick Kane is a very close personal friend of E.C.'s and mine, [a] very fine person, and a director of the bank." When E.C. fell into arrears, the $165,000 became Kane's responsibility. Kane says he thinks E.C. sincerely intended to use the Atlanta money to take Kane off the hook in Bartlesville, as E.C. had promised. "But I was being nice to him and some others were pressing him. Finally he came in and said, 'Dick, I lied to you.' "

The confession did not exactly come as news to Kane. Walter V. Allison, president of the Bartlesville bank, had become very concerned about the loan in December 1969 and had called Kerwin. Kerwin explained that minor defects in title on the Bartlesville house were holding up the Atlanta loan, which certainly would pay off the Bartlesville loan.

The money still had not arrived on March 6, when a federal bank examiner issued his periodic report on the condition of the Bartlesville bank. The examiner instructed Allison to collect the loan, if not from E.C., then from Kane, the co-signer. E.C. supplied a check for $165,000 drawn on his Coffeyville (Kansas) bank account, but told Allison not to process the check because there was not enough money in the Coffeyville account to cover it. As soon as he had the money, E.C. would let Allison know. That failed to satisfy the bank examiner, so Allison called Richard Kane, who swallowed hard and said goodbye to $165,-000 cash.

Arthur Gorman, the contractor, proved much less obliging. E.C. had hired Gorman to renovate the house. On January 13, E.C. had given Gorman a check for $32,860.44 for part of the work, and Gorman cashed the check at the Bartlesville bank. The bank then submitted the check for collection at the Arkansas City bank, on which it was drawn, but the check bounced. So the Bartlesville bank charged the money against Gorman's account, which was too small to cover such a large sum. Gorman had to borrow money to make up the difference, which left him in no peaceful mood. On February 18, he and the bank filed a mechanic's lien against E.C.'s house, claiming title to it until E.C. paid off the debt.

Allison, the bank president, recalls that E.C. did considerable traveling during this time. "On several occasions," according to Allison, "Mr. Mullendore would say, 'I'm sure that I'll be able to obtain funds on this trip' . . . And then he would come back in a few days and he had not been able to obtain funds, but he had another source, and this reoccurred repeatedly." Several times, Allison says, E.C. made appointments to come in and discuss the loan, but Linda would call and cancel the appointments, explaining that E.C. was ill or traveling.

The mechanic's lien that Gorman and the bank filed on February 18 caused severe repercussions at the Fulton National Bank in Atlanta. When the $250,000 take-out commitment arrived from United Family Life, the fine print stipulated that collateral for the loan had to include a first mortgage on the property. Fulton National's men tried to obtain a first mortgage, but discovered that Gorman and the Bartlesville bank had beat them to it with their mechanic's lien. Through this legal loophole, United Family Life could escape its obligation to pay. The sure thing that Jesse T. Collins had accepted was beginning to smell of disaster, and the young loan manager hopped the first plane for Oklahoma to inspect this house that E.C. supposedly had been ready to move into back in January.

"[It] was in the midst of being renovated," he says. "Parts of the renovation had been completed, parts of it hadn't. There was equipment there . . . that hadn't been installed. The skylight needed to be put in in the master bedroom. The plumbing needed to be finished; they had taken out the plumbing and were putting in new plumbing in the bathrooms. The interior needed to be painted. The tile in the living room and entrance foyer had been removed from the floor; the new tile was still in boxes. The room or little cabana-type area that was to be used . . . for the swimming pool needed to be painted and trimmed out. The landscaping needed to be finished. Some of the heating and air-conditioning equipment needed to be installed."

Linda says E.C. met Collins in Bartlesville and "took him around the ranch and showed him the cattle." In Mullendore fashion, she insists that Collins visited the ranch for "pleasure" as well as for business. But it's hard to see how he was pleased. E.C. offered Collins $300,000 in race horses as substitute collateral; the bank appraised those particular horses at $17,500 and turned him down.

After that, Collins's boss, the senior vice-president of the bank, Herbert Megar, suggested the young loan manager might have a brighter future elsewhere. So Jesse Collins left Fulton National to become vice-president of a bank in College Park, Georgia.

And Megar didn't have a first mortgage to collateralize his $250,000 loan, he didn't have a take-out commitment from United Family Life, and he didn't have a promising young loan manager. Couldn't he have filed some kind of second or third mortgage on the Bartlesville house? "Oh boy!" he answers. "There was enough ahead of us that we didn't realize anything from the foreclosure of this property."

The Bartlesville bank foreclosed on the house and sold it at auction in October 1970, a month after E.C.'s death. The original owners, the family that had sold the house to Richard Kane, bought it back for $116,000. This more than covered the $32,860 bounced check but still left E.C.'s estate with Gorman's final $90,000 remodeling bill and a $13,736.25 bill from Thomas L. McCrory, the architect E.C. had hired—to say nothing of Richard Kane's $165,000.

In March 1970, the same month the bubble burst at Fulton National in Atlanta, First National Bank of Tulsa foreclosed on E.C.'s $60,000 loan there and sold his collateral, which was the stock he had bought from John Mecom in the National Bank of Commerce.

The First National Bank of Dewey faced its own decision that month. The Cross Bell was the bank's largest account. George Schumacher, vice-president, says E.C. called frequently to say, "I wrote a check the other day to so and so. I don't think I have the money in my account, but if you will call me when it gets there, I will come down and cover it."

E.C. had secured his loans at Dewey with stock in banks at Pawnee and Cushing, much of it in Gene's name. In March, the Dewey bank sold the stock to pay off the overdue loans.

On March 12, the Mullendores mortgaged thirty registered bulls and 863 acres in Washington County to secure a $50,000 debt in Collinsville. A week later they increased their debt at the Union State Bank in Arkansas City by $200,000.

The young rancher appeared to be out of rope. On February 24, he had asked the Ponca City PCA to lend him $133,000 for feed, $40,000 for taxes, $19,960 for beef stock, $18,452 for equity reserve, and $304,331 for back interest to the PCA, a total of $515,743. In March he received $179,000; the Federal Intermediate Credit Bank turned down the rest.

Meanwhile, dissatisfied as E.C. was with the services that Cohen and Kerwin had provided, the Atlanta agents apparently were pressing him to pay the full remainder of his life insurance premium, plus all sorts of other fees. They presented him with the following bill: $253,500 for his own insurance policies, $33,820 for the children's policies, $40,000 for the loan from Total Learning Institute, $50,000 for the indirect loan from Morris Jaffe, $25,000 (10 percent) for brokering the take-out letter from United Family Life that caused so much trouble at Fulton National Bank, $15,000 (6 percent) for brokering the compensating deposit at Fulton, $9,000 (6 percent) for brokering the compensating deposit at First National Bank of Atlanta, $15,000 (6 percent) for brokering the Fulton loan itself, and $10,500 (6 percent) for brokering the First National loan, a grand total of $451,820.

Against this debt, Cohen and Kerwin credited E.C. with three payments: his original $4,000, the $41,750 from his First National Bank loan, and the $83,125 from his Fulton bank loan. This left a net debt of $322,745, by Cohen-Kerwin computations (or $322,945 by standard arithmetic). Records show that on January 8, 1970, E.C. wrote a check for $50,000 on his account at the Stillwater National Bank to Morris Jaffe, who then endorsed the check over to Cohen, Kerwin, White & Associates. Possibly the check bounced, but at any rate E.C. received no credit for it from Cohen and Kerwin.

The two agents later came up with an IOU that appears to bear E.C.'s signature. It is dated March 27, 1970, and promises payments of $50,000 on April 15, $74,500 on May 15, and $198,245 on July 15.

Kerwin, plagued by tax troubles and still submitting $1,000 a month to reduce his quarter-million-dollar debt from the Mafia caper in Chicago, must have wanted that money badly.

Fifteen "When you run out of legitimate sources to borrow money from," says Eddie King, a Pawhuska Buick dealer and ranch trustee, "you go to some people where you have to take some risks."

E.C. began with a loan from the Metropolitan Life Insurance Company—about as high-class a creditor as one could find. Then he went to Northwestern Mutual, a somewhat more adventuresome operation. Next he tried the banks, first the big ones, then the little, out-of-the-way ones. When he had exhausted that source, he went to money brokers, starting with ones recommended to him by reputable men. Soon he would descend to a lower circle.

In January 1970, John Mecom, Jr., accompanied Linda and E.C. to New York and introduced them to Carl Hess, a broker who, in Mecom's words, "felt there would be no problem." But, Mecom says, "Mr. Hess had some ideas that even E.C. and I did not understand. I still don't understand them, sir; I think that's the reason why it didn't work out. There was a program Mr. Hess had in mind to refinance this with Eurodollars and something else involved, and it was a tax shelter, really, for investors, and something E.C. and I were not familiar with. It was something to do whereby cattle were bought and leased and then bought back. It was a very complex deal. Something I didn't feel fit Mr. Mullendore's program and I don't think he did either."

Someone directed the Mullendores to Jack Kessler at the Oklahoma City office of Equitable Life Assurance Society. Kessler visited the ranch, but a deal never materialized.

Then they consulted Jack Conn, a banker in Oklahoma City and a friend of Mecom's. Linda: "Mr. Conn said the only way . . . to save things is to get Northwestern to release two or three of these smaller ranches and sell them, and E.C. just couldn't face that, you know, because they belonged to his grandmother. And on the way back we stopped on the turnpike and he called Tal Kolb. And Tal said, 'Come to my house in Tulsa. I have a man here I want you to meet that can get the money from the [Teamsters Union] pension fund.' And it was Jim Jackson."

JAMES WILLIAM JACKSON. FBI #532 512 C. Field File No.
    SA [San Antonio, Texas, office] 92–550
ALIAS: James J. Jackson, Jim Jackson
BORN: April 29, 1925, Burlington, N.C.
RES.: Harlington, Tex.
HEIGHT: 6–1. WEIGHT: 300 pounds. Brown hair. Brown eyes.
    Med. complexion
Arrested [youthful offender], Raleigh, N.C., 4–27–43. No
    charge
Arrested, Sheriff's Office, Titusville, Fla., 2–2–57, embezzlement, released in custody of attorney
        Sheriff's Office, De Land, Fla., 3–25–57, grand
    larceny, changed to embezzlement
Convicted, De Land, Fla., 7–19–57, embezzlement, [sentenced to] 6 mos. to 5 yrs., circuit court
Confined, Raiford, Fla., 1–29–58, embezzlement more than
    $50, indeterminate 6 mos. to 5 yrs.
Arrested, Sheriff's Office, Oklahoma City, 6–24–65, fraud
    by wire, unavailable p [prints] contr [contributed to file]
    9–3–68

Arrested, Police Department [apparently San Antonio], 2–24–
   70, possession stolen property, released to liberty
Wears horn-rim glasses.

Tal Kolb says he met Jackson in Tulsa in 1963 or 1964, and
has seen him from time to time since then. "He purports to be a
loan broker," Kolb explains. Jackson had come to Tulsa in
March 1970, "and he was waiting out in front of my house to
talk to me." The Mullendores met with the enormous ex-con that
evening at Kolb's house, then brought him to the ranch. Jackson
said he had just driven in from St. Louis, and only later did they
learn he lived in Texas.

Jackson carved a niche in the memories of all who saw him.
"That sucker weigh close to four hundred pounds," gasped Dale
Kuhrt, the ranch manager. Chub Anderson thought that Jackson
walked with a limp, although it was hard to tell which leg was
limping. "He told me he got it from playing football. He didn't
act like he was agile enough to ever play football, though," Chub
says. Kuhrt scoffs that Jackson had no limp; he just "walks like
a fat man, like it was a hell of a strain to walk, like if you had a
couple hundred-pound sacks of feed on your shoulders all day.
Just damn sure big.

"I only seen him probably for thirty-five or forty-five minutes
one morning," Kuhrt adds. "Tal Kolb brought him out there and
said this guy is gonna help us on this loan and wanted to show
him the ranch. Showed him the horse barn, and he wanted to
see some horses and I showed him a couple studs. He was
supposed to have some horses, but he damn sure didn't know
anything about horses. He had a camera hanging around his
neck like a tourist." At other times, Jackson was seen carrying a
cardboard bucket of Kentucky Fried Chicken under one arm to
ward off hunger pangs through the day.

After Jackson's stop at the ranch, E.C. dispatched him around
the country to find $15 million. While traveling, the fat man
liked to keep a low profile, avoiding known hotels in favor of
little, out-of-the-way haunts and using a female companion as
his gunbearer. Messages to Jackson from the ranch—many of
which contained $500 or $1,000 expense advances—were sent
by wire under the code name "Geronimo." That way, according
to Chub, who sometimes had to send these wires, "you don't
have to show any identification to pick up the wire. You can just
go up to the window and tell him you are John Doe and the code

word is 'Geronimo.' Being's you know the code word, they give you the money."

Jackson himself didn't pretend to have money to lend, Dale Kuhrt says, "but he was supposed to know where to get it. He was just as broke as the rest of them. He would call E.C. up and want him to wire his wife in Texas $250 to buy groceries. We have got quite a few canceled checks [E.C.] gave Jackson."

Linda: "E.C. would call me and say get the cash and send down to the Western Union office and have it wired . . . The code name was Geronimo and it was always sent to the Downtown Western Union Office in California, Los Angeles, or in St. Louis or wherever he happened to be. [His wife] called me and said she was calling from a pay phone and she did not have any money and where was Jim. She could not find him and did I know where and did E.C. know." Although Jackson wasn't on the official payroll, Linda says she assumed that E.C. was sending Jackson $500 a week, in addition to possible large cash payments when they saw each other.

George Ray was at the ranch office chatting with E.C. and Dale Kuhrt one day that spring when Tal Kolb breezed in and announced he was off to California to see somebody about the loan. E.C. asked if anybody had some cash to give Kolb to make the trip.

As Kuhrt remembers it, "We were all broke. And George Ray had always been sincere on trying to help E.C., and said, 'Here, I have got an American Express credit card. He could take it right now.' George wrote out a letter of authorization that [Kolb] could use it and he wanted it back right after the trip. And he never got it back. They gave it to Tal Kolb . . . and then they got hooked up with Jackson and E.C. said go ahead and use George's credit card, and E.C. wrote out some kind of note. And George canceled the damn thing in June. They just went right on using it. And George said, 'They are gonna kill me.' I don't mean kill, but wreck him. They [Jackson and his girl] were staying at this Regent Motel [apparently in Los Angeles], and it would be like $600 in three days."

Jackson's spending impressed even Linda. "He had charged an enormous amount of clothes to this credit card, and one thing and another," she exclaims.

Ray says he received letters from Jackson's lawyer in Los Angeles, "trying to get me to sign different things that he was empowered to use this. They sent me a letter from E.C. to Jim

Jackson empowering him to use my credit card unlimited, and I canceled the card by registered mail when I found out what was going on. Even so, Ray says, it was quite a while before the spending stopped and he got the card back.

When Ray first gave the card to E.C., he already was holding $7,180 in bounced checks the rancher had given him in January and February, presumably for cattle-sale commissions. By the end of the year, Ray says he had paid American Express $9,960 on the debts that Kolb and Jackson ran up, and still owed $8,840.

Did E.C. know that Jackson had a criminal record? Chub: "I think he did. He may not have knew it when he met him, but I think he knew it later."

While Jackson was off talking to the Teamsters or whomever, E.C. needed cash to keep the ranch going and to stave off the more aggressive creditors. Under its usual loan arrangements, the PCA would return most of the money from a rancher's cattle sales, holding back a small part of it to reduce the loan. The PCA's final $179,000 allotment to E.C. in March apparently derived from the $199,000 he submitted that spring from the routine sale of yearlings. But since E.C. was still operating at a deficit, he needed *more* money than the yearling sale brought in, not less.

So E.C. began selling stock from the ranch's brood herd, without submitting the receipts to the PCA. Selling mortgaged property without the consent of the mortgagee is a crime; since the Mullendore cattle were mortgaged to a federal agency, selling them was a federal crime.

"I didn't know any cattle had been sold off the ranch until after E.C. was dead," Gene says now. "Nobody ever told me anything about it. I can't see to count [them]."

Did Gene and Kathleen know? "I am not sure," Chub says. "I was wondering. I always tried to keep my mouth shut around them. I always suspected they might, but I don't know."

Linda (choking with emotion as she tells it): "I remember the day that E.C. decided to sell the cattle. He talked to Gene about it and they agreed it was the only thing to do. In the spring. March or April. Kathleen and Gene both knew and approved the sale of the cattle. They said, 'Go right ahead and sell them, you know we can get the money some place else and pay off PCA, that'd be just fine. That's the thing to do.' I was there."

"Let me tell you something about the cattle sale," asserts John Arrington, Jr. "There's no way that the Mullendore Seniors didn't know that the cattle were being sold, because how else was the place running? There was no other way to get [money]."

George Ray, the one person who more than any other seems to have done whatever E.C. asked him to, arranged to sell the cattle direct to William Lowe at the Tulsa Stockyards, without public bidding. The operation bore earmarks of being clandestine.

Dale Kuhrt: "I sold the yearlings, steers and heifers. Sold the yearling steers to Hatch Peck and somebody else in Emporia, Kansas, on the sixth of April on contract, and all the yearling heifers to Charles Ripley on contract. When [E.C.] started selling cows [the brood herd], I tried to keep the young ones back, and that is the wildest damn thing you ever seen in your life. I didn't know [in advance] what we were getting for them or anything. I never knew who in the hell was paying for them. [E.C.] was there and the buyers were there, and he would leave and tell the guys, 'Whatever deal you and Dale make will be just fine, just write up the contract on it.'

"I could never figure it out. The first time he told me to get a bunch of those cattle in, I told him, 'E., you can't sell those cattle, they're mortgaged.' And he would say, 'It's all right.'

"I always looked for Production and Credit to come out and shut [the ranch] down. And I wish they would have. I know I told Linda one time that we shouldn't be selling those cattle and she said, 'No, he is fine, he knows what he is doing.' But they are a little different kind of family than I have, or you had. They can give each other a cussing one minute and the next be hugging each other."

Linda had rationalized the sale by this time. She decided that everybody sold mortgaged cattle. "There wouldn't be any sales barns around the country if mortgaged cattle weren't sold," she said later.

Chub picked up at least a dozen checks at the Tulsa Stockyards, some of them for $60,000 and $70,000—one for $175,000. He says E.C. directed him to go to the commission office with the name Bill Lowe on the glass door. "I would go, and they got to where they knew me and would have the check sealed in an envelope and hand it to me. [The Mullendores] were always in a rush for these things, I guess, trying to beat checks E.C. had wrote, and I would rush in and rush back to the ranch and E.C. would sign it." With E.C. unable to wait a few days for the cattle sale money, the checks couldn't travel through normal channels; Chub had to race frantically across two states to juggle the transactions. "The Dewey bank wouldn't recognize these checks until they had cleared, you know," Chub explains. "[The bank at] Coffeyville would. [So] I would go to Coffeyville and get a cashier's check and take it into Dewey." On May 6, when E.C. and Chub were out of town, Linda herself went to Bartlesville and handled a $100,000 deal.

George Schumacher, vice-president of the First National Bank of Dewey, who dealt personally with E.C., acknowledges that he suspected the cattle were mortgaged; but he says he didn't ask about it.

By June 30, more than $1 million in checks in E.C.'s name had looped the loop from the Tulsa Stockyards to Coffeyville to Dewey, representing close to half the herd. E.C. always held back his best animals. Burchett, the purported bookkeeper, admits he had no idea how much money was going into and out of the various bank accounts.

Both Linda and George Ray insist the PCA was aware that E.C. was selling the cattle, although Harold Copper, the PCA president, denies it. "They knew this was the only source of operating capital," says Linda. "They had to be aware of it. Also, their field representative was up there all the time and could tell by the grass conditions. Anybody can drive down the road, and if you see the grass is this high (gesturing to her waist), you know there aren't any cattle in that pasture. Harold said that he'd stay with E.C. and help him as long as he could, until he got a big loan to take him out."

Ray says one time he "sold some cattle to the people in Omaha, I can't think of the name of that outfit, and they called Ponca Production Credit and [the PCA] told [them] to go ahead and pay [E.C.] for the cattle, so [E.C.] apparently had something worked out with them."

On the other hand, Paul Jones, the hay-bailing contractor, recalls a day in July when he saw "a PCA man over at the office" who had been sent "to watch that E.C. didn't sell any cattle. They had caught on by then. I was settin' in the office one evening [with] E.C. and Dale and Burchett and [the PCA employee] and a cowboy drove up. I saw E.C. motion Burchett, and he called this guy by name, the PCA man, and sent him out with Burchett to see a horse. [While they were gone], E.C. gave

Dale two $100 bills, told him to 'take the PCA guy to the Snotty Fox [a local tavern] and take care of that son of a bitch—get that son of a bitch drunk. We've got trucks coming tomorrow morning and we don't need him around. I don't care if you have to put him on a plane for somewhere, but I don't want him around tomorrow morning.' E.C. said, when the guy came back, they should take him to a particular pasture—he called it by name—said, 'It's the only pasture we've got any cattle left in.' "

Chub Anderson says George Ray "came up every day it seems like for a long time. [He and E.C.] always seemed like real good friends. But [Ray] introduced me to a man in Tulsa by the name of Lloyd Tucker, and I think he was the start of this whole Mafia bunch. Also a Tal Kolb. I never knew why he [Ray] hung around so much and I think he was possibly making money on the mortgaged cattle E.C. was selling to Lowe. I do know every time they would get ready to ship cattle, E.C. would contact George and George would contact Bill Lowe." (Ray, of course, makes his living by selling cattle for ranchers and had earned commissions from the Mullendores on legitimate cattle sales since E.C. was a boy.)

Ray freely acknowledges that E.C. "always thought he sold them [the brood cattle] too cheap. But he never had any trouble with anyone over it." One of the money brokers Tal Kolb found quotes E.C. as saying "that he had made some sales because of his pressing financial position, that he had certainly been taken advantage of, that he thought the cows that he got a hundred or a hundred and a quarter for were worth maybe two or two and a half."

Linda has said that E.C. told her he was receiving only about half of what the cattle were worth, although she says she never heard him and George Ray disagree about the sales. She says E.C. told her "there wasn't anything he could do about it. They were forced to take whatever they could get. It got to the point that he didn't really want to worry me, you know, about things, and because I would ask him questions about what was happening, how he was getting along with these loan people, and it got to where he would say, 'The less you know, the better.' He said that to me many times."

As Edward Kurtz, the Tulsa CPA, completed his equity statement for E.C., Tal Kolb notified the banks that "the statement will be finalized on Thursday, March 26, 1970, and mailed to all creditors." Kolb told First National in Atlanta, according to an internal memo at the bank, "that the auditor had turned up approximately 10 percent more dollar value in assets, primarily in livestock, and that debts had been reduced by $276,000. Kolb further stated that any creditors' meeting is being held in abeyance until his still unnamed capital source in St. Louis, Missouri, makes the decision about whether it is willing to float an $11–$12 million stock offering."

Apparently Kolb, with help from Jim Jackson's contact in St. Louis, was preparing to convert the Cross Bell Ranch into a publicly held corporation, with money from the sale of stock being applied to the debts. But another memo in the bank's files, in Atlanta, dated May 7, 1970, indicates that Kolb's plans changed. "We today received a call from Mr. Talmadge Kolb in Tulsa, Oklahoma. Mr. Kolb stated that he was having more difficulty than he expected in cleaning up the Mullendore situation, but that he was leaving shortly after our call for Los Angeles, California, for the purpose of arranging a $9 million loan with a bank there. Kolb stated that he succeeded in getting a foundation to hypothecate $9 million in municipal bonds for the purpose of securing a loan from the bank. Mullendore has agreed to allow a trustee to take over the disbursement of these funds, and it is Kolb's understanding that the deal might possibly be consummated within the next week."

The bank "explained to Mr. Kolb that this sounded very good, but we were continuing with our legal action until the loan was confirmed by the other bank. In the event the case came to trial before this confirmation, that would simply be unfortunate for the Mullendores."

At about the same time Kolb was phoning the bank in Atlanta, Chub recalls that E.C. "went to some big bank in Los Angeles; I don't remember the name of the bank or anything." But the rancher returned empty-handed. Linda says [Jim] Jackson "was supposedly working all this time to negotiate some sort of loan for my husband and he always had a different deal, always changing. One time it was, 'Let's get some money and get some bonds.' Then E.C. paid this man in St. Louis, this Stephen Lametta, $5,000, supposedly to get a loan from the pension fund from the Teamsters Union, and then he gave a man in California $15,000, I don't know what his name was or anything, but he was supposedly in a bank there and Jackson got [E.C.] to give this man $15,000 to negotiate that loan. That was a different one again, I guess. And they mentioned that one time about getting some money from the Mormon Church and they had some money in the bank in Salt Lake City."

During the previous year, Chub Anderson, the former cattle rustler and welder, had become something of a taxi driver, shuttling three Mullendore children back and forth to Bartlesville for school sessions that started and ended at a different time for each child. By the last week of May 1970, school was nearing summer recess, and E.C. and his assorted financial aides were planning a new money-hunting junket. Chub was about to assume yet another role: E.C.'s bodyguard.

Sixteen

"WELL," LINDA MULLENDORE SAYS OF HER husband, "he quit drinking for about four years when we got married. He always enjoyed having a drink, and then he . . . quit . . . And when all this, when he kind of realized the money problems, it just got worse."

Chub: "When I first went to work for E.C., I had never known of him taking a drink. I had heard that when he was a high-school boy he drank. People described him as a playboy, but I had never seen him take a drink till probably [1969]. I know that they would go to parties and things. I babysat for them and knew what kind of shape he was in. He might be a little tight or something, but this was at parties or the Bartlesville Country Club, but it never was anything. The next day he was the same old E.C., went about his business, stayed sober."

Mrs. Harrison says the young rancher sometimes tried to confine his drinking during parties he and Linda held in the little house. "I would put a champagne glass on the table for everybody but him, then I would fix him a glass of tea sometimes," the cook says.

Chub: "As [E.C.'s] troubles got worse, his drinking got worse. He tried to hide this from his mother and wife, and he would send me after a bottle of Scotch [his strong preference was for Chivas Regal] and would have it put under the seat or in the trunk. I would drive him around, chauffeur, when he would leave town in a car. He drank a lot of Scotch and water, and beer. As long as he had the money to buy it, he would always do it. I wasn't in favor of him drinking. I mean, I didn't argue with him over it or anything like this, but I would do all I could. A lot of times I would take coffee when we were going some place and, you know, I thought maybe he would drink coffee, he wouldn't drink beer or get him a bottle or anything.

"I don't recall how long ago it was he had been getting worse with his drinking, and his mother would get on to him about it and his wife would get on to him about it. They were having quite a bit of trouble over it, and he did quit. He went for a month, I know, without touching anything. Tab, or Cokes, never any beer or Scotch. But he went to California to get a horse with Wade Navarre from Lafayette, Louisiana . . . that was the first time I knew of him taking a drink, and it wasn't two or three days after that he started drinking again, and it gradually got worse."

Often drunk, seemingly unable to come to grips with how hopeless his financial situation really was, the young rancher maneuvered desperately. In May, he arranged to fly to St. Louis, where Jim Jackson and some others supposedly had readied a loan deal. Chub Anderson drove E.C. to the airport in Tulsa, and, although he hadn't intended to, found himself accompanying E.C. all the way to St. Louis. Recalls Chub: "E.C. was drinking. All the time we were [waiting] to board the airplane, [the boarding attendant] thought I was the fellow going, and E.C. had a drink in his hand and was feeling pretty tight, and the fellow found out that I wasn't the one going, that E.C. was, and he wouldn't let us on the plane. And we had to stay that night at the Sheraton Hotel, and the next morning we left.

"I did know this time that they were trying to borrow some money. I had heard earlier he was trying to borrow as much as $10 million. We stayed all night kind of out to the edge of St. Louis. But we went in town the next morning and [Jackson] took E.C. and I to this building, the Butler Building [apparently, from additional description Chub gives, the *Buder* Building, where several Mafia-connected political figures keep offices, police sources say], but I didn't know any of the names of the people. I knew they were some kind of Italian-sounding name, but I don't remember . . . I think Jackson more or less introduced E.C. to these other people.

"E.C. told me when we went to get some coffee, he wasn't drinking, he told me we were messing with some dangerous people now, and I didn't have a gun on me or anything, but he said he had told these people I had a gun. He always introduces me as his bodyguard. But I never went in the office but one time.

I walked E.C. to the room, their office, with these other two fellows; then he told me to mess around down in the lobby of the building and they went on in this office . . . I didn't see the main man that he talked to. But he was to meet the head man, he described to me as the Mafia in the Butler Building." Chub understood the meeting had been scheduled so E.C. could give the other men some money. "I don't know for what. I don't remember how much for sure, but he called Paul Burchett and had him wire $5,000 to St. Louis. There were three or four of these men went with us when we went back to get this money at Western Union . . . We dabbled around, and Jim Jackson, me, and E.C. were supposed to go to Los Angeles."

The next day Chub and E.C. checked in at the Beverly Hilton Hotel. "Jackson was staying some place else," Chub recalls. "He had just got out of prison and they were trying to keep him hid. I did know Jackson was kind of on the sly. I remember when we was eating in a restaurant at St. Louis about Jackson talking a little bit about, you know, his past life, and he had some girl, you know, that he was traveling with, and I don't believe they were married, and E.C. was asking him something about why he had her around so much, and he was saying something about how easy it was for her to conceal a pistol in her purse."

They went to California to talk with John Parks, Jackson's lawyer, to whom E.C. already had wired $2,500. Bob Huffman, senior partner of John Arrington, Jr.'s law firm, one of the most prestigious corporate law firms in Tulsa, met them at the Beverly Hilton. According to Chub, Huffman "was supposed to go over this money contract thing with them the following day, and I expected to go to some big bank, but we went to Compton, California, and a real trashy-looking neighborhood and a lot of hood-looking colored folk who were wildly dressed, a slum area. But [Parks] did have a fairly nice office in Compton. They hung around the office most of the day, and Bob Huffman was aware of the business. I stayed in a vacant office. It was just a ground-level office building, and it had maybe as many as five offices in it. They told me not to get very far from this building, it was a pretty tough neighborhood, people getting rolled in the streets and things. I remember I walked up the street once about four or five blocks and seen quite a few colored people, they had on the backs of their jackets, you know, *Sons of Watts*, and they looked pretty tough.

"We stayed there all that day and went back to the hotel room and went out that night, and they were wanting to look over

Hollywood and look at homes. We went over in Hollywood to some big hotel where all the movie stars were supposed to go drink. I guess we were going to see if we could see any movie stars. I think all three of us [E.C., Chub, and Huffman] had one drink there. E.C. was drinking his Scotch and water and wasn't drunk but feeling pretty good, and we stayed there a while and we went to Century Plaza. After that they had the Emmy Awards [apparently on television], and E.C. and Bob had a couple more drinks and stayed there a little while, and finally someone wanted to go to this girlie show where they had nude dancers. It was a nice place in Hollywood [later identified as The Classic Cat]. Went into it, don't remember the cover charges, but it was quite a bit just to get in. You would have to order two drinks, and E.C. ordered Scotch and water and I had two straight Cokes. Don't remember what Bob was drinking, but the tab came to nine dollars. We watched these girls dance. And E.C. was getting pretty full by then, you know, and I remember this one— They had different elevations of floors where these girls danced, and one was right behind us about as high as this table, and I remember [E.C.] got up on the table [to get a better view] and was sitting there looking around at this girl, and some fellow [a bouncer] come and asked him if he would sit back in his chair. E.C. had drank one of his drinks and picked the other one up and said, 'Let's go.'

"You had to walk up some steps and up on this platform that was raised and down a hall to get out. [Another] bouncer stopped us and said [E.C.] couldn't take the drink with him, the glass, and E.C. asked him to pour it in a paper cup, and he said, 'Well, we don't have any paper cups.' E.C. did offer to pay for the glass, and he didn't want to sell the glass, either. And [E.C.] just, you know, started to go on, said, 'Well, let's go,' carrying the glass. And the bouncer reached out and got him by the arm. And then we—I don't know, somebody started swinging—and we had some kind of a little scuffle, you know. I got hit with a sap or something up the side of the head, but it didn't really make any injury. E.C. had a big old bruise on his ribs, and I think he got whacked in the mouth that time, too. His mouth was bleeding a little bit." Chub says he doesn't really know what Huffman, the lawyer, who was there when the fight started, was doing while it went on. "Like I say, he could have been there maybe, you know, during the whole time, but [there was] quite a bit of action, and the next thing I remember, the police come running in the door, you know. Maybe he [Huffman] is the one that called the police. They got us outside there, I remember, trying to find out what had taken place, I guess, and the best I remember, the police said something about they couldn't arrest us, and they went over and had a conference with one of these bouncers, he was kind of mad, you know. He had got knocked around a little bit. He didn't like it. He some way placed a citizen's arrest on us.

"Well, the police was there, and—a lot of police—and they was the ones that took us to jail. I just remember this bouncer making a citizen's arrest and then the police came and took over. I don't really know what time it was whenever they put us in jail [the West Hollywood Jail; assault and battery charges were filed against E.C. and Chub, and bail of $345 was set on each of them], but it was about 4:30 [a.m.] when we got out, so we was there probably at least four or five hours. Mr. Huffman, I thought, you know, would probably get us right out, but they threatened to lock him up too, so he went home. But out there, I think they have a policy of whenever they arrest you, they keep you for two or three hours and run some kind of a check on you to see if you are wanted any place before you can get released, and they did later set a bond on us. We never went to trial, he said it was all being taken care of. I know my parole officer found out about it and chewed on me, and I told him what happened and that was all that was ever said." (Paul Jones, the baling contractor, recalls meeting E.C. in a pasture a day or two after the California trip. "Did you ever see a black eye this bad?" E.C. allegedly asked, upon which Jones says he admitted it was quite a shiner. He says E.C. also told him that while they were in jail a wino had put his feet in E.C.'s face. "Chub asked the wino to move his feet. He wouldn't do it. So Chub just popped him one.")

The day after the brawl, Chub continues, "we didn't get much sleep until we had to get up, and I believe we went back to Compton. Rode a taxi across town. I didn't really meet this guy [Parks], I don't think. I seen him. I believe Jim Jackson was there," along with Huffman and a secretary. "They talked over their business some more, and we stayed that night, and E.C. said he had borrowed all the money in California and was real thrilled about everything. He said he was trying to borrow $15 million. E.C. told me he was going to be good to me that night and take care of me and not let me get in any—promised me he wouldn't get drunk that night. And we went to Trader Vic's and I had a couple of drinks. He was wanting me to drink. They [the drinks] were names I hadn't heard of. E.C. told me that I had gone through a lot and he wanted to show me a good time before we left California, and we went out and ate and had a real calm night, a real peaceful evening." Huffman was with them, but not Jackson.

They left California the next day. Jackson "came to the hotel, because I remember we had to ride to the airport with him. He was eating a big bucket of Kentucky Fried Chicken." The fat man stayed in Los Angeles, while Chub, Huffman, and E.C. flew to Oklahoma City and Tulsa, where Chub had left the Continental parked at the airport.

Later, E.C. delighted in telling George Ray about the trip to California. "He said he wrapped a horn around somebody's neck out there, one of the musician's horns, and was arrested," Ray recalls.

Several weeks after they returned, Chub says, "an article came out in *Life*, or maybe *Post*. Some kind of bombing incident. I believe the Bell Telephone vice-president or president's car getting blown up, and supposing the Mafia did it. And E.C. showed me pictures two or three times of these fellows and asked me if I recognized them, and I couldn't remember any of their names. But they were cracking down on the Mafia in St. Louis, and he was showing me pictures of them in this magazine. Well, he said, it was the same fellow he had met in St. Louis. He said they were connected with the Mafia. I am almost certain I could identify two persons.

"All these people look like crime people to me. They didn't have on dressy-looking suits, didn't look like the kind of people to be loaning out big money, to me."

Seventeen   AFTER THE ST. LOUIS–LOS ANGELES junket, Chub became E.C.'s nearly constant companion off the ranch. A virtual member of E.C.'s household, Chub sent his clothes there for Linda or the servants to pack with E.C.'s when they traveled, as they frequently did. At meals, Mrs. Harrison says, "We served him with the family."

Linda: "E.C. was afraid to go on these trips without [Chub],

137

and after he drank so much and everything, he just— And *we* were afraid for him to go. Kathleen and I would always say [to Chub], 'Be sure and drive him,' if they were driving some place. It got to where [Chub] drove him all the time, and drove the children to school, and ran errands for him and did everything—stayed there, rubbed his back, and everything for him. He never stayed [overnight] when I was there. The only time he ever stayed was when E.C. and I would go on a trip and my mother would be there with the children, he would stay . . . back in the boys' room."

Even though he may not, as Linda says, have stayed the night, Chub spent a lot of time around the house during the mornings and afternoons. Looking out across the courtyard, Gene—whose eyesight apparently was good enough for him to see what he wanted to and not what he didn't want to—seethed when Linda appeared with the Adonis-like manservant at the swimming pool. (She says it happened only once, and that Gene exaggerated.)

Throughout the summer, every public action of E.C.'s seemed to evidence absolute faith in his manservant, who took on more and more responsibilities. Chub often seemed to use his bashful, aw-shucks manner and his lack of formal education the way Gene used his eye affliction: as a handy device for excusing himself from talking about matters he preferred not to talk about.

"As far as knowing about his business," Chub says of E.C., "I would just catch little odds and ends when he was on the phone, maybe a few words at certain times, but really hearing the business, no. He would tell me a few things occasionally [when] he had got done, but I didn't ask him about it. I would never eavesdrop because I tried to make a point not to pry into his business. I always thought if he wanted me to know something, he would tell me. Never gave it too much concern. I would hear some people say, you know, [the Mullendores] are going broke, but I didn't know whether to believe it or not. I didn't see hardly possibly how they could."

Sometimes E.C. would remark to his manservant, "I really borrowed a lot of money today." Says Chub: "He was a great hand at telling you enough to make your mind think on something, but he would never tell you the full story on something, and I didn't ask him about it."

Chub says he concentrated on the bodyguarding. "I had my hands full," he explains. "I always drank Cokes when they were drinking. I knew how E.C. was when he drank." Not only did E.C. brag frequently about his gargantuan insurance policy—an invitation to those who might want to exploit him—but Chub had to worry about the fat bankroll in his boss's pocket, secured only by a money clip. "He was very careful about how he pulled it out when he was sober," Chub says, "but when he was drunk, he just pulled it out. He carried a lot of $100 bills. I would always look around to see who was watching. A lot of times it would look like a lot of money. He never carried great gobs of money—usually not over $2,000 in his pocket."

E.C. didn't fool with girls much on these trips, Chub says. "There was always somebody to get us lined up with them, but he never did while I was with him. I did hear them joking about one time he went to Oklahoma City without me, this was in the Holiday Inn West, [he] said that somebody had sent this old girl to his room. I don't know how this old girl got in the room with him, but she stayed a little while and I guess he went to sleep, and he said when he woke up, she had ran off with his—I think—his wedding ring and his watch and some money, but he didn't mention how much money. She was supposed to have been seen leaving his room by the night detective or someone, and the police caught her and they got E.C. up and he had to go to the police station, and he couldn't identify the money, but he did get his watch and wedding ring back."

Neither Chub nor the other servants on the ranch could remain unaware of the Mullendore family bickering as it reached a crescendo that summer of 1970. Says Chub: "The way I would know they were having trouble, I would be staying over at E.C.'s house with his boys and Linda, and E.C. would be over at Kathleen's [and] Gene's house, and I guess they would have a big fuss over him drinking. He would come home later and [Linda] would come over to apologize for the trouble then. Other than when he was drinking, [E.C. and his mother] got along real well. His mother would get on to him quite a bit about his drinking, but it never did help. It always caused a big squabble. E.C. and Linda got along just fine, too, except when he was drinking. She used to jump on him, worse, I guess, the last few months. She said it wasn't doing any good."

Mrs. Harrison says E.C. and Linda "commenced spatting quite a little bit, but what those spats was about, I don't know. I would just hear them swearing at each other, 'cause I can't hear good out of one ear when it's cloudy. I never did pay them any attention when they was arguing, 'cause I figured that went with a marriage." Mrs. Harrison says Linda drank regularly, "but she could take care of herself."

Chub: "Linda drank socially. I don't guess I have ever seen her drunk. They would go over to Gene's house and I think she would probably have drinks over there. I would have the children over at [E.C.'s] house and Mrs. Mullendore [Kathleen] is what you'd call a real social woman, and any time that she has company, she runs up to them with a drink, wants them to feel comfortable. I worked there, but I would say about half the time I would go over there of an evening, she would ask me if I wanted a drink. I think probably about two times is all I ever did. I have never seen Gene drink anything but beer. He drinks a lot of pop, water, and coffee, but I have never ever heard of him drinking whiskey. They all talk about how much he was against drinking, for himself even. He was against smoking, too. He didn't frown on chewing tobacco."

Linda's drinking later became a matter of dispute between her and her in-laws. She says she "used to have a drink in the evening with [E.C.], but when he had this problem, then I quit." Gene asserts that Linda "drank a lot. I have seen her so drunk that she can't see." Kathleen: "Once she was real drunk over here at my house and I helped her get home. E.C. was hungry and wanted something to eat. He was mad at her and hit her, she told me later. That is the only time, because we all do pretty well. Linda and I got along extremely well." No one except Kathleen and Gene has gone on record as saying that Linda drank too much.

Linda has acknowledged, however, that E.C. hit her. "It . . . happened several times, the first time [in the spring of 1970]. He didn't mean it. He would never have struck me if he hadn't been drinking . . . I would try to get him to stop drinking . . . They always say [you] turn on the ones you love the most, and it was always me." (Later, Linda changed the story to say that E.C. struck her only twice, once downstairs and once upstairs in their home, both times when he was drunk.)

Lula Harrison once heard E.C. say, "I got a big insurance on me now so anything could happen to me."

Later, when the insurance companies were fighting Linda's $18 million life insurance claim, they offered such remarks as evidence that E.C. was contemplating suicide, and in the meantime hoping to be wiped out by an accident. Collecting on his giant policies had become the only way his family could save the ranch, the companies would argue, and E.C. realized it. If the companies could *prove* his death a suicide, they wouldn't have to pay off. They also cited such testimony as this:

Talmadge Kolb: "At one time, E.C. and George Ray made a fast trip up to Arkansas City up there to the bank. And apparently there had been some fast driving in it and they were kidding about it. George Ray said something about, 'You've got more insurance than I have,' and E.C., who had been doing the driving, said, 'Yeah, I guess I would be worth more dead than I am alive,' which is a statement that I've heard from other people that are heavily insured. And he said, 'What if we had hit that bridge, Tal? Would they have paid off?' And I said, 'E.C., with $15 million of insurance I don't know. They would sure look hard at your death in any event if you were driving an automobile, or any circumstances of your death would have to be an awful clean-cut deal for $15 million.

"From time to time, he would bring it up, and he had become, as I say, disenchanted with these agents [Cohen and Kerwin] and I probably had put some doubt in his mind. And he asked me, he said, 'Well, what do you think about the company down there [United Family Life]?' I said, 'Well, they're an awful small company, but I'm sure they've got reinsurance [back-up coverage from other companies].' I told him on every occasion that we discussed insurance that it was one of the largest combined policies of coverage that I knew anything about, and in any situation his death would be closely scrutinized.

"At one time, Chub was driving, and E.C. turned to me and said, 'Well, got old Chub driving, so I'm not driving, so you reckon if we got killed they would pay on that?' I said, 'Well, I don't know.' There was a trip back from St. Louis when there was a little altercation on the [small, private] airplane, and I admonished him that it was a dangerous situation, and he said, 'Well, I'm well insured.' It was mentioned ten or twelve times during the course of time that I knew him." Once, recalls Kolb, a former insurance agent, E.C. asked if Kolb could increase his coverage because, in E.C.'s words, "We're going to go for a bigger loan than I [originally planned] and I want more insurance than I got loans." Says Kolb: "I told him I thought he was going to have a hard time making the premium payments on the [policies] that he had and that I felt I wouldn't be able to get him any more insurance. [I told him] to be sure if he wanted to keep [the insurance he already had] that he made the premium payment on it, because with that size policy, if it lapsed, he probably wouldn't be able to get it again."

In late June 1970, Jim Jackson arranged for E.C. and Linda to meet Ed Whitlow, yet another would-be loan broker, in Houston. Tal Kolb also knew Whitlow, but Jackson apparently failed to tell Kolb he was introducing E.C. to their common friend. After several days of preliminary talks involving Jackson and his wife, E.C. and Linda invited Whitlow to their hotel suite. In Houston, the Mullendores normally stayed at an apartment the Mecom family keeps at the Warwick Hotel "for visiting people that are working with us in different areas," and there Whitlow was feted with drinks and dinner. Perhaps too many drinks, as it turned out.

"I was pouring some coffee," Linda recalls, "and suddenly Mr. Whitlow attacked my husband, and naturally he retaliated." According to the chief attorney for the insurance companies that investigated E.C.'s death, E.C. got drunk and "said that Ed Whitlow was a whore and that his mother was a [obscenity], and that's when he hit him." Responded Linda: "My husband was not intoxicated. He had been drinking. We had had several drinks before dinner and wine with the meal." She declined to estimate whether E.C. had downed four, five, or six drinks before dinner. At any rate, after the meal ended with a knuckle sandwich from Whitlow, Linda took E.C. to a doctor in Houston and paid ten dollars to put "some stitches in his chin."

Mecom, Jr., was absent from this fracas, although he had dined with the Mullendores in the apartment a day or two before. "E.C. did get into a disagreement with somebody," the oil heir said later. "I can't tell you the man's name or what it was over. His lip was cut, but that's all I know about it."

Linda and E.C. flew back to the ranch from Houston. Chub stayed home on this trip, or he might have warned Linda about a habit E.C. had developed on airplanes. "They had hijacked a lot of airplanes about the time we were traveling some," Chub says, "and he would joke about it a lot, you know. He would say, 'Well, Chub, we are liable to go to Cuba,' or, you know, just joke. People right around us certainly could have [heard him] if they had been listening, you know."

Linda: "We were flying back from Houston. We changed planes in Dallas. For some mechanical reason or—I don't know, maybe they were waiting for additional passengers, we sat there for thirty or forty minutes and it was very hot. He had

had several drinks in Houston with Katsy and I before he left, and then, of course, they do serve cocktails on airplanes. I would say he was somewhat intoxicated. He was not drunk. And E.C. was joking, and he said, 'As long as it is taking this flight to leave, you would think that someone is going to take it to Cuba,' and someone overheard this and took us off, and I have never been so appalled in my entire life. E.C. and I were both removed from the flight."

Chub got a call to pick them up at the private airport in Bartlesville. "Linda said something about that they had had some trouble . . . He was in a jam, but he kept threatening them, 'Arrest me, you SOB's.' They asked him if he minded if they looked in his briefcase, and he would say, 'Go ahead, but it might blow up.' The airport manager in Dallas was a close friend of E.C.'s and Linda's, and after an hour or so they finally convinced the FBI he was just drunk and popping off. Don McMoy is a [private] pilot there, and that is how [E.C.] got home. They wouldn't let him fly commercial. [Linda] just told me that she would let me go with him from now on. [She told me], 'He is yours from now on, because I cannot handle him.'"

Despite all their money troubles, the Mullendores still seemed unable to learn economy. E.C. was accumulating plenty of bills for luxuries such as chartering private aircraft (the short flight home from Dallas after the "hijacking" incident cost $513). Kathleen continued to be the one Mullendore who tried to break the spending pattern: in June, Julia Gilkey, the maid at the big house, took some time off for illness and never returned to work because, she says, Kathleen told her there was not enough money to pay her former salary. Mrs. Gilkey joined the kitchen staff of the Holiday Inn at Bartlesville.

On June 16, 1970, Linda bought a "14k-gold cowboy pin" from Romano Jewelers for $458.70. On June 5 and 6, she spent $103.65 at the Cinderella Bootery. Peacock Jewelers in Bartlesville submitted a bill for $125.41 for shopping done July 26 through 31; the items included a peridot ring, a dozen glasses, a silver compote, and a silver and mirror plateau. The Mullendores were installing a new lawn that summer, for which the Evergreen Nursery charged $5,033.88. They paid $191 a month to Lynn Pacesetter Pools just to service the swimming pool. E.C., Chub, and a number of the cowboys were visiting a Sedan, Kansas, chiropractor who charged as much as $64 a session. "All the cowboys said it really helps," Linda says. "Well, E.C.

had leg cramps from driving in the car seven hours a day, and he went to the chiropractor, but it was a joke. It was just a fancy excuse for a rubdown."

Meanwhile, Gene made *his* contribution to the budget: a Cross Bell quality birdhouse. According to Linda, Gene just "decided he wanted to have all these birds. All different type of pheasants, all different colors, all different kinds of quail. And he had all the boys go around and plow up eighteen or twenty acres worth of plants for these birds to feed on. And he built a birdhouse—he changed a house that was up there, an old house that a cowboy had lived in, into a birdhouse, with insulators and heat lamps and all. [Decorators installed an inlaid vinyl tile floor.] And the birds were hatched, and this was a hobby of Gene's. Spent $16,000 in one month. I can't tell you why Mr. Mullendore wanted to have the . . . quail or pheasant . . . any more than I can tell you why he wanted to have . . . the race horses . . . Or buffalo or longhorns. [E.C.] told his father there weren't funds available, for instance in the summer of 1970, for something like this [the birdhouse]. And the next thing you knew, the carpenters were up there. Gene fired nine men working on the birdhouse. Nine carpenters. Hired nine different men. He had Mrs. Mullendore drive him in a jeep. He went all over the place. He'd go down and look at the buffalo and longhorns, and these birds."

The horse-racing venture fell on hard times that summer. When E.C. allowed the insurance to lapse on five or six horses he had bought from Melvin Hatley on credit, Hatley sent a truck down to Wade Navarre's stables in Lafayette, Louisiana, to repossess the horses. Hatley then billed E.C. $202,657.21 for moving, feeding, and doctoring the horses, and for the unpaid part of the purchase price. E.C. also owed Dr. Jack K. Frost of Lafayette, Louisiana, $125,000 for other horses.

"He spent considerable more for the horses than the income from the races," observes Paul Burchett, who says E.C. received two winner's checks, one for $850, the other for $2,950. Meanwhile, Navarre, who still stabled about thirty horses for E.C., was holding some $30,000 in bad checks from the rancher. All in all, E.C.'s debts to Navarre mounted to $67,000 by the end of the summer.

Navarre called repeatedly about the bad checks. "Yes," Linda says, "he called on several of the checks. I don't know what the money was for, I guess for feed and things like that. He did call during the summer, and E.C. would say, 'I don't want to talk to

Wade, we will get the money to him.' . . . E.C. . . . always believed that he would have the money. The people [apparently the loan brokers] always promised him it would be there."

"These horses have really torn me up," says Dale Kuhrt. "He has never stopped buying horses at Briarwood. He was buying horses until he was killed."

Other bills were piling up in Paul Burchett's office that summer: $59,000 for feed and fertilizer, and other five-figure bills for bulldozer rental and various ranch expenses; $38,000 to E.C. and Linda, and $14,000 to Gene and Kathleen, from Neiman-Marcus (the unpaid balance from some $100,000 in spending over two years), and bills of $19,000, $16,000, and several of about $5,000 from various other clothing and jewelry stores; a total of $10,000 from six different grocery stores; hundreds of dollars each from various carpenters, repairmen, and animal doctors; $34.30 for shampoo in a single six-week period that summer; and tens of thousands of dollars in other miscellaneous bills, including payments for such luxuries as antiques, floral arrangements, swimming pool repairs, and rodeo supplies.

There were also thirty-one separate notices from the Verdigris Valley Electric Cooperative, totaling $4,196.23. Each monthly notice was headed, "Did you forget to pay your bill?"

Although a few of the whopping clothing bills covered two or three years' spending, most of the bills were recent and indicate just how fast money poured out of the Cross Bell operation. None of the sample listed above had been paid when E.C. was murdered.

Mrs. Harrison, the cook, says that when creditors "came here to collect, they would sit down with E.C. and talk. They seemed to get along in good spirits." Burchett says, "It was the best all-around group of creditors with whom I have ever had any dealings. The only ones that mentioned an attorney were bankers. As long as E.C. was alive, I kept them informed of the progress, and everybody was still staying in there."

A federal bank examiner singled out E.C.'s loan on the books of the Coffeyville State Bank and ordered Coke Harlow, the president, to get rid of it. On May 27—the same day E.C. and Chub sparked a barroom brawl in Los Angeles—Harlow wrote the young rancher: "I must request, E.C., the full pay-off on this note as of the due date, June 8. Please make arrangements somewhere else on this matter so this can be taken care of." The $60,000 debt remained on the books at E.C.'s death.

Throughout the summer, E.C. also was stalling off William Hill at the Union State Bank in Arkansas City. One time, Hill says, E.C. presented "a list of bonds that were being made available to him to use as collateral in order to obtain a loan from unknown sources" of $10 million. On another occasion, Hill visited the Cross Bell and was introduced to a money broker named Talafarro, of whom he heard nothing further.

Despite all the evidence of collapse, E.C. still moved about, even in Pawhuska, as the perennially rich rancher he always had been. "The general populace of this area thought things were running very smoothly," says Eddie King, the Buick dealer and ranch trustee. The Mullendore myth was strong enough to survive innumerable jabs from creditors. Ultimately, only a bullet could puncture it.

According to Linda Mullendore's sworn testimony, the man who threatened to fire that bullet, and end E.C.'s life, was George Aycock, a strange wheeler-dealer who had become the latest in E.C.'s coterie of paid advisers. Aycock denies issuing the threat. But there's no denying he brought more criminals and gunmen into E.C.'s camp, and that E.C. and others associated this group with the Mafia.

Talmadge Kolb had run into Aycock in the lobby of a Dallas hotel in May 1970, and invited him to join in the search for a Mullendore loan. Linda says Aycock is five foot nine, about sixty years old, and "dignified and well-dressed." He has gray hair and wears eyeglasses. Aycock had dealt with Kolb before in Tulsa. "He claimed to have an interest in a ranch" about eighteen miles south of there, Kolb says.

Aycock lives in Prague, Oklahoma, although any number of insurance investigators and newspaper reporters have given up trying to find him there. He has been involved in some odd business transactions, including the purchase and resale of a worthless deed to Tennessee land really owned by other people (Aycock now scoffs, "I didn't get anything out of that," although the recorded value of the deal was $160,000). Another time, federal agents discovered him trying to fence a large amount of stolen stock, which came from a Mafia-organized heist of mail pouches at John F. Kennedy International Airport. In the stolen stock deal, Aycock said he was an innocent broker acting on behalf of two other men, and he testified at the trial that sent the other two to prison. The government never charged him.

Kolb: "[Aycock] told me he was from Cleveland [Oklahoma]

originally, and that he would have a personal interest in it insofar as E.C.'s grandfather had loaned his father some money for a newspaper or something. And some six weeks later, he called me and asked me if I had been successful in getting a loan, and he told me he had a source of money in the Bahamas that he thought would work out."

E.C. and Linda met Aycock only two days after their tumultuous trip home from Houston, during which they had been thrown off a Braniff airliner. According to Linda, Kolb "contacted E.C. and said, 'I have a man I want you to meet that has the money.' And we went down to Tulsa to the Camelot Inn and had lunch and met Aycock up in his room for three or four hours."

Chub came along, apparently as part of Linda's new "you handle him" policy. Chub says he "sat out around the swimming pool" while the others talked business inside, after which he was introduced to Aycock. "I remember him telling me something about being a nice-looking young man, you know, healthy-looking. [He] hoped we never had to cross each other's paths. I didn't know what he was talking about." From that point on, Chub says, Aycock started "staying at the Holiday Inn West in Oklahoma City and carrying on his business from there."

Besides his peculiar remarks to Chub, and his penchant for operating out of motel rooms, Aycock displayed certain other quirks. For example, he seemed to travel only in his private plane, a twin-engined DeHavilland, for which he employed two pilots who kept him nearly constant company. Dale Kuhrt recalls that when Aycock visited the Cross Bell Ranch one day, "he had about eighteen people with him." Dale, like Chub and Linda, was impressed by Aycock's snappy wardrobe.

As Linda recalls Aycock's visit to the ranch: "They landed at the airstrip and E.C. brought him on in, and we went downstairs and sat down there at the dining-room table, and he said if we would sign this note, it was for $200,000, to him, that he would borrow the money in his name and loan it to E.C. Mr. Aycock asked E.C. and I to sign . . . and we did. Mr. Aycock was going to borrow some money from a bank in Galveston, [for] interim financing until he was able to get a larger loan. I signed it, and I knew that it was crooked for him to do that."

Somehow, of course, Aycock never turned up with the interim financing from Galveston. But with the Mullendores' IOU for $200,000 in hand, Aycock promised to keep trying.

Meanwhile, Talmadge Kolb began to suspect with some justi-

147

fication that E.C. was trying to double-cross him (not that E.C. had much cause to be faithful after carrying the unproductive Kolb's high salary nearly six months). Apparently E.C. had arranged with fat Jim Jackson that if Jackson's friend Ed Whitlow produced the loan in Houston, Kolb would be cut out of his promised commission. Linda recalls that "E.C. did not want Tal Kolb to know that he went to Houston to meet Jim."

But Kolb found out about the trip, anyway, and submitted a letter of resignation to E.C. "I feel that recently our lack of contact and communication has left me uninformed on the current status of your business and therefore unqualified to be of any real service to you," Kolb wrote, although Paul Burchett says Kolb continued to pick up his $400-a-week paychecks at the ranch until about August 15. Asked to elaborate on why he resigned, Kolb says, "Mr. Mullendore began to take trips which I was not informed as to where he was going or when he was going and I felt like he was perfectly capable of making those decisions and owed me no explanation, but after some of these trips, information would find its way back to me that he was seeking loans, and I felt that perhaps he had lost faith in my ability to get him a loan."

Actually, Kolb's resignation proved quite temporary, as did E.C.'s renewed faith in Jim Jackson. Although as late as July 8 E.C. wired $14,325 to Jackson's California lawyer, John Parks, E.C.'s disenchantment with the fat money broker soon returned. Jackson had begun running up thousands of dollars in bills on E.C.'s telephone credit card while still struggling to keep George Ray's American Express card operative.

"I would hear [E.C.] cuss him out real good there in the office at the ranch," Ray recalls. Chub says Jackson continued to call in even after E.C. shut off his money supply. At that point E.C. had less than two months to live.

Eighteen "THIS DAMNED GEORGE AYCOCK CALLED E.C. up all the time," says Gene Mullendore. "E.C. told me that he paid him somewhere between $30,000 and $50,000 to get this loan. He was always wanting money. One time he called E.C. up and said he had to have $10,000 to go to Houston."

Chub recalls meetings with Aycock in "a little café back on the other side of the [Tulsa] airport. We met there a lot. They would walk off and talk, you know, Tal Kolb, Lloyd Tucker, and Aycock. They would sit and wait on phone calls in this café, leave, and supposed to come back in two to three days. I got where I knew when we went to meet someone, they may not show up. Lots of times after the disappointment of them not showing up, [E.C.] would stop and get a half pint and ice water. Sometimes beer."

In Kolb's words, E.C.'s "needs at that time had become different from his needs when I first started my association with him." The difference, Kolb explains, was that Harold Copper, the PCA president, "was threatening [E.C.] with prosecution and foreclosure, and it had come to light that there had been a reduction of the cattle without a reduction of the mortgage." Kolb remembers E.C. fretting about jail, complaining over and over, "Copper told me, Copper told me."

Harold Copper confirms that he met repeatedly over the course of the summer with Aycock, Aycock's lawyer John Moran, and Kolb to discuss the Cross Bell loan. One time Aycock and E.C. buzzed into Ponca City in Aycock's twin-engined DeHavilland, picked up Copper, and flew him to Oklahoma City for a meeting with Moran and Kolb at the Holiday Inn.

Copper is rather uncommunicative about what happened. His memories of the bungled Mullendore loan naturally are unpleasant, in addition to which Copper's government job infected him with the bureaucratic dialect. Asked to describe Aycock, Copper says, "He's a very impressionable person."

Q.: Impressive?
A.: Yes, sir.
Q.: What was impressive about him?
A.: He was very businesslike.

Asked if he threatened to close down E.C.'s ranch, Copper replies, "To the best of my knowledge, I told him that my action would probably be in a foreclosure way."

Q.: When did you tell him that and whom did you tell it to?
A.: It would have been probably in July or August, in that vicinity, when things did not develop as we had anticipated that they were going to.
Q.: What do you mean by they "did not develop"?
A.: Well, we felt at that time that possibly some cattle had been moved and not applied to our funds as per se.

149

Q.: What made you feel that way?

A.: Due to the fact that Mr. Sibley [the PCA investigator] was unable to get a count on the cattle gave us a key indicator, as such."

Extensive further questioning elicits that "E.C. so informed me that he had sold some cattle and not applied the funds," whereupon Copper "asked that he pay my note."

Hard as he tries to avoid saying so, Harold Copper had added a backdrop of urgency to E.C.'s life. And against this backdrop, Paul Kelly, the farm manager, remembers overhearing telephone conversations at the ranch office between E.C. and Aycock. "E.C. would say, 'Well, George, can we get some of the money *today*?' or something like this, and it was my thought that [Aycock] must have said, 'Yes,' or 'We'll try,' or something."

One Saturday in August, E.C. and his advisers arranged another meeting in Oklahoma City to do some figuring on the deal. Although the drive wasn't far, E.C. decided to save a couple of hours and impress the others by chartering a plane from Ed's Flying Service in Bartlesville. On the way, he and Paul Kelly touched down in Purcell, Oklahoma, just south of Oklahoma City, where E.C. was breeding twenty quarter-horse mares to a resident stallion and paying, Kelly says, $100,000 or more for the stallion's services. E.C. urged the owner of the stallion to improve grazing conditions, and, ever the showy spender, offered to pay for installing a new kind of grass. Then he and his farm manager flew on to meet the loan brokers, whom they found, naturally, at a Holiday Inn.

E.C. wanted money fast, but as usual his advisers were worried mainly about their own income. Tal Kolb, who had just resigned, says he bounced back from retirement to attend the meeting at George Aycock's request, after E.C. had stopped payment on a couple of expense checks to Aycock. "Apparently Mr. Aycock felt that I could help him collect," Kolb says.

In lieu of the fees that E.C. had shut off, Aycock now demanded that E.C. sign a brokerage contract. Kolb recalls a series of conversations "in the club, in Aycock's room, in E.C.'s room, and here, yonder, and there. And there would be one group and then another group. We discussed whether or not Aycock actually had a source of money, which he kept assuring us that he did." Finally Aycock and his lawyer, John Moran, produced a contract that E.C. agreed to sign.

The contract awarded Aycock 10 percent of the loan he

produced, "plus additional sum of all his traveling expenses, which are understood to be in the approximate sum of $35,000. Said sum is due and payable to George L. Aycock, Jr., in grateful acknowledgment by the undersigned for the valuable services rendered by George L. Aycock, Jr."

Kolb says he told E.C. the contract "was excessive, but I didn't know any way at that point to get around it . . . if he could get the money."

So desperate was E.C. for the loan that Aycock was able to send him chasing across the country to formalize the 10 percent brokerage-fee contract. For whatever reason, perhaps just to give himself more time, Aycock insisted that Linda, Gene, and Kathleen *all* sign the papers. This presented quite a problem. Linda had gone to New York to pick up E.C. IV, who had been staying at a camp for overweight children that summer. Linda herself camped at the Plaza, where she and her mother ran up a bill for $1,019.09. Linda also bounced checks for $320 worth of shoes at a Fifth Avenue store and for her airline tickets. Gene and Kathleen were preparing to go to New York, too, on the excuse that Gene needed a new prescription for eyeglasses. E.C. caught them at the Tulsa airport August 22, shortly before they took off, and collected their signatures on the Aycock contract.

"Well," says Linda, "I come back and met E.C. in St. Louis, and Mother brought Number Four [E.C. IV] back home, and we signed. And Aycock said, 'It isn't any good.' "

Aycock complained that the signatures had been improperly notarized. So E.C. and Lloyd Tucker flew to New York, where they planned to meet Gene and Kathleen at the airport to sign the contract again, this time in front of a New York notary. Then another problem arose.

Linda: "Tal Kolb called and said, 'You tell Gene and Kathleen to get their plane tickets out and show as proof they went to New York, because nobody believes they did.'" Apparently Aycock was arguing that the mixed notarizations, some in Oklahoma and some in New York, would make the contract appear suspicious unless the older Mullendores' airline tickets were also notarized as proof they had been traveling. Linda realized that Aycock was just trying to delay things, but she felt consigned to play the game. So her role was to find Gene and Kathleen by telephone and warn them to bring their tickets when they went to the notary; if they failed to do so, Aycock would use this as an excuse for not procuring the loan. "He thought then that I couldn't get them," she says, "so I called the limousine service at the Plaza Hotel, because I knew the driver E.C. used and he knew E.C.'s parents, and I thought maybe he could find them. [The driver] said, 'Yes, we know where they are, they are right in the Plaza having dinner because they asked us to find a notary for them.' Anyway, I told Kathleen that Tal Kolb said they had to have those plane tickets, they don't believe, which is so ridiculous. Tal said, 'If you don't get the tickets as proof they went up there, the deal is off.' "

E.C. met his parents at Kennedy International Airport, collected their signatures, and paid the notary $100, only to discover that his problems were not yet over. His return ticket called for a flight leaving from La Guardia. After a cross-town dash in a taxi, he caught his plane and arrived back in Tulsa at 4:55 a.m.

"Hell," he told Tal Kolb afterward. "The other one was just as good as this one. My folks signed it at the Tulsa airport. But I guess you have to do whatever they want done if you [want to] get the money."

When the brokerage contract was being negotiated, Kolb says, Aycock "represented that he had someone [a lender] in the Bahama Islands that he had been a mortgage correspondent for, and he gave me the name of a man I don't recall, but there was enough mystery about it to sound good. And this man [was] supposed to be a real-estate owner and dealer in Freeport."

If Aycock called anyone in the Bahamas, however, it never came to light. Instead, after the contract was signed, he summoned David Walker Taylor, a fifty-year-old Methodist minister who liked to dabble in unlisted securities. Taylor had tried many occupations before Aycock showed him the gravy train at E. C. Mullendore's house. Taylor was graduated from the University of Oklahoma Law School in 1947 and began practicing law in Norman, Oklahoma, where Aycock also did business. So they got to know each other. Then Taylor devised an unusual way to make money from wildcat oil drilling. Raising money through the public sale of stock shares in his drilling companies, he bought dry wells. These came relatively cheap, compared to the wells other drillers were buying, the ones that might have oil in them. Although he would never bring in any gushers, Taylor thus had most of the stockholders' money left over to cover his personal living expenses. The downfall of this scheme was imbedded in its very genius. Because other Oklahomans also knew the wells didn't have oil in them, Taylor had to sell his stock to out-of-staters, which subjected him to federal fraud laws. He was arrested in St. Louis in 1959 and sentenced to twelve years.

After his parole in 1965, Taylor headed west and took up the ministry. He held pulpits at the Broadway Methodist Church in Glendale, California, and the Valencia United Methodist Church in Valencia (both are suburbs of Los Angeles). From time to time, he would return to Oklahoma to buy more worthless oil wells. In 1970, when Aycock again looked him up, the Reverend Taylor was peddling shares in these oil wells to his parishioners. In October, a month after E.C.'s death, a state's attorney in Los Angeles would charge Taylor with criminal activity, costing the Oklahoman his pulpit. A year later, in court, he would be convicted of ten counts of attempted grand theft and eight counts of selling unregistered oil shares. But in August 1970, when Aycock brought him to the Cross Bell Ranch, the Reverend Taylor was operating from behind an eminently respectable front.

Taylor did not have $12 million handy to lend E.C. But a few months before, Taylor had introduced Aycock to a Kansas City man who did claim to have access to great funds. Now they decided to call on him again. And thus did Aycock and Taylor lead E.C. to his last money broker—the chunky, pistol-packing penitentiary habitué, Kent Green.

KENT S. GREEN. FBI #621–011–A
BORN: Aug. 12, 1927, Newton, Kans.
OCCUPATION: 1953—factory worker, 1970—building contractor
HEIGHT: 5–9. WEIGHT: 190 pounds. Med. build. Fair complexion. Brown hair. Brown eyes
Arrested, Sheriff's Office, El Dorado, Kans., 6–27–49, grand larceny (cattle rustling).
Arrested, Police Department, Wichita, Kans., 1–24–51, held for Kansas Bureau of Investigation
Confined, State Penitentiary, Lansing, Kans., two counts grand larceny, cattle: 1 to 5 years, 1 to 7 years, consecutive (paroled after 14 months)
Arrested, Sheriff's Office, Wichita, Kans., 3–20–53, investigation, released outright
Arrested, U.S. Marshal, Topeka, Kans., 4–11–57, conspiracy 18USC1343 (fraud by wire), convicted 9–24–57, U.S. Dis-

153

trict Court, Wichita, Kans. [The fraud involved an airliner bomb hoax. George D. Bender, a Wichita used-car salesman and Green's co-conspirator, testified that he planned to board a Trans World Airlines plane at Wichita bound for Kansas City. Green then would call TWA and warn that Bender intended to commit suicide by exploding a bomb that was concealed in his briefcase. Bender would allow crew members to wrest the briefcase from him, but would claim injury in the struggle and would sue for $500,000, charging false arrest and loss of valuable papers in the briefcase, which presumably would be tossed out of the airliner. Before this doubtful sequence transpired, however, Green called both TWA and the FBI and offered to expose the plot in advance for a $5,000 fee.]

Confined, U.S. Penitentiary, Leavenworth, 10–9–57, fraud by wire, three years

Transferred, Federal Correctional Institution, Texarkana, Tex., 12–10–58. Paroled 11–28–59

Arrested, Police Department, Jackson, Miss., 1–12–61, investigation of auto theft

Arrested, U.S. Marshal, Jackson, Miss., 1–12–61, interstate transportation of stolen vehicles (Dyer Act)

Confined, U.S. Penitentiary, Terre Haute, Ind., 5–4–61, transporting stolen autos, 8 years. Paroled after four years, seven months

Arrested, Olathe, Kans., 5–2–70, felonious assault. Pending

The well-pedigreed Mr. Green, while serving time for his stolen-car rap, had shared a cell at the U.S. Penitentiary at Terre Haute with David Taylor, who was in for mail fraud. The two of them hit it off very well. After their parole they kept in touch.

Like Taylor, Green rose quickly in the outside world. By 1970, when E.C. met him, he was developer of Canterbury Gardens, a $1.3 million apartment project in the Kansas City suburb of Grandview. A bank helped finance the project, which Green undertook in partnership with Sal Capra, a prestigious Kansas City lawyer and politician. Capra was a member of the K.C. City Council. E.C. was lured on by Green's association with Capra, because E.C. was told Capra had access to Mafia money. Capra's uncle, Alex Presta, three times convicted of bootlegging in the twenties and thirties, appears on the Kansas City Crime Commission's list of local Syndicate figures. Presta also has a well-publicized connection with machine politics. Capra, his nephew, denies any link to the Mafia, and has never been charged with a crime. How Capra and Kent Green fell into the building business together has never been fully explained. But Green's criminal nature stayed with him, even in this purportedly legitimate business. To collateralize the credit lines Green and Capra used in the $1.3 million Canterbury Gardens project, Green put up shares of stock in the Newport Oil Company, whose president was—the Reverend David Taylor.

Like Taylor, however, Green was due to get his comeuppance before 1970 was over. He and Capra failed in their loan repayments in December. David Taylor's oil stock proved to be disappointing collateral, so Canterbury Gardens was sold at auction. Green's wife had sued him for divorce earlier in the year, and Kansas eventually jailed him for kidnapping her and her mother at gunpoint.

But these misfortunes all lay in the future when Taylor first introduced his former cellmate Green to his old friend Aycock in May 1970. Aycock was trying to cook up a land deal and Taylor thought Green could help; the deal fell through. Toward the end of August, however, Green heard from Taylor again, about a new undertaking. The next day Aycock flew to Kansas City and personally handed Green a letter advising that Aycock had "a valid and outstanding contract with E. C. Mullendore *et al. et ux.* in which it is agreed that I receive a fee or commission of 10 percent of the amount of any loan which may be procured for Mr. Mullendore . . ."

So Green, by Aycock's authority, became E.C.'s new money finder. Aycock and Tal Kolb gave Green quite a publicity build-up, and left E.C. impressed that Green had access to the Mafia millions.

According to Linda, Kolb brought E.C. to Bartlesville on Tuesday, August 25, on the promise they would sign a loan. Then Kolb surprised the rancher by announcing that they were going "to Kansas City to meet the Big Boy." Linda says that Aycock "was constantly referring to someone called the Doctor—'You have to talk to the Doctor. You have to talk to the Head Nurse and the Doctor.' I didn't know whether to laugh at them or what. It all sounded so silly, like a television serial. One minute I was afraid of them, and the next minute it was all so silly it can't be real."

At any rate, Green says E.C. flew to Kansas City that Tuesday with Aycock, Kolb, and Aycock's two pilots, and met him in the office at Canterbury Gardens. "I sent one of our cars over" to the airport to pick the group up, Green says nonchalantly, adding that "one of the office girls" acted as chauffeur. The stocky gangster seldom overlooks a chance to strike a genteel image.

Green says E.C. asked for a $12 million loan to consolidate all his outstanding accounts payable, and that the rancher had brought along a financial statement. "Briefly, we went over it. There was a very rapid page-by-page scanning of the holdings and the assets versus the liabilities and the bottom line on it. He had plans of building a feed lot, and the equipment for it, which he had the elevator for, would involve another $4–5 million. He said his flow of money from Production Credit Association had ceased temporarily. He did need interim financing, and I agreed to look at the financial statement and . . . give him an answer at a later date."

Kolb says they talked for an hour and fifteen minutes, after which E.C. asked, "Is this man a member of the Mafia?"

Kolb: "I said, 'Hell, I don't know.' I was told that during the time Green was in prison that he was a cellmate of some man who was alleged to have had Mafia connections. Whoever that was, I don't know." According to Kolb, Green appeared to okay E.C.'s loan on the spot, but said it would take a few days to convert treasury bills into as much cash as E.C. wanted. So they arranged to meet later in Ponca City.

In the meantime, Green decided to look around the Cross Bell and test the Mullendores' hospitality. So the assemblage flew back to Bartlesville.

Kolb noted that Aycock's plane was too large for the runway at State Line Airport, a small field outside Kansas City. "We took off under, to me, very harrowing circumstances, and I determined I wasn't going back. I had . . . gotten to the point where I was a little shaky about . . . jumping around in these private airplanes. And . . . E.C. and Chub drove a lot faster than I like to drive. [Next] time I told E.C. that I would meet him in Kansas City, but I was going to take a commercial airplane."

E.C.'s trip to Kansas City that Tuesday was so sudden that Chub was left behind and spent the rest of the day trying to catch up. Linda met him as he brought the boys home from school and sent him immediately to Kansas City via Big Ed's charter service. Although he originally was to meet E.C. at Kansas City's swank Muehlebach Hotel, Chub found only a message there to meet his boss at State Line Airport. Wheeling up to the airfield in a taxi, Chub spotted George Aycock's twin-engined DeHavilland and climbed aboard just in time to return to Bartlesville. The frustating chase soured Chub's initial impression of Green and perhaps helped to touch off their bitter rivalry for E.C.'s trust. On the plane ride home, Chub observed that Green sported a big stogie and "a little snub-nose .38. I believe it was a Smith & Wesson. He also had a Browning 9-mm. pistol . . ."

From that day forward, Chub would see through Green in a way that E.C. either could not or would not, and would try desperately to subvert Green's growing influence over his boss.

Once at the ranch, Green got all the proper introductions. Linda says Green told her he owned homes in Olathe and Overland Park suburbs, as well as his suite at Canterbury Gardens. Paul Burchett recalls that Green stopped by the ranch office for thirty or forty-five minutes, but asked few questions. "Evidently he had the figures he was interested in without going through the records," Burchett says.

"The first time I seen him," says Dale Kuhrt, "we were sitting in my house one night and I seen some light in the [grain] elevator and didn't know if someone was stealing something. I put my boots on and went down, and it was E.C. out there showing [Green] around. I imagine at least two weeks before E.C. got shot, [Green] was pretty well there at the ranch all the time. We were over at the office one day and E.C. called me outside and I asked him what that guy was doing carrying a gun around, and he said he has got the source of the money and said he was a double rough character. Said he was part of the Mafia. I took it as kind of joke. I still don't think Green has anything to do with the Mafia. He is too much amateur."

Green arrived at the ranch on Tuesday, August 25, and laid plans for a big meeting in Ponca City that Friday to pay off the PCA loan. Harold Copper, the PCA president, said he'd be glad to get the money. Meanwhile, Green stayed on at the ranch, and once again Tal Kolb felt that E.C. was trying to replace him as financial adviser and deprive him of his ½ percent commission.

That Thursday, E.C. gave Green the traditional spin around inlying and outlying ranches. Kolb went along, relegated to the back seat. Just as the car emerged from the Pawhuska ranch and was to head back to the Cross Bell, where Sal Capra was to meet them for dinner after flying down from Kansas City, E.C. told Chub to swing the car in front of Kolb's mother-in-law's house in Pawhuska. Says Kolb, "I had suspected that I would not be invited to the ranch for that evening's festivities . . . It

157

made me mad. I told [E.C.] that he was deceptive and quite cunning and devious." Capra didn't show up, anyway—he says he wasn't even invited.

Kolb recalls phoning the ranch that night to announce that he would skip the big meeting in Ponca City the next day. E.C. told him "to sleep on it." Kolb says he came to the meeting only after Harold Copper entreated him by telephone to do so.

At the Production Credit Association office, Kolb says E.C. asked him, "Why did you call me last night, Tal, and say what you did?" Kolb says he replied, "Because, E.C., I can never depend on you. Just as quick as you figure you're going to get what you want, you drop me out. I'm tired of the deception."

There followed, on that Friday, August 28, 1970, one of the freakiest episodes in the lore of finance.

Aycock was present, along with E.C., Kolb, Green, David Taylor, Copper, and the PCA lawyer Max Berry. As Green remembers it: "Mr. Aycock called myself, Mr. Taylor, [and] Mr. Kolb off to a private room, described as a board room. He informed us that he had the arrangements made for the loan to take care of [E.C.'s] obligations to the Ponca City Production Credit. [Aycock said] his money would not be available until the following Monday [August 31]." Green says Aycock asked him to issue a check to pay off the PCA immediately. Then, on Monday, Aycock would give Green a cashier's check to cover the check Green would write to the PCA. Green says they talked about possible criminal prosecution for E.C.'s sale of the cattle in violation of the PCA mortgage agreement. Aycock allegedly had told E.C. that Copper "threatened to throw you in jail." Says Green: "That was one of the reasons we went ahead, and rather than wait until Monday, why Aycock said we better go ahead and do it this way today, to get things cooled down."

So, Green says, they left the board room and returned to Copper's office. Copper called the federal bank in Wichita to learn the exact amount E.C. needed—roughly $3.3 million, according to Green. Then came the most important part, calculating the 10 percent brokerage commission for the money finders. To pay the PCA *and* the commission, E.C. needed to borrow $3,665,749. "That's when I issued the check," Green says. "Mr. Aycock assured everyone that funds were available and told them that he had asked me to issue a check, which I did, and that he would cover that check." According to Green,

Aycock said he would obtain the funds "through a Mr. Wilson, who is the general manager of the American National Life Insurance of Galveston."

Aycock says he never promised to cover a check Green issued. He says he did try to obtain a loan for E.C. from American National Life Insurance Company, but that the company was uninterested.

And Copper tells still a different story. He says the men simply walked into the PCA office and plunked down a check for $3,665,749, drawn on the Green Land Company of Grandview, Missouri, signed by Kent S. Green. Copper accepted it. He says the amount was a little less than E.C. needed to clean out the PCA loan, but "that was the amount of dollars they had, or supposedly had," so the PCA took it and agreed to assign its mortgage interest in the Cross Bell Ranch to the Green Land Company, as soon as the check cleared the Grandview Bank. PCA was to receive $3,283,749 of the total. At E.C.'s request, Copper says, the rest would go for commissions. Aycock would get $182,000, David Taylor $182,000, and Talmadge Kolb $18,000. Copper recalls feeling pretty good about obtaining such a substantial payment.

Kolb: "We all formed a procession and went down to the First National Bank in Ponca City, where Mr. Copper endorsed the check for deposit. It was made payable to the Ponca City Production Credit Association. I sat around and waited for them to draw me a cashier's check [for the commission] while Mr. Aycock was working out an idea for a deposit for *his* commission. And Mr. Taylor [for his]."

Aycock reportedly demanded immediate payment of his commission, by cashier's check, but bank officials refused to release any funds until Green's check cleared. It was too late in the day to reach the Grandview Bank by phone.

Chub says he had been waiting outside in the car the whole time. But he remembers E.C. was "happy on the way home. I guess he thought he had made his loan, you know . . . I remember him saying, 'We can rest a little bit now.' It seemed like he was real pleased with what he had done."

Linda: "They came home that day, and he was so happy and said, 'Well, we have paid PCA off.' He said, 'They have got the money, they just didn't get to the bank in time.' That is what Green told him. They had the money, they had the cash, and they didn't get to the bank in time. All these times, Green,

159

Jackson, and Aycock, they always managed to wait until after three in the afternoon or on a Friday. E.C. always said, 'It is too late now, because the banks are closed.' "

The Grandview Bank is closed Mondays also. On Monday, August 31, the bank president was playing golf when a messenger raced out onto the links to summon him to the clubhouse for an urgent phone call. Kent Green, who had returned to Kansas City, says he was out shooting skeet that day when word reached him to hurry back to his office at Canterbury Gardens for an urgent call from the bank president. Harold Copper was in his office at Ponca City when his phone rang, and Tal Kolb and Linda Mullendore were at home when Copper called them.

When Green's $3.7 million check arrived for clearance at a central bank in Kansas City, an official naturally called the Grandview bank president to verify that the check was good. No one has recorded the bank president's exact words, but the fact is, the Green Land Company account at Grandview had less than $2,000 in it. When the bank president called Canterbury Gardens, Green reportedly said he expected the check to be covered by "a $3.6 million dollar check from the Chemical Bank of New York."

When Copper told Tal Kolb that the check had bounced, Kolb says he replied, "Well, that's nice."

Linda: "Harold Copper called me Monday and said, 'Linda, that check was not any good,' and I said, 'I just can't believe it, that anybody would write a check for $3 million and have it not good.'"

Paul Kelly, the farm manager, remembers E.C. laughing about the incident on the ranch the next day. "I guess I am not the only one that writes hot checks," E.C. said. "He wrote one for $4 million."

Green: "I was sitting there waiting for Mr. Aycock, I and the banker, the following Monday [August 31]. The check was there and Mr. Aycock did not appear. In fact, it was several days before anyone heard from Mr. Aycock." Green says they tried to reach Aycock "by telephone, by runner, by carrier pigeon." E.C. phoned and asked, "Where the hell is Aycock?" Replied Green: "I talked to [Aycock's] wife, the Holiday Inn West, the Downtown Holiday Inn, Moran, anybody I could think of." Nobody knew.

Finally, back at the ranch, Green says, "E.C. and Gene and I at one time were on the same connection with Aycock, and at that time I don't recall whether Aycock still told us that he could get the money or finally admitted that he couldn't. I think he finally admitted that he could not get the money. E.C. did not make any comment about being disappointed. In fact, I don't think other than just the acknowledgment that each of them were on the line, other than that passed between them, because I was the one on the spot. I had issued the check. I defined [Aycock's] ancestry to him and what I thought of his ability to perform. That check almost caused the bank to be sold—the Grandview Bank, which I had enjoyed very good relations with."

Reporter Thomas J. Bogdon of *The Kansas City Star* learned that on Wednesday of that week, September 2, Green's teenage daughter brought a $3.6 million check into the Grandview Bank for deposit. This one was drawn on the Lenexa State Bank and carried the signature of a Kansas City woman, not further identified. The bank told Green's daughter that the check would be accepted on a collection basis only, and advised her to take the check to the Lenexa State Bank and obtain a cashier's check instead. The daughter deposited the Kansas City woman's check, anyway, but returned about ten minutes later to withdraw it again, explaining that her father would make other arrangements.

Nineteen THE ALL-AMERICAN FUTURITY, RUN every Labor Day at Ruidoso, New Mexico, is the richest quarter-horse race in the world. According to schedule, the Cross Bell Ranch's spectacular investment in quarter horses was to start paying off at the All-American of September 7, 1970. But in a trial race around the first of September, a bridle broke on the Mullendore entrant, shaking him and throwing the rider, who was badly trampled by other horses. The accident dashed the family's chance to win the big race.

George Ray: "[Gene] wanted to be the man who won the race out in Ruidoso more than anything else in the world. When the bridle broke on their horse, all hell broke loose. It was personally E.C.'s fault [as far as Gene was concerned]."

Coming on the heels of a $3.7 million bad check, the broken bridle foretold a dismal week, the start of a dismal and abbreviated month, for E. C. Mullendore III. In an effort to salvage what he could of the racing situation, E.C. chartered a plane (for $829.25) to Ruidoso, accompanied by Kent Green, Green's chauffeur, and a lawyer from John Arrington, Jr.'s office. Apparently Green had been forgiven for the little mix-up over in Ponca City, having persuaded E.C. it was Aycock's fault.

As for Chub: "I hadn't had a day off in quite a while, and my birthday was the twenty-ninth of August. And I had been invited to a lady's house in Bartlesville for a birthday dinner they were going to have for me, and I left [the ranch] on my birthday and went up to this deal [the party]." Apparently he took a long weekend to recover, because he didn't make the trip to Ruidoso.

E.C. was concerned about the jockey, who was still hospitalized. The lawyer came along to see if the Mullendores could at least get back their $1,300 entry fee. The exact results of the trip aren't clear, but when everyone returned to the ranch and learned that Aycock still hadn't produced any money, the scene could not have been happy. Green drove back to Kansas City in one of E.C.'s Lincoln Continentals, apparently having convinced E.C. of his ability to obtain a loan. The proposed lending source was Sal Capra, Green's partner in Canterbury Gardens (who denies any role in the Mullendore affair). First, however, Green insisted that E.C. find a way to escape his commitment to Aycock. Aycock's whopping 10 percent commission would run an intolerable $1.5 million on the $15 million loan they were seeking. The commission problem occasioned another trip to Kansas City toward the end of the week before Labor Day. (Although witnesses aren't certain about the day and date, the trip appears to have started Thursday, September 3.)

Recalls Paul Kelly, the young, blond farm manager: "I was working in the field, and E.C. picked me up and wanted me to go to Bartlesville with him and pick his car up. And we got to the airport and he said, 'We have got a plane coming in here in a minute and you get on this plane with me. We are going to Kansas City. I have got a Lincoln setting up *there* at the airport [the one Kent Green had borrowed] and I want you to bring it back. As soon as we get up there, you can bring this car back.'

"I called my wife and told her, and we waited around the airport for about an hour and the plane came in—a large plane, with two pilots." E.C. was on the telephone at the time, and "Aycock, he came in this little place there and said, 'E.C., if you are going with us, you better get out here, 'cause we aren't waiting on you.' And E.C. got off the phone and we got on the plane, E.C., Chub, and I, George Aycock, Tal, a man by the name of Dave Taylor, and about three men on there I didn't know and wasn't introduced to."

The atmosphere aboard indicated that Aycock had been forewarned of what E.C. and Green planned to do to his 10 percent commission agreement. Kelly: "There wasn't the usual greetings, and E.C. didn't visit with them on the way up there. E.C., Chub, and I went up to the front of the plane and sat down. Tal, Aycock, and them sat in the back of the plane. There was a rounding bench back there, and they had their heads together. It was my thinking that this was kind of E.C.'s deal, and he should be included. And on the way up, [E.C.] wrote some figures on a piece of paper and showed [Chub and me] some-thousand dollars and he said, 'This is how much they are trying to cheat me out of, and we are going to get it straightened out today.' They weren't including him in the conversation. Then is when I began to wonder what was going on."

Kelly says the men he hadn't met remained silent the whole trip. "One of them sat across the aisle from me, and he sit there and looked out the window," Kelly says; the man was graying, heavily built, and appeared to be Aycock's bodyguard. Kelly recalls that David Taylor talked to him at one point in the flight. "He appeared to be working as Green's attorney. He told me he was an attorney and financial adviser, and he told me about some of the deals he had in Canada with mines, about mining stock, different from the United States, and it was very easy to buy a mining claim and do little work, put in very little money and make money." Taylor apparently omitted discussion of the Methodist ministry, his occupation at the time.

The plane touched down at a small airport southwest of Kansas City, where Kent Green was waiting. With Green was Robert Heid, the "chauffeur" who had flown to Ruidoso with Green and E.C. Today, Green introduced Heid as his "apartment complex manager."

"But he wasn't there just as his apartment manager," Paul Kelly observed. "He was more in the capacity as a driver, and what Chub was to E.C.—kind of kept [Green] out of trouble. He was just a big, overgrown kid, looked like to me.

"E.C., I would say, was kind of nervous over the deal, and he told me that flying up there had made him some-thousand dollars that Tal and George Aycock were trying to cheat him out of on the loan. That they had got part of their money and were cheating, and he got part of it back. When we landed there and went in, E.C. was nervous, and . . . well, the atmosphere made me pretty nervous. It was just a sense that everything wasn't all right. It was in a small airport, and there was a café, and they just went round and round. First E.C. would meet with Tal or Aycock, and then Green would meet with him, and then all of them would get together. There were several small rooms and they were even using the rest room as a meetingplace and they met in the café and they went on for about one, one and a half hours, and everybody congregated in the dining room and we ate. Everybody watched what they were doing and who they talked to . . .

"And George Aycock wanted some cigars and they didn't have any cigars there. So Chub and I were going after the cigars, and E.C. didn't want us to go [which would have left him alone with the enemy]. And it ended up Green, E.C., and I went after the cigars and took them back, and Chub and I sat in the car, and E.C. and Green went and talked to Aycock and gave him the cigars. When [Green and E.C.] came back, this Dave Taylor was with them, and E.C. [told me that] Tal and Aycock would end up with sugar in their gas tanks on that airplane, so don't be surprised, they would crash, and not to ride on it. Of course, E.C. was always trying to act a lot tougher than he really was, but you could tell there was ill feelings in the meeting. He did say this about the airplane. He said they are going to end up with sugar in their gas tanks.

"E.C. had told me on the way up that Green was hooked up with the Mafia and that these old boys he was fooling around with now were just a bunch of gangsters, so watch what you did and said . . .

"We left the airport, it was Chub, E.C., Green, Taylor, and this kid [Robert Heid, Green's chauffeur-bodyguard] and my-self, and went to Green's apartment complex, along Highway 71, south of Kansas City. When we got in this car, I asked E.C. when he wanted me to take it home, and he said, 'This is the only transportation we have right now, so if you take us to the apartment, you can have the car and take it home.' We got to the apartment building in the middle of the afternoon, and E.C. said, 'Well, we don't have any more transportation for Chub and I, so you just wait and we'll let you go home after a while.' I called my wife and told her I wouldn't be home till late.

"And E.C. and Green went in his office and they talked about making several telephone calls, and Taylor and the rest of us sat out in this small room, kind of a party room at the apartment complex, and we visited all afternoon. There was nothing really discussed as far as the loan or very much business at all. Taylor . . . told me that he was called in as a financial adviser to the deal, but it looked to him like the [Cross Bell] didn't have very much of a chance, because . . . the stock was depleted on the ranch, [and] it would take too long to bring it back up to a money-making deal. Taylor said, 'If we are gonna put any money in this deal, he can't be paying all these race horses; that house in Bartlesville, it's gonna go.' E.C. was drinking quite a bit, Chub was drinking hardly any. I had a few drinks along toward evening, I quit, and I wasn't feeling at ease in the whole situation." Kelly remembers that several of the men showed off their guns. Kent Green had two.

"At six, to seven, E.C. decided to go out and eat, and he was pretty well drunk, and we went out to this place. They served drinks and E.C. continued to drink real heavy, and he told me as soon as we got back to the apartment I could go home, and it took a couple hours to get supper and get the drinking all done."

Chub, who was much more at ease through the whole affair, remembers a splendid steak dinner with the five men and several attractive girls Green knew. "And then after dinner we came back to the complex and everybody was sitting around the swimming pool in pool chairs, and I borrowed a bathing suit and went swimming. Everything seemed to be running real smooth. But pretty soon, Paul Kelly come over and told me that E.C. had said something to Kent [that] had made him mad, and said we should try to get [E.C.] out of there. I got up and walked over there and stood by the table, and supposedly Green and E.C. had kind of, you know, had a little hard feeling there some way, but they didn't have any more words to say."

Paul Kelly: "[E.C.] said, 'Well, I have decided to go on home instead of waiting around up here.' And Green said he just didn't believe in doing things that way. He should be up there on business and should remain in a businesslike condition, but it didn't bother E.C. a bit. He just went ahead. During the evening, E.C. continued to drink and about, I suppose, eleven, E.C. went in and made some phone calls from the manager's apartment, and he wanted Chub or I with him at all times. He wouldn't do anything by himself. Most of E.C.'s calls, he didn't get in."

Chub: "I saw that E.C. was getting pretty drunk, and I said, 'E., let's go home.'"

Kelly: "And [E.C.] said, 'Let's go to the Muehlebach Hotel.' I was supposed to go home, and he said, 'You take us up there.'

And he pulled the deal again that he didn't have any transportation, and I called my wife and told her I wouldn't be home that night."

Chub drove the three of them downtown to the Muehlebach in the brown Continental. When they checked in, he recalls, "E.C. was pretty drunk. I talked to E.C. and tried to get him to go to the room, and he wanted to go to the Playboy Club, and [it] was somewhere in the neighborhood of 12:15 a.m."

Kelly: "E.C. was wanting to party, and they came up to the room and wanted me to go with them, and I said no, and I took my clothes off and went to bed."

Chub: "We were just in our Levi's, and I had heard about the Playboy Club and didn't think we could get in, so I said, 'E., I am not going.' He said, 'I am going and will be back in a little while,' so I thought I better go. It was about a block away. Well, they have this elevator there that, I think, all it does is take people to and from the Playboy Club, which was supposed to be the top floor [of the Continental Hotel]. And of course in his condition he was obnoxious, and never cared too much for colored people. And there were some colored people in the lobby. Right before we got on the elevator he said something about, you know, black sons of bitches, and they all looked up at us, and I thought, Boy, you know, here it is. But they didn't get up or anything. They were sitting on a couch in the lobby. And we got on the elevator and were waiting for a white fellow to get on and [E.C.] told the elevator to, 'Come on, we don't have to wait on those niggers.' And I don't think they heard. The elevator got to the top floor and we walked into the club right off the elevator. There was a colored guy standing there checking, I guess, your membership cards when you went in."

Did E.C. have a membership card? "Well, he told them he did, but he didn't have it with him, and of course we were just in Levi's, E.C. and myself, and this colored guy told him that we would have to have ties and slacks on, you know, to get in, and a sport coat. And I told him, 'Well, let's go, E.C.,' you know, always try, you know, to talk him out of things like that. He kept talking to this colored guy all the time, trying to get in, and he offered him some money, I don't know how much, you know, and the colored guy still wouldn't let him in. He said he was sorry, he couldn't do it. We weren't dressed properly. I don't know, they argued around about getting in, and pretty soon the— They had kind of a narrow hall, and the tables were in

166

back, you know, and E.C. just told me, said, 'Come on, we will just get us a table.' And started to walk by this colored guy.

"And he reached out and got ahold of E.C.'s arm, and [E.C.] jerked away and said, 'Let go of me, you black son of a bitch.' And, of course, the nigger, he started swinging then, and he hit E.C. once, and I grabbed E.C., I was just going to, you know, get him back on the elevator and get out of there. I had ahold of E.C. and the colored guy, he hit *me*. So I turned E.C. loose, and we were in kind of a, you know, scrapping around, and two more guys ran up, and I was scuffling around with them, and pretty soon I looked around. E.C.—this colored guy had E.C. down and [was] really thumping on his head, and I ran over and hit him, and knocked him off E.C., and [E.C.] got up, or was wallering around on the floor. Of course, these other guys rushed me again, and I was turning around busy with them.

"The next time I looked around, [the black doorman] had drug [E.C.] on the elevator and he had him down, choking him. I ran in the elevator and hit this colored guy again and knocked him off again, and these other two guys rushed in the elevator, and the elevator operator, he never did get out of the elevator, he just started going down when we all got on. He took the nigger down with him. They had the whole troop. Anyway, we got to the ground floor, well, E.C. was laying on the floor all the time going down, and we was scuffling, and I was trying to keep them back. We finally got down, I never could get him to get up. We got on the ground floor, he still couldn't get up, and they was kind of backed off in a corner then, just watching us. And I had to drag him out of the elevator, because he couldn't— He got hit pretty hard. I remember he was all bloody. His eye was bleeding, and his mouth. He just kind of grinned and said, 'Well, we got her put on us again, didn't we, Chub?'

"And it was raining, I remember, and this— He got to where he could kind of navigate there pretty quick. I was holding on to him, and I told him, I said, 'Well, let's go back to the Muehlebach, E.C., and— Kind of embarrassing, all these nice-dressed people watching us leave the hotel. And I wanted to just run around to the Muehlebach. All we had to do was run around the half a block, you know. But he said, 'No, we will get a taxi.'

"So we was lucky. I thought, you know, the police would be coming any minute. And the first car that come by was a taxi, and we got him stopped. Well, we got in this taxi and E.C. told him to take us to the Red Onion, or some— I don't remember the name of the club, but he was wanting to go to another club. And I told the driver, 'Take us to the Muehlebach.' And E.C. kind of grinned and looked at me, and he said, 'Who's the boss, Chub?' And I told him, 'You are.' And he told the driver again, 'Take us to the Red Onion.' And I said, 'No, take us to the Muehlebach.' And he took us to the Muehlebach. E.C. sat there a little bit, and then he looked at me and grinned. He was beat up pretty bad, his lips were busted and he had a black eye. He got out, and I paid the cab driver."

Paul Kelly: "I had already gone to sleep and they were gone probably an hour, and they came back and E.C. was real drunk by this time. E.C. said they had been in a fight and tried to get in the Playboy Club and that the niggers had thrown them out. E.C. wanted to go somewhere else, and I wouldn't go and Chub wouldn't go."

Chub: "And he called a few people he knew, I guess, that he thought might have a Playboy Club [card], wanting to go back, but nobody seemed to have one. He called two or three of his big-shot friends in Kansas City, and they would tell him to call somebody else. He kept wanting to go some place, but I told him, 'E., let's just go to bed,' and finally I got him in bed and quieted down, and when he did, he finally went to sleep pretty fast."

One man whom insurance investigators say E.C. called was Clifford Noe, an itinerant confidence artist who styles himself "Dr. Noe" and poses as an executive of numerous phony banks and insurance companies. Countless victims have paid good money for the worthless banking certificates and other securities Dr. Noe lugs around in his oversized briefcase. Whether E.C. ever reached Clifford Noe, or what passed between them, has never come to light.

Paul Kelly: "He got up the next morning and said Green was supposed to go to Chicago and fly back in to that little airport [south of Kansas City] and be there in the neighborhood of 10:20." They went to the airport, but Green "didn't show. E.C. was drinking, and Chub and I wouldn't drink one, so he drank all three of them. He would keep insisting and buy you drinks, and Chub would just leave it setting and say, 'No, thanks.' [E.C.] wasn't as vocal with Chub as he was with me. It didn't really make him mad, but he kept offering.

"He was getting pretty well shut down at the airport, and he was pretty obnoxious to be around when he was drinking. I can't stand a drunk when I am not drunk. We just hung around there in the airport a little bit, and he said, 'Check the flights from Chicago.' I went to the rest room and met Chub and he said there were three flights coming in from Chicago, and [they] were on opposite ends of the airport. I told him I would take one end and he took the other, and we were trying to catch Green as he came in, but nobody came in and it must have been one [o'clock]. They were paging E.C. for a phone call, and I couldn't find him, so I took the phone call and it was the [apartment] manager's wife. Green had told her he never planned to come back to Kansas City, he was supposed to meet E.C. in Oklahoma City. So I went up to the bar. E.C. was up there. He just kept drinking. He could still get around pretty good, but you couldn't reason with him. I told E.C. what I had found out and it made him madder than the devil because I had left him by himself. He said he wanted me or Chub to be with him at all times. E.C. told Chub to go check on flights to Oklahoma City, and [Chub] said there weren't any until four. E.C. said, 'I have changed my mind, I want Chub to take that car home and I want you to go to Ruidoso with me.' And I said, 'I am not going.'

"I called a friend of mine in Emporia and asked him to pick me up. I even checked on a job while I was up there, and came on home that night. I told Paul Burchett the story, and he said don't worry about it, just go on and go to work. And Dale [Kuhrt] called me the next day and he said he had seen E.C. in Snyder, Texas, and that there were no hard feelings, to go ahead and work. And on Tuesday or Wednesday, E.C. came in the office and passed it off as a joke. Said, 'What happened to you, we lost you at the airport?' And that is all that was said."

Seeing that Kelly wanted out, Chub gave the ranch manager $40 to get home from the airport. "E.C. was just, you know, running in circles and wallering around at the airport. I didn't know what E.C. and I was supposed to do, you know, he never had told me. But he wanted to go to Oklahoma City then, so we chartered this twin-engine plane."

By the time they arrived, E.C. apparently had forgotten all about his planned meeting with Green. Recalls Chub: "E.C. decided that we would go to Ruidoso. And he wanted me to go call this Don McMoy, in Dallas. He's a pilot for this Lear Jet, it's a charter. And I went and talked to this Don and [E.C.] wanted to know if he could get us in Ruidoso before dark, and he didn't think we could. There wasn't any lights there at Ruidoso, any landing lights, you see, and he would have to fly down in these mountains and kind of in a valley to land.

"And so I went back and told E.C., you know, that he couldn't do it. He said, 'Well, I believe he can,' you know, so he went and called this Don himself, and he said, 'Well, he will be here in just a little bit.' He had talked [the pilot] into coming. It was almost dark when we left here, but they figured they could outrun the light out there, you know.

"And we got out there and it was too dark to land, and we went on over to Roswell, New Mexico, and they had the lights on, and they set this Lear Jet down there. We sent the Lear Jet on home. We didn't have any rental car or nothing. We just sat in there. Some guy at the airport rented us his station wagon, and E.C. was drinking then, you know, still pretty knocked out. I got him to lay down in the back seat, and drove this old station wagon all the way across them mountains back over to Ruidoso.

"We got over there, this Wade Navarre [the horse trainer from Louisiana] was supposed to have us a room reserved. And we got E.C. down, you know, asleep."

In two or three days E.C. had gone virtually nonstop from Ruidoso to the ranch to Kansas City and back to New Mexico.

Apparently the Mullendores, expecting the loan money from Green any day, were preparing to restock the ranch. Linda: "Dale Kuhrt . . . was going to Snyder, Texas, [Saturday, September 5] to look at a registered herd of Hereford [at] the Winston Brothers' there in Snyder, and then go on down to Tucumcari, New Mexico, to look at a commercial herd. So Mr. Mullendore, Sr., said, 'Linda, I want you to go down there to Snyder with Dale and on over to Ruidoso and go to that horse sale so E.C. won't buy any more horses. Keep him from buying any more horses.'" (This recollection by Linda, which seems to contradict some of her other recollections, implies that E.C. favored the race-horse investment and that Gene opposed it. Perhaps both men favored the idea at the beginning, and both grew to oppose it as failure became evident.)

Linda: "So I went with Dale, and when we got there to Snyder, E.C. wasn't there, and Dale and Mr. Winston and I went out to look at this herd and came back. Then E.C. and Chub come in [by a chartered plane from Ruidoso that cost $246.50], and we went back and seen the same herd again so he could see them. Then Dale went on to Tucumcari [on a plane they chartered from Big Ed] to look at the other herd." The rest of the group took off for Ruidoso.

Chub: "They had a big horse sale there at Ruidoso a couple of nights previous to the race on Labor Day. And E.C. went to the horse sale. [The sellers] had their own lounge set up there, two of them. Get those buyers feeling good and they bid more, I guess." E.C. "got pretty full," but apparently bought no horses.

On Monday, Chub, E.C., and Linda arrived at the Ruidoso Jockey Club for the big race. Chub: "E.C. was drinking pretty heavy, and they kept going and talking to different people they knew. I wasn't with him too much. He would go off with this Wade Navarre and they had their own betting centers in the Jockey Club and I was always losing him. When I saw him, he would have me to get him a Scotch and water, and he would see more people there and I would leave, and I didn't keep too good a track of him during the race. He never said anything about betting. The whole trip was a mystery to me. He went more or less, I think, to get away from his worries."

Suddenly Chub, E.C., and Linda were stunned to see George Aycock. Aycock, who was with several girls, two pilots, and a lawyer, explained he was on his way to swing a business deal in California.

Chub observed Aycock, occupying a table, surrounded by "some old girls. One time when I was in the bar, there were three or four more come by to borrow some money from Aycock." Aycock cornered Linda for about thirty minutes that afternoon. Chub watched them from the corner of his eye—but just out of earshot, he says.

Linda: "We were downstairs, I think, watching the race on television. Not the All-American race, but one of the other races, sitting down there at a table. I was never so shocked to see anybody as I was to see him there. He just said, 'You do what I tell you and you will get the money. Do you want to save the ranch and help E.C.?' And I said, 'Yes, but I will never sign anything unless my lawyer looks at it'—because I do not like any of these people, after talking to them over this long period of time. It was obvious that all they were doing was milking E.C. for money, and he said, 'You just use my lawyer and do as I say, and everything will be all right.' Well, he told me that if Kent Green made the loan and did not pay him his commission, that he would have Green killed and also E.C. and I."

Chub: "She told me later that he made a lot of threats to her about their financial situation and said if she didn't do like he wanted, he would have her and the children shot. Some way, Kent Green was supposedly supposed to get [E.C.] $10 million. And Aycock was supposed to get a tenth, which would be a million. Well, the way I took it, they were trying to get by without paying this George Aycock the money, you know, and I guess he was kind of getting nervous about it."

Linda also reported the threat to E.C., who replied, "To hell with him. Don't pay any attention to him."

Aycock denies now that he ever threatened anyone.

Chub: "After this race, I called Don McMoy, and he picked me, E.C., Linda, and Wade Navarre up and took us back to Bartlesville, and took Wade Navarre back to Lafayette, Louisiana." McMoy's bill for the Ruidoso trip came to $2,224.88.

Meanwhile, Kent Green and his girl friend, Ginny Mueller, had spent the weekend with Gene and Kathleen at the Cross Bell.

Linda: "When we got back that night, they were at the airport in Bartlesville, Green and Ginny, and they went back to Kansas City that night [Labor Day]. I told them about it [the threat from Aycock], I am sure that I did. The Greens were afraid, seemed to be afraid of Aycock or something or someone. And E.C. was afraid of all of them, you know, because they had threatened him, he said. I know Aycock did. And you know how E.C. was. He said he threatened them too."

Twenty   KENT GREEN SAYS AYCOCK THREATENED him by a telephone message left with a secretary at the Canterbury Gardens office. "He couldn't get me one day, so he threatened her," Green says.

Undaunted, Green and his girl friend Ginny packed up their .38's and drove back to the Cross Bell in his Eldorado a few days after Labor Day. The Mullendores rolled out the red carpet for them.

Green, queried now about where he intended to get the $15 million he promised to lend to E.C., says, "I had been part of private syndications for issues like this, and also my personal credit will stand in excess of a million dollars." He says he presented the deal to an investment company in Lawrence, Kansas, and also to an associate in New York, and that he "got encouraging replies from both. Neither one turned me down," Green says.

At the ranch, however, Green apparently told a different story. Gene Mullendore says that Sal Capra, the Kansas City lawyer and city councilman, was supposed to supply the money.

Linda: "This is what Green told me. He said the money was coming from Kansas City from a man by the name of Sal Capra, who was getting it from Chicago from a man who they said they called Sam the Waiter. He said the name was a long Italian name and I don't remember what it was, and he told me that it was Mafia money. Green did. He called him Sam the Waiter."

Capra denies even having discussed a loan to E.C. As for Sam the Waiter, the police have never heard of such a character. But Paul "the Waiter" Ricca De Lucia long has ranked among the highest underlords in the Chicago gang world. Green or Linda Mullendore easily could have confused the name.

At any rate, according to Linda, E.C. "always said, 'If this is the Mafia and I can get the money to pay off PCA, then I will be able to'—what he used to call 'buying time'—and 'I can buy more time and maybe get a loan from a legitimate lender.'

"Because I was afraid of these people, I would say, 'E.C., who are these people?' And he would say, 'Just don't ask me.' But he said, 'Yes, it is the Mafia, but don't worry. I will just get the money and I will pay [the PCA] off. Then I will go borrow it from somebody else and pay [the Mafia] off, and we won't have to mess with them after that.' " (When the insurance case neared trial, Linda said she wanted to retract her statements regarding the Mafia, and declared that the story about Sam the Waiter had come to her, not from Green, as she had stressed twice in the quotation above, but secondhand, through Dale Kuhrt.)

Linda says that Green "told E.C. he had been in the pen for income tax evasion. I said, 'E.C. . . . nobody goes to the pen for eight years for income tax evasion,' and [E.C.] said, 'Hell, no, Linda, you know it wasn't income tax evasion. Don't ask so many questions.' "

Linda says she learned about David Taylor's criminal record from Green's girl friend Ginny. "She told me that Taylor built a church and got all this money from these ministers and he was in trouble, and Green told me something about this. He said that [Taylor] embezzled the money."

Paul Kelly: "I told Dale when I came back from Kansas City that if E.C. signed up on that note [took a loan from Green], they would bump him off in thirty days. That was my feelings about the people they were dealing with. They were stringing him along. They were gonna give him hope till all hope was lost."

From the second week in September to E.C.'s death, Kent Green and Ginny Mueller took up residence on the Cross Bell. Ginny was a good-looking bleached blonde in her late twenties, slender but well built. "She was a model," Linda recalls being told, "and ran a modeling school and traveled all over and did special photographic modeling jobs, and after she met Green, she didn't do that any more. She never did say what kind of modeling it was."

Linda says she "wondered about" whether Green and Ginny were married. "I don't know, she just looked like she was just sort of a cheap person. I should not say that, it sounds sort of silly, but she just looked like it to me. But they had matching wedding bands, and they said they were married, and E.C. said they were, and I asked Tal Kolb, and he said yes, and Gene said, 'Why, no, they are not.'

"It did seem unusual to me that Mr. and Mrs. Green carried guns. I was a little disturbed about it, with small children in the house. And I didn't see why they had the guns in the first place." In addition, Linda says, the Greens, like E.C.'s other money brokers, didn't drink much, "but they always wanted to get [E.C.] drunk. He always told them he had a lot of insurance."

E.C. understood the danger—Dale Kuhrt says the rancher ordered Chub to tote a pistol whenever Green and Ginny were on the ranch. But, for E.C., there were only two alternatives to Green's offer of gangster millions: bankruptcy or death (with its incumbent insurance payoff). Either E.C. was blinded to the futility of carrying on with Green, or he kept the hoodlum at his side just to sustain the faith of others, because if the rest of the world stopped believing in Green, it would stop believing in the Mullendores, too. Green was their last hope.

As for why the elder Mullendores trusted the gangster—who stayed in their house because it was roomier than E.C.'s—Kathleen says, "E.C. always brought everyone here. We always lived that way. They promised to get the money. We never thought— He had not been raised not to trust people."

"Mr. Green is very personable," observes John Arrington, Jr.

"He inspires confidence and has an excellent, outgoing personality."

Green roused far more suspicion among the hired help than he did among the Mullendores. Says Lula Harrison: "Mr. and Mrs. Green spent quite a bit of time in E.C.'s home and . . . over at the big house . . . The help over there said she carried a gun, and we was always scared and whispering around about the gun. I think it was a .38. Anyway, it is the same caliber that they said killed E.C. [Ginny] did come out in the kitchen sometimes and tell me how good the food was, but I watched her all the time after I knew she was carrying a gun. I wasn't going to have much to do with her. Linda seemed to be afraid of her. She told me she couldn't sleep good. She said, 'I am afraid of that woman.' "

But no one in the Cross Bell realm perceived the real Kent Green more clearly than did that other ex-convict, Chub Anderson. Chub spurned Green's entreaties to friendship, even Green's offers of a job "with less hours and more money." Says Chub: "I didn't ask him any questions [about the job]. I already knew I didn't want to be associated with him." Chub suspected that after E.C. received a loan from the hoodlum, Green would move in and take control of the ranch. "He said if this deal went through, he didn't want me to quit E.C. or him, so he would have someone he could call and talk to. I think his wife was the last one to really mention it. She was always trying to act so friendly. I didn't care too much for her, but she said, 'Be sure and remember if you want to go to work for us to get ahold of Kent.' The other time he offered me a job, I had waited up with E.C.'s children, and he had walked E.C. and Linda home, and when I left that night, he waited and said if I ever wanted a job, I wouldn't have to be sitting up till midnight."

Chub reported Green's offer to the Mullendores. According to Linda, "E.C. laughed about it and said, 'You should go up there.' But he knew that Chub would never leave him."

Chub says Green was "just hanging around" the ranch with Ginny, just talking to the old man Mullendore. I understand he was trying to find out how many cattle E.C. had, and you know, E.C. was showing him around the place and the acres he owned."

The weekend after Labor Day, Green, Ginny, E.C., and Chub returned to Kansas City on Green's word that the loan money was ready to be picked up. Green went out and came back with a locked briefcase, but since the briefcase almost certainly didn't contain $15 million, or even a check cashable for $15 million, he must have been desperate for a diversionary maneuver as the foursome started the drive back. It was Saturday, September 12. As Linda recalls it: "They were on their way from Kansas City to the ranch. They had a flat tire [near Neodesha, Kansas] . . . and Mr. Green had a heart attack. He had this heart attack, and he was in the hospital."

So E.C. called Linda, Harold Copper, the PCA lawyer Max Berry, Green's lawyer David Taylor, and George Schumacher, vice-president of the First National Bank of Dewey. On the promise of money, the creditors assembled with the others at the hospital at Neodesha.

Schumacher says, "Mr. Mullendore asked me if I would come up there and pick up a check to bring to the bank and get sent off for collection [in light of E.C.'s financial history, the bank certainly would want to collect the funds before cashing the check]. I was down in the lobby of the hospital all day long."

Linda: "I was in the room once or twice. [Green] was under oxygen, and under sedation. He said he had the money and cash in his briefcase, which I did not believe." Taylor asked Green for the money, she says, but Green "was unable to even talk."

Harold Copper: "We went into the hospital and were informed that at that particular time, as I recall from memory, that Mr. Green was under sedation and wouldn't be able to visit with us until sometime after lunch."

So after lunch, the bureaucrat, the banker, the rancher, and their respective lawyers, bodyguards, wives, and sweethearts piled into Green's hospital room. The nurse cleared away everybody but Taylor, Berry, and E.C. Afterward, Copper says, "I was informed by Mr. Berry that they had not completely reached an agreeable situation between Mr. Green and E.C. as far as terms, et cetera, were concerned. I don't know what the conflict was. We came back with what we went with: nothing."

Apparently Green was out of the hospital the next day.

Green brought his manager/chauffeur/bodyguard Robert Heid and Heid's wife Cheryl to the ranch to help him recuperate and open the dove hunting season in Oklahoma. Heid "was a rough-dressed kid," recalls Dale Kuhrt. Kuhrt says the Heids stayed two days and "acted like they lived there."

For the next two weeks, E.C. didn't get his money because of the need to negotiate the terms of his deal with Green. Taking care of Green required that E.C. overhaul his agreement with George Aycock, who naturally wasn't anxious to lose his 10 percent commission.

Dale Kuhrt says he saw one document Green and E.C. signed. "That one was for $12 million. It was three $4 million loans. Then they abandoned that one. I didn't see the next one they made out. They were supposed to have abandoned it, too. They made out another one. Instead of borrowing $12 million through Green, they were gonna borrow $8 million; two $4 million loans."

E.C., Linda, Gene, and Kathleen all signed an agreement dated September 14, two days after Green's "heart attack," calling for a $4 million loan to pay off the PCA and another $4 million loan to buy fifteen thousand head of cattle "to restock the Cross Bell properties." The loans would be secured by the ranch and its livestock, including "twenty-eight head of race horses valued at $1.8 million."

Green says he signed the commitment, guaranteeing to lend the money personally, only so that E.C. could use it to bluff his creditors. He says E.C. knew that he didn't intend to lend from personal funds; Green continued to talk about a $15 million loan from the Mafia.

Meanwhile, it was time to deal with Aycock. According to Linda, Green "said that if we don't get this paper [the commission agreement] back from Aycock and Kolb, we cannot make this loan, because the commission Aycock is asking is too big, a million and a half, and we have to get that paper back."

Although this might have seemed a new stalling tactic, considering that Aycock's commission hadn't bothered Green when he first entered the picture, Green says he had recently become "more aware of what this 10 percent amounted to in relation to the Mullendores." So Green summoned David Taylor, his original go-between with Aycock, to the ranch, and says he asked Taylor to arrange another meeting with Aycock "to renegotiate the amount of the commission, knock it down from this 10 percent to a realistic figure."

From other accounts, however, Taylor's visit to the Cross Bell appears to have been a bit less tranquil than Green describes it. "Taylor got slapped up the side of the head with a pistol," according to Chub, who doesn't recall exactly why Taylor got hit. Then Green, E.C., and Chub took off for Oklahoma City armed with the customary array of handguns plus an M–1 rifle, which Linda thought looked like a machine gun.

Linda: "Kent Green said, 'We are going to get that paper [the 10 percent commission agreement] back one way or another.' Then they left and they go to Oklahoma City and they were supposedly to leave at night and to sneak up on [Aycock] and get the paper back. They all had guns and they had guns in the trunk."

Meanwhile, in Chub's words, "Taylor had called Aycock and told him that Green had hit him." Aycock decided not to hang around. Apparently he called the police, told them some men were on their way to Oklahoma City to kill him, then quickly checked out of the Holiday Inn West.

Green: "When we got to town, it was late, 10:30 or 11 p.m., at least. [Aycock] was not there [at the Holiday Inn West]. Two people that worked for him, pilots, were there, and I told them personally of our appointment. The Holiday Inn West was full, and we went right across the street to the Ramada Inn, and we stayed all night there after my leaving a message with the pilot that we would like to see Aycock. The pilot came across the street and told me he had set up a meeting for 8 a.m. the next morning at the Downtown Holiday Inn, that I was to come alone, that [Aycock] wouldn't talk to anybody else but me. This [was to be] the first time I had seen [Aycock] since the [$3.7 million] check didn't clear. Mr. Aycock told me later that he was fearful of retaliations for his non-performance, and [that was] the reason that he [didn't want to] speak to anybody but myself."

One of Aycock's pilots, a man named Forrester, called George Ray's friend Lloyd Tucker in Tulsa that night. Tucker, the broker who first brought Talmadge Kolb into the Mullendore case, quickly called Kolb again. Recalls Kolb: "[Tucker] said that the pilot had told him that Green and Chub Anderson and E. C. Mullendore III were down in Oklahoma City and that they were looking for Aycock with the intention of doing him some type of bodily harm, and my response to that was that I really didn't think I was interested in becoming involved in the shoot-out at the O.K. Corral—I believe those were my exact words."

Nevertheless, Tucker persuaded Kolb and George Ray to rush to Oklahoma City for an early-morning huddle with Aycock. "We found Mr. Aycock and he was checked into the motel," Kolb says. "We went to the room. Mullendore and Chub had not arrived yet. And Aycock, Tucker, Ray, and I sat down and talked . . . [Aycock] had talked to the hotel manager and told him that he had heard rumors of—that he might be done bodily harm, so the hotel manager called in two policemen and Mr. Aycock went into the office with them. I was not privileged to that conversation. Mr. Aycock didn't seem too greatly disturbed about the situation, and my impression was that he wasn't under any apprehension that he was going to be beat up or shot or anything about it."

Chub says that "Green was the one seemingly wanted the contract back so bad . . . E.C. said he would rather try to *talk* [Aycock] out of it some way, you know . . . But the way I took it, they were gonna pistol-whip [Aycock] around to get that paper back. That is the way Green acted."

When E.C., Chub, and Green drove to the Holiday Inn, Green says, they were startled to find "a portion of the Oklahoma City Police Department, among other things." Gene Mullendore, who heard all about it later from E.C., says that ten or fifteen policemen had ringed the motel. On spotting them, E.C. told Chub to put his .38 under the seat and Green to hide his gun under the armrest. Green left E.C. and Chub waiting in the car and went inside.

Chub: "E.C. and I were sitting in the car. And the police come out and, you know, I could tell they were going to come over our way. They walked out kind of act innocent, and then they walked over and got us out of the car and frisked us. They said that George Aycock, I guess, had told them, you know, that possibly we would be armed. The police found E.C.'s .38. E.C. told them he kept it around for shooting dogs on the ranch, and they didn't get really mad about it. Then they took all the shells out of this pistol and put it in the trunk, and they seen this M–1 carbine and it had a loaded clip in it and they just took the clip out."

Inside, Green was getting somewhat the same treatment. "The police stopped me in the lobby of the motel and shook me down," he recalls. "And then I went on in and sat down, and at that point Mr. Aycock come out of the manager's office and came in and sat down." The brokers congregated in the motel coffee shop. Kolb cowered a few minutes in the manager's office, but finally mustered the courage to join his colleagues.

Green describes the confrontation: "A police sergeant came to the table while we were sitting there. He said there was a gun in [E.C.'s] vehicle and wanted to know if Aycock wanted to file a concealed-weapon charge. Aycock declined."

Then Green says he told Aycock that "we weren't interested in going any further on our end if it wasn't a realistic figure. No investor would invest money having that much [10 percent] taken off the top."

George Ray: "They were trying to come to a settlement. There were a lot of policemen around. Green asked Tucker how much he would agree to take. Tucker told him $40,000. So then he asked me, so I told him I would take $40,000, 'cause I was supposed to get as much as Tucker. And Aycock wanted $120,000, and I don't know what Tal Kolb wanted."

Kolb: "I don't know the round figure, but I agreed to take a substantially less amount than was provided for in the contract. Green made no threats to anybody."

Ray: "Green said they were taking over the ranch and wanted to talk to me mainly about restocking [it]." Ray says he gained the impression that Green personally was going to assume control of the Cross Bell. Then the meeting broke up.

"I never seen George Aycock at this time," Chub says. "But they didn't get the paper back after the police came and gave us that shakedown."

Just before Green, Chub, and E.C. had left for Oklahoma City for the botched showdown with Aycock, they had brought Ginny Mueller over to the little house. Recalls Linda: "She said, 'I am sleeping over here with you. I am going to stay here with you tonight.'

"I didn't feel well and she had a gun in her purse. She said, 'I have my trusty snub-nosed .38, my Bearcat,' she called it. And so E.C. said, 'We better go get Linda a gun.' He did not trust them even then."

E.C. and Linda went to the shelf in the baby's room, but the guns they had stored there were missing. "So," Linda says, "Chub went out and got a gun from some place and E.C. had him give it to me and we went to bed that night and she took this gun out and put it on the night stand. I said, 'I don't know what you are doing, and what you are afraid of, but my little boys get up at night and come and get in bed with me, and you put that gun back in your purse.' And she said, 'Well, do you have a gun?' And I said, 'Oh yes, I have a gun somewhere.'

"Well, I had this gun under the bed, but it wasn't loaded. I did not load it and have it under the bed with the children. But I didn't tell her that because I didn't know what to think of her. I was extremely suspicious and I thought, I am going to have to stay up all night. What is she going to do? Maybe she thinks somebody is going to come over and hurt her, and maybe the children are in danger. And every time I opened my eyes all night long, she was up and walking. This is the only night she stayed there, and they came back from Oklahoma City the next day.

"Anybody like Kent Green and his wife that go around with loaded guns in their purses and in their back pockets all the time, they are afraid of somebody, or something, you know. She showed it to me when I took her to the beauty parlor in Bartlesville . . . the day after she spent the night with me. She just opened her purse right there and showed it to me as she was under the drier, and she said, 'I wonder what anyone would think if they could see this' . . .

"I believe she said that they had been married five weeks. [Green] called her his bride. [E.C.] accepted them for what they were. He thought they had money and it did not make any difference to him."

E.C. and Green had negotiated a deal with each other, and had renegotiated the deal with Aycock. Green again was out of excuses for not issuing the loan.

Chub: "[Green] kept promising that it would be there any day, the money, you know. He would have the money any day. Enough to pay the loan off at Ponca City, which I understood was about $3.5 million. We kept going places to meet him. He was supposed to show up with the money, and a lot of times he would call and say, well, he was delayed, his man didn't show up, and just everything happened to him to delay things."

Soon after their return from Oklahoma City, perhaps the next day, E.C., Chub, Green, and Ginny set out again for Ponca City, allegedly to pay off the PCA loan. Chub: "Tal Kolb and Tucker and George Aycock were there. They weren't supposed to even be there, but I guess they were trying to get their percent of the loan. Their car was sitting in the parking lot at the Production Credit office. The best I remember, they was in the car. I believe it was a surprise to E.C. that they were there. Well, they had a couple of guys [with them] that Kent Green was supposed to have known, being, you know, toughies. They were waiting at the PCA office and E.C. got the idea of having the police check them down, and E.C. had me pull up to the police station. And when he got out, Green [who faced kidnapping charges in Kansas] said, 'E.C., don't go in there,' and E. said, 'I am going in.' And Green got out and went with him."

Green: "E.C. was concerned when he witnessed the arrival of

Aycock, a man later identified to me as Wayne Padgett [identified by Tulsa papers as 'a crime figure'], a third party who was identified to me I do not know the name of, and Tal Kolb. E.C. went to a police officer and told him that he was alarmed about his safety. He told him he felt these people were out to harm him and wanted to know what to do about it."

Chub: "We wasn't there, I guess, when the police, you know, went down and searched them. But they wanted to find out if these two fellows they had with them were armed, you know, or anything." There is no record of police having taken any action against Aycock or the men with him.

Linda: "The day they went over there [to Ponca City] to pay that off, E.C. said that Tal Kolb and George Aycock were all there in Ponca City, and that was the reason they didn't pay it off, because Green said he would not go in there."

Talmadge Kolb, on the other hand, says Green had called and invited him to come—an indication Green staged the whole incident to give himself another excuse for not coming up with the loan. Kolb says he saw Green that day "at the Production Credit. He left to go see Mr. Mullendore and did not come back. After we had waited an hour or an hour and a half, I saw [Green's] car in the parking lot at a grocery store, and I walked down and met him while he was on the public telephone calling somebody. And he said that E.C. was not coming out. And I said, 'Fine, I am going home.' "

Whatever the reason, all parties agree that Green failed to produce any money that day. E.C. still faced foreclosure by the PCA.

Then, according to Gene Mullendore, "Green wanted to go to Kansas City. I don't know what he wanted to go there for. He said, 'Let's go up there and see the boss, and find out when he can come down.' I got hold of Chub and Linda and told them I wanted them to go with E.C. Green told Linda and Chub that there wasn't room for them [in the airplane], that it would be too crowded. I don't know why it would be too crowded. Linda said that would be all right, three in front and three in back, said the back is bigger than the front seat. 'No, you can't ride, it would make it too crowded.' "

Linda: "I wanted to go, and E.C. wouldn't let me. He said he would take Chub, and they were going up there and get Bob and Cheryl [Heid]. This Bob was Green's bodyguard. And they left and E.C. was feeling badly, so anyway, they left and said they

would come back that night. And after thirty or forty minutes
the telephone rang and it was Chub. I said, 'What do you
mean—you didn't go? You let them take him and you didn't go?'
And he said, 'We got in the plane and Green said there wasn't
room for [me].' And I thought, Well, now [E.C.'s] drunk and
they have got him and they won't bring him back. But they did.
They brought him back. I went over to the office [at the ranch]
and called Canterbury Gardens and talked to Green and talked
to E.C. and so did Kathleen. We told him not to stay all night.
He wanted to stay all night. We told Green to bring him right
back, and E.C. said no, not to bother him, but Kathleen and I
both said to Kent on the telephone, 'You bring him back to this
ranch tonight,' and they did. They brought this other couple
[the Heids] with them.

"E.C. met . . . Sal Capra . . . in Kansas City, and he said
when he came home, he said, 'We are really going to get something done. I have talked to the head man and he is going to
help us out.'" Later, Linda said she doubted that E.C. really had
met Capra, and for his part, the city councilman absolutely
denies it. Capra also says he never heard of Sam the Waiter.

After E.C. was virtually abducted to Kansas City, his family
and friends worried more than ever about his drinking, afraid
that he would make a sudden decision or sign a document
without knowing what he was doing.

Dale Kuhrt: "The last two weeks before he got shot, [E.C.]
stayed pretty full [of whiskey] all the time. That was Green's
excuse for not getting the deal finalized. I quizzed [E.C.] a lot
about it. I was always asking him, 'Are you sure that so-and-so
has any money?' I couldn't see it. I was just concerned about
[E.C.'s] money. I figured the guy was just taking him for a ride.
I said several times, 'Why don't you check on him some more?'
and he kept assuring me Green had it. Green would always have
everything ready to go and something would always happen.
One time Green said they were gonna send all this money down
to the bank in Pawnee, and they all went to Pawnee, and
nothing showed. I called Paul [Burchett] that day and told him
to call the bank in Kansas City and see if the money had been
sent, and the bank had heard nothing of the deal.

"It always made me wonder why that son of a buck carried
this gun around, and here this guy was out here wearing a little
Western hat that maybe cost three dollars, and you didn't really
know if he was a dangerous character or drugstore cowboy, or

what he was. When I flat asked him why Green carried that gun, [E.C.] said he is a double tough and has the Mafia behind him."

Twenty-one

ON SEPTEMBER 8, 1970, NORTH-western Mutual Life Insurance Company wrote to Harold Copper, president of the Ponca City Production Credit Association: Unless E. C. Mullendore III paid $366,000 principal and interest on the insurance company's loan by December 1, 1970, "Northwestern Mutual intends to call the note due and demand payment in full . . . We have been advised that your association is financing Mr. Mullendore's operation . . . In view of the past payment record on this loan, we felt that this letter was necessary (copy to E. C. Mullendore III)."

Minutes from the board meeting of the Ponca City Production Credit Association, September 17, 1970: "The loan of E. C. Mullendore III was discussed and President Copper informed the board that approximately eleven thousand cattle had been sold and the funds from the sale diverted elsewhere and not applied to the PCA loan. President Copper informed the board that the FICB [Federal Intermediate Credit Bank] had been notified of the shortage. After considerable discussion of the loan and upon motion by Director Moore, seconded by Director Pfrimmer, and carried, that the loan of E. C. Mullendore III be called and that he be required to start selling his remainder chattel security with the funds being applied to his loan. Sales to start immediately and to be completed by October 15, 1970. He is to sign a written agreement to the effect and his submitted plan of liquidation of his machinery and real estate to pay off the loan in full. Submitted plan must be acceptable to the Board of Directors and is to be submitted on or before October 15, 1970."

Copper notified the FBI about the missing cattle, and agents promised to investigate. Then, Copper says, he summoned E.C. and informed the rancher that PCA would not pay the Northwestern loan, and instead would close down the Cross Bell Ranch. According to Copper, E.C. took the news "very much in stride," and "felt that he had refinancing arranged to take care of his indebtedness."

At about the same time, George Aycock was calling the ranch

to complain about the bounced expense checks. E.C. already had paid Aycock $30,000 in "expense money," but stopped payment on an additional $7,000 after Green blamed Aycock for the $3.7 million check debacle at PCA. This stop-payment on checks to Aycock caused the Cross Bell payroll checks to bounce on September 1. As Paul Kelly explains it: E.C. said that "he had given those shysters a check and that they had it laying in Dewey for collection and that he wasn't going to pay the check until he got ready, and that [he was] going to put that money in there and just pay specific checks. And the bank wouldn't do it that way. If [he] put [money] in, they would pay first come, first served. That's why the payroll checks bounced for one day. So [E.C.] took the money from the bank and paid us in cash."

Paul Burchett, the bookkeeper, says Aycock called several times about the uncollected checks. "He wasn't in a bad mood, but he sure wanted the money," Burchett recalls.

Aycock wasn't the only one. Big Ed, the pilot, wanted $3,129.92, and other pilots had submitted bills mounting into the thousands of dollars. A Fifth Avenue shop that one of the Mullendore women had patronized on the New York trip demanded $1,150. Wade Navarre, the horse trainer, had filed suit in Louisiana for $36,000 that E.C. owed him, and another Louisianan, Dr. Jack Frost, had filed a foreclosure action on some horses he had sold to E.C., who hadn't kept up the payments.

Meanwhile, Jim Jackson's freewheeling use of E.C.'s telephone credit card, mounted atop the Mullendores' normal heavy chitchat to Katsy in Houston and various stores in Tulsa, had set the local phone company to wondering about the Cross Bell's $7,500 balance. E.C. wanted the company to weed out Jackson's bills, reportedly more than half the total, but the company insisted that the ranch was responsible for all of them. So in mid-September, Ma Bell cut off all outgoing service from the ranch and left the lines open for incoming calls only.

"I thought it would end in bankruptcy," George Ray says. "I talked to E.C. about it in the last six months [of E.C.'s life], after he started on that splurge of buying them damn horses. I told E.C. that a loan such as he was trying to get, that what this ranch would produce couldn't possibly pay the interest, much less any amount on the principal. I told him that it was an impossibility. He thought he would pull everything out of the fire, that everything would be fine. That was his last words to me, at least." Ray says he last talked to E.C. on September 18 at the Hominy (Oklahoma) Sales Barn, where E.C., Green, and Chub had gone to shop for cattle to restock the ranch. "We had a cup of coffee," Ray says. "They said they was down there checking the market."

The Mullendores' financial reputation had suffered so greatly that even Retail Credit Company learned about it. On September 14, the credit investigative experts issued an updated report on E.C. "Prior to about one year ago," the report said, "the subject's financial reputation was above reproach; however, he has had several financial reverses in this time due to heavy personal spending and poor business management. His financial reputation is quite questionable in this area at the present time. He has sold off several thousand head of his livestock and has also sold several thousand acres of land [apparently untrue] in order to meet pressing financial obligations and due to having very little operating capital. He has been known to have written several insufficient-fund payroll checks and his employees now have to go to the bank that the checks are written on to cash them. We have contacted a local department store in Bartlesville and their records show that the subject's wife and daughter [*sic*] owe over $4,600 to this store and they have since December of 1969, and [the store has] turned this account over for collection.

"Prior to about one year ago, the subject's net worth was estimated to be about $37 million, consisting of his land, livestock, and investments. Business and personal sources contacted during this investigation stated that . . . at the present time . . . the subject's net worth would be estimated at around [figure unreadable] to $10 million. Very little of his net worth can be used as operating capital, however, and that has been his main financial problem of late."

Dale Kuhrt: "[E.C.] and his dad hadn't taken a drive all summer, and he picked up his dad and drove around the ranch and even looked at that grave spot. You get to thinking that something was gonna happen and he knew it. The way I got the story from Mr. Gene, they drove around, and hell, I don't know, he told me that they drove up to that hill, and Mr. Gene said something about him and Mrs. Mullendore, that when they passed on, said that would be as good a place as any to be buried. And E.C. said, 'Well, if it's good enough for you, it's good enough for me. This is where I want to be buried.' Knew what was gonna happen."

George Ray: "I don't think E.C. was afraid of anybody. I never knew of him fearing for his life."

Sometime early in the third week of September—just before or just after the Oklahoma City trip—Linda Mullendore packed her bags to leave the ranch. But, for reasons she has never explained, she stored them in a closet and stayed on.

Chub: "I would really say [E.C.] couldn't hold his liquor too good, you know. Usually in the afternoon he would get pretty well out of it. Right within a month or two before his death, he got pretty bad. He drank Scotch and water. Whenever he would run out of water [and] we were [driving] somewhere, we would stop at these Dairy Queens and cafés, just anywhere he could get ice and water, you know, and he always kept usually a bottle in his briefcase or trunk.

"I could handle him about as good as anybody. We didn't argue over it, but I could talk him out of a lot of things, you know. His mother was always telling me if we were away just to manhandle him, you know, put him in the car and bring him home. But you just don't do your boss that way. They was always afraid the public was going to see him drunk, you know. They were pretty sensitive about it. I always tried to keep him out of the public when he would get like this, but he would always want to go some place and people would see him like that, and I guess everybody found out about it. His mother used to tell me to keep him from it, but there wasn't any way to keep him from drinking. I talked to him a few times. I said, 'E, why don't you get your business first?' And he said, 'I always do business better if I drink first.' I couldn't reason with him.

"A lot of times, he wouldn't drink anything before around 10 or 10:30 [a.m.], and a lot of times he would drink a couple of beers first, and I think it would kind of get him primed, you know, and he would start drinking Scotch."

"When E.C. got back from Kansas City," recalls Paul Kelly, "he drank all the time. When you would go up there in the morning, he would already be pretty well fixed."

To persons who weren't around E.C. constantly, the drinking problem didn't seem bad. Even Paul Burchett, the accountant, failed to notice it. Pawhuska residents say the young rancher came to town to buy things or pay bills during September and appeared sober.

But Linda says Kathleen had to nag him. "And so did I. I mean, you know, about the drinking. We all tried. But there wasn't anything we could do with him. Nobody could. He would just lay down and go to sleep and we knew that [if he woke up], he would go jump in the car and run into a tree or something. Everybody tried to take care of him."

Lula Harrison remembers going into Linda's bedroom one morning, and "she had a bruise on her nose. She told me he struck her, but you know, that's two-sided." During the third week of September, Mrs. Harrison reports, E.C. even had an argument with Chub. Linda was upstairs at the time. Mrs. Harrison says she couldn't hear the substance of the argument, but that E.C. "came on into the kitchen" afterward, complaining about his manservant. "He said, 'I bought that so and so a car. He didn't know me, but I bought him a car.' I said, 'Come and eat, you are hungry.' And he came out of there talking to [Chub], but I didn't know what they were saying." A little later, she says, Chub returned alone. "Chub was always quiet, but he came in the kitchen and said to me there was too much tension, too much pressure. He said, 'I am going to quit this job.' I said, 'Chub, if there is too much pressure, the hired help ought to know about it. We ought to quit if there is that much pressure.' But he didn't tell us nothing. If Chub had listened to me, he wouldn't have been in this. I said, I would get me a different job, and get yourself straightened out and go back to your family. He stayed right on 'cause they was pouring the money on him. Whenever they would think he was going to quit, they'd give him more money, and that was tempting when you can make a lot of free money throwed to you."

Until that week, Mrs. Harrison says, she had never seen Chub drink. But then, "I saw him take a drink a couple of times with Linda. She fixed it and they sat down and she talked with him."

After dark on Friday, September 18, Mrs. Harrison says she observed Chub enter Linda's bedroom, while Linda was in it, and close the door—something she says she hadn't seen before. "Chub's in there and they closed the door," she recalls telling the cleaning woman. In a while, she says, the manservant emerged. (Linda says she called Chub into the bedroom to supply him with a jacket long enough to cover the gun he was wearing; she says she didn't want the maids to see the gun.)

The next evening, Linda recalls, "We were sitting on the back porch at Mr. Mullendore's. Kent Green, E.C., and I [were] out there and his mother was trying to calm him, and he was drinking and everything."

Kathleen: "We were out on the back porch, and he was mad

at Mr. Green. I said, 'E., my goodness, you have probably blown this deal.' "

Green says the argument was over drinking, and that E.C. told his mother, "Well, you know so much more than I do, well, you run the place."

Linda: "He said he was leaving and everything, and he slammed the freezer door shut real hard and stomped and ran out of the house. So Kent Green went after him."

Green: "He left by the front door, jumped in the red Lincoln, roared up the driveway from Gene's house, turned the corner to the right to his [own] house, lost control of the Lincoln, went down over the retaining wall on the right-hand side of the road, and then came back up, lost control again, and made a full circle through his yard on the north side of the flagpole, made a 360-degree turn, and roared off down the road."

Green says Kathleen asked him to follow E.C. in another car. "[I found him] at the Dutchman's [a bait shop that sells beer] on the north end of Hulah Lake, drinking. I asked him to come home with me. He would not do it, but he did agree to let me take him to Mike Burkhart's [the home of a cowboy], which I did. I asked Mike to say with E.C., and told him that [E.C.] had had a misunderstanding with his mother and needed to get away for a while."

Linda says that after Green left the big house to follow E.C., Chub was ordered to pursue them in a third car. "We were afraid he would have a wreck or something." Still not satisfied, Linda herself drove off in Kathleen's car to see if she could help. She met Green and Chub on the road, and says Green told her, "Now, he is all right. We found him. He went to Mike Burkhart's house and he is just fine and [Burkhart] is with him." Linda: "I said, 'Where did he go?' and [Green] said, 'Don't make me lie to you. Don't worry, he will be home pretty soon.' "

Burkhart, an Oklahoma State graduate, was virtually an assistant foreman, working under Dale Kuhrt. Paul Kelly, the farm manager, was at Burkhart's house that night. Kelly says it was "the first real indication that E.C. and Green weren't getting along. My wife and Mike and Mike's wife were there, and we were gonna play cards, and E.C. and Green came in. It was seven or eight o'clock, and E.C. told Mike to get his shoes on and go with him, he wanted him to drive him around. And Mike told him he was gonna play cards. E.C. said, 'Well, I need you.' And Green [told E.C.] to leave Mike alone and he would take E.C. home. And [Green] asked me to go over and move [E.C.'s] car from the Dutchman's bait shop, and I said yes. I swore after going to Kansas City [the night of the Playboy Club fight], I said I would never go [with E.C. again], but I felt sorry for Mike and I said I would go. And [E.C.] squatted over by my chair and said, 'Let Mike go with me this time. I don't want you to go. Your wife is gonna have that baby there and I don't want you to go.' He was pretty drunk. Green said, he was real apologetic, said he had never done things this way and he wasn't used to people drinking like this when they were trying to do business, and as soon as he could get something done, E.C. was gonna have to straighten up or get out. Then they left.

"There is about three things that really helped influence my opinion [about E.C.'s murder], and that is E.C. telling me not to ride home on that airplane, that they will have sugar in the gas tank; E.C. telling me about Tal, Aycock, and them trying to cheat him out of the money, whatever the amount was; [and] Green saying over at Burkhart's that night [that] he is going to get E.C. sobered up and get him signed up or his ass would be out. Green [said], 'If I am gonna put my money in down here, I am gonna have a say about what goes on, and I am gonna be down here.' "

Mike Burkhart, the assistant foreman/cowboy, says he and E.C. drove off together in the Lincoln. E.C. asked Burkhart to spend the night with him in a motel. Says Burkhart: "He had had an argument with Linda and his mother, he said, and he was mad. That is all he told me. We met Chub there about the Cross Bell sign [on route 10] when we were going back toward Bartlesville, and we stopped there and talked to him. He was worried about E.C., and Mrs. Mullendore and Linda was worried. [E.C.] told Chub not to tell them anything, but to tell his dad that he was all right. He was pretty drunk. He didn't tell Chub where he was going.

"We stayed at a place on the highway, near the Holiday Inn. When we got out at the motel, he said he had two pistols in the back of the car, and he opened up the car and looked for them. And they weren't there. He was pretty drunk. Evidently he had had them there at one time."

At about 10:30 that night, Burkhart says, they called Linda at home and talked to her and Chub there. E.C. "didn't want me to take him home, he wanted Chub to come and get us. He gave Chub the wrong motel evidently, or Chub misunderstood him. [Chub] did not show up."

Linda: "Gene said, 'You send Chub down there after him. He

has no business being down there, you go and find him.' [Chub] went and then called me and said they were not there, and I don't know whether he went to the wrong motel or what."

Says Burkhart: "E.C. passed out right after he talked to [Chub] on the phone, woke up about eight the next morning." Driving home from the motel, Burkhart and E.C. stopped at the home of Chub's brother, who was mechanic for a stock racing car that E.C. sponsored. The next weekend the race track at Caney, Kansas, would feature a novelty race in which the sponsors were supposed to drive their own cars. Burkhart remembers E.C. joking that "his insurance [company] wouldn't be too happy if he drove in that race, but he was going to, anyway. He had his life insured for $15 million."

Burkhart: "We came back to my house, probably about ten that morning, and he let me out. Linda came about fifteen or twenty minutes later and wanted to know where he was at. She was worried about him. And I told her he was all right and that he had left to go home. She said that she was going into town to pick up the oldest boy. She was driving the yellow Cadillac— no, she was driving the two-toned Cadillac that belongs to Gene."

Linda: "Mr. Burkhart said [E.C.] had been gone ten minutes and I asked if he was all right, and [Burkhart] said, 'He has only had a few beers.' I said I wanted to thank [Burkhart] for taking care of him and everything. Mr. Burkhart is a fine man. Then when I got home, E.C. was home in the kitchen, drunk. I don't know how he could have been drunk on a few beers, but another thing, Green was giving him pills. He told me they were ten-milligram Valium. Some of them were blue and some were oval tablets, pale bluish green. I think that if Mr. Burkhart was right and he only had a few beers, how could he have been drunk when I got there? It only takes ten or fifteen minutes to drive from Mr. Burkhart's back home. I stopped at the bait store and I asked Kent Green what he was giving [E.C.], and he said it was just Valium, and it wouldn't hurt him. Green pulled it out of his pocket and told me that was what he was giving [E.C.] and he had given it to him the night before. I said, 'You know you are not supposed to take any kind of drug with alcohol, and anybody knows that.' No wonder [E.C.] was so wild."

During the previous week, Linda says, she had "discussed with E.C. the problems that he was having, the fact that Mr. and Mrs. Green were there and they had guns with them. This bothered me, and I also asked him to stop drinking. He said that he would. This [was] probably about the fifteenth of September. Before, I had always believed, as he did, that these people would be able to provide adequate financing. By this time I realized, I assumed . . . that they did not have the money. I felt that if he stopped drinking, he would realize this."

Gene: "She would gripe all day long, he would come over and tell me about it."

Kay Sutton, Lula Harrison's eighteen-year-old granddaughter: "When we were packing bags one day, she told me I had to pack the baby's bag and she said she was afraid; that they had been threatened and she was afraid for herself and the kids. That's why she was leaving. She asked me not to tell anyone, though. She didn't want E.C. to find the bags because she didn't want him to know she was leaving. It was all planned, it looked like."

Linda: "He told me the night before [Saturday night, September 19, the night E.C. spent at a Bartlesville motel with Mike Burkhart] that he wouldn't blame me if I left, that I should leave, that maybe he would change. I could see that [the money brokers] didn't have any money, that the agreement they wanted me to sign would have wiped him out in two years. The Greens' agreement was two years of [paying] interest only, 10 or 11 percent, and a balloon payment [of principal] at the end of three years. There was no way it could work. The cattle had all been sold. There was no way [the Mullendores] could have repaid [Green]." In other words, if E.C. signed, the ranch almost inevitably would be lost for failure to pay the loan back in a lump sum, as called for.

Kay Sutton: "Well, see, E.C. had been drinking [Sunday, after his return from Bartlesville] and Linda had said something to him and he was swearing back at her and she went over to Mrs. Mullendore's."

Kathleen: "Linda always has said, 'I am going to quit bitching at E.' I can't believe she did that. She came over [that Sunday] and said, 'E. is awful mad,' and I asked her what about, and she said she didn't know. She just said, 'You and Mr. Mullendore will sure be mad at me for what I am doing.' I told her, 'You could never make us that mad,' and she said, 'Yes, I am.' [I thought], Well, by golly, I will go over and see if there is anything wrong. E. was sitting in the living room and said he sure was glad I came over and to have a cup of coffee. Linda had followed me over, and she came and sat down beside him and put her arm around his neck and he put his arm around her waist, and I thought, What the heck."

But after Kathleen returned home, the seemingly placid situation deteriorated. Kay Sutton: "[Linda] seen Chub go over the hill, and my brother went after him, and we had to take care of the children while Chub talked to E.C. and put him to bed, I think. But then he got up and went over to his dad's."

Mrs. Harrison: "He went to his parents', and [Linda] ran upstairs yelling to [Kay and the cleaning woman], 'We got to go, we got to go.'"

Chub: "I was taking care of the boys. [Linda] had these colored maids working for her, and they gathered up three or four suitcases and went out and loaded them in a station wagon [the Mercury that E.C. had bought from Leon Cohen]. And there was kind of a mad haste. She took the four children. She had an Eldorado they took, too. E.C. was over at his father's. He was drinking heavily."

Kent Green: "Approximately 3:30, 9/20/70, Linda took the Mullendore station wagon, the Cadillac Eldorado, I was told she took a TV set and clothing and two or three of the domestic help, and left the ranch property."

They drove to Edna Vance's home in Pawhuska, Mrs. Harrison recalls. "Seems Mrs. Vance had her bag packed, ready to go, too. Throwed her bag in the car. They was all ready to go. I don't know how long they had been getting ready." Then they dropped off the servants—a long walk from home, Mrs. Harrison notes caustically—and headed for Tulsa.

Linda: "That Sunday I could not talk to him. His parents knew [about her going], but he did not know. He was drinking. I did not even try to talk to him. I left because I thought that it would make him realize that he would have to stop drinking, and that he would have to stop dealing. When I left, I did not leave him. I left the home, and I always thought that I would come back."

Twenty-two   IN 1970, THE ATLANTA INSURance agency of Cohen, Kerwin, White & Associates, Inc., became part of a worldwide fraud network organized by several dozen professional securities swindlers. Starting in the late 1960's, the organized con men stole hundreds of millions of dollars through the sale of worthless securities issued by corporations that they themselves had created, which had no real assets; in 1974 they were still operating.

When federal and state law-enforcement agencies began to investigate the fraud network and pored over files taken from the Cohen-Kerwin office, they encountered the names of Morris Jaffe, the Texas financier, and E. C. Mullendore III. The results of these inquiries into the Cohen-Kerwin office would greatly confound Sheriff Wayman's efforts to unravel E.C.'s murder.

Cohen and Kerwin first encountered the organized swindlers in late February or early March 1970, two or three weeks after E.C. was hospitalized with the flu. Apparently, the encounter occurred under less than friendly circumstances. A Cadillac-renting, country club-crashing golfer and con man named Henry Timbrook managed to swindle the two agents out of $80,000 in a sinister duel of wits. Timbrook, working out of the organization's headquarters in Fort Lauderdale, Florida, originally lured Cohen and Kerwin into investing $150,000 in a golf-product company Timbrook proposed to start. But the Atlanta agents smartly double-crossed him, persuading Timbrook to take only $80,000 cash and the other $70,000 in the form of some worthless stock—specifically, the shares in Satellite Three-in-One Corporation that originally had been issued to John Mecom, Sr., who bought them from Morris Jaffe. The share certificates that Cohen and Kerwin provided Timbrook still had Mecom's name on them; how the agents laid hands on the certificates has never been disclosed.

Because the Satellite shares were worthless, Cohen and Kerwin apparently thought at this point that they had conned Timbrook out of $70,000 worth of golf-product stock. They were presumably startled when they learned the golf-product stock was just as worthless as the Satellite stock, leaving them net losers by $80,000. They quickly traced Timbrook to his superiors in organized swindling, Harold Audsley and Byron Prugh, two Missourians who worked from a rented suite of offices in Fort Lauderdale. From early spring to mid-fall 1970, Cohen, Kerwin, White & Associates joined Prugh and Audsley in a series of confidence schemes that allowed Cohen and Kerwin to try to recoup their loss at the expense of others.

The six foot six, 217-pound Prugh had important contacts in the Chicago underworld, so Kerwin may have known of him even before the Timbrook incident. Prugh had just gone bankrupt in Kansas City erasing $7 million in debts he owed in the community as a result of some business transactions. Now he was living in a $350,000 house on an inland waterway in south Florida. Audsley lived a bit more modestly, but had important contacts among swindlers in Europe and Latin America. Together they put the Atlanta agents in touch with perhaps the most demonic intelligence in the realm of fraud: Philip M. Wilson. Wilson was in the midst of a spectacular series of schemes in which he and a cooperative lawyer would legally incorporate a "bank," "insurance company," "mutual fund," or other firm; then bribe an accountant into certifying falsely that the new company was worth hundreds of millions of dollars; then print up bank drafts, insurance policies, fund shares, or whatever, and sell or cash them on the American and world market at almost pure profit.

Wilson was always interested in meeting contacts like Cohen and Kerwin, who had connections with many legitimate businessmen. A legitimate businessman could take some of Wilson's worthless securities to a bank and collateralize a loan with them, as Wilson himself usually could not do because he had a criminal record.

So Audsley and Prugh delivered large quantities of Wilson's printed-up securities to Cohen and Kerwin, who wanted their $80,000 back. The instructions were to use the securities to obtain loans for business clients from banks in Europe or the Bahamas. There, loan officers would be less able to detect the phoniness of Wilson's securities than U.S. bankers would be. Cohen and Kerwin were to cut huge brokerage fees out of the loan proceeds, keep 20 percent of the fees, and return the remaining 80 percent to Audsley, who would give Wilson a proper share.

Culling over their clients to use as fronts in cashing Wilson's phony securities, Cohen and Kerwin did not exactly have to cull very hard before they came up with E. C. Mullendore III. At one point during the spring of 1970, E.C. and Linda filed rush applications for passports for what Linda says was to be a combination pleasure and money-borrowing trip to Europe or the Bahamas. She says she knows nothing more about it except that the trip was canceled.

After Kerwin's correspondence with a bank in Germany collapsed, Audsley and Prugh sent an aide from Phoenix to negotiate a loan in the Bahamas for E.C., secured by Wilson's phony mutual fund shares. Apparently that deal fell through, too, although Kerwin and Audsley picked up $27,600 on the side selling worthless shares of an inactive metals concern that the Phoenix man was manipulating on the over-the-counter stock market.

Meanwhile, Philip Wilson, who had supplied the phony mutual fund shares for E.C.'s loan, had grown impatient with the Cohen-Kerwin agency's inability to raise money with the shares, and demanded them back. The funds were called First Liberty Fund and the Allied Fund for Capital Appreciation (AFCA). Apparently, Kerwin had sent the shares to Europe to try to obtain loans, and Wilson thought the loans had gone through and that the Atlanta agency was trying to cheat him out of the proceeds. On June 5, 1970, Kerwin received a telephone message from Wilson, taken down by a receptionist at the agency. The message read:

"BAD NEWS FOR THE JEWS—Vigilantes coming Monday to tear you, Cohen, and office apart. Found out from reliable source in Rhode Island that 280,000 shares of AFCA not in your possession."

If violence occurred, however, it was never reported.

While dealing with organized swindlers, Cohen, Kerwin, White & Associates continued to sell life insurance. The agency put $20 million in business on the books of Alexander Hamilton Life, which made Cohen and Kerwin the biggest producers the company had. Alexander Hamilton gave the agents a $250,000 advance on future commissions, with the money to be earned or repaid by October 1, 1970. A Hamilton subsidiary took over a $500,000 outstanding bank loan to Cohen and Kerwin (the subsidiary paid off the bank, and Cohen and Kerwin agreed to pay the money back to the subsidiary). Cohen claimed publicly that he had sold $150 million in life insurance, close to a record. He said there was "one man in Ohio who has sold more, but that man is seventy years old."

Such was the pattern of success that Morris Jaffe arranged in the summer of 1970 to provide the boys with their own life insurance company.

First Financial Life Insurance Company had broken away from its parent, Fed-Mart Corporation, in the mid-1960's. Jaffe had continued to operate it from his headquarters in San Antonio. For a while Mickey Mantle was a director of the company. In October 1968, Jaffe sold a controlling interest in First Financial Life to a new group, Nashwood Corporation. Jaffe continued as a director until the following April, when a full Nashwood board replaced the former Jaffe board.

The Nashwood directors of First Financial Life made an impressive array: Waggoner Carr, former attorney general of Texas; Tom Thomas, then an associate in Carr's law firm; John Osorio, former chairman of the Texas Insurance Commission and former president of National Bankers Life Insurance Company; Sam Stock, current president of National Bankers Life; and Joe Novotny, an associate of financier Frank Sharp, president of the Sharpstown State Bank.

Despite these blue-ribbon credentials, however, the Securities and Exchange Commission in 1971 charged all five men and Nashwood Corporation itself with stock fraud and corporate looting involving the Sharpstown State Bank and National Bankers Life. The scandal rocked Texas. A federal judge, acting on a complaint from the SEC, enjoined the five men and Nashwood from violating the securities laws. Sharp pleaded guilty to making false entries in the books of his bank and selling unregistered securities. Criminal charges against the other men, who pleaded innocent, dragged on into 1973.

In June 1970—while the alleged manipulations were taking place but seven months before the scandal erupted in public—the Nashwood group sold its controlling interest in First Financial Life to Cohen, Kerwin, White & Associates. In effect, this returned control of the company to Morris Jaffe, who became chairman. At the time, First Financial Life had sixteen thousand policyholders and $900,000 in assets.

Cohen and Jaffe bought large quantities of First Financial stock shares. Smaller buyers included Richard Korem, Kerwin's brother-in-law, who had been lawyer and money handler for Kerwin's bankrupt Ford agency in Chicago, and Arnold B. Rubenstein, the urologist who had doctored phony medical reports for the Cohen-Kerwin insurance business.

Around the Cohen-Kerwin office, First Financial Life often was referred to simply as "Fifi." Cohen became president, under Jaffe, the chairman. Fifi hired Kerwin as a $1,000-a-month "special consultant," although Jaffe and Cohen barred him from the board of directors because of his criminal record. Cohen's own criminal record seems to have bothered no one.

In addition to Cohen and Jaffe, the directors included John

Mecom, Jr., E.C.'s brother-in-law; Dr. Rubenstein; Ernest Morgan, a former United States attorney in Texas and a friend of Jaffe's who represented Kerwin in his income tax troubles; Joseph Freed, owner of Freed's Furniture Store, Dallas's second largest, who sold cancer insurance policies as a sideline; Charles W. Windham, a former rancher whom Jaffe had hired to help run his big shopping center in San Antonio; and Donald Worden, a San Francisco lawyer who represented some of the athletes Kerwin was trying to sign to insurance policies.

Although the men who controlled First Financial Life supposedly included the world's greatest insurance salesmen, they seem to have paid more attention to promoting First Financial's publicly traded stock than to selling policies. Premium income, which totaled $1.2 million in 1967, dwindled to $8,586 in 1970.

Through the summer of 1970, Nashwood's Tom Thomas, the former attorney general's law partner, helped Kerwin launch Fifi on the securities market. Thomas was corporate attorney for a Dallas brokerage firm called Main Street Securities. He persuaded C. V. Mercer, a principal in Main Street, to meet Kerwin at the First Financial Life office in San Antonio. As a result of the meeting, Main Street agreed to market First Financial stock. Recalls Mercer: "All over the U.S. there was a lot of demand for First Financial. Hundreds of people were buying and selling the stock. There were a lot of brokerage houses involved." But as for Main Street, he says, "We were selling short."

By the fall of 1970, selling seems to have been a wise thing to do. The stock price had been rising steadily through the summer. Kerwin bought and sold shares every few days. Thomas sometimes participated in the trading, too. The price peaked at $5.75 a share October 29. From that point, the investors needed parachutes. The stock was quoted at twenty-five cents a share at the end of 1971.

The stock promotion reeked of gimmickry. The Cohen-Kerwin record of life insurance sales looked very good on paper to potential purchasers of the stock, just as it looked very good to insurance companies that advanced the agents hundreds of thousands of dollars in expected future sales commissions. But the policies that Cohen and Kerwin issued lost money rather than made it for the underwriting company. Perhaps because they knew this, Cohen and Kerwin did not write policies on the insurance company that they and their partner Jaffe controlled. Instead, whatever policies the two wrote continued to go to

Alexander Hamilton Life, which in no way benefited the outsiders who bought stock in First Financial.

Ever since Cohen, Kerwin, White & Associates had opened its doors in Atlanta in 1968, the agency had made money by siphoning off exorbitant fees from the loans it finagled for business clients like E. C. Mullendore. This income was limited by the amount of money that banks and other institutions were willing to lend to Cohen-Kerwin clients. If business loans weren't forthcoming, neither were the exorbitant brokerage fees.

During the spring and summer of 1970, Byron Prugh and Harold Audsley, the two swindlers from Fort Lauderdale, showed Kerwin and Cohen a new way to make money from the loan brokerage business. Prugh and Audsley established the insurance agency as a front for the most profitable confidence scheme of recent years, the advance-fee loan racket.

The racket works by encouraging businessmen to pay fees out of their own pockets, in advance, for loans that actually never materialize. To be convincing, a swindler operating such a racket needs a phony financial institution that promises to give loans. Audsley and Prugh suggested that Cohen and Kerwin join them in creating a firm with a large, fictitious portfolio of assets, similar to the worthless "mutual funds" Philip Wilson had created. The fictitious lending firm would advertise that its assets were available for loan to businessmen, who might apply for funds through various loan brokers across the country.

Cohen, Kerwin, White & Associates not only accepted the Audsley-Prugh idea but improved on it. Rather than create a phony lending institution, as Audsley and Prugh suggested, the Atlanta agency proposed to use Texas Trust Company, an investment bank that Morris Jaffe had owned for many years in San Antonio. Apparently Jaffe never had activated the bank, and it had no offices or assets; yet any businessman who checked up on Texas Trust would find that it was officially registered with the state of Texas as a bank (though not a commercial bank—a private investment bank). What a perfect front for a fraud operation!

As a typical advance-fee swindle, Texas Trust would issue, not loans, but loan commitment letters. Suppose a developer applied for funds to build a shopping center. For a fee, Texas Trust would issue the developer a letter guaranteeing that when the shopping center was complete, say in two years, Texas Trust would lend enough long-term mortgage money to pay off the developer's short-term commercial bank loans. Because of this commitment letter, issued before the start of the project, a commercial bank might be willing to lend short-term funds for construction, whereas it might not make the loan without a guarantee from a long-term lender to take over. Commercial banks and conservative investment firms often divide the job of financing construction projects in this way. Therefore, a businessman may be willing to pay $30,000 to $100,000 in fees to a loan broker to obtain a commitment letter. Of course, the businessman and his bank expect the letter to come from a legitimate investment firm, not from a fraud like Texas Trust. But loan brokers insist the fee must be paid before the businessman learns which investment firm will issue the letter. The brokers say that if the businessman knew the name of the investment firm before he paid his fee, he could make his own deal with the firm without compensating the loan broker.

So, according to plan, Audsley, Prugh, Kerwin, and Cohen would solicit businessmen to pay blind fees for commitment letters from a purportedly legitimate investment firm. Actually, the letters would come from Texas Trust, which didn't have the money promised in the letters. But it would be two years before the money was due, and in that time Audsley and Prugh figured that Texas Trust could attract millions of dollars in brokerage fees. Meanwhile, anybody who ran only a cursory check on Texas Trust would come away satisfied.

Morris Jaffe recalls that Kerwin came to him in the spring of 1970 and asked to buy legal rights to Texas Trust, the inactive investment firm. Jaffe says he turned Kerwin down and that he never activated Texas Trust. (Records show that, in January 1970, E. C. Mullendore issued a $10,000 check to Texas Trust, though no one has said what the check was for or who collected on it.) Despite Jaffe's reported rejection of the idea, Cohen, Kerwin, White & Associates proceeded to set up an advance-fee loan swindle employing Texas Trust.

Kerwin handled the paper work, as he always did. Under Audsley's instructions, he located a certified public accountant—Herbert E. Woll of Atlanta—who attested that Texas Trust had $17.1 million in assets. Some of the purported assets were worthless, swindler-issued stock or mutual fund shares supplied by Audsley and Prugh. In addition, Woll wrote in his certification, "Texas Trust Company owns 100 percent of

Cohen, Kerwin, White & Associates Inc., and 70 percent of First Financial Life Insurance Company."

Prugh instructed Kerwin on how to divide the brokerage fees with various loan brokers around the country who would refer clients. He also supplied Kerwin with printed forms for the loan applicants to fill out. "It is going to be easy in most cases to require that these applicants purchase life [insurance] policies from you in the amount of the loan, which is an added goody," Prugh wrote.

Prugh wanted the Cohen-Kerwin agency to sell policies on an insurance company that Audsley would register in Switzerland, and to sell shares in a mutual fund that Audsley would incorporate in Panama.

> The reason that you can do this, and not Harold and I [Prugh wrote] is that you have the assets, and MOST IMPORTANT, you all check out beautifully, as will the Texas Trust Co. in a short period, after you complete the financial statement and clear it with Dun & Bradstreet.
>
> Have lots of loans ready to go; must get with you soon.
>
> Love and kisses,
Byron

In September 1970, Prugh wrote:

Dear Leroy,

We need a little better communications with you, as we are ready to explode on these loan commitments. There is a lot of money in this, cash, ready to go now. Of course, all we can do is generate interest, which is now nationwide, and then we have to screen all applications, which we are now doing, 7 days a week, 15 hours a day. Harold and I met at 7 a.m. and quit at 10 last night.

Today we have three sets of people coming in, one from Miami with some pretty good loans, three from Columbus, Ohio, with some dandy deals, about $10 million worth, and some people this evening from L.A. It is unbelievable the interest. [Apparently the people visiting Prugh were independent money brokers who had compiled lists of clients seeking loans.]

We must get ready to write some commitments, which only you can do on Texas Trust letterhead. Please let us know when you are ready, we will come there and go over all the deals with you. We have them in good shape so it won't take too long, but we are about ready to do this, within a few days . . .

Best regards,
Byron

Not until October did the actual sale of Texas Trust loan commitments begin. Before then, E. C. Mullendore III was dead.

By September 1970, Cohen had settled his $223,237.14 debt to the Internal Revenue Service, although neither he nor the IRS will disclose the amount they compromised on. Carol Kerwin, Leroy's wife, visited the H & S Fur Company in Chicago September 12 and paid $795 for a "natural morninglight mink jacket"; a month later she returned to buy a "natural blackglama ranch mink coat" for $2,195. The agents were living it up.

Police who later raided the Cohen-Kerwin office found a memo apparently written by Cohen, indicating the matters that preoccupied the agency that September 1970. The memo is entitled "Things to Go Over with Leroy Kerwin" and begins:

1. Mink coat for Mother
2. Amount of money Tom Thomas owes us
3. Stock regarding son
4. Money in safety deposit box
5. Cars for parents
6. Amount of money owed us by Mullendore
7. Amount of money owed us by Morris Jaffe—let's let him know how much he owes us
8. Matter pertaining to United Family Life regarding renewals
9. Diamond rings for wives

The list continues in similar fashion. But item 6, the money owed by E.C., is especially striking in this private memo. Apparently Cohen and Kerwin still sought to collect on the $322,745 that E.C. had pledged to pay them the previous March. (The $322,745 consisted of the full premiums for E.C.'s $15 million in insurance policies from United Family Life; the full premiums from the four children's policies from Alexander Hamilton Life; plus the $90,000 in loans and $74,500 in brokerage fees due to Cohen and Kerwin; less the $128,875 that Cohen and Kerwin already had received from the bank loans they arranged for E.C.)

Also present in the Cohen-Kerwin files were three checks from E.C. totaling $322,745. If collected on, they would have repaid the debt. Apparently E.C. had written the checks in advance and dated them forward to January 8, 1970, May 15, 1970, and July 15, 1970. Except for the January 8 check, this was the schedule he had agreed to in March. Apparently Cohen and Kerwin never submitted the checks for collection, perhaps because E.C. told them he did not have enough money on account to make them good.

The check of January 8, for $50,000, was made out to Morris Jaffe, who had lent $50,000 to E.C. with funds he himself had borrowed from Cohen, Kerwin, White & Associates; Jaffe's signature appears on the back of the check, endorsing it over to the insurance agency, which would cancel out the indirect loan. But the check is not endorsed by Cohen or Kerwin, indicating they never cashed it.

If E.C., in fact, owed the agents $322,745 in September 1970, the money certainly was needed. Kerwin still owed the Internal Revenue Service a substantial debt. Moreover, Kerwin had fallen behind in his monthly payments to Associates Discount Company in Chicago on the Sterling-Harris Ford obligation. Associates reminded Kerwin's old mob overlords, Larry Rosenberg and Leo Rugendorf, that if the insurance agent continued recalcitrant, the debt would revert back to them. By September, the Chicago Mafia organization may well have been pressuring Kerwin.

In addition, the end of September would bring due the repayment of $750,000 in loans and advances that Cohen, Kerwin, White & Associates had received from Alexander Hamilton Life and its subsidiary.

When a businessman faces such substantial debts, he naturally combs his receivable accounts for sources of cash. For Cohen and Kerwin, that might have meant looking west, toward Tulsa.

Twenty-three A DAY OR TWO AFTER MOVING off the Cross Bell Ranch, Linda Mullendore established a residence in Tulsa and filed suit for separate maintenance against her husband. Oklahoma women who intend to divorce their husbands often move to Tulsa, where courts are kinder to divorcees than they are in rural counties. Linda later contended that she left E.C. only temporarily, to encourage him to sober up, and that she always intended to return. Doubters, however, have pointed out that Oklahoma law requires a person to live in a county for thirty days before filing for divorce, so that divorce actions customarily begin with a suit for separate maintenance.

The Osage County sheriff's office assigned Deputy Bill Mitchell to serve Linda's suit on E.C.

Chub: "I had seen this deputy sheriff down on the road and knew he was trying to serve some papers on E.C. Well, I asked him what kind of papers he had, and he just said he had some divorce papers he was going to serve on E.C. [E.C.] was aware, I guess, of [their] trying to serve papers on him, because he stayed hid, you know, when they would come to the house. He wouldn't ever answer the door or anything. He would have me answer the door and tell them that he wasn't home.

"[Linda] was trying to keep in touch with me," Chub goes on. "I had got [her] number from this attorney that she hired and I called her. They was worried about Kent Green, you know, getting these [loan] papers all signed, and Linda had said that's why she had left him. When she found out this deal was supposed to be closed, she said I would have to find some way to get those [separate maintenance] papers served. She said if he gets these papers filed on him, that Kent Green couldn't tie up their ranch, you know. I guess as long as they had got this [separate maintenance] filed, the [loan] E.C. signed with Kent Green wouldn't be legitimate . . . without her signature, you know."

Linda still worried about the terms of Green's contract. The Mullendores were to receive an $8 million loan, and would be required to repay $12.8 million principal and interest in a mere five years, including a final balloon payment of $6.5 million in 1975. Since the ranch couldn't produce enough income to make the payments, the property would be at Green's mercy. Regardless of Linda's ultimate intentions, she had to stop Green from getting a stranglehold. If she planned to divorce E.C., she would want her share in the family holdings. Even if creditors forced the ranch to be sold at auction, millions of dollars might remain, after payment of bills, to divide at the divorce settlement. But if E.C. increased his obligations by adding $4.8 million in interest payments to Kent Green, the extra debt might eat up any remaining equity and leave Linda penniless. On the other hand, if Linda, as she said, planned to return to E.C. when he came to his senses, she still would want to protect him from obligating himself to the cutthroat from Kansas City. Under either circumstance, she needed to assert her legal claim to the ranch and thus prevent E.C. from signing it away without her consent. To make her claim official, she needed to get the papers served on E.C., and she implored Chub to help. He was only too willing.

Chub says he "talked to Bill [the deputy], and I thought maybe I could fix up some kind of deal" to trap E.C. where the papers could be served, but in a way that the rancher wouldn't realize Chub was plotting against him. Chub rationalized his betrayal, convinced he was acting in E.C.'s best interest. "[It] didn't matter if E.C. ducked the papers or not," Chub explained later. "He would get them eventually. I didn't want to see him and Green get in some kind of deal."

Lula Harrison says Chub talked to Linda every day that week, although Linda says it was only three times. Once, early in the week, Chub called to warn Linda that "Kent Green thought she was in Tulsa, and he was going to try to find her. I heard him telling E.C. that he had found a blue Eldorado in the parking lot of the Mayo Hotel, and I thought possibly it was hers and it frightened me, because, you know, I thought he might be going to do something to the children and her. He appeared to me as being kind of an underworld man, and a man if people didn't agree to what he wanted, he would force them to do it."

According to Kay Sutton, Mrs. Harrison's granddaughter, who accompanied Linda, they were at a Holiday Inn—not the Mayo Hotel—when a message arrived, possibly Chub's. Says Miss Sutton: "Linda went down in the lobby and she got a phone call. About fifteen minutes later she came up and said, 'We have got to leave because E.C. knows where I am.' And we had to rush and pack everything and leave right then. I think we left half of what we had. We got downstairs where the cars were and she was putting the wrong key in the car and we had to break the window of the station wagon to get in, and then we left after we got everything in the car. We went to some apartment building. Didn't have very much furniture in it or anything. We stayed there and went to, I think, her lawyer's secretary's [apartment] and stayed there." After two nights with the secretary, they moved to a rented house.

Chub felt as strong a desire as Linda did to subvert E.C.'s arrangement with Kent Green. Says Chub: "I asked [Green] one time what would happen if E.C. couldn't make the first payment, and he said they would come in and tell [E.C.] to get what clothes and get out, and I was pretty worried about what would happen. E.C. was threatened, I know. I remember he asked Kent Green one time if—what would happen if he couldn't make these payments after he had borrowed the money. He referred to it as the nut-cutting, and Green told him, well, they would just come in and move him out. I one time asked E.C. if he really stopped and realized what he was getting into. It kind of bothered me that he would get tied up with people like he was meeting. And he just kind of grinned and asked me, he said, 'You are not crapping out on me now, are you?' That's all he said, you know. I didn't say anything. I was [scared]. This Green carried this pistol with him a lot, you know, and ordinary business folks just don't do things like that."

Another time E.C. remarked, "Chub, we aren't scared of all these threats, are we?" Recalls Chub: "I didn't know what he meant. He was drinking and I asked him what he meant and he wouldn't answer me."

As ever, when caught on the defensive, E.C.'s impulse was to lash out. He decided to file a divorce suit against Linda before she could serve her separate maintenance suit on him. But there seems little doubt about his true feelings.

Recalls Mrs. Harrison: "E.C. couldn't understand why [Linda] ran off. He was pitiful, like he wanted to cry." Once, she says, he came into the kitchen and recounted for her a conversation with Chub in which he had threatened to name Chub as "the other man" in the divorce suit. "I said he never should have told Chub that," Mrs. Harrison recalls, "and he said, 'I know.'"

Chub says E.C. appeared unconcerned about Linda's absence. "He was a little bit drunk and it didn't bother him much at the time. He asked me a couple of times where would she go, anyway, and I didn't have any idea either." Although Chub had Linda's phone number, he concealed it from E.C. He suggested innocently that E.C. ask a friend of Linda's in Bartlesville, but the friend hadn't heard from Linda. Says Chub: "I think [when] he found out she had filed on him, whatever it was she filed, he was going to file for a divorce in Pawhuska, and that's when he and Kent Green went and seen these attorneys. Kent Green seemed more interested in it than he did."

Tuesday, September 22, Chub drove E.C. to Pawhuska, where the rancher signed papers at a lawyer's office and officially filed for divorce. Meanwhile, Chub was sent on some errands and promptly discovered that the Cross Bell's credit problems had begun to come home to Osage County.

Chub: "E.C. had his horse-race check [winnings from one of the quarter horses], a $2,900 check, and told me to go cash it. I

[went] to fill up the car at the Texaco station, and this fellow told me the credit had been shut off, and so I paid for it out of my pocket. I went down to this bank by the Manhattan [Restaurant] and they didn't have a director [available to approve the check], so I called [E.C.] at [the lawyer's] office. E.C. took the check and I think he was getting low, down to two or three hundred dollars, and after he got through talking [at] the lawyer's office, we went down to the bank and got his check cashed, and he told me to pull into the Texaco station. [E.C.] went in and got the owner and brought him out and said he wanted him to meet Chub Anderson. I don't know why. The owner said he heard some stories and had got scared, and E.C. had him figure up his bill and paid him in cash, $302. After we left this station, we went to the Apco station and fixed it up so he would have credit, and he told Doodle, the cowboy, they had switched stations." Later that day E.C., Chub, and Green went shopping at the Dewey Ranch & Rodeo Supply store. That night Chub slept at E.C.'s house as the rancher asked him to do after Linda left.

Chub: "Green had been giving [E.C.] some kind of little sleeping pill and he would go to sleep immediately. [Tuesday] night Green had given him a couple of those and he had gone to sleep about six. I went on and went to bed around 9:30, and he had been sleeping till six or seven of a morning. I had been sleeping back in the back room where the twin beds were. He woke me up at two the next morning and had a drink in his hand. He was already dressed, and he said he had to go down and see a Dan Crautch in Bartlesville, and Kathleen had left him a note to be there before five the next morning.

"Supposedly this Crautch had put in a new air-conditioning unit, [replacing one] that went haywire, and wanted his money. He was fixing to leave on a trip. And I guess E.C. had promised him he would pay him before Crautch left. And we went to Bartlesville and neither one of us knew where Crautch lived. But we looked his house up, and somewhere around four o'clock, probably, or 4:30, we found him. And E.C. paid him somewhere in the neighborhood of a thousand dollars in cash for the air-conditioning unit he had put in. [E.C.] was awful good about keeping his word. When he told you he would do something, he would try to do it."

On Wednesday, September 23, the phone company cut off all incoming as well as outgoing service to the ranch, including the two mobile telephones used in ranch work. Recalls Chub: "I do know they got a letter from the telephone company saying another unauthorized credit card, not Mullendore's, had been used to call the Mullendore ranch and [they] were trying to find out the name of the party using his credit card. And my own personal opinion was George Aycock was using it. Calls had been made from Norman, Stroud, Oklahoma City." Paul Burchett, the bookkeeper, went to the phone company office in Bartlesville and offered to pay them in cash at the end of each day, but the company refused to provide service until E.C. satisfied the back bills.

Meanwhile, on Wednesday, Jim Gose, a cowboy, recalls gathering some of the remaining cattle for shipment to the Coffeyville Stockyards for sale. "We was getting ready to wean some calves and yearlings, and threw them together. Moved some over in pens, cut some dry cows out of the wet cows, that was about it. We gathered some black Angus bulls, and I guess that they was shipped."

The same day, E.C., Green, and Chub went to Ponca City to buy guns. Chub: "We had missed a couple of guns and [E.C.] was wanting to replace them. He had two .38's, and they had been in the trunk of his car a lot. And I would kind of keep an eye on them. But they just turned up missing. You know, there's a lot of people work around the ranch, and I just thought maybe somebody probably taken them. They were both Smith & Wessons, .38's. One of them had a wooden handle that was beavertailed, checkered, if you know what I mean. And the other one was some kind of bone handle. He had three different cars he was driving, you know, and I couldn't remember which trunk they were in last or where they had last been.

"And Kent Green was wanting to buy another gun for hisself. He claimed he had given his to Ginny. And I guess they thought they were in some kind of danger, and he was really the one wanting the .38 that E.C. purchased. E.C. bought it and Kent Green took it. And I told him I had lost the other one and E.C. wanted me to get some kind of a small gun. This fellow at the first gun store didn't have one, and E.C. told me to go across the street [to U.S. Surplus & Loan, a pawnshop] and [see] if I could find me a .38. And I went across and this fellow had a Colt Cobra, and I wasn't very fond of it, and I saw this .25, and went back across the street and told [E.C.]. He told me to go across and buy it, and I told him I couldn't [because Chub was on parole]. And he understood and gave me his driver's license and a $100 bill and told me just to buy it and sign his name, which I did, and brought the gun back and gave it to him . . . [E.C. and Green] bought two boxes of .25 automatic shells . . .

"Kent Green took the .38 that E.C. bought, you know, and Kent gave Ginny the gun he had that he brought from Kansas City. He had brought a snub-nose with him, and she was supposed to have carried this in her purse, I guess. But I know he did have two .38's.

"We went outside of Ponca City and shot the gun. E.C., Kent Green, and myself. I wouldn't say that E.C. was a good shot. Green was. The way I would classify him, he was an expert. I can shoot rifles real well, but I never shot pistols very much and wasn't [a] very good shot with a pistol." Chub says he was able to hit the target with the .25 "if I laid it down over the car and squeezed hard, but to just throw it up, it didn't seem like it shot good."

Lula Harrison says she thinks she may know what happened to one of the missing guns Chub talks about. That same Wednesday, September 23, Della Boylin, the cleaning woman, found a large pistol under a sofa cushion in the den at E.C.'s home. Says Mrs. Harrison: "She yelled to me, scary. She said, 'Is this the real thing?' I said yes. Della said, 'Now I know I'm quitting.'" Mrs. Harrison says she and Mrs. Boylin hid the gun in an ironing board closet so that whoever had hid it under the sofa cushion wouldn't be able to find it. Mrs. Boylin went home, never to return. Mrs. Harrison also left, but returned later to iron all of E.C.'s clothes and fix him a dinner of Mexican-style beans and corn bread, plus several days' supply of his favorite stew for after she had gone. They had a long talk.

Mrs. Harrison: "Only thing E.C. said was, Linda left and he didn't know why. Said, 'What would she do that for?' He said, 'I have got to find her because I want her to sign some papers with me. Do you think she's in Tulsa somewhere?' I said, 'I don't know where she is. She could be.' I understand he went out looking for her one night. He sat down and said, 'This is the worst day I have ever had in my life. I don't know why she left me.' He ate a big dinner. I told him that he ate more than I had ever seen him eat. He said, 'You are the best cook in the United States.' He left and went on to bed. Chub gave him a rubdown or something. I washed up the dishes and left."

On Wednesday or Thursday, Harold Copper of PCA visited the ranch. He says Ginny greeted him at E.C.'s house and told him nobody else was home, so he left.

Kent Green tells a much different story—a story of bribery—which Copper stoutly denies. Says Green: "Copper came to the ranch headquarters, and it took place at E.C.'s home. He come up there to the door. Myself and E.C. is the only ones I can recall being there . . . He was pushing and had been pushing, and he had said he would have to turn it over to Wichita, the home office of the Federal Reserve, where the bank is, and [he] couldn't control it any longer. And so we asked him what it would take . . . to buy time . . . and he told us, so we paid. I paid. One hundred $100 bills. He came back that afternoon to get it. I had to fly clear back to Kansas City . . . I went to the bank and cashed a check. I can show where it was withdrawn from my account. We didn't have any choice. E.C. was driven up rather tight at that moment, I mean, short on funds, and we needed to get the necessary time to get him refinanced, and if it cost $10,000, it would cost $10,000. Copper wouldn't even give us a receipt for it." Authorities have listened to Green's story and doubted it.

On Thursday Linda went to see Jack Givens, her lawyer. As she walked into the Fourth National Bank Building, where Givens kept his office, a fat man walked in front of her and she thought she recognized him to be Jim Jackson. "He had on a black overcoat and I saw him as I was behind him and he walked around to get in the elevator. I thought I would just stand back and see where he was going. I thought maybe E.C. had called him to come and find me. At that time, Tal Kolb walks out of the elevator, right past [Jackson], and they didn't even acknowledge that they knew each other. Tal saw me, but Jackson never did, so I went into that installment loan building and ran back, took an elevator to the basement, and called the lawyer's office and said, 'I have just seen two of these hoods in the lobby. What am I going to do?' And [the secretary] said, 'Stay right where you are.' I walked down the hall to the Trust Department and Jack Givens's secretary came down and got me, and then we took the elevator up to the third floor. We got out and I walked down that ramp because she said they were watching the elevators, and I walked down to the parking lot. That is quite a coincidence for them both to be there when

Jackson had been in California all this time as far as I was concerned."

Tal Kolb says he never was in the Fourth National Bank Building with Jim Jackson.

That same afternoon, Dale Kuhrt says, he "had Mike Burkhart calving heifers, and Green, E.C., and [Green's] wife were there, and [E.C.] was gonna take Mike. And I said, 'What are you gonna do, kidnap Mike and leave my damn heifers here?' And he said, 'Yeah, I need Mike.' Green wanted him to go to Miami or [somewhere] so those people wouldn't be able to serve him [the separate maintenance papers]. I went out and checked the heifers."

Burkhart: "Back at my house Thursday about four o'clock, E.C. and Green's wife was waiting for me, told me to pack some clothes for about three days, and Green came in a little bit later before we left. He seemed to be the one making the arrangements. Had E.C.'s car all greased up. Green told E.C. to let me carry the money and that he would follow us to the county line. [But] I never did see [him] after we left. E.C. was drinking, but he was pretty sober. We went to Kansas to a little town just the other side, north of Neodesha. We were to be there three days, supposed to come back Sunday.

"He got drunk. I imagine he drank pretty close to half a fifth of Scotch and a couple of beers. He always gave me the money, every time. There was pretty close to $1,000. I didn't count it. He never did say anything about being threatened, but he acted like he was a little bit scared."

Burkhart says that while they were driving to Kansas, E.C. showed him a contract, "but I didn't pay much attention. He was telling me the ranch was going to be all right. All he had to do was sign, and at that time he intended to sign it. That is what he told me, but I don't know whether that was Green's contract. He didn't mention Green's name. I just supposed it was Green 'cause he was there."

They checked into a motel and Burkhart says E.C. called his parents and his sister in Houston. Katsy told him she thought she could persuade Percy Foreman, the noted trial lawyer and a friend of the Mecoms, to handle E.C.'s divorce case.

"E.C. got sick along about 11:30, I guess, and I took him to the hospital," Burkhart says. "He was drunk, they wouldn't take him, and he said he had heart trouble. I brought him back home, got home about 1:30 [a.m., Friday]."

Plenty had happened while they were gone.

Twenty-four

On Thursday, September 24, 1970, an enraged Gene Mullendore fired Chub Anderson.

Dale Kuhrt says he returned home from checking heifers at about 5:30 that evening and was surprised to see some ranch hands milling about the office. "My wife came out there and said Green had been over and wanted me to come to Mr. Gene's. And I went over—and Green had taken Mrs. Mullendore into Copan to make a phone call—and Gene was just fired up and said, 'Go over there and tell Chub to get his stuff and get out of here right now. He wasn't here when he was needed to go with E.C.' I went over and told Chub that Mr. Gene was madder than hell, and told him what he said, and Chub said it didn't make him much difference."

Chub: "[Gene] must have thought I was supposed to devote all my time there. I had a flat on my car and I had left to go to Copan to get my spare tire fixed. E.C. was over at his folks', had been over there all day, or, you know, quite a length of time . . . And [while I was gone] E.C. had got drunk and decided he wanted to leave, you know, get out of there real quick where they couldn't serve him any papers, and he had got this Mike Burkhart to take him. When I got back, [Gene] sent Dale Kuhrt over to tell me to get my things and leave, you know. I knew what kind of pressure the old man was under, and it wasn't much of a shock to me. Dale told me that Green had been poisoning Gene [Gene's mind], running me down, and [Dale] thought Green was behind me getting fired. But I didn't give it too much thought. I knew Gene would flare up and get mad. This was the first time he had ever done it to me, but I had seen it happen to other guys. Dale said, 'Go ahead and stay up there for tonight,' and we would get hold of E.C. tomorrow. And I said no, I would stay with my brother in Copan. I gathered up the few things that I had, didn't move everything, but gathered up some clothes and left. It didn't shock me too bad at this time. I really more or less felt relieved. I had been under a lot of pressure."

One more thing comes to Chub's mind about that Thursday: in the morning, before Chub left the ranch to fix the tire, Kent Green had come over and repeated his offer of a job, "for less hours and more pay." While they talked, Chub says, Green's eyes concentrated on the gun in Chub's pocket. Once again Chub turned down the job offer.

Green's version of the firing: "Mr. Mullendore asked [Chub] if he was aware that he was expected back at noon to take a trip with E.C., and he admitted that he was aware of it. He did not come back. He had no explanation for that, and Gene told him to get his things and get off the place. [Chub] got in his Chevelle and drove off the ranch property."

Gene Mullendore: "I fired the son of a bitch because he wasn't on the job. He was delinquent about a lot of things."

Dale: "[Chub] had been living with [E.C.] and his drinking, and it had been a strain on him. And Chub had a lot of stuff to move and I told him [that Gene] wanted me to bring the keys back to him. Chub . . . was gonna come out the next morning and get his stuff. I kind of forgot about it that night. And about 10:30 Green was ringing my doorbell." Green said he was relaying instructions from Gene that Dale should notify Green as soon as Chub arrived in the morning. It made Dale suspicious: "I always felt that Green sat over there and aggravated that man from seven till ten, poisoning that old man against Chub, wanting Chub out of there."

Gene: "[Kent Green] didn't like Chub, I know that. He never did say anything about firing him, but he did mention that Chub was always in the way every time when they was trying to talk business. As far as being mad at Chub, I am more disappointed. He [was] not doing what he [was] supposed to be doing. He [was] supposed to drive E.C. and go with him. E.C. liked Chub. I know Chub respected E.C. and E.C. trusted Chub. Chub had taught his boys how to shoot. E.C. was higher on him than I was. I don't trust him."

When Chub left the ranch Thursday afternoon, he must have headed straight for a telephone to call Linda. Linda had moved secretly into a private apartment in Tulsa a day or two earlier because of Chub's telephoned warnings that Kent Green might have discovered the name of her hotel. But Chub was kept advised of her new phone number. Recalls Linda: "Chub called and said that Green and these people were trying to get rid of him to get to E.C. He said, 'They are trying to get him to sign these papers.' And I said, 'Just stay with him and don't let them hurt him.' He said, 'I don't walk from my car to the shop without looking around and without my gun.' And if he said that, he was afraid. Well, he said, 'I have been fired. Gene fired me because I wasn't here to take E.C., and I think Green put him up to firing me.' And I said, 'You go back out there. I don't care if Mr. Mullendore did fire you, you go back.' "

Mike Burkhart recalls that when he and E.C. returned to the ranch at about 1:30 or 2 a.m. Friday, "Green was in the house, and his wife. [E.C.] rang the doorbell and Green came to the door, and he was in a house robe, and he was staying there. [E.C.] went on in. He didn't really say anything. The main thing that was on his mind was that divorce suit."

Green says he and Ginny were staying in E.C.'s house because the servants had left and E.C. didn't want the house unattended. After Burkhart left, the three of them stayed up talking for about two hours, "about the horses and things of this nature, not business," Green says. "At that time, [E.C.'s] greatest concern was his loneliness for his wife and his children, and that's basically what we talked about. E.C. was upset by the fact that Chub had been discharged, very upset. The reason, one, was that he thought possibly Chub could be quite detrimental in the pending [divorce] action between Linda and E.C., and the second reason was that they were going to sell some cattle that he had already sold on paper to Chub, and he certainly didn't want Chub running off with his money."

Green is referring to some Mullendore cattle scheduled for sale at the Coffeyville, Kansas, auction that Saturday. Because word had gotten out that Mullendore livestock was mortgaged and couldn't be sold, E.C. arranged to conceal the ownership of the cattle. He transferred title to Chub, who then would sell the cattle in his own name and convey the money to E.C. The cattle were expected to bring about $20,000. There's a problem, however, with Green's story that Chub walked off with legal title to $20,000 of Mullendore cattle. Both Dale Kuhrt and Paul Burchett say that E.C. didn't sign the cattle over to Chub until the next day, Friday. E.C.'s anger over Chub's dismissal probably grew out of a deep and genuine liking for the manservant.

If Kent Green had gained momentary advantage in his struggle with Chub on Thursday, he lost it on Friday (September 25).

214

Early that morning Chub encountered Paul Kelly at the Barnett filling station in Copan. They discussed Chub's firing and Kelly's own desire to get off the ranch. Recalls Chub: "I remember he was getting pretty scared up about this Green, because he had some relation that knew of this Kent Green and his reputation, and Paul said some of his relations had told him that if they were him, they would get their things and leave there."

Kelly says he already had discussed the situation with Dale Kuhrt. "The phones were shut off. Everybody said the electricity was shut off. It was getting where we couldn't get diesel fuel to farm with, and E.C. was staying drunk, and the story got around that the Mafia had made the loan and were gonna take over, and everybody was scared. You didn't know if the next payday was good, or who you would be working for."

According to Kelly, Chub "said something is gonna happen out there. Chub was scared of Green." As Kelly remembers it, Chub suggested that Linda left the ranch because Green frightened her—not because of anything E.C. did. Chub "said he wouldn't have ever quit, but this is maybe the way out. He told me he didn't think he would go back out there and work, but he owed E.C. the respect to go back and talk to E.C. He said, 'They have been good to me.'" Then Chub headed for the ranch.

Dale: "When Chub came over to get his stuff, I helped him . . . put it in his car. That was on Friday. Green got over there about the time we got everything loaded up. That car was full, and he came over and just waited, said he sure felt sorry about Chub, what happened the night before. And pussyfooting around there. Chub was all ready to go into town, and Green told him, 'Now, Chub, I have got a better job for you, just go on up to Kansas City,' and Chub told him, 'No, thanks.'"

Chub: "Dale Kuhrt, the ranch foreman, come over and told me not to leave without seeing E.C., and I wasn't really mad at anybody, I didn't see I had done anything wrong, you know, but all the things that I had done for Gene Mullendore, and then he lose his cool that quick, I was kind of disgusted with him. But thinking as much of E.C. as I did, I went over to see him. [During the whole time I worked for him], we never did have a harsh word of any kind. And he told me that Gene couldn't fire me, that I was working for him, not Gene, and that he didn't want me to leave. And he told me he would get his boys back, and he wanted me to stay there and take care of his boys. He asked me if I was going to stay, and I said, Well, I wouldn't ever quit him just because his dad had got mad at us, so he stuck out his hand and we shook hands, and that was our agreement. That was Friday morning, because I remember he asked something about if I had anything I wanted to do that night, and I told him, Well, yes, Copan was playing their first football game. He said fine, he would see me at eight in the morning. And I went Friday night and watched the football game at Copan."

Dale Kuhrt was there for at least part of the conversation, and brought up the planned sale of cattle at the Coffeyville auction the next day. Originally, E.C. had proposed to sell the cattle in Kathleen's name, in case the sale barn officials knew that E.C. had mortgaged all of his own cattle. But, Dale says, "when Chub and I were getting ready to leave the house, he said, 'Don't have the check made out to my mother, have it made out to Chub.' I had to go over and catch the trucker and told him whose name to put the cattle in."

On his way out of the ranch, Chub again encountered Bill Mitchell, the deputy sheriff who still was trying to serve E.C. with the papers from Linda's suit. "I was talking to him," Chub says, "and he asked if I could help him find some way. And I told him, 'Well, he's pretty busy running here and there.' He was home at the time, but I told [Mitchell] he would probably be going to the races the next night, stock-car races, he was supposed to go drive a stock car he was the sponsor of. And [Mitchell] was going to be sitting waiting on him the next night to serve the papers on him, catch him on the road, you know, when he got home from the races."

Chub: "I think on that Friday or something, Green was still expecting, or told E.C., that some other man was coming. He talked about a Sal Capra from Kansas City."

Sal Capra, the Kansas City city councilman who was Green's partner in the Canterbury Gardens apartment project, says Green never even mentioned the Mullendore matter to him. But Gene and Kathleen clearly expected Capra to fly in with the money. That Friday evening they remember the beginnings of what would become the final argument between Green and E.C.

As Gene Mullendore tells it, E.C. had wanted to buy some land in Kansas and Green had promised to pay the bill of $23,000 as an advance on the umbrella loan. Green went to Kansas and returned saying he had bought the land, but E.C. fretted, "Well, I am worried about that piece of land. Green went up there and said he bought it, but didn't give me a receipt, and I don't think he paid for it. Green never done a thing about it, just lied to me like a dog." So on Friday, September 25, Gene says, "E.C. told [Green] that he wasn't getting anything done and that [E.C.] was getting tired of [Green's] lying to him." More words followed.

That night Green and Ginny moved off the ranch and into the Holiday Inn at Bartlesville. E.C. had reserved a couple of rooms there in the name of Sal Capra.

Green: "I stayed in the Holiday Inn at Bartlesville, Oklahoma, in room number 419, and I stayed there under the name of S. A. Capra. E.C. was experiencing a great deal of pressure within his family, excluding his wife, to get something done, you know. He had met Mr. Capra and knew that Mr. Capra was possibly going to work with me on the financial arrangements, and he had some conversation which I am not privy to with his mother about this. And Sal Capra was supposed to come down on Thursday or Friday or Saturday night, or something like that, to visit the ranch. [E.C.'s] mother had been at him pretty heavily again, and E.C. called up for that reservation himself and asked me to go in and stay there, 'just to get Mom off my back.' " In other words, the motel reservations would provide at least the appearance of an actual visit by Capra. We have only Green's word that E.C. made the reservations in pretense rather than in expectation of an actual visit.

Gene says he and Kathleen asked Green and Capra to dine at the ranch with them that Friday night, but that [Green] declined, because, "Well, [Sal] eats kosher food." Capra, of course, is Italian-American.

Mike Burkhart says Green drove E.C. over to the Burkhart house for a visit at about 6 p.m. Friday, then left alone. E.C. wanted Burkhart to drive him home. "We got in his car, the Lincoln, and before we got there, he asked me, when we got to his house, if I would go through and check the rooms. He didn't think anybody was there. I told him I would. He never did tell me why he wanted me to. When we got there, his mother was there and she had supper cooked for him, and I went on home."

Gene: "Night before E.C. was killed, she took some food over there, some hash and some red beans. Chub was supposed to be with him."

Kathleen: "E.C. told me, 'These people are sons of bitches, I am through with them. I have had all I want and they are just riding me for everything they can get. I am tired of them. I am through with them, all of them.' I said, 'More power to you, E., whatever you do is sure fine with all of us.'"

Twenty-five   AT EIGHT O'CLOCK ON HIS LAST morning, Saturday, September 26, 1970, E.C. drove to Copan with his mother to make a phone call from the nearest pay booth. The ranch itself was incommunicado thanks to the unpaid phone bill. Gene says he isn't sure whether E.C. was trying to reach Percy Foreman, the high-powered Houston lawyer Katsy had suggested to handle the divorce case, or to reach a doctor in Houston who was planning to operate on E.C. to correct a floating hernia. The hernia had been discovered that summer after E.C. complained of intestinal problems.

Lula Harrison recalls that at some point Saturday Kathleen called her and said E.C. wanted her to return to work. "In a few days we are going to have everything straightened out," she quotes Kathleen as saying. "Yes, in a few days we will have the bills paid and everything. We will be just like we were." According to Mrs. Harrison, "They had a big loan coming through then. I don't know if they got it."

Mike Burkhart recalls that E.C. dropped by his house with Chub at about 9 a.m. They drove to the home of Mrs. Kilbie, a neighbor, to discuss again E.C.'s lease on part of the Kilbie ranch. They stayed about an hour.

Meanwhile, Dale Kuhrt was supervising a cowboy crew loading cattle for the sale at Coffeyville. "I had to go to the west side that morning and see if they got those bulls in," he says. "I called the trucker from Sedan [Kansas], and the rest of the cattle were hauled in horse trailers." He met E.C. and Chub in the office about noon, and they wrote a formal bill of sale to Chub. "I was wanting to eat lunch," Dale recalls, "and E.C. had been drinking pretty good by noon that day." Chub confirms that E.C. was "pretty full" and delayed the proceedings.

What happened during the next six or seven hours depends on who's telling it. Paul Jones, a nearby rancher who baled hay for E.C. on contract, came to collect a $14,897.91 debt for services and equipment. Jones—tall, lanky, and prematurely bald—says he arrived about 4 p.m.; Chub says it was well before one. Jones was struck by the dissension that was building toward the murder that night; Chub's account glosses over the tenseness in the air.

Jones: "I went to Dale Kuhrt's house [where the office was] to try to make good on two checks they gave me. [On previous occasions] Burchett would say, 'Tomorrow we're gonna get our money.' And I'd be there in the morning and he'd say, 'We'll have it at 1 p.m.' One time he said, 'The money's on the road, we should have it in the bank before it closes.' This went on for two weeks. That Saturday is when they were supposed to have the money. Well, Burchett said, 'Kent Green is over at the house now. He's the guy who's going to take the thing over. You ought to see him about the money.' " So Jones went to E.C.'s house and found, he says, an argument. "E.C. and his mother were really into it, shouting at each other. E.C. had a drink in his hand and was two thirds shot. E.C. said he was going to leave, and she said, 'You be sure to be back. We've got a lot of business to do.' [E.C. said], 'I want Paul to go to Copan with me.' She asked me a couple of times, 'Don't you want to watch the football game?' [E.C.] said, 'Damnit, I told you we were going to go to Copan. Let's go. Paul, you drive.' Kent said, 'I'll drive.' E.C. said, 'No, we don't need you along.' We left Kent standing there."

Jones, E.C., and Chub drove off in the rust-colored Lincoln Continental, with Chub behind the wheel. Jones noted that E.C. usually rode in the yellow Continental. "E.C. said, 'Now, Chub, step on it,' and of course Chub would do it. He was going 110 [miles an hour] on the straightaways." Jones says that E.C. and Chub normally liked to drive at such speeds, even on a narrow two-lane road like route 10 to Copan. "E.C. took a big old dip of this Copenhagen [his chewing tobacco]. In his own car [the yellow one], he usually carried a coffee can around to spit in. This car didn't have a coffee can, so he opened up the door to spit out—this is going ninety miles an hour. Chub grabbed him by the arm and pulled him back, and said, 'If you got to spit, do it out the window or on the floor. Don't go opening the door.' He sounded a little disgusted with [E.C.]. Then E.C. took something out of a briefcase and took a drink out of it. We went into this service station [Barnett's Sinclair], and some of the local boys were in there. E.C. went up to the guy that ran the station and he says, 'I've got to make a phone call, could you ask them to leave?' I started to leave, too, and he said, 'No, Paul, I want you to hear this.' First he tried to make it on his credit card and they wouldn't take it. Then he tried to make it collect [to Percy Foreman], and Mrs. Foreman wouldn't accept the charges. He said his sister was Mrs. John Mecom. He still had to borrow [the money for the phone call] from Chub. Foreman wasn't there, so [E.C.] said he would call back at seven. Then Green and Mrs. Mullendore pulled up to the station. He motioned at them with his hand to leave. They took off north. So E.C. came out of the filling station, said, 'Come on, let's lose those sons of bitches.' So we went out . . . to see a race car E.C. was sponsoring."

Chub: "He was supposed to have drove this race car in Caney [Kansas] Saturday night. So he wanted to go over . . . and drive the car [apparently for practice]. This car that he sponsored belongs to my brother, so we went out to my dad's to see if it was out there, and [my brother] had just left with it . . ." They found the car at a service station where Chub's brother was adjusting the rear-end alignment. "I told him to take his time," Chub says, " 'cause I didn't want E.C. driving in the car since he was drunk. I talked to [E.C.] and talked him into going home . . ."

Paul Jones: "On the way back, [E.C.] and I had a conversation about the money deal. He said, 'It doesn't look like I'll be getting any money.' But he said they would be cutting hay soon, and he told me to take the hay and sell it, 'till you get your money. I want you to have your money.' "

(There is importance and irony in what Jones remembers hearing: *It doesn't look like I'll be getting any money.* That is the only solid indication that E.C. had given up on Green as a lending source before he died. Gene and Kathleen observed that E.C. was angry at Green's delays, but not that he flatly had lost faith in Green as a source of funds. Every other person who quotes E.C. directly on the subject says E.C. went to his grave convinced that his loan was on its way. Later, a consortium of insurance companies spent hundreds of thousands of dollars (one estimate said more than a million) on an investigation designed to prove that E.C. planned his own murder. The alleged reason: dying was the only way he could get funds to save the family ranch. And yet the insurance investigators apparently never talked to Paul Jones—who could have given them their one substantial piece of testimony on a suicide motive. Jones never gave a deposition in the insurance case. Only the methodical work of Sheriff George Wayman linked him to the murder day, and the quotes from Jones in this chapter are drawn from an interview the author conducted in Jones's home.)

Jones says that when they arrived back at the ranch after the trip to Copan, he wanted to hop in his car and go home, but E.C. insisted he return to the little house. "And downstairs," Jones exclaims, "there are Kent Green and this blond woman cleaning their guns on the [dining room] table! E.C. says, 'What are you doing?' Kent said, 'Oh, we've been out behind the barn practicing.' And E.C. said, 'Practicing for what?'" Apparently Green didn't answer. "E.C. sat down in his chair and went into a stupor," Jones says. "I was feeling pretty uncomfortable. I walked over to Dale Kuhrt's house."

Chub remembers taking two trips to Copan that day with Paul Jones, but seems confused about the timing of them. Jones recalls only one trip. Chub says the first time they returned, "I thought [E.C.] was going to go to bed, and he went into the house and told me to go on to Coffeyville and pick up the [cattle sale] check. He laid down to take his nap and I went over to the ranch office. I think it was about one [p.m.]. Dale had told me it would be around five [before the check was ready], and I went back to Copan and called, and they said it would be around eight. Some of the stuff we had over there would be the last to sell and it would be around eight before the check was ready, so I went back to the ranch. Paul Jones was with us." That's when Chub recalls the encounter with Kent Green and Ginny and their pistols. "We sat around there for quite a while and around six [p.m.] E.C. went upstairs maybe to use the bathroom. I got up and told Green I was going to Coffeyville to get the check. They were wanting this check. E.C. was drinking and I didn't want him to go, too, and I told [Green] to have Ginny lock me out [lock the door behind him]."

Paul Jones: "While I was setting there [at Dale Kuhrt's house], Chub Anderson come walking across the lot to his garage apartment. He was over there just a few minutes; then he came on over to Dale Kuhrt's. Chub said, 'How do you feel about those people?' I said, 'I really don't know.' He said, 'Boy, every time I turn my back on those sons of bitches, I can just feel a knife or gun going into me.'" Chub left, and a little while later Green and Ginny drove off in a green Eldorado. Then Jones says he himself left the ranch and didn't return that day.

By Green's account, the afternoon went much more pleasantly. "Ginny wanted to go shopping," he recalls, "so we went into the shopping plaza on the east side of Bartlesville and she did some. We came back, spent some time with E.C. over at [his] house. Kathleen was over at the house. And we left about five o'clock. There was a show that we had all seen several times and wanted to see again at the theater behind the Holiday Inn. *Giant.*" (The movie *Giant*, based on a novel by Edna Ferber, tells the story of a baronic ranching family, especially the triangular struggle between the scion of the family, his beautiful wife, and a handsome, muscular ranch hand—portrayed in the film by Rock Hudson, Elizabeth Taylor, and the late James Dean.) Green says he and Ginny went to a Chinese restaurant, saw *Giant*, and returned to their motel. He stoutly denies that he and E.C. argued, or even held "heated discussions," either that day or the day before. He denies that E.C. complained about his failure to produce the loan money. E.C. and Kathleen were "already committed to go up to Caney and watch the stock-car run; that's the only reason we were not together" that night, Green says.

Gene and Kathleen Mullendore say that at about 7 p.m., after Chub had left to pick up the check for the cattle in Coffeyville, Green and E.C. had a flare of tempers. The argument supposedly occurred in E.C.'s house, but the stories are inconsistent about who was present.

Gene: "E.C. told Green, 'You have stalled me as long as you are going to stall.' He asked me, 'Do you care if I run that son of a bitch off?'" Although this seems to imply that Gene was present at the argument, other things that he and Kathleen say indicate he wasn't. According to Gene, who spews out his emotions in a manner not conducive to factual questioning, E.C. told Green, "You either get on or get off by 9 a.m. in the morning. I don't want you to come out to the house, you just call me up." Gene says that Green "was so mad he was shaking. E.C. gave him a cussing. Mrs. Mullendore can tell you because she was there."

Kathleen's version, like her husband's, is more emotional than consistent. At times she refers to her own role in the argument, but when asked about it specifically, she says that Green and E.C. were alone in E.C.'s house and that she heard about the argument later from E.C. At another point, she says Ginny was present. Possibly E.C. and Green confronted each other more than once during the day, in different settings.

Kathleen says Green told them that "Sal [Capra] and his driver and an attorney" would show up at the ranch for a meeting the next morning, Sunday, September 27, and that the money would be there. "But E. was mad at him that night. He said, 'This is it. I am through with all of you. You either get on the pot or get off.' Green said, 'I came back to tell you that I am leaving and going back to Bartlesville like you asked me to. I don't know if I will be back or not.' "

Apparently Kathleen spoke with Green out of E.C.'s presence. "I didn't want him to get away. We were all going to get together the next morning. I didn't know E.C. was mad [at Green]." She recalls saying, "Oh, please do come, we have all this set up here." Green then said, "[E.C.] told me that he wanted us to show up with the money," and Kathleen says she replied, "Isn't that what you are planning to do?" Then, she says, "he turned right around and faced me and said, 'Yes, we will be here.' "

So Kathleen said, "You all plan to have dinner with us in our home." But she says Green declined, and she explains: "This man [apparently Capra] is a very strange man. He eats with no one. He eats only kosher food. What about the Holiday Inn? How does he eat there? I don't know where you would get kosher food around here. Mr. Green said he wouldn't know, either, but I do remember the other day there was a delicatessen truck there and I asked if he knew the name, and I thought, I would go to that delicatessen. And he said he didn't notice. But I think they were such liars. You can't believe anything they tell you."

She says Green told her he was staying at the Holiday Inn that night to meet Sal Capra, and that he would come back the next morning. As to why Green stayed around the ranch so long to begin with, she says, "You can't dream up [the] excuses that man could dream up for staying out here. I was all for it. I felt that if I could help by keeping [him] here under my thumb, fine. He was very nice around the house. He was as little trouble as anyone." For Green, the Cross Bell was a cozy retreat from the Kansas kidnapping charge he was dodging. It was across the state line and a law unto itself.

Kathleen says she last saw Green that day at 7 p.m. "I walked right past him. He was going down the steps." She says he made it a point to tell her that "all the doors [to E.C.'s house] were locked."

After Green was gone, Kathleen recalls E.C. saying, "I am through with these people, and I mean through."

At about twenty minutes to eight, they left for the races. E.C. had four hours to live.

Kathleen: "We got to Copan at ten minutes to eight. He had an eight o'clock telephone appointment and he didn't get his party, so then we went on to Caney. I think he was going to call his doctor or his sister." (More likely, it was Percy Foreman, who later told the *Tulsa World* that E.C. had spoken to him from Caney, Kansas, at about 8 p.m. "He was not at all despondent," Foreman recalled. "He [said he would] be able to get to Houston by 6 p.m. Sunday, and couldn't get here sooner because he was tying up a loan.")

Kathleen: "When he came out of the telephone booth in Caney, he said, 'I am going to take you to the automobile races.' That was all the conversation about the telephone call. We stopped and got a beer, a Coors and a Bud, and we went to the automobile races and stayed there for a while. I really don't know how long, but it could have been as long as an hour."

All through the preliminary races, Kathleen says, she was hoping E.C.'s car "would be torn up so he couldn't drive it." Finally, time came for the race in which the sponsors were to drive. E.C. climbed into his machine and Kathleen recalls the tense moment. "He said, 'I am going to drive the car in this race,' and I said, 'Oh, E., your dad would be so mad at me if I let you drive this car. Your life is way more valuable to us than that $1,000 car.' 'You think so, Mama?' 'I sure do.' Then he got out. [He] made arrangements for somebody else to drive the car, and we started on home. [We stopped in] a beer place on Main Street. We were getting a beer when E. said, 'Just a minute, some of my boys are in here.' I suppose he was in there five minutes, enough to pay for it. We hadn't drunk that whole can of beer when we got home, because apparently he had taken his own in the house with him. He had left my empty can in the car. I asked him if he would come stay all night with us, and he said no, that he would rather sleep in his own bed."

While E.C. and Kathleen were at the races, Chub hadn't made out very well at the Coffeyville cattle sale. He says he "got over there at the sale and messed around and when 8 [p.m.] came, I went up to the window and asked for my checks. And this fellow asked me if I was Chub Anderson and asked me to come in the office and sit, and said Ponca City Production Credit had called and said that there wasn't to be any Mullendore cattle sold unless the check read 'E. C. Mullendore III and Ponca City Production Credit.' I told them, well, I had bought these cattle to the best of my knowledge. Ponca City had called [E.C.] around the fifteenth or maybe just a few days before [to warn him not to sell any more cattle], and they [E.C. and Dale] made this bill of sale out [back-dated] to the twelfth of September. Dale

Kuhrt, E.C., and I signed the bill of sale. And I showed [the officials at Coffeyville] this bill of sale where I had bought these cattle on the twelfth, and they were going to go on and give me the checks. So they had some of the checks all ready to give me, and I got to thinking I would get in a jam over it, and [that I] would leave the checks and the bill of sale and go home and tell E.C. what had happened. And I left all the checks and the bill of sale and told them if it got cleaned up he could send me the checks."

Harold Copper says he got a call Saturday morning, the twenty-sixth, from the sales manager at Dewey Mill & Elevator, who "wanted to know if we had a security interest in the cattle that E.C. might be selling at Coffeyville. I told him that if E.C. was selling the cattle, that we definitely had a security interest in them. I, in turn, called the sale barn at Coffeyville, informing them that if E.C. was selling some cattle, the checks should be made both to Ponca City Production Credit and to E.C. III. I heard no more from them until late that evening. My wife received a phone call [and] I was out of town, so I returned his call when I arrived home—this was approximately midnight. And he informed me that a person by the name of Damon Anderson had a bill of sale for the cattle and he was selling the cattle. I had no idea at that time who Damon Anderson was. I knew who Chub Anderson was. I didn't know who Damon was."

Chub says he arrived back at the ranch around nine or nine-thirty. He went to "E.C.'s and the door was unlocked. And I called down to see if anybody was home and went down to E.C.'s room to see if he was asleep, and the brown car was gone and I walked across to Gene's."

Gene, when asked what happened the night of the twenty-sixth, says: "That was the night E.C. was— It was Saturday night. I was watching the Texas Tech game on TV. I know the first half was over, the second half had started, and Texas had scored again. They were just running over Texas Tech in the second half. [Chub] stayed probably between five and seven minutes, not over seven minutes. Sat in a rocking chair opposite my little table, and he sat there real close to me. And he said, 'How are they getting along?' And I said, 'Well, Texas Tech has done pretty good the first half, but this second half is going to be a different story because Texas is just too tough, they have too many men, every man they put in is better than the one they took out, and the way they was gaining all the time—' "

Yes, interjects a questioner, but what about Chub?

Gene: "He sat there for about five or seven minutes, took his coat and hat off, and walked out there and put it on the piano bench, which was very unusual. I never knew him to do that before. He always put it over on the divan where the coats and hats are supposed to be put, but he pulled the bench out and put his coat and hat on the piano bench. He said, 'My legs are a little stiff, and I am going to get up and walk around a little bit.' I said, 'Sit down and watch the game for a while. E.C. and Mrs. Mullendore will be back in a few minutes.' He said his leg hurt him and walking kind of made him feel better, but I interpreted it that it made him nervous—a few days before that I had fired him. And I said, 'That is all right, Chub. Walk around if you want to, but E.C. and Mrs. Mullendore will be back in a few minutes and I want you to go over there and stay with E.C. That is what your job is, to stay with him.' He had been off longer than was necessary. E.C. let him off and he hadn't been taking care of the boys, 'cause Linda had taken the children and run off somewhere, leaving E.C. and filing separate maintenance. Like to have killed E.C., because he didn't know where she was or what she was doing. Just a few days before that, she was so drunk . . ."

Chub: "I walked out and here come E.C.'s car, and they drove around and circled the shop and drove back to E.C.'s. The yard was pretty lit up. E.C. got out of the car and . . . Kathleen was driving around to her house . . . When I walked across to E.C.'s house, he sent me back. He had forgot and left his snuff in the car Kathleen had drove around to his father's house. I went back across, and this was before Kathleen had gone in the house, and we said a few things, and I told her I had to get a can of E.C.'s Copenhagen from the car. And I got it and walked back to the house, and E.C. was standing out in his front yard taking a leak. I would say he wasn't as drunk as I have seen him, but he was certainly too drunk to drive a car. We both went in the house and went downstairs, and I do remember checking both doors at this time, *always had me check both doors and see that they were locked* [emphasis added]. Both doors were locked and we went downstairs and he fixed him a drink, and I don't remember if he carried a Coors in or not, but his mother had bought him some and I seen him so many times with drinks in his hands, I didn't pay much attention. And we sat downstairs and talked how his mother didn't want him driving the race car."

Chub had especially bad news for E.C. that night—news that

might have infuriated the rancher. Chub hadn't collected the $20,000 E.C. was counting on from Coffeyville, and the money might be sent instead to the PCA. There has been speculation that E.C. needed the $20,000 to pay brokerage fees to Green and Capra the next morning, or that he intended it to cover a $16,000 check, already mailed out, to keep his life insurance current. The first two of his three $5 million policies were more than one year old and were into their thirty-day grace period. The policies would expire October 4—just one week away— unless $16,000 in premiums were paid to United Family Life. E.C. also might have wanted the $20,000 to meet the month-end payroll. In any event, he wanted it badly. But Chub insists the subject never came up that night because E.C. "was drunk, and I was going to tell him the next morning."

Suddenly, Chub recalls, E.C. said, "Oh, hey we're going to Houston tomorrow to meet Percy Foreman, the famous attorney." Then, Chub says, "He wanted to go to Copan to make a phone call and call Don McMoy [the pilot] in Dallas. And he did have this fellow's card [McMoy's business card]. He went back and got hisself a jacket and brought one of his out and told me to wear it. The best I remember, it was kind of a cream-colored corduroy. We left the house, *didn't lock it or anything* [emphasis added], out front. And the only car out front was my car [a maroon 1970 Chevy that E.C. had bought for Chub]. And we got in it and I was driving and we left for Copan." Chub says they left at about 10 p.m., but Dale Kuhrt says he saw them drive off at about 10:30.

"We got on the county line hill east of the ranch, right about three hundred yards east of the Osage–Washington county line. We both seen a car parked off the highway, and as we approached the car, it turned on a red light, and E.C. told me to step on it and outrun him."

At this point Chub faced a difficult decision. He had arranged this trap with Bill Mitchell, the deputy sheriff who was trying to serve papers on E.C. Linda had told Chub the papers would establish her legal rights and prevent E.C. from signing the ranch away. Apparently Mitchell had missed E.C. on the way back from the races and had hung around until now. As Chub recounts it, he considered that "they were supposed to close this deal. I knew they were supposed to be waiting on this Sal Capra to come the next morning. I thought it would be helping E.C. if I did, you know, help get the papers served on him. But then again, I just didn't want to do him that-a-way, you know?"

So Chub made his decision. He extinguished the headlights and stomped on the accelerator. "We turned on a road north . . . [The deputy] chased the car approximately two or three miles and got lost in the dust, and didn't get to serve the papers. After you go north for about four or five miles, you hit Sand Hills Road that goes to Chautauqua, Kansas, and I told E.C. we could go back down by Jim Gose's house and take a back road that goes through the pasture back to [E.C.'s] house. So he wanted to stop at Jim's house when we got to it, about three eighths of a mile from the Sand Hills Road. And we couldn't hear any cars coming."

Chub was still driving without headlights, to elude the deputy, and had a pistol stuck in his belt. He says he carried it whenever they left the ranch.

Jim Gose says E.C. and Chub reached his house at about 11 p.m. "I was just a ranch hand. I live in a trailer house. Me and my wife get to bed about 10:30. [We] just got to sleep good and I heard the car come in from the north. It was driving pretty fast. They pulled up to our porch and I flipped the light on. It was E.C. He was hollering, 'Let me in, Jim. Don't turn the light on.' I turned the light off. I let E.C. in and Chub stayed out by the car. They pulled the car right up there by the porch. Chub was looking back to see if anything was coming, I guess. E.C. said, 'The law was after us.' I let E.C. in the house. He said, 'Do you still have a telephone?' I said, 'You bet,' and he asked if he could use it. Just sitting there and talking, and before he made the telephone call, we had the lights off, he was talking about the troubles about his wife divorcing him. [E.C. said], 'I just want to show you something. Open the icebox door.' Where we had just a little bitty light. He showed me a piece of paper [a newspaper clipping] where Linda was suing E.C. for divorce. 'You think I haven't got double trouble.' It was then a piece of paper dropped, I guess out of a newspaper, it was in a newspaper, that Chub [who had come in by then] said, 'Damnit, E.C., don't be dropping that. It is too important to be dropping around like that.' I don't know what the paper was—at the time I didn't pay any attention to what it was."

Asked about it later, Chub said he didn't remember anything about a dropped piece of paper at Gose's house.

Then the three of them, not wanting to turn on a light for fear that Mitchell, the deputy, might still be prowling about, again opened the refrigerator door a crack to read Don McMoy's telephone number off the business card E.C. was carrying.

According to Gose, E.C. "called an airplane pilot and asked him to meet him, and I thought he said in Bartlesville [Chub says at 2 p.m. the next day], and I thought he said to wait. 'I might be a little early and I might be a little late. Don't tell anybody who you are going to pick up. If you got to tell anybody, tell them you are picking up Chub.' I would say he was intoxicated. He was pretty lit, I would say. I don't know if he was staggering, he didn't walk around that much to tell if he was staggering. He just apologized for getting me up that late, that was about it. Chub kept trying to get E.C. to come on. Chub just looked after E.C. like a big brother or something. Kept trying to get E.C. to go. Chub was sure not drinking. Just asked for a drink of water. Sure wasn't drinking that I could tell. Acted embarrassed, to me. E.C. apologized for waking me like that, kept apologizing. Chub acted embarrassed, E.C. acting like that. Asked him to come on."

Gose says he can't remember whether the men took off their hats when they came inside, or whether Chub had a jacket on, or what color it was, because the lights were off. He says they left on the ranch road toward E.C.'s house at roughly 11:15 or 11:20. "It is between four and five miles to the ranch house. It would probably take ten minutes unless they were really driving fast. You come down through a pasture. You got to open two gates to get on down to the ranch."

Chub: "We headed on down the road toward the main ranch, and we kind of circled around number-four pen, where the horses are, up from E.C.'s house, and we could see there weren't any cars, and we got out and went in and locked the front door. I don't remember for sure if I locked the [other door] going out to the playpen or not. The first time Kathleen brought him home, I do distinctly remember locking both doors, but the last time I locked the front door, *but don't remember about the other door. I never paid a awful lot of attention to it* [emphasis added]."

Twenty-six   Dale Kuhrt and his wife had

played cards at the Mike Burkharts' that night until 10:15 or 10:30, then had come home and watched television. At about 11:45, Chub appeared at Kuhrt's door, still wearing his white hat and the cream-colored outdoor jacket. He was dripping blood.

Dale: "He was ringing that doorbell, bawling, and said, 'Help, we have got to get E.C. to the doctor. He's hurt bad.' When I opened the door, he was standing there all stooped over and his hand was on his arm, and blood was squirting out between his fingers pretty bad, bleeding like hell. I was just looking at blood and wondering who was gonna get shot next. He stated, 'Get a gun and come on. We have got to get E.C. out of the house.' And I went in and got a .22 we had in the house and probably dropped fifteen bullets trying to load the thing, and got in my pickup and drove up to the house."

Chub: "I told him E.C. had been hurt real bad, and he seen blood all over me, and all over my arm, and he kind of, you know, panicked. The best I remember, maybe he didn't have on his boots. And I ran back across— I happened to remember this .32 under E.C.'s car seat, parked over at his mother's, the one they had drove earlier, and I ran over and got the .38—or the .32—out from under his seat and went back to his house. And I went out, looked out across the parking lot, and didn't see anybody. And I ran back downstairs and looked at E.C. again, and I could tell he was still—that he was still breathing, but you know, he was hurt real bad. I could hear him gurgling, he had his mouth open, and I picked his head back and could see how bad he was hurt. And I ran back upstairs, and Dale came at that time, and he went downstairs, we both ran back downstairs, and I remember him saying something about, 'Oh my God, we got to get hold of an ambulance and call the sheriff.' Well, he said he was going to call the ambulance and the sheriff. And we didn't stay there but an instant and ran back upstairs, and I told Dale I am going to the doctor, and I went out and got in my car and took off for Dewey. He went back to his house. I think he went back to get his pistol. He was naturally pretty shook up."

Dale: "[I] ran in and downstairs, and I seen him, slid down off the couch, sitting with his rear on the floor, with his knees kind of up. When I looked at him, he had his head back, blood coming out every direction. He was still breathing. His mouth was wide open. You could see a great big hole right here [pointing to his forehead between the eyes]. Other than that there was blood everywhere. All [Chub] could keep saying was, 'We have got to get him up to the pickup and get him to the hospital.' And I counteracted that and said no, we wouldn't want to move him. 'Let's get some help.' All I could think about [was], 'Are we gonna get shot any minute?' He said, 'I have got to get to a doctor,' and I said, 'Yeah, go on, and I will call the sheriff.' Chub left first, and I went over and told my wife to lock all the doors and stay inside. Then I left, and Chub was about a half a mile ahead of me. I could see taillights ahead of me about a half a mile on the Mission Creek Road. I got to thinking where the nearest phone was and went to Bill Armstrong's. I got to thinking, They are going to pick us off going down that road. I never seen a damn thing. I was driving like hell and hoping it didn't come through the window. I guess I was just a coward, but goddamn, when you're driving down the road and know somebody is shooting people, all they had to do was stand along the road and shoot."

When Kuhrt reached the Armstrong residence, he made a decision that would surround the murder investigation with blunders. Although E.C.'s body lay in Osage County, Kuhrt, apparently acting from instinct, called the Washington County sheriff's office in Bartlesville, which was slightly closer than Pawhuska and had a hospital. At 12:10 a.m. (by sheriff's records), Kuhrt told an officer "to get an ambulance and all the goddamned deputies they could out there." Then, he says, he

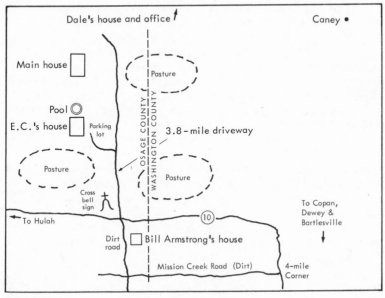

not set to scale

"went on up to Max Foreman's and woke him up and asked if he had a gun, we might need some help down there." Kuhrt says he arrived back at the Cross Bell sign just as the ambulance and deputies were pulling onto the ranch.

Chub also headed for Washington County, where his father had owned land for many years and where he had friends among the sheriff's deputies. Chub says he was holding his arm tight. "I could feel a lot of blood inside of my clothes, and blood all over my coat. After I got in the car, I let [my arm] hang. It was hurting pretty bad then." In Dewey he encountered Henry James Catron, an elderly Dewey policeman he had known many years. Chub left his own car and got into Catron's.

Catron says Chub approached him at 12:16 a.m. "He said, 'Take me to the hospital. I have been shot.'" On the way to Jane Phillips Hospital in Bartlesville, Chub told Catron that E.C. had been shot by strange intruders. He "said there was two men, one tall with a high forehead, gray-haired, and the other man was chunky and sort of curly-headed, dark, and the kind of clothes they had on, he said he just couldn't remember. White men. He said, 'I shot at them as they went out the door.' I said, 'In this shoot-'em-up, where did you get shot?' And he said, 'In the shoulder.' And he sobbed, and then he said, 'Will you do me a favor?' And I said, 'What is it?' He said, 'Will you check on E. C. Mullendore and see how bad he's hurt and let me know at once?'"

Chub remembers he was still carrying the two pistols. The .25 "was kind of small and I had stuck it in my pocket. I didn't even really realize having it." The .32 pistol was in his belt. "I really wasn't aware of having it, but after I got in the car, I was in quite a bit of pain, and I remember feeling it in my stomach. I pulled it out, and I don't remember whether I laid it on the floor or laid it on the seat, but I did tell [Catron], 'Here is this pistol,' you know."

Catron was driving fast and had the siren going. He says he didn't know the pistol was in the car until much later, when he was startled to find it and thought it must have fallen out of Chub's clothing by accident.

According to Chub, a sheriff's deputy and a highway patrolman "was there waiting on the Dewey police car when we got to the emergency entrance" of the hospital.

Larry Silver had been a Bartlesville policeman for eleven years, the last ten of which he had worked part time as an ambulance driver for Mercy Ambulance Company. His next-door neighbor, Gene Klutts, was employed by the Federal Bureau of Mines, but also augmented his income with part-time work for the ambulance company. Silver and Klutts were home watching television the night of September 26.

Klutts: "[We] work a shift together, and we keep an ambulance there at our two houses where we can leave out of there. And [Silver] came over and knocked on the door, and he said, 'We got a call to make.' So I grabbed my shirt and a jacket and put it on, and got in the ambulance. Well, we was going through Dewey, I can't remember exactly where it was, but we met the Dewey police car and he was coming in, and he said, 'Well, I've got one of the boys here.' So we, you know, started shutting ours down, because there's no need to run on up there and burn up a tank of gas if somebody has already come on in. But they said, 'No, go on up there.' They said, 'E.C. is still up there.' "

Racing at speeds of more than one hundred miles an hour, the ambulance screeched to a halt in front of E.C.'s glassed-in porch seconds after Dale Kuhrt and Washington County Deputy Sheriff George Hughes had arrived. (Osage Deputy Mitchell, unable to serve his summons, apparently had gone off duty.) Kuhrt was on the porch, waving them on, Klutts says. "Dale had a big pistol stuck in his gun belt there, and [I] wondered, you know, kind of what the deal was, and Larry asked him."

According to Silver, Kuhrt responded that "there had been a shooting. He pointed to the front of the house and said, 'Look at this.' " They saw six bullet holes in the glass door to the porch. "The comment was made that there had been a pretty good shoot-out or something up there," Silver says. "I asked him where Mullendore was. We thought that he was supposed to have been hurt."

Kuhrt told them E.C. was downstairs. The well-furnished lower level of E.C.'s house contained the den, dining area, and kitchen. But Klutts thought Kuhrt was pointing to a basement, which only added to the general fear. As Klutts recalls it, "Dale said he had went down to the first landing there, and could see E.C. sitting up next to this couch. He said he didn't go on down. He said he sat there on that first landing. He didn't know if anybody was down in there or not."

Silver: "[I] asked if [E.C.] was dead or alive, and George [Hughes, the deputy] said he didn't know. But the other man [Kuhrt] said, well, he had been down there earlier [and] he thought [E.C.] might still be alive. And we said, 'Let's go down and get him. We've got to get him out of there and to the hospital.' [Kuhrt] said, 'Well, we don't want to go down there yet. We don't know if whoever done this is still down there.' So we had some discussion. Well, we've got to go down there and get him out regardless of what happens. [But] no one wanted to go."

Klutts: "Larry said, 'Well, let's not rush into anything here, right real quick.' So he asked George for his pistol."

George Hughes, the deputy sheriff, apparently trembling, gave his gun to the ambulance driver, who proceeded into the house. Silver inched through the living room and led the other three men down the stairs.

Klutts: "On the way down there, Larry said, 'Well, I will go down in here. You can come on behind me. If anything happens, light on up the stairs.' I told him he didn't have to worry about that, I would leave."

When Silver and Klutts reached the den, they looked back and saw Kuhrt and Deputy Hughes still cowering on the landing. The would-be heroes tell slightly different versions of what happened.

Klutts: "Larry was in front with the pistol, and he was more concerned, you know, he was scanning the room, looking if they was still down in there. While Larry was doing this, I went to E.C. He was leaning up against the divan with his head back and he had his right hand clutched like, you know, like he had been in a fight or something. And his left leg was junkered back underneath his right leg, kind of like Indian squat or something, and his right hand, or his left hand, was down toward his kneecap, somewhere like that. He was awful bloody."

Silver: "I went directly to Mullendore and tried to see if there was any kind of a pulse or anything at all on him, which I didn't think there was. His body appeared to me to be still very warm, and I noticed he had what appeared to be a wound between his eyes and massive head wounds. I am not a doctor." So Silver called up to Deputy Hughes on the landing, "George, what do you want me to do? If it's just been a matter of minutes, if there is any chance at all, the last chance is to get that resuscitator on him." Hughes answered back, "Get him on it if you think there is a chance."

Klutts: "After Larry had made his little sashay through the room there, he came to me, and I guess he stick George's pistol in his hip pocket or front pocket or something, or his jacket pocket, and he asked me, 'What do you think?' And I said, 'Well,

234

it's possible he is still kicking, but I am not sure.' And he said, 'Well, let's get him out of here and get that resuscitator on him.' And I said okay. So we then started moving him. Just the two of us. Larry, he had noticed this fist clenched, and he said, 'We ought to put something around it.' I guess that's where his police training came out. He was thinking there might have been something in there, so he wanted to put some towels around it, and so we wrapped one towel around in there, and Larry said, 'Give me that other towel and we will go ahead and wrap it around on him.' So we wrapped two towels around his clenched fist."

Silver and Klutts couldn't get a stretcher down the narrow stairway, so they had to carry E.C. up by hand. Klutts says that Hughes and Kuhrt didn't enter the room where E.C. was murdered until two more deputies arrived.

By this time, Washington County police radios were buzzing with talk of E.C.'s shooting. Among those tuning in were Osage County Sheriff George Wayman and his deputy, Rudy Briggs. They raced toward the scene in separate cars, Briggs in the lead. But just as Briggs roared into the main ranch gate from route 10, the ambulance roared out of the gate the other way and off into Washington County, carrying with it the corpus delicti from the biggest criminal case in Osage County history.

De Los Pettit, whom everyone calls "Pig," a fifty-six-year-old game ranger, had been parked in an alfalfa field along the dirt road connecting route 10 with the Mission Creek Road. He and another ranger had waited in the alfalfa field for more than an hour, watching for deer poachers, when their police radio crackled with news of trouble at the nearby ranch. They drove directly to the scene, where they found Dale Kuhrt and some deputies searching the grounds outside E.C.'s house, looking for a gun. So they joined the search.

Pig Pettit: "We looked around and we thought we found a gun. We had a flashlight, and we shined it and saw the butt end of a gun. Somebody said, 'Here's the gun. Don't touch it.' Dale said, 'Well, that's a kid's toy gun.' " And it was.

After what he estimates as twenty or thirty minutes of this, Pig asked, "Has anyone checked on the old couple? They could be dead, too."

"I am not going to do it," Dale replied.

"Well, I will," said Pig. "I know them real well."

So Pig and Dale went together to the door.

235

Pig: "Dale says, 'Well, there is no light on.' And I said, 'Well, I believe I'll tear the door down.' And about that time, Kathleen said, 'Who is it?' And I told her and she said, 'Just a minute.' She flipped the light on and stuck her head around the door and said, 'Oh, I'll let you in.' I told her there had been an accident over at E.C.'s, that they had shot him and Chub both, and she said, 'Oh my land, how bad?' And I said, 'Well, I don't know, really.' She run upstairs and hollered at Gene that they had been shot, and they called me up there. And I explained to Gene that Chub had drove to the hospital. And I helped Gene get dressed, and I told Gene, 'Now, Gene, the shooting is bad.' I didn't want to tell him that the boy was dead. So Gene said, 'Here, help me load this gun.' And he got an old German Luger-type gun, and I said, 'There ain't no shells.' And he got some shells, and he handed me another gun, a pistol, snub-nosed, looked like a .38. And I said, 'This thing is not loaded either.' And he got some shells, and I loaded it and laid it down on the bed. And he handed me a big, old, pearl-handled .45, looked like an old Colt, and I said, 'This is not loaded either, Gene.' And he said, 'Isn't that a———.' And he kind of cussed a little, and he said, 'Not a gun loaded!' And he stuck it under the mattress of the bed. And when Kathleen came in, he gave her the little snub-nosed gun and she put it in her purse, and he put the big German Mauser-type Luger in his pocket. And I drove him to the hospital in their Cadillac."

Twenty-seven

BARTLESVILLE IS A PHILLIPS town. You drive down Phillips Boulevard, can't miss the Phillips Building, and arrive at Jane Phillips Hospital, more likely than not powered by Phillips gasoline.

Kathleen Wheat, a licensed practical nurse, was working the 11 p.m.–7 a.m. shift at the hospital the night they brought Chub Anderson into the emergency room. He was wearing blue jeans, and his jacket and shirt had been removed, showing a boxer's physique. She scrubbed his wound. The black powder burn that ringed the bullet hole in the back of his arm, at the shoulder, wouldn't wash off. The other hole, in the front of his arm, slightly lower and toward the outside, was so small she didn't even notice it.

236

"First he was sitting on the side of the bed or the table down in the emergency room," recalls Mrs. Wheat. "He acted like he was going to faint or something, and the night supervisor, she was at the telephone, she said, 'Grab him and lay him down.' So I laid him down there on the cart, the table they have in the emergency room. And I tried to clean him up. He had blood on his arm and I washed it off, and where he had put his hand up to his face, why I washed that off. [He said], 'When they bring Mullendore in, take care of him first. He's worse than I am.' He said quit on him and take care of Mullendore. I had left the emergency room and had gone out, and just as I came back in, somebody said, 'Why, here comes Mullendore now.' Anderson says, 'Oh, Gene, please don't tell on me.' Just as they brought Mullendore into the emergency room. I had just come back through the door when he said, 'Oh, Gene, please don't tell on me.' "

E.C. had on blue jeans, a mostly white shirt with blue-and-orange vertical stripes, and an outdoor jacket with a leather paneled front and green cloth back. His face was bloody and his hair sticky and matted with blood. There was a circular powder burn around the hole in his forehead.

State Trooper Bill Dunlap arrived at the emergency room in response to a police radio call from George Hughes, the sheriff's deputy. Dunlap says Chub was wobbly and complained of feeling faint. But Chub poured out his story about hearing a shot, running downstairs to find E.C. bleeding, being shot himself, and finally giving chase to two murderous intruders, whom he described as young men. Then the wounded ranch hand begged Dunlap, "Don't leave me. Will you stay with me?"

"I will stay with you," Dunlap replied. At one point, Dunlap says, Chub pulled back a curtain to look at E.C. and sobbed, "He was like a brother to me."

Nurse Wheat: "When I got [Chub] upstairs [to his room on the third floor], there was blood on his clothing. He had some tobacco in his shirt pocket. It was in a round container about an inch deep, and it had blood all over it, and I put it in his drawer. Then, when I took his pants off, you know, when you go to hang up men's pants, things fall out of their pockets, so he had some change in his pocket and I got some bullets out of his pockets. I put the change and things in the drawer, and I took the bullets downstairs and gave them to Mr. Hughes [who had arrived at the hospital by this time]. I believe there was six bullets. He had some bills, but I don't know how many he had. They counted it and I believe they said he had $300. [Chub] wanted to see Jimmie Holt [the Washington County sheriff, who knew him]. Someone had told him that Jimmie Holt was home sick. He tried to talk to George Hughes, but I don't know what he talked to him about. They went into the recovery room and talked. He gave Hughes a little gun."

Trooper Bill Dunlap also talked to Chub in his hospital room that night, and recalls, "He kept referring to, that it was Mafia, and at one time while he was talking he asked me if I will pull the shade. His bed was next to a windowsill, or over by it, and if I will pull the shade because he said they would try to get him . . . He said that Mr. Mullendore, the dealings that he had had, that he believed that some of the people he was dealing with were Mafia." Chub told Dunlap and Hughes about the gun incident at the Holiday Inn at Oklahoma City, and mentioned Kent Green. Going through E.C.'s pockets, the two law officers found a loan commitment signed by Green. Dunlap recalls that the commitment was for $12 million; Hughes says it was for $8 million. They also found $999 cash in E.C.'s jeans.

Gene Klutts says he talked to Chub after bringing E.C. to the hospital. "I asked him, 'How are you, Chub?' And he says, 'What is E.C.?' And I said, 'Well, they are working on him over there.' And he said, 'He's dead.' He was, to me, visibly shaken. He was crying, he was weeping. He wanted a cigarette. I told him, 'Chub, you know I don't smoke.' Finally, I think, the technician gave him one."

Pig Pettit brought Gene and Kathleen into the hospital. "They wouldn't tell us nothing," he recalls. "Gene and Kathleen went in the little waiting room. Of course, they were pretty nervous, and Gene was getting a little rowdy because he couldn't get to see anybody. We sat there approximately fifteen, twenty minutes or so and talked, and they wanted me to get ahold of Kent Green. [Kathleen] said, 'Now, you can't get him by calling Kent Green, you will have to go through Mr. Capra,' and I wrote it down, took the number. And we didn't have any change. And the special investigator, [Arnold] Moreland, he had something to do with the Washington County sheriff's office, I handed him the card and told him, 'You make this telephone call,' which he did, and handed me back the card. Then she wanted me to get ahold of Mrs. Vance and Linda. They didn't have any change. None of us did. So I got my state credit card out and called Mrs. Vance in Pawhuska, and they didn't answer. Kathleen said, 'Well, I told you, Gene, that Linda is in Tulsa.' " So Kathleen called John Arrington, Jr., who called Jack Givens, the lawyer in Linda's separate maintenance suit, who called Linda at about 2:30 or 3 a.m.

Kent Green says Kathleen called him personally at about 2 a.m., and said, "Kent, can you come over?"

"And I said, 'Well, yes, what's wrong?' She said, 'Well, E.C. has had an accident.' I said, 'Well, where are you at?' She said, 'Right here at the hospital in Bartlesville.' And I said, 'Well, what happened?' and she said, 'He's been shot.' I said, 'How bad is he?' And at this point she broke down and said, 'I don't know how bad he is. They won't tell me. But I think he's dead.' And I immediately dressed, went over to the hospital."

Kathleen confirms that she spoke to Green at the Bartlesville Holiday Inn after Pig Pettit dialed the number, and that Green promised to "be right there, and that was about all. It took him an awful long time to get there [Gene says an hour and a half, probably an exaggeration]. He said he got mixed up and went to the wrong hospital."

When Green finally arrived at Phillips Hospital, he immediately asked Kathleen how Pig Pettit had been able to contact him at the Holiday Inn, since the phone was registered to Sal Capra. "I had already told Pig about Mr. Capra," she recalls, "and Mr. Green said, 'Oh no, you didn't say anything about Sal, did you?' And I said, 'Oh no.' That is when he told us that he had a prison record. 'I sure don't want Sal mixed up in this,' [Green said]. I never answered him and neither did Gene. Someone told him, one of the officers told him, that they wanted him to stay around. 'I will stay around, right here,' [Green said]. He did. He was awfully excited. I walked right out there and told Pig, 'Don't tell him that I told you about this man. I have told [Green] a lie, that I have not mentioned [Capra's] name or anything.' "

Nurse Wheat remembers Kathleen as "a gray-haired lady, a heavyset lady. She came upstairs and wanted to see Mr. Anderson, and I said we weren't allowed to let anybody go in to see him, you know, if we didn't know the people, and she says, 'Well, I just want to see him. I want to ask him one question.' I went to get permission from one of the RN's on the floor to see if it was okay for her to go in. When I came back, she had already gone in. There was quite a few people in the room, around five. Somebody said the Osage police officer was there. George Hughes was there. I think Bill Dunlap. Mr. Mullendore. When I would go in to take Anderson's vital signs, they were quiet, and they were just sitting there in the chair or standing against the wall."

Kathleen: "Chub was absolutely wild that night." His wildness impressed her because it was so unlike his normal placid manner. Dale, too, was upset, she says, but he always "goes to pieces. There are people who do panic," she explains. But Chub ordinarily wasn't one of them. Green remembers that "Chub was visibly and emotionally upset. He did not appear to be in any great pain."

Chub says, "I do remember [Gene] or Kathleen, one, said that E.C. was dead, when they came in." But he says he doesn't remember Kathleen's asking him any questions. Of Green's visit, Chub recalls, "I believe he said something about, he asked me, was it Aycock. I told him it wasn't. I would have known Aycock's build. He wasn't built like the two fellows I seen. They were just both about the same size, medium built is the—about the only description."

Pig Pettit remembers that hospital authorities finally decided to break up the convention in Chub's room. "They run us out of the operating room, said, 'He has to go to bed,' " Pettit recalls. So Gene and Kathleen asked to go see E.C.

By this time, one other important figure had arrived at the hospital: Arnold Moore, Bartlesville's leading funeral impresario. Osage morticians doubtless dreamed of dead Mullendores, and before the eyes of Arnold Moore rose the vision of a $20,000 funeral (actually, the Mullendores contracted many of the arrangements independently and buried E.C. on ranch property, so Moore's ultimate bill came to a mere $8,042.90). With the job in his hand, but not yet in his pocket, Moore set about to impress the dead boy's parents. When Moore got word that Gene and Kathleen wanted to view the body, he reached it first and began a demonstration of his art. Trooper Dunlap says he saw Moore cleaning up E.C.'s body—specifically including the clenched right hand, which Silver and Klutts had so carefully wrapped in a towel to preserve whatever evidence it contained. Pig Pettit also says he saw someone—whom he does not identify—wiping off E.C. with a towel. The Mullendores apparently were satisfied with the clean-up work because Moore got the funeral. Later, Moore told Sheriff Wayman that he had received no instructions from anyone about not touching the corpus delicti that night.

Gene Klutts, the ambulance driver, says he "told the sheriff of Osage County about the fist," and that Sheriff Wayman had replied, apparently by radio, "Well, that's good. Keep it there until we can get somebody there to remove anything in it." But Klutts and Silver drove E.C.'s body from the hospital to Moore's mortuary, and as they placed it on the embalming table, Klutts says he was startled to notice the towel was open and the hand partially cleaned up. "Somebody cleaned him up there at the hospital," Klutts says. He says Silver instructed Gene Hackler, the attendant at the funeral home, that Sheriff Wayman wanted the body left undisturbed. Silver himself says he told both Hackler and Arnold Moore personally that Wayman didn't want the body embalmed or evidence touched, "didn't want to disturb nothing," until after an autopsy was performed.

Gene Hackler says he worked at the funeral home without sleep all night Saturday and all day Sunday, preparing three or four other bodies besides E.C.'s. He says he received no instructions from anybody about not touching anything. He just went ahead and set up the embalming and cosmetic equipment.

Meanwhile, Gene and Kathleen left the hospital. According to Kent Green, "Gene asked me to go out [to the ranch with them afterward], and also a deputy sheriff went out, because the thought at that time was that these individuals that purportedly had done this were still possibly about. And I did go out."

On the way back from Bartlesville, Pig Pettit recalls, Kathleen said, "Oh my land, I want to call the telephone man." So they stopped in Copan, and from a pay booth Kathleen convinced Ma Bell to restore service to the Cross Bell Ranch.

Kathleen: "On the next morning [Sunday], that was the twenty-seventh, Green and his wife was going back to Kansas City to get some clothes, and he said to her to take his gun and asked me if he could borrow one of my guns, and I said, 'sure.'"

Just four days earlier, Green had coaxed a gun out of E.C. in Ponca City by saying he had lent his own .38 to Ginny. But Kathleen didn't know that, so Green collected yet another gun right after the murder. Asked later what happened to the .38 she had been given, Ginny said she had lost it.

Upon getting the gun from Kathleen, Green and Ginny drove off in E.C.'s yellow Lincoln. "I think maybe he went back to Bartlesville," Kathleen says. Later, Ginny went to Kansas City in Green's Eldorado and Green returned to the ranch.

At 6:30 a.m., Mike Burkhart says Green knocked on his door. "He said, 'E.C. and Chub have been shot,' and wanted me to get my pistol and come over to the house to guard. He never did say what, just to guard. I did, as quick as I could."

Later that morning, George Ray saw Green guarding E.C.'s house, and before the day was out, Green was even hobnobbing with John Mecom, Jr.

Burkhart ran into Dale Kuhrt as he arrived at the ranch compound. Light was just breaking, and they made a startling discovery. "You could tell where anybody went from the dew on the grass," Kuhrt recalls. As the beads of dew glistened on the grass, they could see clear footprints where anyone had walked the night before. In some areas, where the ambulance and police cars had driven, Kuhrt says, "you wouldn't have found nothing." But if someone had entered the house through the door to the children's playpen, the one Chub thinks he might have left unlocked, the footprints would be there. And if someone had fled through the grass behind the house, the footprints would reveal it. Only the driveway itself would hide the tracks.

Kuhrt: "We couldn't find any fresh tracks. [In the back yard, the playpen area], we couldn't see anything for footprints that night and couldn't see anything the next morning. We looked along that whole fence [lining the driveway between the houses and route 10]. That fence had dew on it, and if somebody [had] grabbed that fence and tried to climb it, we would have been able to see it. It would have pulled the dew off it."

Burkhart: "We saw where Chub had gone across the lawn to Dale's house, but we found only that one set of tracks. We couldn't find anything in the grass. We looked all over, out in the pasture, we couldn't find any more."

At 11:45 a.m. that Sunday, T. F. Dukes, the Osage County prosecutor, returned home from church. The phone was ringing. Until then, nobody had told him that E. C. Mullendore had been shot to death.

Dukes dashed to the ranch, then to the Moore funeral home in Bartlesville. "When I went into the room where the body was," he says, "there was an attendant working on the body, and cleaning him up, washing the body. And I told him to stop immediately, I wanted to observe the body. He had been working on the hands, and I observed some stuff in [E.C.'s] right hand. And I told him to stop immediately and wait for a technician." Dukes says he called Paul Sterling, a technician for the Oklahoma Bureau of Investigation, who drove right over. E.C.'s fist, Duke says, "was closed, and what I would call rigor mortis, and as I observed the hand, it was clutched, looked like a clot of blood and debris and hair. The technician took it."

Cross Bell Ranch, extending as far as the eye can see. Arrow 1 indicates main house. Arrow 2 indicates house where E.C. was murdered; road to right was getaway route

POLICE DEPT
WICHITA KANSAS
21900
1-24-51

Kent Green

Pictures of the following people
were unavailable to us:
  Leroy Kerwin
  Leon Cohen
  Talmadge Kolb
  Jim Jackson
  David Taylor

Sheriff George Wayman

Cowboys leading riderless horse past Cross Bell flag at half-mast at E.C.'s funeral

Cattle watching funeral procession moving up the hill to E.C.'s burial

Chub surrendering to a U.S. Marshal

Gene and Kathleen coming out of Grand Jury hearing; Gene Stipe in the background

Linda and her lawyer, John Arrington, on the back stairs to the Grand Jury room

But Sheriff Wayman says the technician's sample failed to produce results. He and Dukes later complained that the body had been embalmed before doctors could perform an autopsy or examine blood samples. They blamed the mortuary for preventing certain important tests. Sterling concurs, though he also blames the lawmen for failing to take charge quickly and firmly enough. The mortuary denies doing anything out of the ordinary, and points to the mixed-up police work.

The confusion only sharpened the doubts in Sheriff Wayman's mind about Chub Anderson's story. He decided that as soon as the funeral was over, he would call the young ranch hand in for rigorous questioning. Some kind of charge would have to be filed against Chub.

Twenty-eight

LINDA MULLENDORE SAYS SHE wanted to go to the ranch early that Sunday morning, after hearing of her husband's death, but "I was afraid for me and the children." She had already lived through a harrowing week. Even if Jim Jackson, the ex-con, was hundreds of miles from Tulsa, he wasn't out of Linda's mind, and she thought Jackson and Tal Kolb had been following her. So, at John Arrington, Jr.'s suggestion, she hired Gary Glanz, a strong-arming, lock-picking, former Tulsa policeman who had shrugged off the restraints of the law and gone into private detective work. She wouldn't leave her apartment that Sunday until Glanz arrived with the first of a series of off-duty cops he hired to protect her.

Kay Sutton, who was staying on to do domestic chores for Linda, recalls that "she drug around the house half the morning until they took her up to the ranch. When I saw her, she seemed upset. I didn't know what was wrong with her. After she left, Mrs. Vance said E.C. had got killed and that Chub was wounded but he would be okay."

John Arrington: "The morning after [E.C. was killed], I went to the ranch with Linda and Gary Glanz to express my sympathies, and the first thing I was told by Gene was to go to Atlanta and make sure those [life insurance] premiums were paid. I didn't even discuss it with Linda. She was in a state of shock." But Arrington was at Linda's side when she confronted her father-in-law.

243

Linda: "Gene said, 'I want to make a deal with you. We'll split everything down the middle. You take half and I'll take half. The insurance money, the land, and the cattle.' I couldn't even discuss it. I was in shock for three or four days. I had to go to the funeral home. The children hadn't even been told. I was appalled."

Arrington: "Nobody knew anything about the extent of the indebtedness, how much was owed. He was very insistent that I draw up a document that day. He said, there's no reason it should take any time. 'You draw up a document. You're a good lawyer, supposed to be.' He became very abusive to Linda when she didn't want to talk about it. It was our idea to just run the ranch the same as ever. We couldn't understand why he kept wanting to split everything down the middle. We knew he owned 80 percent of the land." (E.C. had acquired the remaining 20 percent during the 1960's in his own name.)

Linda: "Gene thought that title to all the land was in E.C.'s name, which would have meant that I would have gotten half and the children would have gotten half and he wouldn't have gotten anything. Five or six years before, he had told E.C. to start transferring all the land into his name. E.C. never did anything about it. He felt like if he transferred everything, his dad would feel like he didn't really have any place. E.C. worshipped his father."

Arrington: "As soon as I knew this, I explained to him that the land had not been transferred. There would have been tremendous gift-tax problems. So [Gene] was going to get the land, anyway."

But the land was $10 million in debt. This naturally brought up the subject of insurance. E.C. had bought nearly $1 million in life insurance before he met Cohen and Kerwin, but most of it was pledged against bank loans. He had acquired three policies totaling $15 million in Atlanta. The premium payments had been due September 4 to renew $10 million of this insurance for a second year. (He had taken the additional $5 million policy in December 1969, after the insurance company had rejected Linda's application for medical reasons. That policy was considered paid up through December 1970.) E.C. died the night of September 26–7. But the policies had a thirty-day grace period, which meant that the September 4 policies stayed in effect until October 4 to give the Mullendores an extra chance to pay the premium. Although the full second-year premium on those policies would have exceeded $100,000, Paul Burchett, apparently on E.C.'s instructions, had submitted a check for $16,000. John Arrington, Jr., explains that this small amount was the "net premium" due under a special provision that allowed E.C. to borrow on the cash value of the policies. Why the policies should have held a cash value when E.C. had paid scarcely anything for them is part of the murky agreement E.C. made with Cohen, Kerwin, and United Family Life, an agreement never fully explained.

The $16,000 check Burchett sent to United Family had not yet cleared the bank. Gene was worried that the ranch account lacked sufficient deposits to pay it, and he wanted to cover the check with the $20,000 earned from the sale of cattle in Coffeyville the day before. Somehow Gene knew that Chub hadn't collected the $20,000, although Chub was still in the hospital and would insist later that he hadn't discussed the matter with anyone the night before.

As to whether the cattle had been sold specifically to raise money for the insurance premium, the answer may have gone to the grave with E.C. Gene is unwilling or unable to say. Strangely, the insurance companies, though bent on proving suicide, never pursued the curious question of why the Mullendores might have committed fraud against the PCA, sacrificed part of the dwindling cattle herd, and diverted $16,000 of precious capital just to make a down payment on keeping E.C.'s huge life insurance policies in force a little longer. The companies chose instead to adopt an alternate theory: that E.C. signed the cattle over to Chub to pay the ranch hand for helping E.C. in a suicide plot to collect the insurance. But Paul Burchett insisted that there was never any question but that Chub would return the cattle-sale proceeds to the ranch.

Arrington: "We can't say what the $20,000 was [intended] for. We just knew there was $20,000 available. We were just told there was a premium due. I knew that death relieves the obligation. But out of an excess of caution, [Gene] did express himself very forcefully that we should go to Atlanta. There would be a couple of minutes when he would cry, and then he would express himself the same as ever."

On the instructions of Arrington's law partner, James Kincaid, Paul Burchett rang Harold Copper on the phone and told him about the $16,000 insurance premium check. Burchett said he wasn't sure the Mullendores had enough money on deposit to cover it, and that in any case the bank would have frozen E.C.'s account upon his death. "We wanted to be sure there wouldn't be any slipup," Burchett says, "so I called him and said, 'Now we have this money, enough to pay the premium, and I want to ask you right now if we can use that money to pay the premium.'"

Copper, in what he later described as a gesture of sympathy, agreed to release the cattle-sale funds. This sent Dale Kuhrt dashing to Coffeyville, where he collected the sale checks, then back to get Chub's endorsement on them. Arrington then hopped a plane to Atlanta, where he personally met the $20,000 as it arrived by wire. But United Family said the cash wasn't required. E.C.'s account there was paid up when he died; that much was not in dispute.

This crisis settled, there began a hunt for the insurance policies. Two $5 million policies were known to be at the two Atlanta banks holding them as collateral. But Edward Kurtz, the Tulsa accountant who had prepared a financial statement for E.C. the previous spring, was startled to get a phone call from Arrington's law firm asking the whereabouts of the third $5 million policy. He said he didn't know.

In this state of confusion, only two days after E.C. was buried, John Arrington, whose law practice normally involved the representation of large corporations before government regulatory bodies, went winging back to Atlanta in quest of the two hoodlum insurance agents who might hold the key to the Cross Bell Ranch. Linda Mullendore, despite her shock, gathered the emotional wherewithal to accompany him.

They met not only Leon Cohen—who, it turned out, had held on to the third policy—but also James Foreman, president of United Family Life Insurance Company. Both men assured them all three policies existed and that the insurance money would be paid in about ninety days. Linda also checked in at the First National Bank and Fulton National Bank in Atlanta, where E.C. had assigned two $5 million policies to collateralize loans. Linda: "I went to the bank and I told them that as soon as the insurance money was paid that they would get their money [a foregone conclusion since the bank held an assignment of the policy as collateral for the loan] and I wanted to thank them for loaning the money to E.C." She and Arrington also took time to examine the terms of the document E.C. had given the bank.

"How is the tension up there now?" Sheriff Wayman asked Paul Kelly a week after the murder.

"Someone say 'boo,' I am already gone," Kelly replied, and

added, "If Linda doesn't put that insurance money in there, [the ranch] is lost, because right now, as far as my end of it, we aren't doing a thing. We can't get diesel fuel to run our tractors. I think the fuel man would bring it out, but you don't know when he would get paid. I am not gonna cause a businessman to lose money. The old man is trying to authorize [it], but I don't think he has the right."

Needing cash to run the ranch until she received the insurance money, Linda applied to the PCA for another $100,000. On October 7, the PCA agreed to lend the money and took an assignment of the third $5 million policy as collateral.

On October 2, Kathleen announced to the papers that the Mullendore family was "not about to give [the ranch] up now. Everyone in big business has to borrow money. It is not at all uncommon. If you are not in debt in a small way, you are not making progress. The affairs of this ranch will be straightened out, and it will be preserved both as my husband and our son intended."

Meanwhile, the murder investigation had moved from its bungled first stages into even further confusion.

Henry Catron, the aging Dewey policeman who drove Chub Anderson from the outskirts of Bartlesville to the hospital after the murder, delivered some of Chub's personal effects the next day to Osage County Deputy Sheriff Rudy Briggs. Only after Briggs brought the gear back to Sheriff Wayman's office did he discover what may have been the most important single piece of evidence in the case. Briggs says he was inspecting Chub's hat when he saw something glisten from the right front brim near the band. Eyeing it closely, Briggs says he determined that it was a small piece of human bone stuck on the hat among some blood. The piece of bone was roughly diamond-shaped—about the same size and shape as a small piece of bone missing from E.C.'s head. If Briggs could get the bone sample analyzed, and it was proved to have come from E.C., that would establish that Chub was with E.C. when the rancher suffered his fatal wound, rather than having come upon E.C. afterward as Chub had told everyone at the hospital. That might solve the whole case!

Briggs set the hat aside in the sheriff's office and typed up his official report, including a line about the hat and about the thing that appeared to be a piece of human skull. Then he left the office. Later, he says, he returned to get the hat to take it to the Oklahoma Bureau of Investigation crime lab for analysis. And, he says, the bone was missing. In an interview with the author, Briggs theorized that one of the other deputies tried on the hat as a joke and knocked off the crucial evidence without ever having noticed it was there. It was never found.

Briggs says he and Sheriff Wayman decided to keep the incident secret. Perhaps they could use it someday to surprise Chub into confessing. They didn't even tell the Osage County prosecutor's office about the piece of bone, Briggs says, because that office had shown such a propensity for leaking information and misinformation to the press. Indeed, it had.

For example, an assistant prosecutor inspecting E.C.'s body at the funeral parlor observed that the gashes on the top of his head were U-shaped. Somebody suggested that the gashes were in the shape of the bottom half of the Cross Bell Ranch brand— the bell part with the cross removed. So the assistant prosecutor told questioning reporters that E.C.'s assailant had beaten the young rancher over the head with a branding iron. It made a hell of a good story and was widely printed.

On sober reflection, and in the absence of a branding iron, Sheriff Wayman later concluded that E.C. had been slugged with the butt end of a pistol, which also would have left a U-shaped mark. Possibly, he thought, it was the same .38 pistol, still missing, that had sent the bullet through E.C.'s forehead, and that—just before or just afterward—had hurled another bullet through Chub Anderson's arm.

Deputies found a spent .38 slug behind a cushion of the divan E.C.'s body was resting against, and another imbedded in the wall behind E.C.

After the authorities had finished "going over the place with a fine-tooth comb," Lula Harrison brought Kathleen inside, took her over to the ironing board cupboard, and gave her back the pistol Mrs. Harrison had hidden there the week before the murder. No one had touched it. Mrs. Harrison says she doesn't know what caliber the pistol was. It went back into the family gun collection.

Osage County Prosecutor Dukes was confronted that week by a television camera and a reporter asking him to explain his criticism of the investigation conducted by Washington County officials immediately after the murder. "It would probably take a treatise to answer that question," Dukes said. "It was badly handled, and I made an exhaustive investigation as to find out why, and whether or not it be surreptitious or ulterior motives, and even a lot of *that* evidence would be confidential and private and probably shouldn't be divulged until the crime is settled and disposed of, because it might hurt some individuals and might also hinder the investigation."

On September 29, Dukes complained to the *Tulsa World* that there were "too many motives and clues." But the next day, he told the *World* he had received "some very startling news" and "critical evidence. We've reached a most satisfactory point in the investigation," he said. "We're all very hopeful that we will get a solution much quicker than we thought, unless this blows up in our faces. I'm optimistic we're on the right track, and as a lawyer, I've reached the point where I don't want to take any chance on violating anyone's civil rights. There is a question in our minds just how many are involved and if some could be from out of state."

On October 1, Dukes expressed "cautious optimism" to *The Tulsa Tribune.* The prosecutor declared, "I've reached the point that . . . well, it's just fantastic. I can't believe it. As a lawyer, I've reached the point that I cannot tell you any more right now. There is a question as to just who and how many people are involved. But the thing that shocks me is that it fits in with what you have printed in the *Tribune.*" The *Tribune* had printed nothing more than a cursory summation of E.C.'s financial difficulties and his search for a loan.

That same day, October 1, Sheriff Wayman brought Chub Anderson in for questioning. The Osage County courthouse, where Wayman keeps his office, sits on a high bluff overlooking the rest of Pawhuska. To enter the front door, the visitor on foot must climb an enormous embankment of stone steps. Most people ascend the steep, sloping driveway to the back door. By either route, you are going to arrive gasping and panting for breath, while Wayman greets you fresh in his air-conditioned office. He always has the advantage. Beside Wayman's chair is a metal spittoon for the long swills of juice from his chaw of Beech Nut. He uses the spittoon every three or four minutes.

Chub answered questions from 10:55 a.m. until 6:07 p.m. that day, pausing only for the stenographer to limber her knuckles occasionally. No lawyer was present. This is what Chub said had happened after he and E.C. returned from Gose's house the night of the murder:

"We went downstairs and he was hungry and said let's go in here and heat something to eat. Somebody had a big crockery of stew on the stove and a big bowl of beans, and he had turned on the stove and was heating this up and he had got out a couple of trays to fix us a plate, and I told him I wasn't hungry. I was tired and wanted to go to bed, and he told me he had a headache and wanted me to go find some Alka-Seltzers. I went up to his bathroom and found a bottle and took it downstairs, and all that was in it was two styrofoam spacers in it. I told him I would run back upstairs and look for some more and he said no, after he ate he would feel better, anyway. I talked to him there for just a little bit. Few words were said, and he started stirring this stew and beans and eating out of the crocker and hadn't dished any in a bowl yet, and I went on upstairs, and the house was kind of cold. Two or three days before this, Dale and I came in and Gene was lying downstairs with a blanket, in E.C.'s house, and wanted me to see what was wrong with the heating, and the pilot light had blown out of the furnace and I had lit it at that time, and I guess it had blown out [again]." Chub dwelt on the temperature apparently to parry Sheriff Wayman's curiosity about why he kept his hat and coat on the whole time. E.C. also had his coat on when he was shot.

"It was fairly chilly and I went upstairs and was drawing my bath water, and I was gonna turn on this heater and heat up the bathroom, and I had just turned off the bath water and got out the towel and [I] heard the shot—what I thought to be a shot. I ran back downstairs and I could see E.C. before I got down the stairs. He was sitting right in front of the couch with his head propped over forward, and immediately after I entered the room, I felt the shot, and [it] knocked me over forward, like somebody hit me real hard with their fist; then I felt a burning, and I wasn't down but just an instant and I heard somebody running up the stairs out of my view and I jumped up and I had a little .25 automatic in my belt, and as I got to the top of the first flight of stairs, I could see somebody run down the porch, just got a quick glimpse of them, and I ran on up the steps, out on the porch, and I shot, I don't know how many times, five or six times. And they were immediately out of sight again, running east. Then I ran to where I had shot at them and looked out and couldn't see them, and then I ran back to the head of the stairs outside, and I hesitated a minute before I ran up to that. They ran up the driveway. The last time I saw them, they were just below the low-water bridge. The same moment my gun was emptied, I took off, running for Dale's house."

On questioning, Chub said he was within five or six feet of where E.C. sat propped against the furniture when he felt the shot enter his arm. He had seen no one out of the corner of his eye from the time he came downstairs. He thought the shooter was "real close" to him. "It was real loud. My right ear rang for a long time." He said he was "kind of facing E.C. and the couch. I just ran down the stairs, dumbfounded, standing in front of the couch." When he fell, "I think I might have hit the edge of the couch, but I did not fall on [E.C.]. More or less in front of the couch." He said he had been in the house perhaps twenty minutes and was upstairs drawing the bath water for "ten or fifteen minutes" when he heard the first shot.

Sheriff Wayman struggled for a description of the assailants. "I can't tell you if they wore suits or not," Chub said, "but they were dressed in slacks and had on dark coats. I am almost sure they were bareheaded. I couldn't tell you if they had on boots or not. They were probably maybe my height, maybe not that tall. E.C. always turned out the lights to save on the electric bill. I couldn't swear to which ones were on or off, but it wasn't too lit up downstairs." Chub said he heard no voices, either upstairs or downstairs.

The sheriff left the interview with a lot of unanswered questions. By Chub's account, he and E.C. had been in the house the second time—after returning from Gose's—for just about as long as they were in it the first time—after E.C. returned from the car race with his mother. Why, then, did Chub take his coat off the first time, so that when they went out he had to put on a different coat, and yet the second time keep his coat and hat on? By Chub's account, he had finished drawing the bath water and turned it off before he heard the first shot. Aside from the peculiar circumstance that Chub still had his hat and coat on and a gun in his belt, why were there only three to four inches of water in the tub when investigators arrived that night? Could Chub have been drawing the water the first time he and E.C. were home and been called away suddenly when E.C. wanted to go make a phone call?

Both Lula Harrison and Julia Gilkey insist that E.C. and his entire household, including Linda and Chub, had practically a fetish about keeping doors locked. "E.C. did not at no time leave the doors open," swears Mrs. Gilkey. "I used to get mad. You would be taking something over there and could not get in for love or money." How could E.C. have driven off that night to make a phone call, leaving the house open?

Considering the unusual design of E.C.'s house, a converted cabana, would professional killers have descended the stairway into the den, from which there was no other exit, leaving E.C.'s armed bodyguard between them and escape? With neither the television nor the radio on, wouldn't they have heard Chub drawing the bath water and thought to take care of him?

The assailants allegedly fled through two sets of sliding glass doors. The first set led from the living room onto the glass-enclosed porch, and the next set from the porch to the walk. Immediately outside the second set of doors, the walk turned right, alongside the house to the parking lot. If the intruders had run straight, across the yard, instead of turning along the walk, they presumably would have left footprints in the dew. No footprints were found. Chub says they followed the walk to the parking lot. Why, then, did he empty his gun shooting straight ahead through the second set of doors? He said his aim was off because the wound in his right arm forced him to shoot left-handed. But if the door was partially open to allow the gunmen out, would all six shots have gone through the glass, as they did, instead of through the opening? Chub said he started shooting "just as I had come out the first glass door going onto the porch. I did see the backs of someone going out the door." But he agreed "they could have been out of view" by the time he got the last shot off.

Sheriff Wayman would have liked to put Chub's story to a

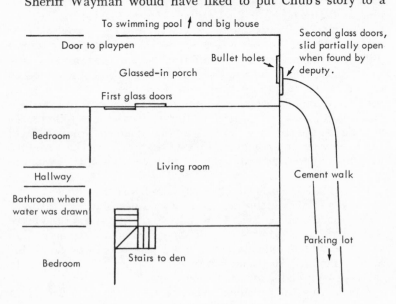

To swimming pool and big house

Door to playpen

Bullet holes

Second glass doors, slid partially open when found by deputy.

Glassed-in porch

First glass doors

Bedroom

Living room

Hallway

Cement walk

Bathroom where water was drawn

Stairs to den

Parking lot

Bedroom

252

scientific test. For example, a laboratory technician can spread paraffin on a man's hands and tell with considerable accuracy whether the man has fired a gun recently. Guns leave powder traces that paraffin can detect. If a test had shown that E. C. Mullendore had fired a gun shortly before he was killed, that might have given new insight into how Chub got shot in the shoulder. Suicide pacts aside, the theory then might have been that E.C. shot Chub just after they arrived home, perhaps in the midst of an argument. After all, they had plenty to argue about. Possibly E.C. found out about Chub's failure to collect the $20,000 at Coffeyville, or about Chub's attempted betrayal of E.C. to Linda. Possibly Chub debated too strenuously against E.C.'s plan to sign an agreement with Kent Green the next morning, giving Green claim to the ranch despite Linda's absence. If E.C. took the first shot, intentionally dealing Chub a minor wound, one could theorize that Chub grabbed the gun out of his boss's hand in a rage after months of abuse and retaliated. On the other hand, since the angle of Chub's wound practically ruled out self-infliction, a negative paraffin test on E.C. might have lent considerable weight to Chub's tale about the intruders. Moreover, a paraffin test on Chub's right hand might have had some bearing on the lingering suspicions, since Chub said he shot only with his left.

Sheriff Wayman says he ordered a paraffin test on E.C.'s hands while the body still lay at the mortuary. He says the test results were inconclusive because the funeral attendants had already cleaned off E.C.'s hands. Apparently, no test on Chub's right hand was ever ordered or taken.

In the absence of scientific evidence, there remained only tough cross-examination to quiet the doubts about Chub's story. But nearly one year would pass before an experienced trial lawyer finally got Chub Anderson under oath in the witness chair to talk about the Mullendore murder.

Twenty-nine   IN THE WEEKS AFTER E.C.'s death, Linda says that she and her insurance lawyer, John Arrington, Jr., went to the ranch "three different times to discuss financial business. I planned to move back immediately, and take the children back. We tried to run the ranch the best way we could. And Gene just . . . well . . . E. was the only person who could talk to his father. [Gene] wouldn't listen. Not to me, not Kathleen, not anybody."

Arrington: "There were two basic problems. First, with E.C. gone, there was no insulation, there was no buffer any longer, [between Gene and] Kuhrt and the people who were trying to run the ranch under our direction. [Second], since E.C. had been running the operation, the debts were for the most part in his name . . . His estate was the only entity that could operate the ranch up there legally. We rushed into court, got all the necessary orders that authorized us to carry on the business. Linda went to PCA, and in order to get a loan of $100,000, which we felt would tide us over until the policies could be collected, she assigned an interest in a policy, and they made us secure their entire loan. Nobody else would have loaned money under any circumstances."

Linda: "No one would loan Gene money."

Arrington: "We were trying to operate the ranch. Well, there was continuing friction, continuing interference, continuing objection to whatever we tried to do . . . Every other day there would be a new objection. [Gene would] call up Dale, call me . . . call [Linda] . . . and talk for a long time. It made it extremely difficult, and we did everything we could to placate him and keep him informed, but he was not able to stand the idea of someone else running his ranch. I mean, E.C. was just an extension of him, as far as he was concerned, but when it was actually someone else running the ranch, no one could do it right."

November 1970 brought reverses to various persons connected with the Mullendores. Osage County Prosecutor T. F. Dukes, leaving a trail of unfulfilled promises about solving the murder case, was voted out of office in his bid for re-election.

John W. Mecom, Sr., was forced to surrender his worldwide oil empire to a federal bankruptcy court, after more than a year of financial difficulty. Basically the empire remained solid, and Mecom would refinance it and take it out of bankruptcy a year later. But in the 1970 credit crunch, several banks called their outstanding loans to the Mecoms, who were caught without cash. Certainly they were in no position to help their kin in Oklahoma.

The probate judge in Pawhuska granted Linda Mullendore a $1,000-a-month allowance for her and the children to live on.

After rent and groceries, the allowance wouldn't buy very many fur coats at Neiman-Marcus. And Linda may well have shed a tear or two when the auctioneer's hammer fell on her dream house in Bartlesville.

But the worst disaster of all had occurred in a conference room at O'Hare Airport in Chicago. There, a week or so after the murder, representatives of six major insurance companies— Connecticut General Life, Continental Assurance, Republic National Life, Occidental Life, Lincoln National Life and General Reassurance Corporation—had gathered to discuss the $15 million claim of Linda Mullendore. They considered it the largest single life insurance claim on record in the United States. Little United Family Life, in Atlanta, had kept only $40,000 of the total policy on its own books. It sent the remaining $14,960,000 to General Reassurance Corporation, which distributed the risk among more than one hundred companies around the country. No company held more than $500,000 of the coverage. Insurance companies often reinsure large policies in this manner so that no one of them can be crushed by a single giant claim. The network of underwriters on the Mullendore policy agreed to let representatives of the six designated companies determine strategy for all of them. In that airport conference room, the six men voted to fight. They took time to chart their legal course carefully and waited until February to notify Linda that they were rejecting her claim. But by November, their intentions had become evident.

That's when the phone calls started from Atlanta. Leon Cohen and Leroy Kerwin needed money. They had an IOU from E.C. for $322,745. They knew that if the insurance companies challenged the manner in which they had issued E.C.'s policies, Linda would need them to testify on her behalf. Several times they called to ask for a guarantee that their note from E.C. would be paid when the insurance policies were made good. Linda says that Cohen and Kerwin didn't talk to her about testifying, and that she doesn't recall that they threatened her. Of course, she says, she "was very upset at that time" and might not recall. But threat or no threat, neither Linda nor John Arrington needed reminding that in the event of a lawsuit, the two hoods would be sharing their canoe and had better be paddling in Linda's direction. So on November 24, 1970, Leon Cohen was invited to settle himself on the sofa in John Arrington's well-appointed office in Tulsa.

Linda: "I came down to the office, and Leon had been there

for quite some time, and he asked me if I would sign the note. He told me that he was in financial difficulty, and this would help him, and E.C. owed this, and I said, 'Certainly, I will be happy to sign the note.' And that was all."

Although E.C. had agreed to pay only $322,745, Linda's note was for $350,000, to be paid as soon as the insurance was paid. Linda explains that the extra money represented "interest" in an amount that she, Cohen, and an Arrington law partner had "arrived at."

Linda: "Leon Cohen was a friend of my husband. He came to me and told me that my husband owed him this money and asked me to sign a note because he himself was in financial difficulty, and because of their friendship I signed the note, and I would be happy to sign other notes if I had been asked."

By December, relations among the Mullendores, already strained, simply collapsed. Says Arrington: "After I told [Gene] it was his land, he kept on saying, 'There's got to be a settlement. There's got to be a contract.'"

Linda: "I didn't care if any of the land was in my name. We offered to divide it in any way, between Katsy's children and my children—any way that would have insured that my children would get some of that land. Gene told me he never wanted any of my children to set foot on the ranch again."

Linda says Gene even insisted that E.C.'s Osage Indian headright be transferred back to Gene rather than passed on to the children. Because of E.C.'s Indian blood, however, the law forbade transfer of the headright except through a will.

George Ray: "They could not get together without Gene bemeaning her, blaming her for E.C.'s death. It finally became impossible for Linda to go back to the ranch."

Arrington: "We offered to give them *all* the cash if they would agree to leave that land to the children. But [Gene] would not agree to any agreement that would have assured Linda's children land. We finally saw there was no other solution than to settle for cash."

So in December the Mullendores signed an accord under which Linda would get $5 million of the $15 million insurance, the lawyers for her and for the family would divide $500,000, and Gene and Kathleen would get the rest; Gene and Kathleen would get all the land except the Sedan, Kansas, ranch, and, in return, would indemnify Linda against all the debts accumulated during E.C.'s lifetime. Linda had signed on almost $9 million of the ranch's indebtedness, and still other creditors were likely to materialize if she collected the insurance without a prearranged settlement. Under the agreement, she would move onto the Sedan ranch—5,000 owned and 2,500 leased acres—and let the creditors line up at Gene's door in Oklahoma. Their own position thus cemented, and with Cohen and Kerwin virtually under contract, all three Mullendores prepared to face the united forces of the American insurance industry. Linda and her mother moved into a private house in Tulsa, under tight security arrangements. On February 10, 1971, United Family Life formally notified her they were denying the claim on grounds of fraud. Primarily, the company said that E.C. had misrepresented his financial condition to the Retail Credit Company investigator whose erroneous report led to issuance of the policies. On February 23, Linda, joined by First National and Fulton National Banks of Atlanta and the Ponca City Production Credit Association, sued United Life to force payment. The struggle was on.

Meanwhile, Sheriff Wayman and other authorities were trying out theory after theory to explain E.C.'s death. Could angry creditors have murdered the rancher so they could collect their bills from the proceeds of the insurance? The sheriff posed the idea to Dale Kuhrt and Paul Burchett, who dismissed it flatly. Except for one or two bank officers, E.C.'s creditors were most amiable, they said.

Was E.C. the victim of a Mafia contract? Tulsa police received a tip from Cleo G. Epps, sixty-six, known as the Queen of Bootleggers. Mrs. Epps, a long-time organized-crime figure in the Tulsa area, had been leaking information to the authorities there in recent years—the exact arrangement is still a secret. But Mrs. Epps mentioned in one of her briefing sessions that two Jewish men had come to Tulsa late that summer looking for a professional killer they could hire. That was all. Osage authorities never got to question Mrs. Epps; she had given her last performance as an informant. She disappeared from the scene in November and, on February 24, 1971, was found dead at the bottom of a septic tank.

Then there was the possibility of a love triangle. Sheriff Wayman asked repeatedly if Chub and Linda had been having an affair. These were some of the answers he got:

Kathleen: "Well, I don't want to . . . all I can say is that they went fishing, hunting, and frog hunting all the time together with the children, and went to Tulsa together. Coming home that night [after the murder] the first thing I thought of was Chub, and I asked Gene if he thought he could . . . but now I don't know. [E.C.] was not a hand to ever talk about it to me."

George Ray: "I have heard rumors and I have heard some sly remarks, and I passed them off. I certainly didn't believe it. Just some sly remarks among the cowboys."

Mike Burkhart: "I have heard some, just kind of joking about Chub and Linda having a little affair. I don't know if anyone knew anything. It didn't make any difference whether they did or not, they would still be joking about it. He was around the children a lot, taking them to school."

Mrs. Harrison: "I don't know. You know, people think something is wrong when there isn't nothing wrong. When they was together, the boys was all with them. When they would go swimming or sunbathing and hunting or horseback riding, they was all together."

Mrs. Harrison, however, also cited remarks by both E.C. and Katsy indicating that they suspected Linda, Jr., was not by blood a Mullendore. Alarmed over recurring rumors that Chub, not E.C., was the father of her fourth child, Linda eventually brought the ranch hand to a doctor for a blood test. The test was risky because it might have proven inconclusive, serving only to throw more fuel on the rumors. But Linda came away with a doctor's certificate attesting that Chub couldn't possibly have fathered her baby.

A reporter asked Gene Mullendore about Chub and Linda and he replied, "There's a lot of difference between getting up on the stand and saying, 'I know this,' and when they say, 'Why do you know it?' It's just surmise. You can't bring a fellow up on surmise. Sure, you would have gotten mad. I would have gotten mad. But E.C. never talked about it. He had learned to be close-mouthed. He kept his troubles to himself. I think I can answer your question, but it wouldn't do any good until after this [insurance case] is over. You come on down here after it's over and I'll tell you what I think." After the insurance case was over, Gene canceled the invitation.

Unable to find solid evidence on the love triangle theory, the sheriff dropped it. Whatever the truth, it would matter little in court, anyway. No one who met her would believe that the prim, charm-schooled, status-conscious, would-be princess from Pawhuska had seriously considered a permanent relationship with a welder who had a prison record and lacked a formal education, even if he did look like Mr. America. And if Sheriff Wayman could establish a factual case against Chub, he would have a plethora of other motives to choose from without resorting to a love triangle.

On October 25, 1970, Chub Anderson was arrested and charged with a parole violation for firing a pistol the night E.C. was murdered, and for having another pistol with him in his car as he drove to the hospital. Early in December, he went to jail for several days in lieu of $10,000 bail on an additional charge of violating federal gun laws. When he had bought his pistol in Ponca City, he had given false information, using E.C.'s driver's license instead of his own.

Things indeed were looking down for Chub until Patrick A. Williams entered his life. Williams was a rather high-powered lawyer for a ranch hand facing misdemeanor charges. He had served as district attorney of Osage County, and chief prosecutor of Tulsa County, then entered private law practice with David Hall. In 1970 Hall was elected governor of Oklahoma, and Williams was master of ceremonies at the inauguration.

With all the publicity attendant to the Mullendore case, Williams managed to churn up enough enthusiasm to defend the ranch hand in super style. After Chub had made bond, Williams decided to prepare for trial on the federal gun charge by clearing Chub's record of the cattle-rustling conviction. Then Chub would be able to testify for his own defense without disclosing a criminal past. Moreover, by wiping out the rustling conviction, they would automatically dispose of the parole violation charges. So Williams filed to vacate the 1965 conviction on the grounds that police failed to advise Chub of his constitutional rights before interrogating him, as the 1966 Miranda decision required them to do. Also, Williams said, Chub "was never advised that, notwithstanding a plea of guilty, he had the right to appeal the case."

Williams never got to establish whether his argument was sound. A red-faced prosecutor from Washington County arose before the judge and confessed that his office could "not exactly" oppose the appeal because it had lost the records from Chub's case. So the conviction was overturned by default. Had he been aware of it, the prosecutor might have offered the judge Chub's stenotyped statement to Sheriff Wayman. The sheriff had asked Chub, "Who did you steal the livestock from?" to which Chub had replied, "I don't recall the fellow's name at this time," and then had proceeded to describe how he had committed that crime and two similar thefts. But Chub didn't have a lawyer present at that session either, so Williams probably would have won out, anyway.

With the rustling conviction overturned, the path was clear for a sterling performance by Williams and Chub at the gun trial in Oklahoma City in March. Despite clear testimony that Chub had bought a gun using E.C.'s driver's license, the jury acquitted him on his eloquent plea that he had only done what his boss had asked him to.

Chub would have to take the witness stand a few months later, however, and this time he would be questioned about the murder of E. C. Mullendore.

Thirty   ON JUNE 13, 1971, TORONTO, CANADA, WAS just thawing from the previous winter's snows. Some thirty-three miles north of the city, a bottle collector was walking a lonely backwoods road when he spotted some human toes protruding from the muck off to the side. The body connected to those toes had decomposed so badly that police spent four days, cutting off finger after finger and soaking them in fixing solution, before finally obtaining the one print that said it was Leroy Kerwin.

Police in Atlanta had listed Kerwin as missing since December 3, 1970, when he boarded a plane for Toronto and didn't return. Whoever met him at the airport had pumped two bullets into his head.

The authorities didn't have to wait long to satisfy their suspicions that Kerwin's murder was Mafia work. On June 24, some shoppers in a Montreal suburb complained of the stench coming from the trunk of a car abandoned in a parking lot. Opening the trunk, police found the rotting body of Theodore Yanovich. They knew Yanovich, alias Teddy Young, as a loan-shark enforcer for the Cotroni family, which controls organized crime in eastern Canada.

The authorities concluded that Yanovich, who knew Kerwin,

killed him and then was executed himself. Shivering in that Canadian December night, the dim-witted muscleman had given up spading the frozen turf before making sure that Kerwin was deep enough to stay buried. With Kerwin's fate known, the police were certain to come asking questions that Yanovich might have been able to answer, about who ordered Kerwin to his untimely end. So, presumably, Yanovich was done away with.

Concerned as they were by Kerwin's demise, government agents were even more interested in what a migrant worker found in a ditch two miles from the body: Kerwin's briefcase. This black attaché case, its triple combination lock broken but its contents preserved from the winter's snows, bulged with documents, many of them incriminating. The papers ranged from multimillion-dollar insurance agreements to the sale contract for Mrs. Kerwin's Maltese dog, Princess Mitzi. They tied Kerwin to his swindler friends in Florida and his prominent businessman friends in Texas.

The attaché case contained securities, endorsed and in marketable condition, with a face value in the millions of dollars. There were stock shares in worthless corporations, such as the inactive metals company that Kerwin and Audsley had been selling stock in, and there were shares in Morris Jaffe's First Financial Life Insurance Company. There were documents relating to the Texas Trust Company swindle. There was the original copy of the $350,000 IOU that Linda Mullendore had given to Leon Cohen just ten days before Kerwin vanished. And there was a hand-scrawled note, written sometime before December 3, which said, "Arr. prob. for Chubb."

Law enforcement authorities called this mass of evidence the Kerwin Papers. On June 23, 1971, the papers were the subject of an all-day seminar at the Georgia State Capitol, involving representatives of the FBI, the Securities and Exchange Commission, the Postal Inspector's office, the Comptroller General's office, the Ontario Provincial Police and four Georgia state agencies. This meeting produced more questions than answers. Promised indictments never came. Georgia investigators later complained that after giving themselves a two-month crash course on corporate finance and insurance operations, they were told by the state attorney general to drop the case because it belonged to federal jurisdiction.

The papers make up part of a jigsaw puzzle, fitting together

261

with other papers found in Florida, Georgia, and Texas. Some pieces of the puzzle are still missing, but the picture is clear. It shows Leroy Kerwin's world crashing down around him.

On November 6, 1970, (Mr.) Nola White, first assistant attorney general of Texas, effectively broke up the Texas Trust Company scheme. White wrote letters on that date to Morris Jaffe, the San Antonio financier who owned Texas Trust, and to Herbert Woll, the Atlanta accountant who worked with Cohen and Kerwin, demanding an explanation for the complaints that were pouring in to White's office.

The suckers who had paid Audsley and Prugh tens of thousands of dollars in Fort Lauderdale for Texas Trust loan commitment letters had begun taking the letters to banks to use as collateral for loans. The letters promised that Texas Trust would pay off the bank loans after a year or two. Of course, the letters were virtually worthless because Texas Trust was virtually worthless.

White, the assistant attorney general, and Jaffe differ sharply over what happened. Jaffe insists that Kerwin devised the swindling scheme without telling him. Jaffe says he was furious at Kerwin when he learned of it. "A banker notified me that he had received an inquiry from another bank regarding Texas Trust on a [loan commitment] letter. I decided to go to the attorney general of Texas. The letter that you saw from the attorney general's office was composed by me and requested by me so that I could confront Mr. Kerwin."

White, however, denies he talked to Jaffe at all before sending out the letters that demolished the Texas Trust con. "I had two or three different banks over the state to call this office wanting to know about this company," he says. "That's what caused the letters." On checking Texas Trust's corporate records, White says, "I found they had practically no assets—something like $25,000 total. After I found out what they were worth, I called the banks immediately. In a very short period of time, there would have been actual loans." He says the loans he learned of totaled $320,000, and that three "prominent Texas banks" were involved, although he won't name them.

"Insofar as I know, there were no loans made in Texas," White says. "I have heard since then that this same group of people fleeced a lot of men in Florida and Georgia with the Texas Trust Company. I advised Mr. Jaffe of this matter. He had already talked to the FBI about it because of the repercussions from some transactions in Florida. Mr. Jaffe did offer to go over his records with me, but I was unable to tell anything at all about them. On the surface—on the surface, that is—it would appear he had clean hands in the matter. Since I knew that he was in touch with the FBI or they were in touch with him, I figured I would leave the matter." The investigation apparently stopped there.

Considering how much there was to find out, particularly about the fraudulent Audsley-Prugh operation in Fort Lauderdale, and considering that the FBI usually succeeds when it tries hard, the federal government appears to have paid scant attention to the Texas Trust matter. Authorities weren't reminded of it until the discovery of Kerwin's briefcase in Toronto the next spring. Even then, without Kerwin's testimony to explain the documents, many questions remained unanswered.

Kerwin's name was there alone on the correspondence of Texas Trust, as it was on the correspondence of Cohen, Kerwin, White & Associates. Kerwin's job at the agency was to handle the paper work and correspondence. Cohen and Jaffe steadfastly denied—as they deny to this day—that they knew anything about the Texas Trust operation until the banks complained. They blame it all on Kerwin.

Kerwin's friends did not stand by him in his time of adversity. Jaffe says he fired Kerwin from the consultant's job at First Financial Life immediately after the attorney general's office sent its letter November 6. On November 9, Cohen signed a new contract with Alexander Hamilton Life's marketing company, specifically excluding Kerwin from participating in Cohen's commissions. "Mr. Kerwin will make his own arrangements with Hamilton," the contract said. Kerwin began negotiating with Hamilton's lawyer for a contract, but died before they agreed on one. Meanwhile, First Financial Life appointed Cohen personally, not the Cohen-Kerwin agency, as its exclusive agent.

Cohen and Kerwin even prepared to sell their insurance agency, and negotiated a contract with National Processors, Inc., of Dallas. Like so many other things Cohen and Kerwin arranged, the deal looked shady. According to its corporate charter, National Processors was organized to sell meat, meat products, and seafood, rather than insurance. The company's registered agent is listed as J. H. Jones, 1001 Sargeant Road, Dallas. The telephone company reports no listing for a J. H. Jones at that address.

Tom Thomas, the partner in Nashwood Corporation, also was

involved. He had left the Waggoner Carr law office to form his own firm. In November 1970, the Sharpstown Bank scandal, which would involve both Thomas and Carr, was still two months from public disclosure. Thomas says he continued as Leon Cohen's attorney until that November, when he switched over to represent National Processors in buying the insurance agency from Cohen and Kerwin. Thomas says the deal fell through after Kerwin disappeared December 3, because the principals of National Processors—he won't name them—found out that Cohen, Kerwin, White & Associates was not worth the $3.5 million that Herbert Woll, the accountant, said it was worth.

Until the date of his disappearance, Kerwin continued to share the office with Cohen in Atlanta. A document found the next spring showed that they were planning to buy large quantities of suits, sportswear, and other clothes for themselves that December and charge them to the agency as Christmas gift expenses.

Kerwin was preparing to move to Dallas, however. He and his wife contracted to buy a house there for $70,000, and he was in the process of buying the Freed Furniture Store, Dallas's second largest, from Joe Freed, a director of First Financial Life Insurance Company. Kerwin visited the store the day before his fatal trip to Toronto. To represent him in the Freed transaction, Kerwin said he had hired—who else?—Tom Thomas. A secretary in the Cohen-Kerwin office later told Georgia police that Thomas was scheduled to meet Kerwin immediately after his return flight from Toronto—the flight Kerwin never made. Thomas denies this.

Kerwin had two announced pieces of business to take care of in Toronto: securing a loan to buy furniture for Art Powell, the former Buffalo Bills football star, and arranging one of his special $1 million insurance policies for John Barry, a Toronto tavern owner and showman. Powell and Barry were among many clients Cohen and Kerwin obtained through a friend of Kerwin's in Chicago who represented professional athletes in their business affairs. The friend, Barry Rimmerman, was such a valuable source of clients that he would get phone calls from Morris Jaffe when the Texan was in Chicago, and airline tickets from Kerwin, who got them free from Alexander Hamilton Life.

Art Powell, the football player, ran up a bill for $5,480 at the furniture store Kerwin was buying. (Powell says now he was "amazed" to learn of Kerwin's past from newspaper accounts of the agent's disappearance, and adds, "I wouldn't have bought tiddledywinks from him if I had known where he was at.") Joe Freed, not having sold his furniture store to Kerwin yet, was nervous about extending so much credit to Powell.

Powell, like many other athletes, often hung around the Humber House bar in Toronto, which was owned by John Barry. Kerwin intended to fly to Toronto the next day anyway to discuss the proposed $1 million insurance policy on Barry, so Kerwin arranged to ask the tavern owner to guarantee Art Powell's credit note to Freed Furniture for $5,480.

Barry had started out as a miner in Sudbury, Ontario, but rose fast in the world. While running the Humber House, he began producing grandstand shows at the Canadian National Exhibition in Toronto, where he provided such prominent entertainers as Tom Jones and Engelbert Humperdinck. He had met Kerwin at a party at Rimmerman's house in Chicago and mentioned that he wanted to borrow $500,000 to buy and revamp an old film studio near Toronto. Naturally, Kerwin explained that the first step was to take out a huge life insurance policy. According to newspaper reports published in Toronto, Kerwin tried several times to obtain a loan for Barry from a Toronto bank, using worthless swindler-issued mutual fund shares as collateral. Barry says he "didn't pay any attention to what security they were offering the bank. The bank manager said no, and that's all there was to it."

Whether Barry was a lure used to bring Kerwin on his fatal journey north is something police never have been able to establish. Barry says he was reluctant to sign for Powell's furniture, and that he doesn't know what Kerwin wanted to talk about concerning the insurance policy. (One item might have been the premium. Barry says he paid $4,040 to Cohen and Kerwin as full premium for one year. Alexander Hamilton Life says it normally requires at least $25,000 for one year on a $1 million policy. Barry now says he has received his $4,040 back from Cohen and that the policy was never issued.)

At any rate, although Kerwin purportedly flew to Toronto to see Barry, he was to meet someone else at the airport first for another brief bit of business. Authorities never discovered the nature of that business. Kerwin's secretary told police she took a phone message from the man who was to meet Kerwin, but that she couldn't be sure of his name. It was a long name, hard to pronounce. It wasn't Barry, she said.

The name almost certainly belonged to Kerwin's killer. Stewardesses on the flight Kerwin took to Toronto say he planned to return on the next flight to Atlanta, leaving at seven the following morning. He had wanted to return even sooner, they say, but no flights were scheduled. The stewardesses say Kerwin traveled first class (after all, it was free), worked out of his briefcase, and drank two Jack Daniel's during the flight. He refused his dinner, asking them to give it to a serviceman in the tourist section. He was dressed characteristically in slacks and a green pullover sweater with a suède front. Kerwin left the plane about midnight, after which he probably spoke to no one but his murderer.

Theodore Yanovich was a character straight out of fiction. He owned a lavish wardrobe of suits, which he called "fronts," believing they would give him a good image. He kept his back and leg muscles in trim by toting thousand-pound weights around a local gym. He would not allow a stranger to walk behind him. In restaurants he always sat with his back to the wall, facing the door.

Shortly before Kerwin's murder, Yanovich had gone to work promoting a heavily overpriced stock, Buffalo Gas & Oil Company, which was being sold on the Canadian market. Buffalo had some oil leases in Ohio, but little if any income from them. Its largest inside stockholders were two Atlanta men (both of whom denied knowing Cohen or Kerwin) and Carl Rosen, head of Puritan Fashions, the well-known sportswear company in New York. Yanovich's overseers in the Canadian stock promotion had links to the Audsley-Prugh operation in Fort Lauderdale. Yanovich's direct supervisor, Leonard Varah, had participated in a previous stock manipulation with two men who helped promote Control Metals Corporation, the inactive Arizona metals company whose worthless stock Kerwin and Audsley had been selling all year. Yanovich probably had met Kerwin before, although police couldn't establish that positively.

When Kerwin got off the plane in Toronto, he was carrying fifteen Control Metals stock certificates, totaling 184,000 shares, fully endorsed and ready for transfer. Some law-enforcement agents have speculated that Kerwin intended to swap stock with Yanovich, acquiring shares in Buffalo Gas & Oil, and paying for them with the shares of Control Metals, or shares of First Financial Life, which Kerwin also brought to Canada, endorsed by various registered owners and ready for transfer. Other authorities point out that every swindler carries a sheaf of negotiable assets in his briefcase on the chance he might run into a sucker—thus, perhaps, Kerwin was carrying his odd assortment of papers by coincidence.

Two other, more sinister explanations have been offered for the strange collection of papers in Kerwin's briefcase that night. He may have been trying to blackmail someone in connection with the Texas Trust fraud. Kerwin possessed embarrassing and possibly incriminating evidence against men who were casting him aside. Both Cohen and Jaffe knew Carlos Marcello, the New Orleans Mafia boss. Harold Audsley has operated in Marcello's territory, too. Could Marcello have ordered Kerwin's death?

On the other hand, the Mafia in Chicago may have ordered it. Kerwin may have been trying to buy his way out of debt with the only resources at his command—Linda Mullendore's IOU and the dime-store stocks—which may explain why they were in his briefcase. Kerwin's briefcase also contained an order from a federal judge in Chicago commanding Kerwin to appear in court December 1, 1970, regarding the unpaid debt to Associates Discount Corporation of $228,523.32. Both Kerwin and Associates Discount knew that Milwaukee Phil Alderisio's organization wanted that debt canceled. Leo Rugendorf and Larry Rosenberg, the lieutenants who once supervised Kerwin, would be asked to pay the money if Kerwin didn't. Yet Kerwin had fallen behind in his $1,000-a-month installments. Attached to the court order in Kerwin's briefcase was a letter from Malcolm Gaynor, the Associates Discount attorney. It was dated November 13, 1970, and said:

Dear Leroy,
We are in receipt of your check in the amount of $1,500.
We are notifying the . . . court that the citation . . . is being withdrawn. However, this is only on the understanding that you will be straight with us within two weeks.
cc: Mr. Leo Rugendorf, Mr. Larry Rosenberg

On November 20, Rosenberg mailed his copy of the letter to Leroy Kerwin without comment. The letter and envelope from Rosenberg were in Kerwin's briefcase when he disappeared December 3, six days after Gaynor's two weeks were up. Gaynor says he received no response from Kerwin to his letter.

A few months after Kerwin disappeared, a St. Louis mobster and con man named James Boyd bragged to his attorney that *he* had killed E. C. Mullendore III, and said he did so at the request of Philip Wilson, the Mafia-connected swindler. Wilson had delivered phony mutual fund shares to Leroy Kerwin for use in collateralizing a loan for E.C., and had threatened Kerwin for failing either to return the worthless mutual fund shares or to pay for them. Boyd's braggadocio omitted details of how he supposedly pulled the job in Oklahoma—and didn't even mention why, exactly. Evidence never turned up that E.C. had received any money through Wilson, though at least one police detective in Florida surmises that a bad debt may have existed anyway. Boyd, a purported bombing expert, also hinted broadly to his lawyer that the wired Cadillac that blew up a telephone company vice-president in St. Louis about the time E.C. visited the Buder Building there with Jim Jackson was actually intended for Philip Wilson, who was visiting the same building that day in the same model and color Cadillac. There was no further verification, and Boyd wasn't believed. He later was indicted for running a phony Panamanian-based "bank," which Wilson was using in an advance-fee swindle.

Until Kerwin's body was found, Cohen and Jaffe told police they doubted their partner was dead. They said they suspected Kerwin had taken a lot of money from the agency and run off, perhaps to Israel.

Cohen called police at one point to report that Sidney Shine, an Atlanta man, and Lawrence Block, a local pilot, had conveyed a message to him from the Mafia in Chicago. The message was that Kerwin had been murdered and stuffed in a car trunk in Chicago because he failed to pay a debt to the mob, and that if Cohen didn't make an immediate $35,000 installment on that debt, he also would wind up in a car trunk in Chicago. Block and Shine say they merely passed the message along and don't know anything else about it. They say they didn't tell Cohen to pay the $35,000 personally to them.

Whatever Cohen's feelings when Kerwin's body was unearthed, he probably was relieved when Canadian police returned Linda Mullendore's $350,000 note, which had been lost with Kerwin's briefcase. Kerwin having died, Cohen stood to collect the money alone. He submitted the note promptly to the court in Oklahoma, where it was put in a pile with some $10 million in other Mullendore debts that awaited the insurance payoff.

In June 1971, John Arrington, Jr., and Linda Mullendore visited Cohen to discuss his pending testimony in the insurance case. At about the same time, Cohen resigned as president of First Financial Life, which was being placed in conservatorship. Jaffe continued to list Cohen as a director of the company, at least through July.

In 1972, Cohen continued to operate the same insurance office in Atlanta that he had shared with Leroy Kerwin. He wouldn't say which companies he represented, although Alexander Hamilton Life insists it certainly was not one of them. "All this publicity is killing me in the insurance business," Cohen lamented to a reporter.

Herbert Woll, the accountant whose inaccurate $17 million balance sheet enabled Texas Trust to start business, apparently had been forgiven. Woll insisted he was merely victimized by Kerwin the same way everyone else had been. In 1970, Cohen and Jaffe were complaining that Woll signed the Texas Trust papers behind their backs, but, in 1972, Woll still shared the office and receptionist with Cohen.

The receptionist still answered the telephone with her throaty trademark, "It's a *wonderful* day!"

Richard Korem, the lawyer who handled so many of Kerwin's business affairs, and whose sister Kerwin had married, died in December 1971, apparently of a heart attack.

Nola, the topless go-go dancer Kerwin befriended, left her $300-a-month apartment after Kerwin's disappearance, before the next month's rent came due. Atlanta police learned she was gone when she failed to turn up for a lie detector test they had scheduled. They haven't found her.

In August 1971, testifying in Linda's insurance case, John Mecom, Jr., said he was still a director of First Financial Life. A surprised lawyer asked Mecom, "Isn't that company under conservatorship now by the insurance commissioner of Texas?" Mecom replied, "I don't know. I have not discussed it with Mr. Jaffe in a long while." A few months later, Mecom's attorney announced that the young oil millionaire had resigned from the board at First Financial Life "for personal reasons."

Morris Jaffe says he bought out Leon Cohen's interest in First Financial Life and that Cohen no longer is affiliated with the company. Jaffe says First Financial has more than $800,000 in liquid assets and that he still hopes the company will flourish. He continues to defend his business acquaintanceship with Carlos Marcello. And he has offered to pay a reporter's way to Texas "to thoroughly investigate me. And if you can find where I have ever been involved in any type of illegitimate dealings, I will buy you a Cadillac limousine and hire a chauffeur to drive you back."

Thirty-one

SINCE GENE WAS GOING TO GET THE land after the insurance case, he formally took over management of the ranch from Linda and her lawyer, John Arrington. The day he did so—January 15, 1971—Dale Kuhrt left the ranch for good. "Gene didn't care for him," explains Paul Burchett. Burchett himself stayed on only until June.

Debts continued to pile up. During the delay in the insurance case, interest alone was adding $3,000 a day—about $1 million a year—to the bills that ultimately would have to be paid.

Trusted friends were turning against the family. According to Linda, Wally Noel wanted to buy out E.C.'s $100,000–$150,000 investment in Noel's Pizza Huts for $45,000. Then, she says, he sued the estate, claiming E.C. hadn't paid on certain bank loans that the rancher had co-signed for Noel. Linda was furious. "E.C. gave Wally everything he had," she complained. "His house, his car, all the working capital in the Pizza Huts."

Under the daily stress, Linda's own agreement with Gene and Kathleen, seemingly final, began to fall apart. Communications between the households ceased, and each blamed the other. Linda says she gave her telephone number—one of the best-kept secrets in Oklahoma—to Kathleen and Katsy, so that E.C.'s children could meet their grandparents from time to time. But, she says, the older Mullendores never called.

Twice in March, Gene telephoned Coke Harlow at the Coffeyville State Bank and complained about his daughter-in-law. The real purpose of the calls, Harlow says, was to wheedle the bank out of some money. As collateral for a loan, E.C. had assigned the bank an interest in a $131,000 investment Kathleen had inherited in Texas. The investment produced intermittent checks of $7,000, one of which had just arrived and was claimed by the bank. Gene said the ranch needed the money to buy hay and feed, but Harlow was having no part of that argument.

Harlow says Gene told him that Linda "had received $600,000 from insurance and that she had paid some of the debts, including Mr. Hill over at [the] Arkansas City [bank], and that he thought that I ought to call Linda's attorneys and demand payment on our note." The debts Linda had paid, of course, were to banks that held collateral liens against her other insurance policies; she could not have collected on the insurance without paying them. But Gene wanted all the insurance money applied against the ranch's debt.

According to Harlow, Gene cursed out Linda and Dale Kuhrt over the telephone. Recalls the banker: "He told me that they were not staying with [the family] over at the ranch, and that he thought she ought to be taking a hell of a big part in this thing. He was hurt that Linda was not taking on this bad debt of the ranch, that they weren't getting along very well, and that she had gone her [own] way, and [Gene and Kathleen] were going to stay there and fight the thing out. He made mention to me that they were not getting along as a father-in-law and a daughter-in-law should with his four grandchildren." But Gene did not mention the agreement the family had signed the previous December, denying Linda or the children any interest in the Cross Bell Ranch.

In April the caldron boiled over. Gene and Kathleen went to court to intervene in Linda's insurance suit, imperiling her rights to the money. On April 15, they filed bankruptcy papers on the Cross Bell Ranch, listing debts of $9,785,146.24, plus other debts in amounts not known. After court-appointed appraisers examined the ranch in May, assets were listed at $9,472,335.50, including $8,080,205 in land, but not including the $10 million agreement with Linda over the insurance. Until United Family Life paid Linda's $15 million claim and Gene received his $10 million share, the ranch couldn't operate without protection from its creditors. So U.S. District Judge Allen Barrow agreed to place the ranch under the federal bankruptcy laws. As long as the protection lasted, the creditors would have to wait for the insurance check before they could collect bills from the Mullendores. Later, it appeared that Judge Barrow's appraisers had conducted their estimates of assets with extreme conservatism. That summer, even the least valuable livestock, for example, sold for more than twice its appraised value.

On April 23, Linda asked the court to prevent the Mullendores from entering her insurance case and to void the agreement she had made the previous December giving them two thirds of the insurance money. That agreement, made under duress, "constituted illegal extortion," her court papers now said. Arrington, writing on her behalf, seemed undeterred by his also having been her counsel the previous December. Now he argued that Linda had signed the agreement in December only because Gene had "insisted . . . that Linda Vance Mullendore should pay all debts, and that if she did not fully comply with his demands, he threatened that he would prevent the payment of the insurance policies by telling falsehoods and engaging in deceit. These threats, accompanied by slanderous verbal abuse and attempts to cause Linda Vance Mullendore extreme mental anguish, continued until Linda Vance Mullendore signed, against her will and true intentions, the purported settlement agreement. Mr. Mullendore has repudiated said agreement by alleging to numerous persons that he will obtain all the insurance proceeds and that all property, whether real or personal, belongs to him."

Explained Linda later: "[Gene] told me that he would call the insurance company up on the telephone and tell them that the proceeds from all the insurance belonged to him, and that he would prevent payment of the proceeds to me."

On April 24, Linda resigned as executrix of E.C.'s estate, which was hopelessly bankrupt. The estate had virtually all of the ranch's debts, and few of its assets, since the land was mostly Gene's. But Linda continued to work on a spectacular sale of quarter horses she was staging for the estate.

Under the agreement in December, Gene was supposed to receive E.C.'s thirty-three race horses. But when the insurance payment was delayed, problems arose. As Arrington explains it, "Most pressing was the fact that the trainer [Wade Navarre] had run out of money and was no longer able to properly care for the animals, and their value would decline rapidly. Furthermore, the valuable mares would foal later in the spring, and subsequent potential buyers would look askance at foals born in Louisiana, which has an unfortunate reputation for colt-switching."

Arrington and Linda consulted Ellis Gragg, an Oklahoma quarter-horse breeder, who advised them to bring the horses back to Oklahoma and sell them at the famous Haymaker sale May 22. Linda and Arrington obtained permission from the creditors who held liens on the horses. (For the most part, these were the men E.C. had bought the horses from in the first place.) Then they made plans with television star Dale Robertson and his brother Chet, who run the Haymaker sale.

Arrington, Linda, and Ellis Gragg traveled to Lafayette, Loui-

272

siana, to get the horses. Recalls Arrington: "Ellis checked the condition of the horses (which was bad) and noted the markings of the yearlings (to make sure we got the right ones). By this time, the trainer [Navarre] was asserting a claim of over $57,000 for unpaid feed, veterinary, and training bills, and stud fees, and had attached the horses through legal action. We retained legal counsel [in Louisiana] and bargained the trainer down to $25,000 in cash plus three horses and a foal, which we estimated to be worth at most $18,000. In order to obtain the necessary funds to 'ransom' the horses from the trainer and prepare them for sale, Linda borrowed $50,000 from a Tulsa bank, secured by . . . one of the horses, Ruby Charge. (We later learned that a [government] bank examiner had disapproved this collateral for the loan, only days before the mare and her foal sold for $100,000 in the Haymaker sale!)

"The remaining twenty-five horses located in Louisiana were brought back to Oklahoma in three large vans [under cover of night], accompanied by a veterinarian (in case Ruby Charge foaled en route) and a lawyer (in case other Louisiana creditors attempted to attach them). The announced route was changed after the vans began rolling on March 8 in order to foil attachment attempts [apparently creditors were chasing Linda and her horses all the way to the border], and the promise of a steak dinner persuaded the drivers to keep moving until the Sabine River was crossed into Texas at Shreveport in the early morning hours of March 9." The party arrived safely in Oklahoma City later the same day.

The horses sold at the Haymaker for $660,550. Arrington says that amounted to $213,500 more than the debts on the horses and the cost of the sale. But the three horses that E.C. had paid record prices for in October 1969 all went back to their original owners at a substantial loss to the Mullendores. Sea Nymph's price dropped from $105,000, which E.C. had agreed to pay in October 1969, to $85,000; Chickamona's price dropped from $111,000 to $75,000, and Paula Laico's from $125,000 to $63,000. The difference, a total of $118,000, amounts to an eighteen-month rental fee.

The law in Georgia, where E.C. bought his life insurance policies, says that if a company delays in paying a claim that is later found to be proper, the company must pay 25 percent extra as a penalty. So Linda Mullendore's lawyers decided to sue under Georgia law, which they were entitled to do, even in

Oklahoma, where the suit was filed. That way she could seek not just $15 million but $18,750,000. They also filed a $50 million suit alleging bad faith on the part of the reinsurance companies that had chosen to fight the claim, but a federal judge threw that suit out of court, declaring that the case offered plenty of room for honest doubt. Both sides were entitled to a trial.

When a widow sues to collect on her husband's life insurance policy, an out-of-state insurance company seldom walks into court as the good guy. The average juror has a life insurance policy of his own, and expects that it will be paid on mere proof of death. He doesn't want to establish a precedent honoring the tricky wording in the fine print. So, regardless of who is suing whom, or the rights and wrongs of the case, the burden of proof usually is going to rest on the insurance company.

Adding to Linda's natural advantage, many people on the jury roll, from the florist to the feed dealer to the domestic help, had an interest in getting the Cross Bell Ranch's debts paid. Or he had a relative or friend who had an interest. A $19 million payout by out-of-state insurance companies would have about the same effect locally as if Congress passed an economic assistance bill to redevelop the Osage.

To help surmount these obstacles the companies hired Vip Crowe to represent them. For the past forty or fifty years, Vincil Penny Crowe had been the one man whom an Oklahoman in serious trouble most wanted to have on his side. Though seventy-three years old, he was still tough as a Hereford's hoof and headed the state's largest law firm, with thirty-five lawyers. In truly big cases, he often was beseeched for help by both sides and chose the better offer. Recently he had defended a state supreme court justice charged with income tax evasion, and defended Apco Oil Corporation in a state price-fixing suit. He also taught the men's Bible class at his Methodist church.

Linda's lawyer, John Arrington, Jr., was born in Pawhuska but studied at Princeton. He went to Harvard Law School, as did his chief partner in the insurance case, James Kincaid. The last thing the insurance companies wanted to look like was Ivy League. Vip Crowe learned law Oklahoma-style. He says the first client who walked into his office in 1921 was a tenant farmer who complained that his landlord had ordered him out of a field he was plowing. Crowe excused himself, went into another office, and called an older lawyer for advice. "Tell the man to tell the landlord to go to hell," the older lawyer instructed. "Can you do that?" Crowe says he asked. "Sure," the other lawyer replied. Crowe says he did, and "I never heard from my client again." Vip Crowe's was the face the insurance companies wanted to wear into court.

Gene and Kathleen Mullendore countered by hiring powerful politicians to represent them. Local papers called their chief trial counsel, State Senator Gene Stipe, "the most controversial state figure in the last three decades." Long a ruling figure in the legislature and a political prop behind U.S. Speaker of the House Carl Albert, Stipe had recently returned from Vietnam, where he successfully defended a marine private on charges of murdering sixteen Vietnamese women and children. He was an outspoken foe of liberal Senator Fred Harris and the antiwar wing of the Democratic Party. Beside Stipe on the Mullendores' team was J. Howard Edmondson, who, in 1958, at the age of thirty-three, had become the youngest governor in Oklahoma history. Following the death of Senator Robert S. Kerr in January 1963, Edmondson resigned as governor—nine days before the end of his term—and the ascending lieutenant governor appointed him senator. Edmondson filled out Kerr's two-year term. Howard Edmondson's brother Ed Edmondson later became a congressman. In November 1971, with the trial in the Mullendore case scheduled for December, Howard Edmondson died of a heart attack.

The court-appointed receivers in bankruptcy for the Cross Bell Ranch also intervened in the insurance suit, and were represented by James Ellison, the law partner of the publisher of the *Tulsa World*. The *World,* the area's morning newspaper, had devoted much less coverage to the case all year than had the afternoon *Tribune.*

The insurance companies needed unassailable proof of fraud to convince a jury that Linda didn't deserve to collect. To develop such proof, the companies scheduled an extensive series of depositions by potential witnesses in the case. The deposition-taking continued all summer in 1971, and allowed Crowe to find out by question and answer, under oath, just what the witnesses would say.

By the time the first depositions were taken in June, a veritable army of high-powered lawyers had been assembled to represent the various factions. A federal judge in Atlanta counted seventeen lawyers who sat in on the testimony when the deposition-taking caravan flew there from Tulsa to spend a week gathering evidence. The caravan continued on to Detroit, New Orleans, and even Seattle, the Siberia to which Retail

Credit Company had sent Ed Miller, the credit investigator who had reported E.C.'s worth at $37 million. Following this circus every step of the way were Linda Mullendore, who didn't miss a word of the voluminous testimony, and Joseph Howell, the sixty-year-old part-time rancher who reported the case for the *Tribune* and missed very few words. Howell and a number of the attorneys are on the short side, and when the tall, dominant figure of Linda led the procession into court, it often looked like Snow White with an extended trail of eighteen dwarfs. Her demeanor was queenly. According to Jim Sturdivant, a Tulsa attorney who was helping Vip Crowe, Linda dressed "like Jackie Kennedy. Very high-fashion, excellent taste, never a hair out of place, often in blacks and whites, never sexy or revealing. She's one of the most striking women I've ever seen." She also wore her badge of loyalty, a small gold pendant in the shape of the Cross Bell brand.

The insurance companies set about to establish that E.C. committed suicide, possibly with the help of others, to allow the family to collect on his policies and save the ranch. Like many policies, E.C.'s contained a two-year suicide clause removing the companies' obligation to pay in case of a self-willed death within that time. "It's as good a case of suicide as I've seen," Vip Crowe bellowed to reporters in characteristic style. Proving it was something else. One key indicator might have been the sequence in which E.C. suffered his wounds. If he was shot through the head before he was beaten, that would lend considerable weight to the theory that someone had gashed his scalp merely to plant evidence of a struggle that never occurred. On the other hand, if the bloody blows had been delivered *before* he was shot, one would be hard put to believe that E.C. had submitted to them willingly.

Jim Sturdivant is convinced that certain tests on the body might have determined whether the beating came before or after the gun shot. The pattern in which the blood clotted around the various wounds might have indicated whether E.C. was dead or dying before the wounds were delivered. But to produce results, a doctor or trained technician would have had to conduct the tests immediately after the body was found and before it was cleaned up and embalmed. The tests were never conducted. (Paul Sterling of the Oklahoma Bureau of Investigation says he doubts such a test was possible.)

The only hard evidence the insurance companies had was the Retail Credit Company report, a cornerstone of their argument that the Mullendores were trying to defraud them. Everyone agreed the report was way off base. But that was a long way from proving that the Mullendores had caused the false report by lying. The companies argued, for example, that E.C. had concealed the ranch mortgages totaling $8 million to Northwestern Mutual and the PCA. The trouble with this argument was that the mortgages were available on public record where anyone could go see them. Howell, the newspaper reporter, found them in a day, right after E.C. was killed. Miller, the credit investigator, apparently never looked. Whose fault was that?

United Family was understandably miffed, since it had relied on Retail Credit, which claims to serve "virtually every large life insurance company and practically all the major auto, fire, and casualty insurers." Retail Credit employs 15,000 persons and lists annual sales of $200 million. W. Lee Burge, president of Retail Credit, said his firm had used the same procedures investigating E.C. that it used in other cases. "There was a reasonable amount of investigation through various sources," he said, complaining that he was being second-guessed only because an error had occurred on "the case of the century."

As the insurance lawyers questioned witness after witness, Linda's investigator, Gary Glanz, set about gathering evidence in his own fashion. When the author of this book went to Oklahoma to cover the case for *The Wall Street Journal*, Glanz broke into my room at the Downtowner Motor Inn and rummaged through my belongings while I was out one day. He later reported back to his employers that I was "genuine," whatever that means. Apparently he could tell I was a reporter by the faded condition of my washables and the bargain labels in my suits, although a phone call to New York would have done him. What other mission I might have been on trudging around northeastern Oklahoma in 95 degree heat, has never been suggested.

According to an attorney in the case, Glanz also busted his way into the swank parlors of John Mecom's hotel suite in either Houston or New Orleans and sorted through Mecom's and Katsy's belongings. If he found anything, it never appeared as evidence. Linda now says—and at one point testified—that Glanz's work hasn't given her any idea who shot E.C.

Linda and the Mecoms followed the insurance investigation carefully. Just before Crowe, Sturdivant, and the fifteen other deposition takers went to interview E. M. Radcliffe, the Memphis money broker who had arranged loans for both E.C. and the Mecoms, Katsy telephoned Radcliffe and told him not to furnish any information about their financial affairs. The day before Leon Cohen was scheduled to testify in Atlanta, Linda, Arrington, Kincaid, Glanz, and an aide from a local law firm dropped by to talk to the insurance agent in his office. Presumably they didn't just chat about the weather.

The deposition-taking caravan found Kent Green back in familiar surroundings, the Kansas State Penitentiary at Lansing. He was serving an indeterminate sentence of one-to-fifteen years for possession of a pistol and failure to appear at a hearing on the assault and kidnapping charges that had been pending against him all summer of 1970. His friend Ginny Mueller had moved to Oregon.

The day in Lansing began unpleasantly for Linda when she was confronted by a process server. The Home State Bank in Kansas City, apparently unable to serve a summons on her in Oklahoma, cleverly had filed suit against her in Johnson County, Kansas, knowing she would appear there for Green's deposition. E.C. hadn't repaid the bank for his $100,000 loan, arranged for him by his old college fraternity buddy, Dudley McElvain, the bank's vice-president.

Everyone was impressed by Green's demeanor in prison. Says Jim Sturdivant: "Green is a guy who walks in and takes charge. He has an air about him that he's a responsible guy. Even in the penitentiary he walks in, arranges the table, tells the guards to go bring everyone coffee." At one point, when some lawyers complained that too many documents were being passed around and that they needed a copying machine, Green spoke up, "I have one in my office upstairs." During the testimony Green was smoking a cigar and had other cigars in his shirt pocket, along with pens and pencils.

When asked to name the various business ventures he was associated with, Green replied, "I still have interest in corporations, and due to the presence of the news media, I see no advantage to you, myself, or the Mullendores in involving any of these corporations in this kind of publicity. None of them were involved. They are all legitimate and most of them are public-owned [part of the stock had been sold on the over-the-counter stock market]."

Green also accused the insurance companies of trying to bribe him. He said that W. Dewbre, the chief legal counsel of Republic National Life, had told Donald L. Dorei, Green's own lawyer, that Green could get $150,000 in loans on future

construction projects, "or by some other method, if I cou[
supply names and dates and places of conversations betwee[
people and E.C. that might have brought about his death." Po[
sibly, the offer allegedly went, Green could help prove that E.[
paid Chub to perform the murder. "I kind of felt like I was bein[
bought," Green testified. "I'd have had to manufacture evidenc[
because it didn't happen that way, to my knowledge. [E.C[
loved living too well." Dewbre, the insurance lawyer, denies th[
whole story.

Finally, Green was asked if he had any opinion about who di[
kill E.C. He replied, "We are in the penitentiary, gentlemen. Th[
very thing you are asking me to do, I couldn't make it to tha[
front gate without three knives sticking in me."

Thirty-two

As the months passed, Sheriff[
Wayman's interest in the Mullendore case never wavered. He
continued to scout for evidence that might justify an arrest.
Among other things, he was intrigued by the recollection of one
of his deputies, Rudy Briggs. Sorting back through the excite-
ment of the murder night, Briggs was convinced Chub had told
him at the hospital about driving from the ranch to Bartlesville
along route 10. Yet Dale Kuhrt had mentioned that night that
he thought he saw Chub's car proceed straight out of the ranch
driveway, across route 10, and down the dirt trail that led to
Mission Creek Road. The next day Briggs had gone to question
Chub again at the manservant's house and had been startled to
hear Chub's story conform to Dale's: he had crossed route 10
and taken Mission Creek Road to where it joined Highway 75
just north of Dewey; there the policeman found him and brought
him to the hospital. Briggs felt certain—and still does—that
Chub had talked to Dale in the interim, realized the discrepancy,
and changed his story.

Suppose Deputy Briggs's recollection was correct. Why,
Wayman wondered, would Chub change his story about the
route he took to the hospital? If Chub had deliberately lied,
Wayman could imagine only one reason for it. Perhaps Chub
had thrown the murder weapon away en route and wanted to
divert the attention of authorities away from the spot where he
had thrown it.

For weeks, without a single leak in the press about what they were doing, Wayman and his deputies combed fifteen miles of backwoods road, looking for that missing .38 pistol. They dredged eight creek crossings along both route 10 and the Mission Creek Road. They could find no gun.

One August evening in 1971, temporarily out of leads in the Mullendore case and tired from other work, Sheriff Wayman came home, undid his tie, turned on the television set, pulled off his cowboy boots, propped his feet up, and sat back to watch the evening news. Suddenly he saw on screen the faces of Gene Klutts and Larry Silver, the ambulance crew that had taken E.C.'s body from the ranch to Phillips Hospital the night of the murder. Silver was telling a story that almost dumped Wayman out of his chair.

Silver: "As soon as we left the immediate area of the ranch house and got on the main gravel road going out away from the house [the driveway], we had traveled just a very short distance and these headlights come on behind us, and they were very bright. In fact, they were on brights, and this car stayed up with us and on our back bumper all the way out and outside the main gate and on the highway, and I thought maybe it was a deputy or something going to follow us to the hospital. And we got to hollering at them on the [police] radio, 'Whoever you are, turn your lights down on dim and get off our back end. If we have to stop, you are going to hit us.' And they wouldn't respond." So Silver said he and Klutts called the sheriff's office in Bartlesville and said, "If you can, contact your cars or whoever this is up here to get off our back bumper."

According to Silver, the sheriff's office said, "Well, all the deputies that's up there are out of the car.' So we advised them that someone was following us, and for somebody to pull him over and get him off of us. And couldn't get no help, so I was going to pull over just before we crossed a little metal bridge and find out what his problem was, telling him he was blinding me, which I couldn't see to drive. It wasn't a full-size car, I could tell that from looking at the mirror. It was a smaller car, possibly a Mustang or a Cougar, something of that size. When I started shutting the ambulance down [to pull over], he made a hard right and took off. There is, I believe, a road back there, a gravel road that a lot of people use as a shortcut to go back around and come in ahead, south of Copan. That's the last we

saw of that car. And we still— I don't have any idea who it was."

Sheriff Wayman's jaw was still slack when he heard Klutts add that the mystery car "would have to [have] come off one of the pastures. We were traveling probably eighty or ninety miles an hour. We came off the ranch road. We probably lost him right there about the Caney River bridge, and he must have turned back on Mission Creek Road and took back that way."

Sheriff Wayman had worked on the case in Washington County for several days after the murder and was in close touch with the Washington County sheriff's office. Why hadn't Silver and Klutts come forward earlier? Wayman immediately questioned Rudy Briggs, his own deputy, who had tuned in to the Washington County sheriff's radio while speeding toward the ranch that night. Briggs insisted he never heard the conversation described by Silver and Klutts, though he may have been out of the car and in the ranch house by the time the conversation occurred. Wayman himself had probably tuned in to the Washington County radio by the time the ambulance was pulling out of the ranch, and he never heard the conversation either. And if the mystery car had entered the road from a pasture, why hadn't it left tracks in the dew that night? Every inch of pasture along the four-mile drive had been searched. Nothing ever came of Silver's mystery car story.

Not knowing what to do about the story now that eleven months had passed since the murder, Wayman decided to wait and see what would happen September 2. That was the day Vip Crowe, maybe the best trial lawyer in Oklahoma, would try to break Chub Anderson's story from the witness stand in a pre-trial deposition.

First, however, Crowe was scheduled to face Linda Mullendore.

Thirty-three   LINDA AND HER IN-LAWS HAD patched up their legal differences in June, signing a new agreement very similar to the one they had signed in December 1970. There hadn't been any real problems, Gene insisted to a reporter; the cause of the disagreement "was just some lawyers trying to get in on the jackpot."

But the bitterness continued, deeper than ever. Linda said she wanted her children to see their grandparents and says she even urged Katsy that summer to intervene to persuade the Mullendores to call her. Kathleen told a reporter she hadn't "the slightest idea" where Linda was. "I know you're going to think this is terrible, but the only time we ever see her is in court," Kathleen said.

The worse the bickering got, the better the insurance companies liked it. Perhaps Crowe could make the Mullendores do each other in.

This is how Joseph Howell of *The Tulsa Tribune* described Linda at her deposition Thursday, August 26, and Friday, August 27, in the grand-jury room of the U.S. Courthouse in Tulsa: "Poker-faced, deadly serious, poised, and seldom smiling. Most of the time her eyes were hidden by black-framed sunglasses, but when she removed the glasses to read a copy of her statement to the sheriff at Crowe's insistence, fire often flashed from her dark eyes. She seldom responded with a direct answer to Crowe's interrogations and was reprimanded repeatedly for volunteering information. Rather than saying yes or no, Mrs. Mullendore preferred to explain why."

For two days, Vip Crowe and Linda Mullendore engaged in what was mostly a psychological exercise, a clash of wills, the kind of contest neither of them was experienced at losing. Linda, who bitterly resented questions about what she considered her private life, characteristically responded in barely audible tones. Crowe would not let her get away with it. "I can't hear you at all," he kept saying, urging her to speak up. When he asked her to read one of E.C.'s tax returns into the court record and she didn't want to, she complained, "It's hard for me to read this Xerox." Shot back Crowe, "That's the copy that your attorneys furnished the defendant, and I found it a little hard to read, too."

Linda's steadfast refusal to admit that her late husband had any faults at all must have infuriated Crowe as he sought to establish some simple truths about E.C. Testified Linda: "He never did drink very much, Mr. Crowe. Occasionally at parties and things, you know." Asked about the brawls E.C. got into, Linda explained, "These people just attacked him, so naturally he retaliated." Crowe fared poorly trying to get her to discuss business. "I always signed everything E.C. asked me to sign" was her explanation for how her name got on certain documents. Crowe couldn't even get her to admit that E.C. had been

282

unable to borrow money from the various loan brokers, including Carl Hess, Jim Jackson, George Aycock, and Kent Green.

Crowe: "Did you have any luck getting any money from Carl Hess?"

Linda: "There was adequate financing available."

Crowe: "Did E.C. have any success in getting money from Carl Hess?"

Kincaid: "Don't shout, please."

Linda: ". . . he did not fit his needs."

Crowe: "I will ask you if E.C. was ever able to borrow money through any of those sources or from them."

Linda: "He—at different times there were sources available to him through these people."

Crowe: "My question was, was he ever able to borrow funds from any of these people we have named."

Linda: "No, he never did, because again, the deal did not suit him."

But in many instances, Crowe could work not just from common knowledge but from the seemingly candid statement Linda had given to the sheriff the week after E.C. was killed. Although the statement was not formally sworn, as the deposition testimony was, and although Linda never signed the sheriff's statement, it had been taken down by a stenographer and there were witnesses.

Crowe read into the court record sections of Linda's earlier statement. "Q.: How long had E.C. been on the bottle? A.: Oh, it has been bad for about a year, I know that. Longer, but not like it has been."

Linda: "Of course, Mr. Crowe, you realize when this statement was taken, it was only six days after E.C.'s death. If [the answer] is here, I obviously gave it. But that's not right. That's not correct."

Crowe asked her if the statement she had given to the sheriff was untrue. "Yes," she replied. "There are many places where I was incoherent because I was in rather a state of shock at the time."

So, through the long afternoon, Crowe took her tortuously through her previous statement and got her to retract answer after answer. She repudiated her statement that E.C. had bought the insurance policies in Atlanta so he could borrow money. "E.C. purchased the insurance for estate tax purposes," she now proclaimed.

As for her statement that E.C. told her he had paid George

Aycock close to $30,000, she now said, "This is an assumption on my part, and I now think—I know now that probably this is all the money that he gave to all of the people."

Crowe: "Now, Mrs. Mullendore, you have said that your answer . . . is an assumption on your part. [Reading her previous answer]: 'He told me that he had given him close to $30,000.'"

Linda: "I may have assumed that E.C. told me that."

Crowe: "You said he told you, didn't you?"

Linda: "Yes, sir."

Crowe: "Did he tell you?"

Linda: "I don't remember that he did tell me that, no, sir."

When Crowe reached the part of her statement where she described warnings from E.C. to stay away from the various loan brokers because they were dangerous, Linda broke in, "I don't think this is really fair."

Replied Crowe: "I can't hear you."

Linda turned to Arrington and Kincaid, her attorneys, and protested, "The fact that I was never sworn and I never signed it, I don't see what difference it would make—"

Crowe: "Listen, this is not a proper place for conversation between you and your attorneys."

Linda: "I don't see that this makes any difference. I don't—"

Crowe: "It makes a difference to me, Mrs. Mullendore."

Sometimes, when Crowe had facts at his command, he still could not get Linda to admit their meaning—even the simple point that E.C. was short of money. Crowe badgered her to confirm that E.C. had been unable to make his $380,000 annual payments to Northwestern Mutual when they were due, December 1, every year.

Crowe: "You know he did not make it, do you not, on December 1, 1968?"

Linda: "I don't know, but that isn't unusual, because many times—"

Crowe: "You say you do not know?"

Linda: "No, no, no. I believe I heard you say that he didn't, and that it was twelve days late or something like that."

Crowe: "I will ask you if it isn't a fact that payment was not made until the middle of January of 1969, not within twelve days."

Linda: "I am not aware of that."

Crowe: "You are not? . . ."

284

Linda: "I know now. I did not know then."

Crowe: "When did you learn that it was six weeks late when payment was made?"

Linda: "I don't remember. I really don't."

At times, Linda was protected from Crowe's rigorous examination by her lawyers, and even by Willard Gotcher, who, with State Senator Stipe, was representing Gene and Kathleen. The insurance companies, for example, wanted to prove that Leon Cohen had arranged the policies on behalf of the Mullendores, not on behalf of United Family Life—in other words, that his closest allegiance was to the customer, explaining his part in providing the company with wrong information.

Crowe: "Have you ever heard of Leon Cohen?"

Linda: "Yes, sir, he is their agent, United Family's agent."

Crowe: "Did I ask you that?"

Gotcher: "That was a good answer, Mr. Crowe."

Crowe: "If a witness is going to volunteer, maybe so. It's her stark conclusion. [To Linda] I didn't ask you that, did I?"

Linda: "I am awfully sorry."

Kincaid: "Mr. Crowe, please don't shout at Linda."

Crowe: "The lawyer seems to get so much pleasure out of her answering questions that are not asked, maybe that's not her fault. I think Mr. Gotcher—"

Gotcher: "Mr. Crowe, I don't quarrel with her. Shout at me, I will shout back at you. She can't."

Sometimes Arrington overprotected her, and at one point even apologized to Crowe for calling the older lawyer unfair. Crowe devoted considerable questioning to Linda's court petition of the previous spring accusing Gene of "slanderous verbal abuse."

Linda: "At that time the entire family was very distraught over the death of my husband. He sometimes uses very strong language, and I have no intention of repeating it."

Crowe: "The court said you were to answer the question [as to exactly what Gene said].

Linda: "I just can't answer that, Mr. Crowe. This language was very strong and it's not language that I use, and it would embarrass me to repeat it."

Crowe: "Well, is there any of it that was included in a slanderous verbal abuse that you can repeat at all?"

Linda: "No."

Crowe asked if she ever used profanity. "Rarely," she replied.

285

Then Arrington broke in angrily. "You are trying to create dissension in the family when we got all of our differences settled and everybody is going forward."

Crowe, who, of course, was trying to create dissension in the family, recalled Linda's earlier statement to the court that "Mr. Mullendore has repudiated said agreement by alleging to numerous persons that he will obtain all the insurance proceeds, and that all property, whether real or personal, belongs to him." Who were the "numerous persons"? Crowe wanted to know.

"I can't remember all the names," Linda replied.

Crowe reminded her that she already had mentioned Dale Kuhrt as one of the persons.

Linda: "But I don't like to embarrass my friends, Mr. Crowe."

Crowe: "You said you couldn't remember. You didn't say you didn't want to embarrass them."

But Crowe could get no names other than Dale Kuhrt's.

At perhaps the key point in his questioning, Crowe tried out his suicide thesis.

Crowe: "As a matter of fact, Mrs. Mullendore, he was at the end of his rope financially at that time, wasn't he? He had no money. He made— He could get no loans, and he was selling mortgaged cattle, and he was threatened with a prosecution and he was threatened with a foreclosure by Ponca City Credit Association; isn't that all true?"

Linda: "My husband always believed that he would be able to procure a loan to take PCA out. He never gave up and he never stopped trying."

Crowe: "He had no source of it, no place to get money."

Linda: "He never believed that. He always believed that these people would come—"

Crowe: "Did you know of any place that he could have gotten money at that time?"

Linda: "I don't know—I don't remember. But I know that he felt that the money was forthcoming, that he would have the money."

Crowe: "You do know, do you not, that at that point everyone had turned him down for a loan that he had been fooling with for six or eight months, and that he also—"

Linda: "No, they hadn't."

Crowe: "Ma'am?"

Linda: "Mr. Green testified at Lansing he felt that he could still arrange a loan for E.C."

Crowe: "You know there wasn't any money forthcoming from any of these sources, don't you?"

Linda: "I don't know that."

Crowe: "Well, did he get any?"

Linda: "I don't know. I was gone for six days before his death. I don't think so. I don't know."

Thirty-four
CHUB TOOK THE OATH AND slouched casually in his chair. He was not a man to be formal. Vip Crowe fumbled through his papers, found the ones he wanted, and approached the witness.

"Everybody thought Chub was going to crack that day," Jim Sturdivant recalls.

When Crowe was a prosecutor back in the 1920's, the court-rooms weren't air-conditioned, and Crowe, the bulldog, was especially good in summer. Tie loose, sweat beading, he could outlast a recalcitrant witness. He had successfully prosecuted some locally famous criminals, including cop-killing bank robbers like the Kimes Gang.

Pat Williams, Chub's own politician-lawyer, was there, and had told the Crowe team that his man had only two things to hide. Chub would answer no questions regarding his attempt to sell $20,000 worth of Mullendore cattle in his own name, or regarding his daredevil driving to escape the process server on the night of E.C.'s murder. Both were crimes Chub conceivably could still be prosecuted for. Except for those two specific incidents, Williams said, Chub was ready to have his story put to the test.

Crowe let Chub ramble on about what had happened after he and E.C. had returned from Gose's house.

Chub: "He just said we would be going to Houston the next morning. We sat down and watched a little bit of TV, you know. Downstairs in his living room [the den]. And I don't know, we was there maybe fifteen minutes, and his maid, he called Lula, had made a pot of—looked like stew, still sitting out, and he told me he was going to heat him some stew before he went to bed and eat a bowl of stew. And I told him I thought I would go on upstairs and take a bath. And I went on upstairs. He had brought him a bowl of that stew back into the living room and I believe he had sat down and eaten that bowl of stew. He was sitting in one of those black leather chairs. I believe he had went back to the kitchen when I went upstairs. I didn't really look around to see if, you know, find anybody, but I hadn't seen anybody else in the room.

"I always wore a hat around. We still had our jackets on. The air conditioning had been on [he told Sheriff Wayman, remember, that the pilot had blown out on the furnace] and it had turned kind of cool. I think I had a hat on, also. Well, I drawed my bath water and put some bubble bath in the water, and prepared to take a bath."

On questioning, Chub said he had made no move to undress. He was still carrying a gun "in my belt. I think I took it whenever we left. I don't remember for sure, but I believe when we left to go to Copan, we had it." When Crowe asked whether Chub had been carrying a gun all week, Williams shut off the questioning: another possible law violation, even though Chub had been cleared by a jury of gun violations that occurred after he bought the .25 pistol on Wednesday.

Crowe turned the questioning back to the bath. Chub said he had shut off the water. "They had a ceiling heater, a little old round thing that blowed hot air down, and I had turned it on, too. You could hear it, but it wasn't noisy."

Q.: Did you take a bath?
A.: No.
Q.: Why didn't you?
A.: I heard what I thought to be a shot.
Q.: Was the water running then?
A.: No.

Chub said he heard only one shot. "I ran downstairs where E.C. was. He was sitting on the floor at the end of the divan. The best I remember, his feet was stretched straight out in front of him and his head was slumped over forward. I started to him. Well, just as I entered the room, I got shot in the right arm, and I fell over forward, and of course I knew right away I had been shot, and jumped up, and I heard steps on—someone running up the steps behind me, and I turned around and got the gun out, ran upstairs, and as I got to the top of the steps, they were on the glass porch in front. I just caught a glimpse of them going to the other glass door that leads outside, and I ran to the first glass door and shot at them."

288

Q.: How many did you see?

A.: Two.

Q.: Did you see their faces?

A.: No, sir.

Q.: Did you see them in the room when you went in?

A.: No, sir, I didn't.

Q.: Where did you first see them?

A.: At the top of the steps. They were on the porch, headed north down the porch.

Q.: Was that before or after you got up?

A.: After I got up.

Q.: Then, as I understand you to say, you heard somebody coming down the stairway?

A.: No, I heard someone running up the stairway.

Q.: Up the stairway. You did not hear anything before that of persons other than after you were shot?

A.: That's right.

Q.: I guess you know where the bullet entered your arm and where it exited?

A.: Yes.

Q.: Would you tell us?

A.: Yes. It entered right here [indicating] and came out here [indicating].

Q.: You are indicating that it entered in the back part of your arm just below the shoulder?

A.: Yes.

Q.: And came out in the front part of your arm?

A.: Yes, sir.

Q.: Did you go to E. C. Mullendore before you ran out and shot at them?

A.: No.

Q.: You hadn't reached him?

A.: No.

Q.: How far were you from where he was?

A.: Oh, approximately three to five, six feet, something like that.

Q.: You saw him?

A.: Yes.

Q.: What did you see, if anything, about his condition before you were shot?

A.: Well, naturally it was kind of hard to explain what you think, but—

Q.: No. You just tell us what you saw, if you remember what you saw.

A.: He was sitting on the floor with his head slumped over, and I knew he had been hurt. I could see blood.

Q.: You saw blood?

A.: Yes.

Q.: Do you know whether he was breathing then?

A.: No, I didn't know at that time.

Q.: Did you later find out he was breathing when you returned?

A.: Yes.

Q.: Was he still alive, at least as far as breathing was concerned?

A.: Well, I could hear a gurgling sound and knew that he was still alive.

Q.: You made no examination of him until after you had been upstairs?

A.: That's right.

Q.: And about how many shots did you fire, do you think?

A.: Well, I think this gun held eight shots, and I don't know if it was fully loaded or not, but I think it was.

Q.: What gun were you using?

A.: The .25 automatic.

Q.: Was that the one you had bought at Ponca City?

A.: Right.

Q.: Whenever you did carry a gun, did you carry that gun after you bought it as distinguished from other guns?

A.: Yes.

Q.: That is, it was your gun and that was the one you kept with you when you had a gun?

A.: That's right.

Q.: Now, was the glass door open off the porch, that went off the porch upstairs?

A.: We locked it when we went in.

Q.: Do you know whether it was open when you were shooting at these people?

A.: Well, they went out the door, yes.

Q.: Did you see them go out the door?

A.: Well, just as—I started shooting just as they were going out the door.

Q.: And do you know where the bullet holes were where you did fire, Mr. Anderson, by later examination or otherwise?

A.: Well, I did see them later.

Q.: And they were through the glass, were they not?

A.: Yes.

Q.: Do you know whether you fired any shots through the open door?

A.: No, I don't.

Q.: I guess you hit nobody with your shots, did you?

A.: Well, I don't know.

Q.: Didn't know then, but you didn't see any evidence of anybody being shot?

A.: No.

Q.: Do you remember which hand you were shooting with that night?

A.: My left hand.

Q.: Was that because you had been shot in the right arm?

A.: Yes. It was pretty numb.

Q.: How far upstairs or up in the upper part of the house did you go at that time?

A.: I went plumb outside.

Q.: You went clear up the stairway and then out on the porch and outside of the porch?

A.: Yes.

Q.: Did you go through the open glass door?

A.: Yes.

Q.: Did you see anyone after you got out there?

A.: Yes.

Q.: Where were you when you last saw anyone?

A.: As you go out the glass door and turn east [right], there is a sidewalk that goes out and it leads down some steps, a flight of stairs, and I ran to the end of those steps as they was running out across the parking area, and the best I recall, I shot two or three more times there.

Q.: Did you see anyone at that time?

A.: Yes. I could see them running out across the parking lot. But there was only one gaslight outside, and it wasn't, you know, real bright.

Q.: Did you see two men?

A.: Yes.

Q.: Could you give any description of them?

A.: Well, I didn't really see them that well. They were just average-sized men. [Catron, the Dewey policeman, recalls a much more thorough description Chub gave on the murder night.]

Q.: Would you be able to identify them if you saw them?

A.: No, sir, I couldn't.

Q.: Did you see any blood out there at that time, where you had shot anybody?

A.: No.

Q.: Did you see any tracks there?

A.: No.

Q.: What did you do after you run outside then?

A.: Well, I went back downstairs and could see E.C. was hurt real bad. [Note that, in his statement to the sheriff, Chub said he ran immediately to Dale Kuhrt's house before returning to E.C. Crowe never picks up on this.]

Q.: Did you go to him at that time?

A.: Yes.

Q.: Was that when you determined he was still breathing?

A.: Yes, and even after that, when I got back, he was still breathing, after I had went to Dale Kuhrt's house.

Q.: He was still breathing then?

A.: Yes.

Q.: Well, did he ever, at any time, say anything?

A.: No.

Q.: You heard no sound?

A.: No voice at all.

Q.: No voice. Did you examine him when you went to him after you had been upstairs?

A.: Yes.

Q.: What was his condition?

A.: Well, I ran over and picked his head back, I could see blood dripping from his head, and I could see a hole in his forehead.

Q.: You have indicated practically between the eyes, was it?

A.: A little above, yes.

Q.: What else?

A.: I knew he was hurt pretty bad, and I ran to Dale Kuhrt's house for help.

Q.: Did you see any other injuries except the bullet hole?

A.: Not at that— No.

Q.: As I understand it, you had— What, did you place his head against the divan in back of him?

A.: Well, I ran up to him and got ahold of his head and pulled it, you know, lifted his head up, is when I seen the hole in his forehead, and I don't remember how I left his head.

Q.: But was that the only injury you saw at that time?
A.: Yes.
Q.: And was the bleeding from this gunshot wound?
A.: The best I could tell, yes.
Q.: Had it bled on his clothing and floor?
A.: I could see it drip down on his jacket and on his Levi's.
Q.: He had on a jacket and Levi's?
A.: I believe he had on a leather jacket, the best I remember.
Q.: How long were you there at that trip?
A.: I just ran back downstairs, and I could see that he was hurt real bad, and I wasn't at his side over probably ten seconds at the most.
Q.: Then what did you do?
A.: I ran to Dale Kuhrt's house.

Then Chub described how Dale came over, how they looked at the body, and how they decided that Dale would call for help while Chub headed for the hospital. Chub said he found his Chevy in the parking area behind E.C.'s house. "And I took his driveway on to number 10 highway, and a dirt road on down, winding around, hits Highway 75, which leads into Bartlesville." (Note—see diagram, page 231.)

Q.: Were you on Mission Creek Road that evening?
A.: Yes.
Q.: How far did you go on the Mission Creek Road then?
A.: Approximately three miles, I guess.
Q.: And where did it lead to, where you left Mission Creek Road?
A.: It leads directly down to what they call the four-mile corner, four miles north of Dewey on Highway 75.
Q.: I believe you had stated that you went straight across the number 8 bridge?
A.: Yes. It's on that route, what they call number 8 bridge. It's a bridge that crosses Big Caney River.
Q.: Is that on the Mission Creek Road?
A.: It's right before you get to the Mission Creek Road.
Q.: And then did you follow the Mission Creek Road around across several bridges, until you got back to the Four Corners [Four-Mile Corner]?
A.: Yes. About three bridges, I guess. You cross Big Caney and Little Caney and Mission Creek, all on this same road.
Q.: You took that route?
A.: Yes.

Q.: You didn't go in on Highway 10, then, to Copan?

A.: No.

Q.: You started toward that highway, didn't you? Did you start to go in on Highway 10?

A.: No.

Q.: And then decide to go the other way?

A.: No.

Q.: I don't quite understand where you said you went from E.C.'s driveway. You mentioned Highway 10, and I—

A.: I went across Highway 10. See, Highway 10 is the road that goes to Hulah Dam, and E.C.'s driveway, it runs into Highway 10 and then goes on south, the dirt road goes on south, down the Mission Creek Road, back into Highway 75, that goes into Bartlesville.

Q.: Was there any particular reason why you didn't take Highway 10 into Copan that night, if you remember?

A.: No, I was just driving fairly fast and ran on across it, before, you know—

Q.: Before you realized it? And did you drive fast on Mission Creek Road?

A.: I realized it. Well, I was afraid to drive too fast, but I— After I had went down the road a little ways, I noticed some lights behind me, on the Mission Creek Road, or going toward the Mission Creek Road before I got to the number 8 bridge.

Q.: Was that Kuhrt's car?

A.: Well, we figured it was, later. He went down that road to make phone calls. At a ranch south of E.C.'s place. Bill Armstrong's.

At this point, Crowe, something obviously up his sleeve, pulled one last trick.

Q.: And then you got to Copan, did you not?

A.: I didn't go through Copan.

Q.: You got to Copan, somewhere there where you met the—

A.: I met the Dewey—

Q.: I am sorry. Dewey is what I was thinking about.

Chub was locked firmly into his story. He didn't take route 10, which looped through Copan. He took the Mission Creek Road, which cut into Highway 75 between Copan and Dewey. Crowe had taken Chub as far as he could that day. But in ten days, Crowe was going to unveil a surprise for Chub about the Mission Creek Road on the murder night. In the meantime, Crowe was in for quite a surprise himself.

Thirty-five
lawyers had been meeting informally around a table on Sunday
afternoons to discuss strategy. Sunday was the only day they
all could take time out from the press of details to think about
the case in general. August 29, 1971, was their Sunday of
Serendipity.

Jim Sturdivant says it wasn't even clear who first noticed the
crucial evidence on which the case was to turn. Several heads
just bobbed up at once around the table.

They had been going over dates, trying to get the myriad of
events into the proper chronology. They were talking now about
Ed Miller's credit investigation. Miller had spent one full day at
the Cross Bell Ranch interviewing E.C. and Linda. One lawyer
found a copy of Miller's report and read the date on it: September 4, 1969.

September 4. Wasn't that date on the bottom of another
report? The form was quickly produced. September 4, 1969,
was the day Dr. Michael T. Schlossberg claimed to have given
E.C. a thorough medical examination in Atlanta, Georgia. What
the hell?

The two doctors, Schlossberg and Rubenstein, had been approached by the insurance companies soon after E.C.'s death.
And they say they had seriously considered telling the truth. But
each of them called Kerwin, and Kerwin talked them out of it.

Schlossberg: "I asked Mr. Kerwin what this is all about. He
told me that this man had been killed, and he showed me a
Xerox copy of my medical exam. And I told him I didn't do this
exam, and he says, 'You better tell them that you did it. Otherwise you'll be in a lot of trouble.' "

Not only did Schlossberg and Rubenstein give stenotyped
statements to an insurance investigator confirming their original examination reports, they even charged the insurance companies a fee for the office time taken to give the false
statements.

Now, nearly a year later, on September 2, 1971, while Chub
Anderson was testifying in Tulsa, William Majors walked into
Dr. Schlossberg's office in Atlanta. Majors was an attorney for
United Family Life Insurance Company.

Schlossberg: "[He] told me [he] didn't think I did the examination. I said, 'You're right. I didn't do it.' "

Majors immediately sat Schlossberg down and took a written

statement from him. On his way out, Majors told Schlossberg that he had better see a lawyer.

That night Schlossberg telephoned Rubenstein, who recalls that Schlossberg said "something to the effect that a gentleman was in his office and presented him with the fact that they wanted the truth told about Mr. Mullendore. And he told the truth about Mr. Mullendore. And he felt that they would be coming to visit me also if I did an examination which was false on Mr. Mullendore. I was worried about this examination because of the publicity that had been given to this particular case, and because of the statement that I had given and I believe I signed to [the insurance investigator]. I was very relieved that [the truth] had finally come [out], because if I didn't expect it now, I'd expect it ten years from now. I'm glad it happened. As soon as [Majors] walked into my office, I got very nervous. I was just afraid, scared." Rubenstein canceled his office hours that day and gave Majors a statement.

Schlossberg and Rubenstein suffered thirty-one-day suspensions of their medical licenses in May 1973, by order of the Georgia Composite State Board of Medical Examiners.

John Arrington: "It turned on the medical. We felt that we had sufficient evidence to convince a ball park on the finances [the Retail Credit report], and if the insurance company was misled, it was their own fault. We were thinking in terms of a $13 or $13.5 million settlement. Then the medical— It was as big a surprise to us as it was to them."

Jim Sturdivant: "They kind of laughed off everything we threw at them except the medical."

This was the irony of it: Under Oklahoma law, the medical exams wouldn't have been so important. But Arrington had opted for the case to be tried under the rules of Georgia law, because it entitled Linda to the $3.75 million penalty for delayed payment. And Georgia law was very clear about the medicals. The third $5 million policy, based on two false medical exams, was invalid on the face of it. The judge probably would have to throw it out of the trial before the jury even looked at it. The other two policies, each with one genuine medical exam and one false one, could go to the jury, but under a cloud. In July, the insurance companies had offered a $7 million settlement and Arrington had told them it was out of the question. Now the momentum had shifted. But the companies had two more cards to play before getting down to negotiations.

First, Vip Crowe came up with his stunner for all the people who had been combing Chub Anderson's testimony seeking clues about the murder. On September 13, Crowe brought to the witness stand Pig Pettit, the game ranger who had wakened Gene and Kathleen the night E.C. died.

Pettit testified that he and John Lowery, another ranger who backed up his story, had parked in an alfalfa field that night by the junction of the Mission Creek Road and the road leading north to the ranch. They had stayed in the car from 10 p.m., keeping a careful watch for deer poachers, and didn't leave until the Washington County sheriff's radio announced trouble at the ranch, on information phoned in by Dale Kuhrt. Then Pettit and Lowery drove straight up the dirt road to the ranch.

Pettit testified that all evening long they saw only three cars. The first came from the north, on the road leading from the ranch, and turned *west* on Mission Creek Road, away from Dewey, toward the little town of Bowring. The second and third cars each came from the east, from Dewey, and continued along Mission Creek Road toward Bowring. Pettit swore, unequivocally, that no cars came from the north and turned east, as Chub Anderson had sworn that his car did.

What Chub might say in response to that would wait for the trial, scheduled for December, when the ranch hand would have to take the stand again. But then came the question of whether a trial would ever occur.

Vip Crowe's final tactic was a motion to dismiss Judge Allen E. Barrow from the case. Barrow also was judge in the Cross Bell bankruptcy case, and the insurance companies claimed it was a conflict of interest. Payment of the insurance policies would solve the bankruptcy problem.

On May 7, 1971, Judge Barrow had told Gene Mullendore from the bench, "You know, I think you are a fine gentleman. It is critical that we have your complete support." Replied Gene: "I certainly will cooperate to the fullest." Barrow said on that occasion that he would like to appoint Katsy to manage the ranch, because she had been active on it ever since her school-girl days as an equestrienne. (Katsy did spend considerable time at the ranch that summer, but a professional manager was appointed.) The insurance companies also accused Barrow of lunching with Linda's attorneys, attending a horse sale with members of the family, and meeting privately with the family's attorneys. On October 7, Barrow denounced Crowe's motion as "scandalous and offensive" and refused to disqualify himself.

The insurance companies took their case to the U.S. Court of

Appeals and won. Judge Barrow was out. From his bench, he denounced the appeals court decision as "ridiculous," although he later seemed to vindicate it by publicly proclaiming the following prejudices: "The ranch is in beautiful condition. I consider the ranch a part of the historical heritage of Oklahoma. I hope it can be preserved." Obviously, no one with such a view could sit impartially on the insurance case.

So the appeals court sent in a new judge, James Meredith, whose customary bench was in St. Louis. Judge Meredith, in effect, told the lawyers to get together and settle the thing or he would hold them to the December trial date.

One more obstacle arose. On October 14, Vip Crowe, who had just turned seventy-four, was indicted in Oklahoma City on charges that he tried to fix a case involving a one-way-street designation that was being contested before a local zoning body. After the case had spawned some large headlines, the witnesses against Crowe were discredited and the charges were withdrawn.

In December, a week before the insurance trial was scheduled to start, the seventeen lawyers locked themselves in for several days of intense bargaining, and finally shook hands on a deal for $8 million. John Arrington and five other lawyers representing Linda's interests had insisted that $8 million was the minimum that would fill Linda's needs and leave enough to give the ranch a fighting chance at getting out of bankruptcy, which it had to have if the deal was to keep Gene's support. The money was paid in the middle of January. Linda got $3 million. Fulton National Bank in Atlanta automatically received $304,247.51, and First National Bank in Atlanta, $158,936.81. That left about $4,536,816 for the trustees in bankruptcy. They held the money and tried to arrange a new mortgage of manageable size that would put the ranch back on its feet.

Immediately after the settlement, John Arrington left his wife of twelve years and their four children. The legal bonds were snipped quickly and deftly. Arrington's wife filed suit against him for divorce on December 31, charging that they were "incompatible" because of "the conduct of the defendant." Arrington waived his right to answer and agreed to a pre-negotiated settlement providing his payment of support of $125 a month for each child and undisclosed alimony and property division.

In June, apparently the earliest lawful opportunity, John Arrington and Linda Mullendore went to Colorado and were married. They returned to Tulsa to live. He maintains his law practice.

In February 1972, a joint Pawnee–Osage county grand jury convened to investigate the murder of E. C. Mullendore III. For more than a year, people had been saying that once the insurance case was settled, the Mullendores would start talking.

They came, and testified: Gene, Kathleen, and Linda. What they said is secret, as are all grand-jury proceedings. But whatever it was couldn't persuade the grand jury to indict anyone. The loudest testimony may have been Chub's silence. Chub had been working as a welder in the Dewey area. When the grand-jury investigation materialized, he got a job in Caney, Kansas, just across the border, and didn't bother to drive back to Dewey at night. They had to serve him his subpoena in Caney; he didn't have to answer it. For Oklahoma to lay hands on him, he would have to be extradited from Kansas. By the time that process could be completed, considering there were no formal charges against him, the grand-jury term would be ended. So the grand jury went home without hearing from Chub and without charging anyone in E.C.'s murder. Chub moved back to Dewey. The new Osage prosecutor, William Hall, promised to call another grand jury, but as of this writing that has never been done.

Meanwhile, John Mecom, Jr., his own business affairs getting back in the black, promised to take an active role in rescuing the Cross Bell Ranch. He made a big display of shelling out $30,000 for the prize Hereford bull at the American Royal Stock Show in Kansas City, indicating that it was the beginning of a program to restock the ranch.

On May 15, 1972, Judge Barrow approved an $11.2 million bankruptcy plan. In addition to the $5 million from the insurance, the receivers would raise $1.2 million from the sale of livestock and other ranch property (but no land), $1.4 million from bank loans, and $3.6 million by refinancing the Northwestern Mutual Life mortgage. But haggling over details dragged on past May 31, Northwestern Mutual's deadline for making the loan, and Northwestern Mutual refused to extend the deadline. John Mecom, Jr., announced he would look for a lender in New York to take Northwestern Mutual's place in the plan.

Meanwhile, Mecom's old associate at First Financial Life, Leon Cohen, had another brush with trouble in Atlanta. On June

9, 1972, police broke into a room registered to Joseph Russell at the Atlanta Cabana Motor Hotel. John F. Inman, chief of police, later identified "Russell" as Joseph Spatuzza, a Chicago mobster who had come to Atlanta the previous evening "to pull a job and get out quick." FBI agents and state investigators who searched Spatuzza's room found amphetamine capsules and $1,848 cash, Inman said. Spatuzza was charged with drug possession and using a false name at a hotel. Inman said that Spatuzza had been picked up at the Atlanta airport, upon arrival, by Fred W. Sans, identified as a sixty-seven-year-old part-time restaurant employee, who was driving a 1969 Cadillac with license plates registered to another car. He was charged with concealing the identity of an auto. Several years earlier, Sans, who then ran the Peerless Provisions store in Atlanta, had figured in a $50,000 deal by which Cohen, Kerwin, White & Associates had helped bankrupt a Covington, Georgia, bank. According to Chief of Police Inman, the man who told Fred Sans to pick up Joseph Spatuzza was Leon Cohen. Cohen wasn't arrested or charged.

A month later, Cohen's old mentor, Morris Jaffe, offered his own money to buy creditors' claims against the Cross Bell Ranch for sixty cents on the dollar. He sent the following letter to the creditors: "On behalf of certain friends of the Mullendore family, I would like to offer to purchase from you your claim against the above bankruptcy estate. Since we would like to see this bankruptcy matter concluded at the earliest possible date, and due to possible future costs and necessary delays in actual collection, we have decided to assist the family in clearing this matter more expeditiously. So as to assure you that this is being done in good faith and as a gratuitous gesture, I hereby pledge that if the bankruptcy estate is ever in position to pay a greater amount on your claim than I offer and pay you in connection with this letter, any excess will be returned to the bankruptcy estate, so no one will ever profit from the transaction other than possibly the Mullendore family."

Linda was furious when she heard about the offer, and contended that she had given up $5 million of her insurance money on the understanding that creditors would be paid in full. Jaffe later announced that "quite a few" of the smaller creditors had accepted his offer.

Apparently John Mecom, Jr., couldn't find the big bank loan he was looking for. According to reports, potential lenders all insisted that the ranch have professional management and Gene wouldn't quit. So on October 17, 1972, another bankruptcy plan was filed. This one provided for sale of 20,000 acres of outlying lands, including the Sedan, Fairfax, and Pawhuska ranches, which would pay off enough debts for Gene to keep the main Cross Bell Ranch on his own terms. What remained to be seen was whether Gene would ever, finally, sign his name to a land-sale deed. All he did in court was *promise* to sign.

Says Eddie King, one of the bankruptcy trustees: "The ranch is workable. I don't know if it's Gene, or it's me, or it's somebody else, but somebody can run that ranch. You just need better management."

A reporter who asked Gene whether he could run the ranch was told, "You're goddamn right I can run the son of a bitch, and I *will* run it. Who do you think put the son of a bitch together?"

Gene kept his thirty or forty buffalo and sixty or seventy longhorns on the ranch. And he kept his bitterness. Says Frank Raley, the Pawhuska rancher and druggist: "Some of the people he had helped for years wouldn't have anything to do with him now. He drove into town in a red Cadillac with Julia Gilkey's daughter a few weeks ago. He said, 'All of my friends have deserted me. They killed my son.' I said, 'The best brains in the country have been working on it.' He said, 'They haven't done a damn thing.'"

Linda: "It's difficult to explain to your children why their grandparents won't—they haven't sent a Christmas card or a present since the settlement. It's the very last thing E.C. or either one of us wanted. He always wanted the children to live on the ranch."

In 1972, Gene ordered a thirty-foot monument erected over E.C.'s grave, so that it would be visible from the main highway. George Ray says that the contractor who fenced in the memorial area was stunned afterward when Gene told him to submit his bill to the bankruptcy court, where it would lie waiting with all the others. The monument itself hasn't been built.

Linda still visits the grave on rare occasions. But on Judge Barrow's instructions she will do so only in the company of the local United States marshal.

Epilogue and Acknowledgments

In December 1973, Gene Mullendore died. The scalding foot wounds he had suffered while bathing in Hot Springs, Arkansas, in 1969 left him dead of blood poisoning four years later. It was a crowning death to a stubborn life: if he had sought medical help in time, he could have been saved easily. Just before he died, he agreed to lease the Cross Bell Ranch to L-B Land & Cattle Company, a subsidiary of Lacy Management Corporation of Kansas City, Missouri, which planned to make it the center of a large purebred Hereford cattle operation. The lease established a reliable income for the ranch, and enabled the Mullendores to borrow $4 million from Equitable Life Assurance Society. This money was expected to pay off the ranch bankruptcy, including $500,000 as an advance on needed improvements. The leasing company planned to graze about $600,000 of cattle profitably on the main ranch, 35,000 acres after Kathleen's house and grounds had been set aside. With the semiannual lease payments of $214,000, Kathleen and her heirs—whoever they will be—are expected to be able to pay off the Equitable Life loan and have $60,000 a year on which to live.

There is one hitch. Joseph Howell of *The Tulsa Tribune,* who continues his intensive coverage of the Mullendore case, says that new claims have threatened the ability of the $4 million loan to cover the Mullendore debt. An $800,000 inheritance tax has been filed against Gene's estate, and some $1 million in legal fees is being demanded by Gene's attorneys, State Senator Gene Stipe and Willard Gotcher. But Howell says that Judge Allen Barrow has ordered an appraisal to determine the just amount of the inheritance tax and that Kathleen may sue to reduce it.

Under the lease agreement, L-B Land & Cattle Company will acquire a one fourth interest in the ranch after twenty years and the right to initiate a buy or sell move at that time, based on the company's appraisal. When the company sets a price on the ranch, the Mullendore heirs will have the right, at their choice, either to buy out the company's one fourth interest for cash or sell out their own three fourths interest to the company for cash.

The only objection to this plan, Howell wrote, came from

Matthew Kane, Jr., of Pawhuska, a lawyer who represented five unsecured creditors with claims totaling $175,000. Matthew Kane was, by coincidence, the lawyer E.C. hired during his final week alive to file the divorce action against his wife.

The three outlying Mullendore ranches were sold at auction, with Linda Mullendore making a desperate effort to recoup them for her children. Although she risked her entire insurance fortune, a Colorado man, Donald F. Lebsack, drove the price up to $3,460,000—an average of $190 an acre—and took the land. Linda promptly bought another ranch, of 5,600 acres, near Sedan, Kansas, and hired Mike Burkhart as foreman and sole employee. She says she considers the new ranch small consolation for her loss at the auction—"When your name's Mullendore, you don't want just any ranch." But she says she told Burkhart, when he took the foreman's job, "It wasn't just to ranch. It was to train these boys, Whatever they want to do when they grow up, they'll have the opportunity to carry on the tradition."

Everything in this book is true—at least as the persons quoted recount it—except for a few fictionalized pages at the beginning of chapter 5. Because E.C. was dead before I stumbled onto the story, I felt the need to add just a touch of imagination to color in a stronger picture of him. Even so, the words that come out of his mouth and the incidents that happen to him in those pages are true to life as related to me by people who knew him; all I did was put them in the context of a single morning.

I regret that I never met Gene or Kathleen Mullendore face to face. Their numerous offers of interviews, dinners, and hospitality—which I always accepted—were inevitably balanced by the eventual withdrawal of the offers, usually accompanied by sudden and inexplicable bursts of cursing and threats by Gene over the telephone.

The most important source materials for this book were the thousands and thousands of pages of depositions, affidavits, and law enforcement interviews from the Mullendore case. Studying and organizing these materials was difficult, because U.S. District Judge James Meredith of St. Louis ordered all books and records of the Mullendore case sealed and ordered participants to discuss the case with no one but him under penalty of contempt of court—judicial behavior that should not be tolerated in a democracy. It wasn't. I only regret that Judge Meredith's threat of contempt prohibits me from thanking publicly the lawyers and court figures on various sides of this many-faceted case who enabled me to open the record.

While the written record laid the factual foundation for this book, these pages would have been dry indeed without interviews. Remarks from some interviews have been woven among quotations from the court testimony of the same person almost interchangeably (although attention always was given to any contradictions between statements of the same speaker in different forums).

I particularly want to thank the widow of E. C. Mullendore III for her cooperation. Linda Arrington didn't want this book published. But she realized that she had become a public figure before I ever ventured into Oklahoma, and in the interest of accuracy, she graciously consented to lend some time. I will let her explain in her own words: "The only reason that I've said all right now, that I'd talk to you, is that I feel you can't write this unless you have someone that knows how E.C. was, what kind of person he was. He wasn't a party boy or a playboy. So much has been said, and people talk, rumors get started, that simply wasn't true. And that's the only reason I'm talking to you."

Special thanks also to Mrs. Mildred Mullendore Adams for her fascinating recollections of her remarkable father. And for especially gracious offerings of time from Mr. and Mrs. George Ray, L. C. Mueller, Mrs. Bessie Johnson, Sheriff George Wayman, Frank Raley, Richard Kane, Mr. and Mrs. Paul Jones, Joseph Jarboe, Mrs. Lula Harrison, Mrs. Julia Gilkey, Rudy Briggs, Mrs. Sabra Smith Branstetter, Mrs. Geraldine Clark, Eddie King, the current residents of the old Erd Mullendore estate (whose names I neglected to take), to those persons besides the lawyers mentioned above who asked not to be identified, and especially to Joseph Howell, who contributed hours of enjoyable conversation as well as his newspaper reports; to Windsor Ridenour of *The Tulsa Tribune* for help with the photographs; to *The Tulsa Tribune* and *Tulsa World* for use of their libraries, and to John Joseph Mathews, the Indian historian. Mr. Mathews's history, *The Osages, Children of the Middle Waters* (University of Oklahoma Press), would be excellent background for *The Mullendore Murder Case*.

I would like to thank Chub Anderson for his offer of an interview, and express my regret that the sudden death of his father in a work accident while I was in Oklahoma in 1972 led him to withdraw the offer.

The Mullendore Murder Case was the outgrowth of articles that first appeared in *The Wall Street Journal*, November 23 and 24, 1971. The investigation that produced these articles originally concerned Leroy Kerwin, the Atlanta insurance agent. But Jack Cooper, then industrial editor of the *Journal* and now on its editorial-page staff, sensed from my initial notes and memoranda that Kerwin's client E. C. Mullendore III was the more interesting story. If Cooper hadn't put me on a plane for Tulsa, where I could make this judgment myself, the book probably wouldn't have come about.

Nor would this book likely exist had not the newspaper project received the support and indulgence of Glynn Mapes, the *Journal's* New York bureau manager; Frederick Taylor, the managing editor; and Michael Gartner, then the page-one editor and now executive editor of the Des Moines newspapers. To Cooper, Mapes, Taylor, and Gartner, sincere thanks.

Thanks to David Thaler, friend and editor-publisher of the *Bayshore* (N.J.) *Independent,* for many helpful editorial suggestions.

And thanks most of all to my wife, Martha Kwitny, who contributed comfort, encouragement, and countless improvements to this manuscript and every other aspect of life.